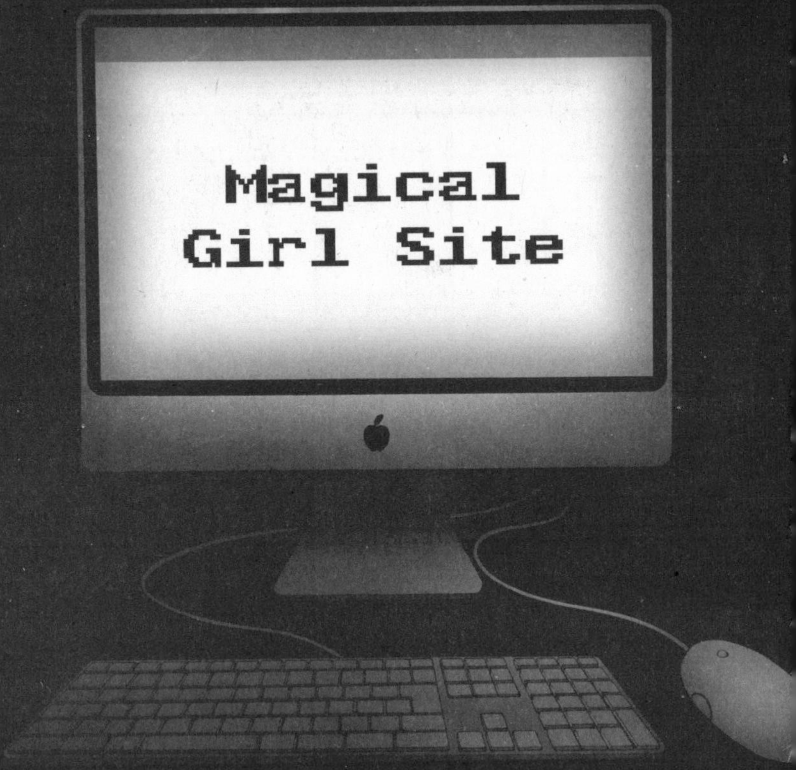
Magical
Girl Site

VOLUME 8

AUTHOR
KENTARO SATO

SUMMARY AND CHARACTER INTROS

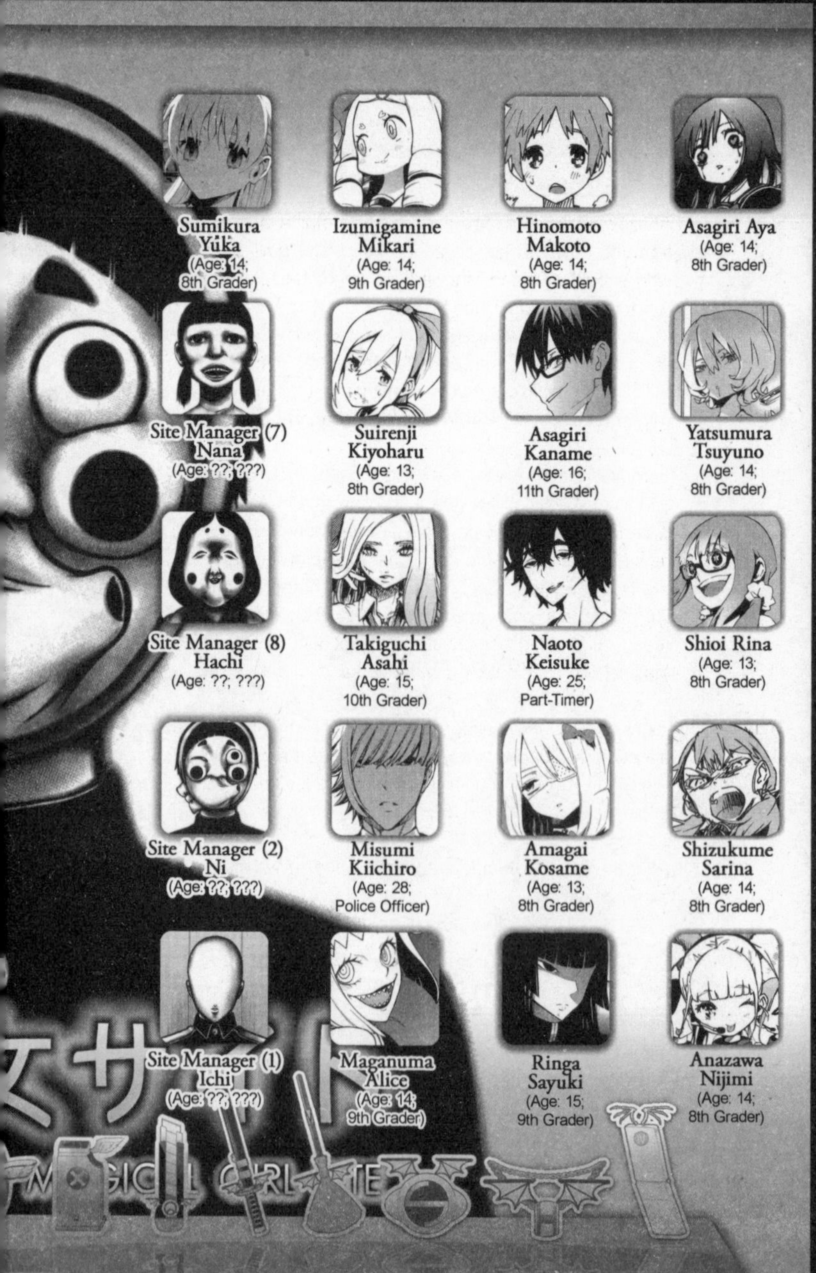
Sumikura Yuka (Age: 14; 8th Grader)
Izumigamine Mikari (Age: 14; 9th Grader)
Hinomoto Makoto (Age: 14; 8th Grader)
Asagiri Aya (Age: 14; 8th Grader)
Site Manager (7) Nana (Age: ??; ???)
Suirenji Kiyoharu (Age: 13; 8th Grader)
Asagiri Kaname (Age: 16; 11th Grader)
Yatsumura Tsuyuno (Age: 14; 8th Grader)
Site Manager (8) Hachi (Age: ??; ???)
Takiguchi Asahi (Age: 15; 10th Grader)
Naoto Keisuke (Age: 25; Part-Timer)
Shioi Rina (Age: 13; 8th Grader)
Site Manager (2) Ni (Age: ??; ???)
Misumi Kiichiro (Age: 28; Police Officer)
Amagai Kosame (Age: 13; 8th Grader)
Shizukume Sarina (Age: 14; 8th Grader)
Site Manager (1) Ichi (Age: ??; ???)
Maganuma Alice (Age: 14; 9th Grader)
Ringa Sayuki (Age: 15; 9th Grader)
Anazawa Nijimi (Age: 14; 8th Grader)

Magical Girl Site

Magical Girl Site 7

Display Images

Summary

Anazawa Nijimi's death triggered a tearful Aya to push away from the reality of her situation--until Shizukume Sarina, a girl who should be dead, showed up before her. Sarina returned Aya's wand and told her that she should use it to take down Magical Girl SITE. Maganuma Alice, the girl who saved Sarina, and Sarina herself, are plotting together to assault Magical Girl SITE in secret. Now Aya and her friends are moving forward with one objective: to rid the world of Magical Girl SITE.

Surprise Attack--Alice's plan was simple. Attack them quickly and as efficiently as possible at the one time that a site manager is certain to appear: when they are delivering a new wand to a new Magical Girl. There would be no attempt at capturing one this time; the group's only goal was to fight them. Learning that the managers only operate in their assigned geographical areas, Alice used her private SNS account to find a potential Magical Girl candidate: Sumikura Yuka.

Right on time, the manager appeared at the junior high school attended by Sumikura Yuka, where Aya, Sarina, Sayuki, Asahi, Rina, and Kiyoharu confronted the manager and blasted them to pieces.

After the dust cleared, Manager Ni's body turned into...
a human girl?!

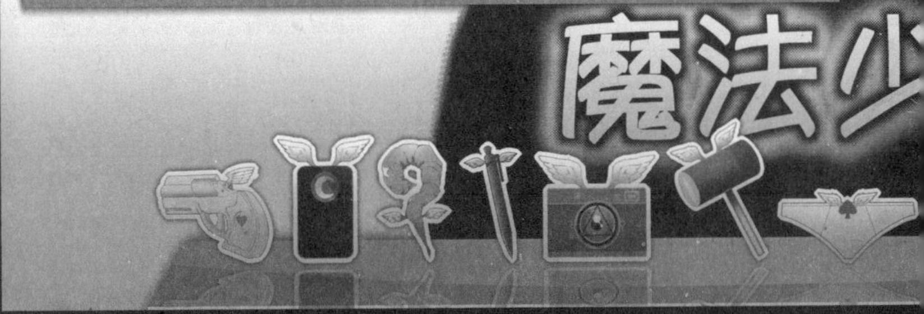
魔法少

SEVEN SEAS ENTERTAINMENT PRESENTS

MAGICAL GIRL SITE

story and art by KENTARO SATO

VOLUME 8

TRANSLATION
Wesley Bridges

ADAPTATION
Janet Houck

LETTERING AND LAYOUT
Meaghan Tucker

COVER DESIGN
Nicky Lim

PROOFREADER
B. Lana Guggenheim

ASSISTANT EDITOR
Jenn Grunigen

PRODUCTION ASSISTANT
CK Russell

PRODUCTION MANAGER
Lissa Pattillo

EDITOR-IN-CHIEF
Adam Arnold

PUBLISHER
Jason DeAngelis

MAHO SYOJYO SITE Volume 8
© Kentaro Sato 2018
Originally published in Japan in 2018 by Akita Publishing Co., Ltd..
English translation rights arranged with Akita Publishing Co., Ltd. through
TOHAN CORPORATION, Tokyo.

Seven Seas books may be purchased in bulk for promotional, educational, or
business use. Please contact your local bookseller or the Macmillan Corporate
and Premium Sales Department at 1-800-221-7945, extension 5442, or by
e-mail at MacmillanSpecialMarkets@macmillan.com.

Seven Seas and the Seven Seas logo are trademarks of
Seven Seas Entertainment, LLC. All rights reserved.

ISBN: 978-1-626929-82-1

Printed in Canada

First Printing: March 2019

10 9 8 7 6 5 4 3 2 1

FOLLOW US ONLINE: *www.sevenseasentertainment.com*

READING DIRECTIONS

This book reads from *right to left*, Japanese style.
If this is your first time reading manga, you start
reading from the top right panel on each page and
take it from there. If you get lost, just follow the
numbered diagram here. It may seem backwards at
first, but you'll get the hang of it! Have fun!!

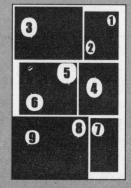

ENTER.50 A NEW MYSTERY

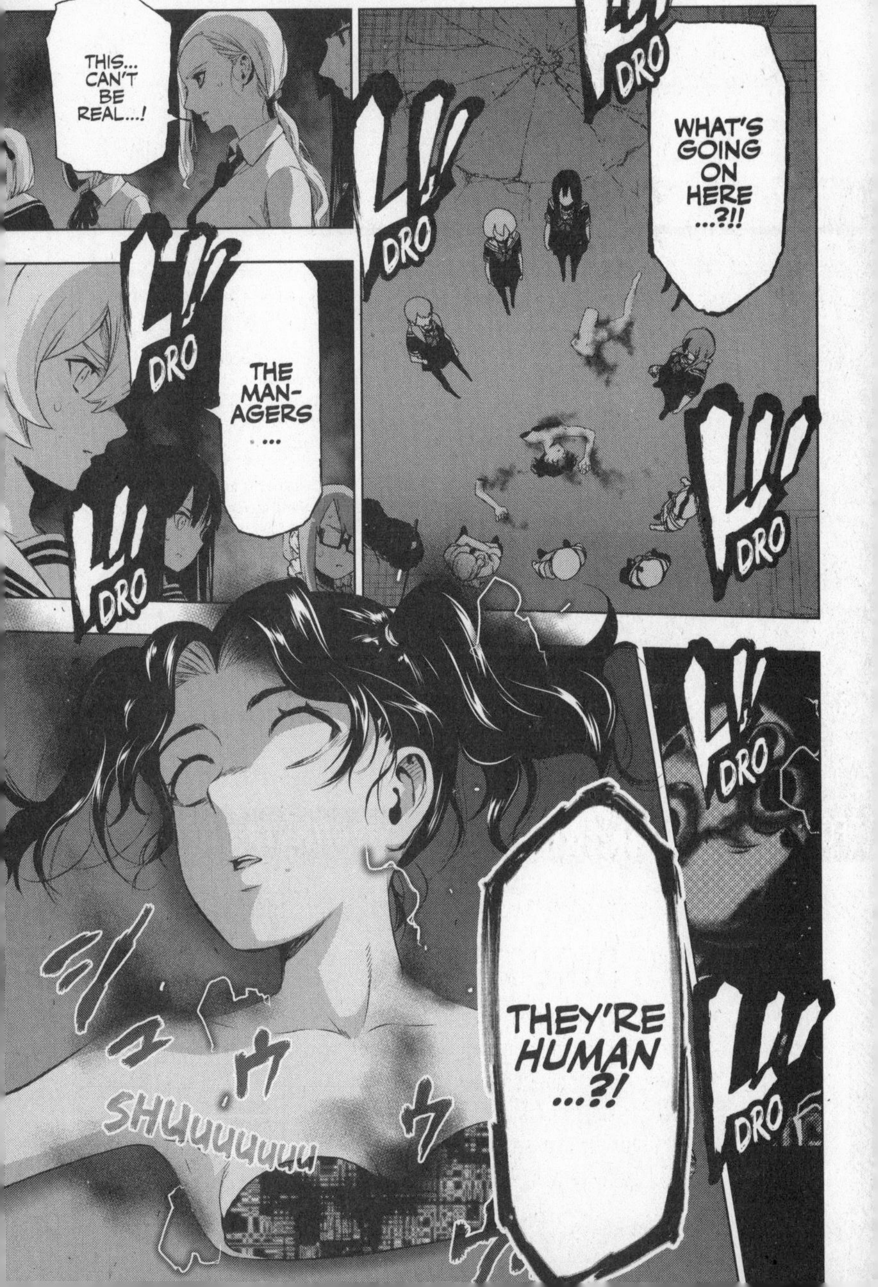
DRO
WHAT'S GOING ON HERE ...?!!
DRO
DRO
THIS... CAN'T BE REAL...!
DRO
THE MANAGERS ......
DRO
DRO
DRO
THEY'RE HUMAN ...?!
SHUuuuuuuu

ENTER.50 A NEW MYSTERY

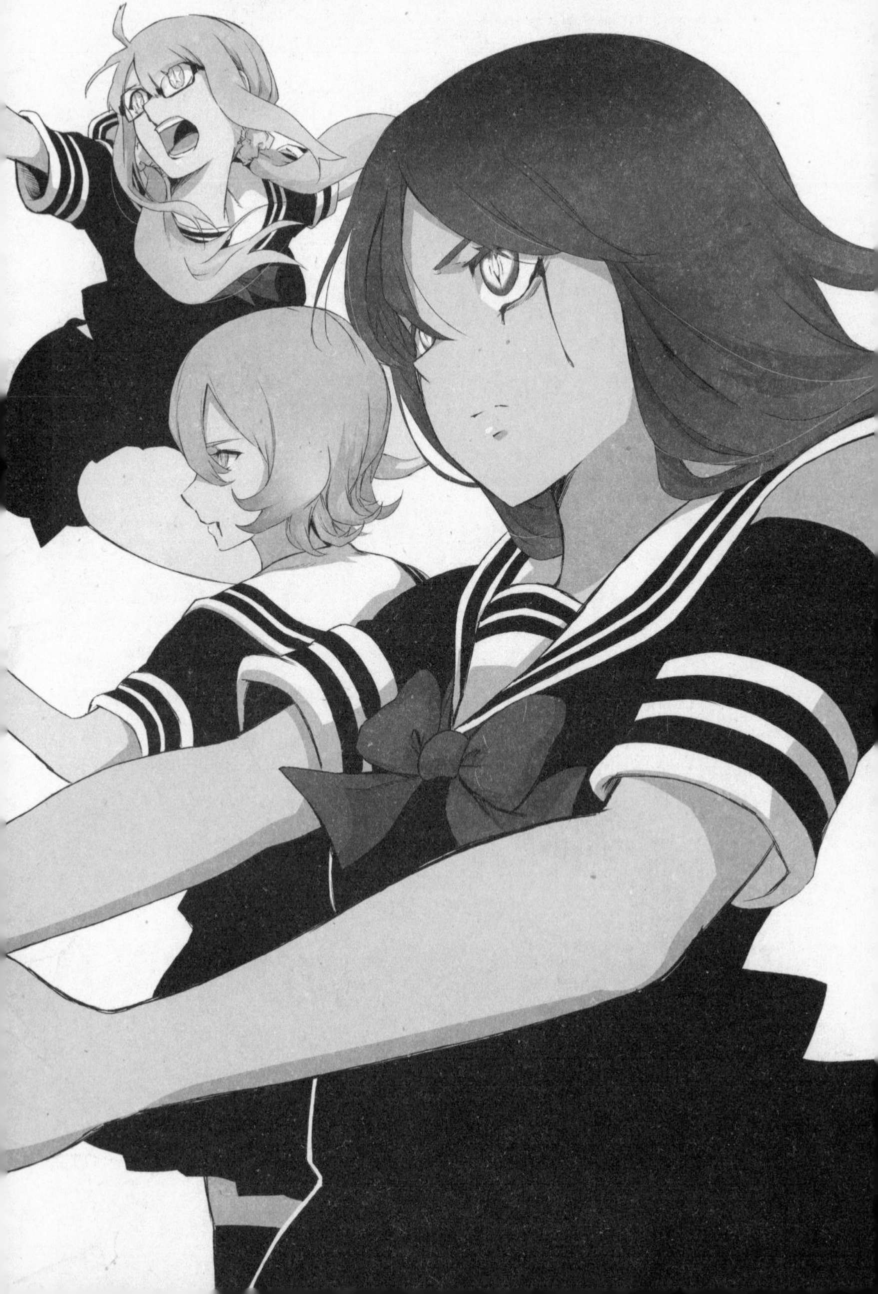

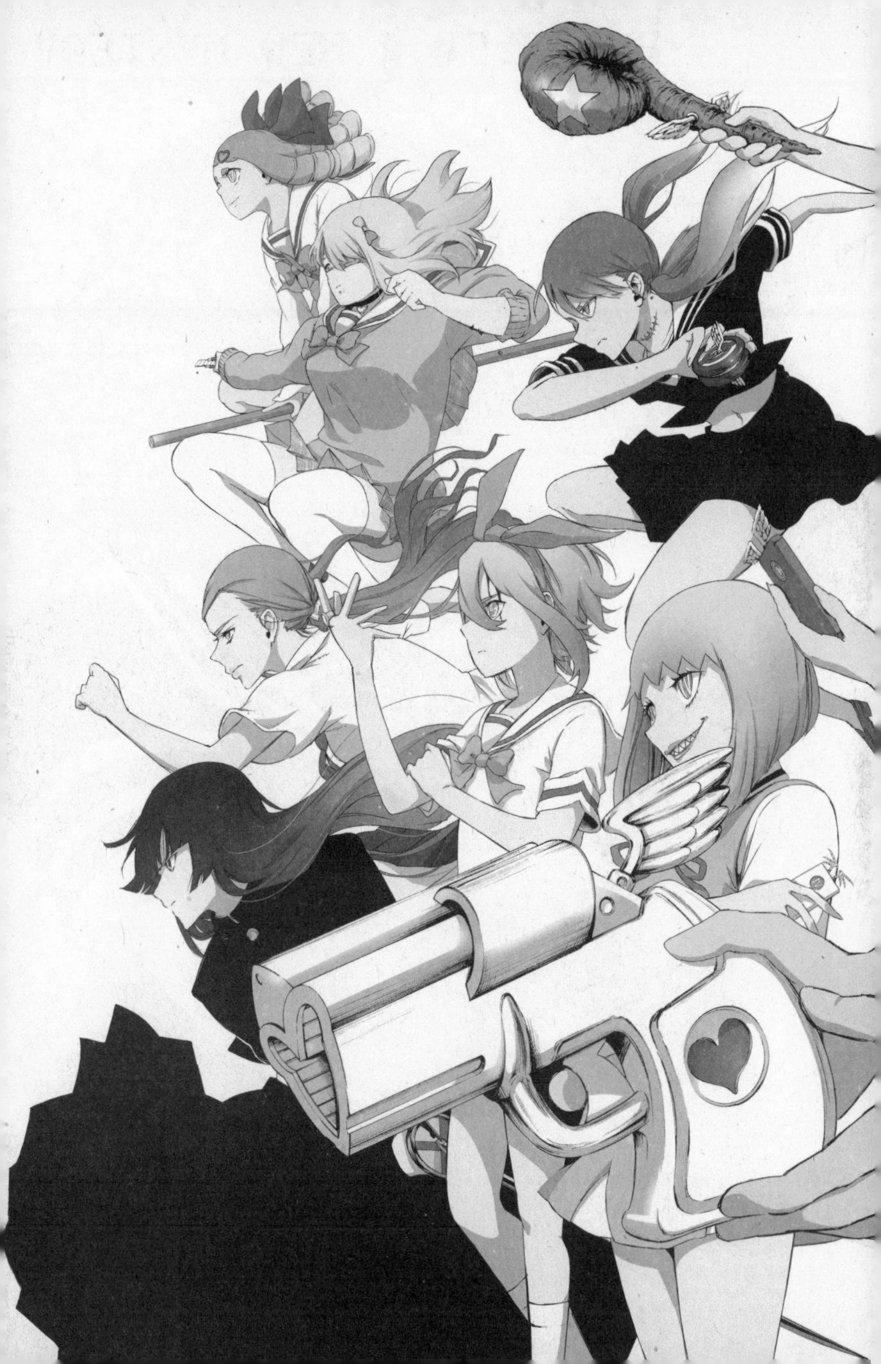

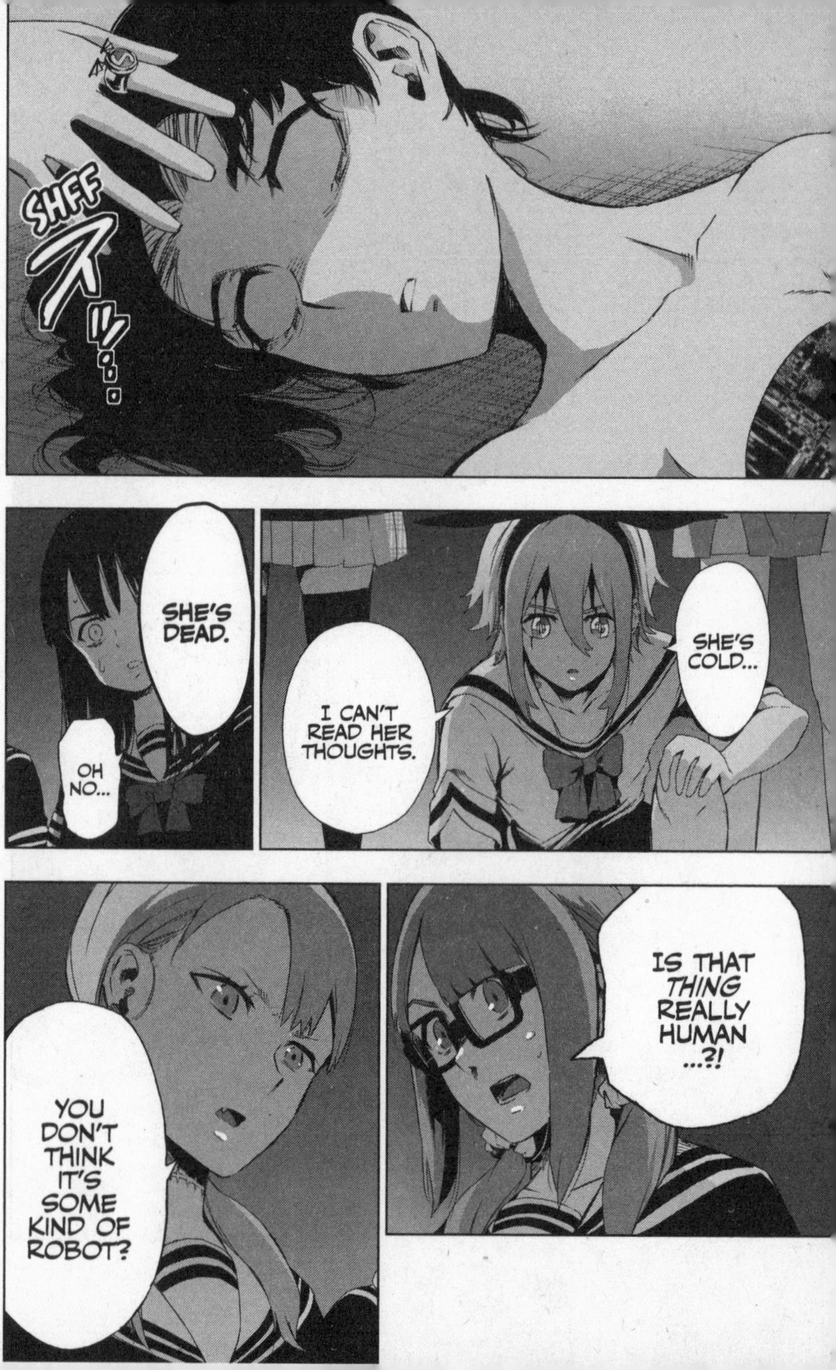
SHFF
SHE'S COLD...
I CAN'T READ HER THOUGHTS.
SHE'S DEAD.
OH NO...
IS THAT *THING* REALLY HUMAN ...?!
YOU DON'T THINK IT'S SOME KIND OF ROBOT?

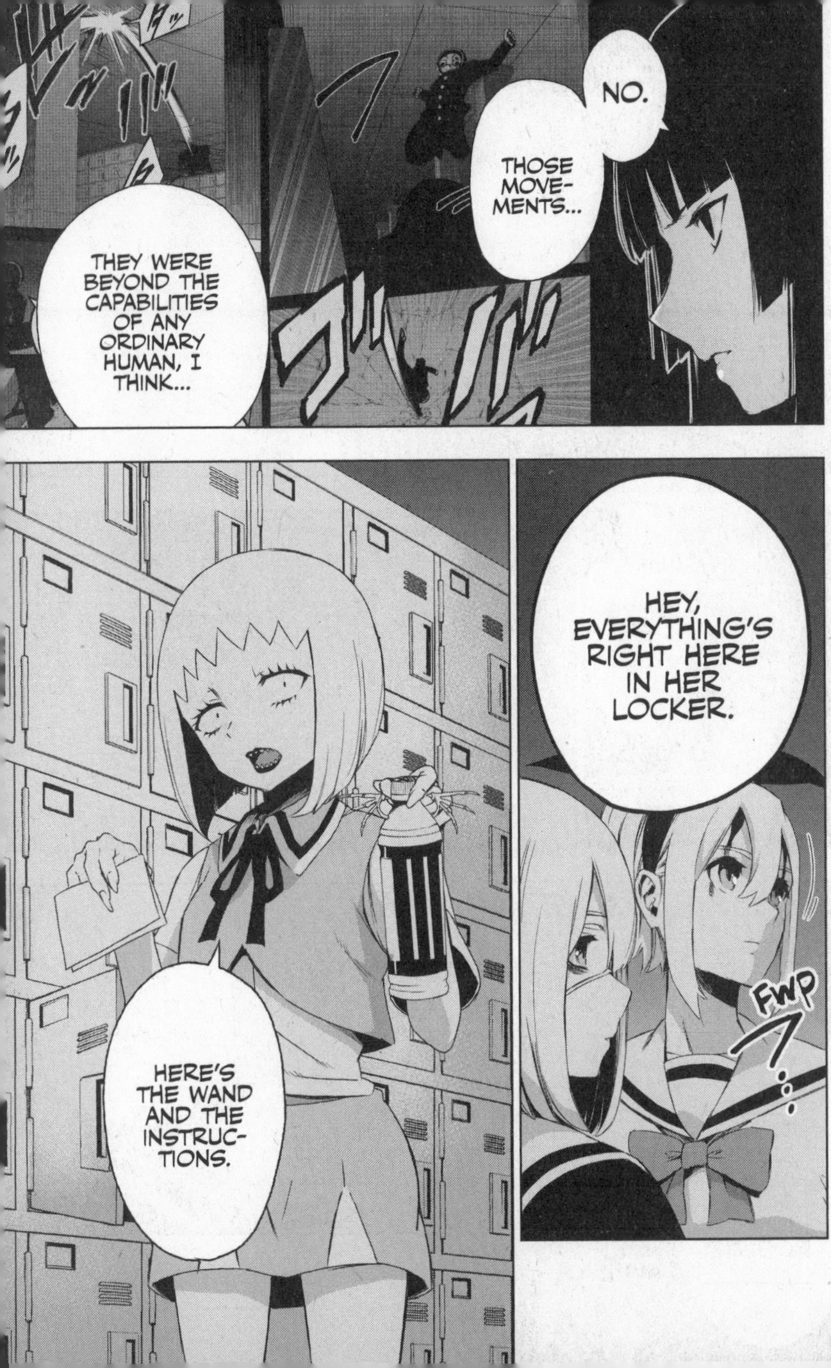
NO.
THOSE MOVEMENTS...
THEY WERE BEYOND THE CAPABILITIES OF ANY ORDINARY HUMAN, I THINK...
HEY, EVERYTHING'S RIGHT HERE IN HER LOCKER.
FWP
HERE'S THE WAND AND THE INSTRUCTIONS.

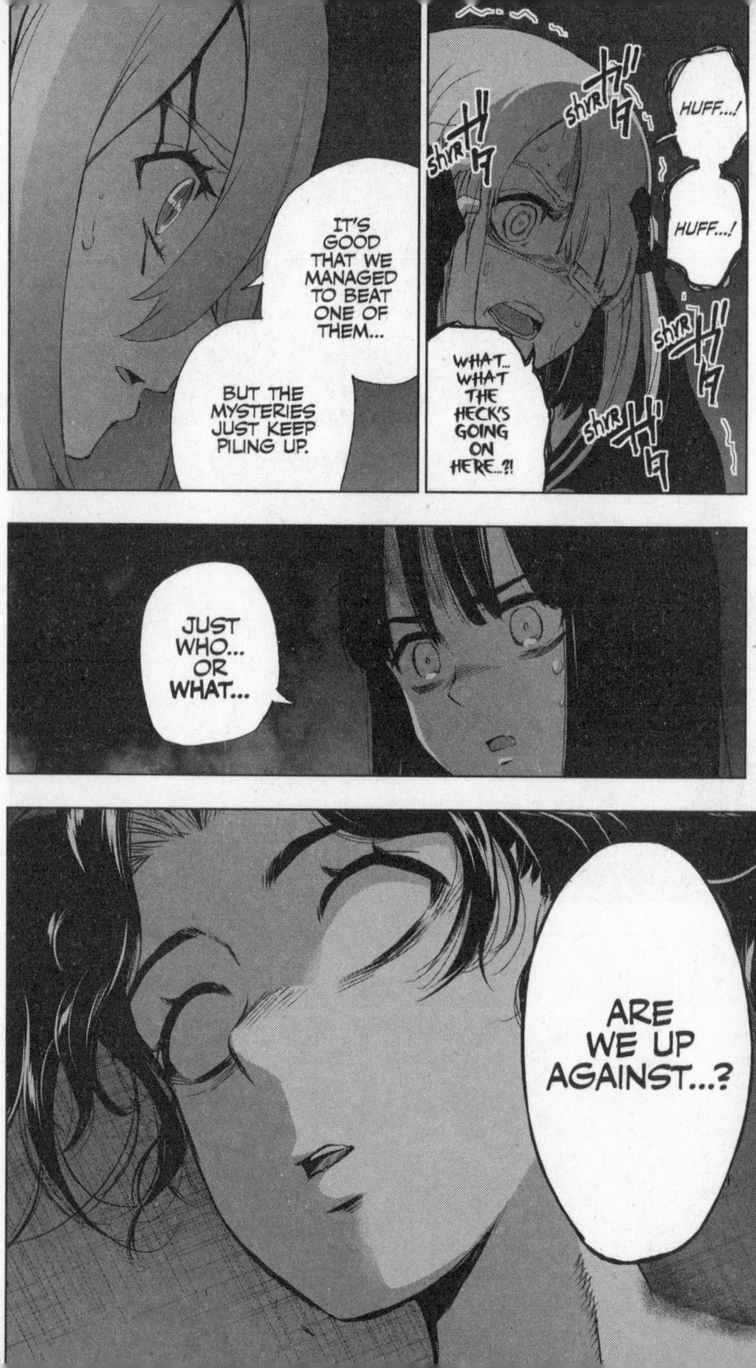
HUFF...!
HUFF...!
shyR
shyR
shyR
shyR
WHAT... WHAT THE HECK'S GOING ON HERE...?!
IT'S GOOD THAT WE MANAGED TO BEAT ONE OF THEM...
BUT THE MYSTERIES JUST KEEP PILING UP.
JUST WHO... OR WHAT...
ARE WE UP AGAINST...?

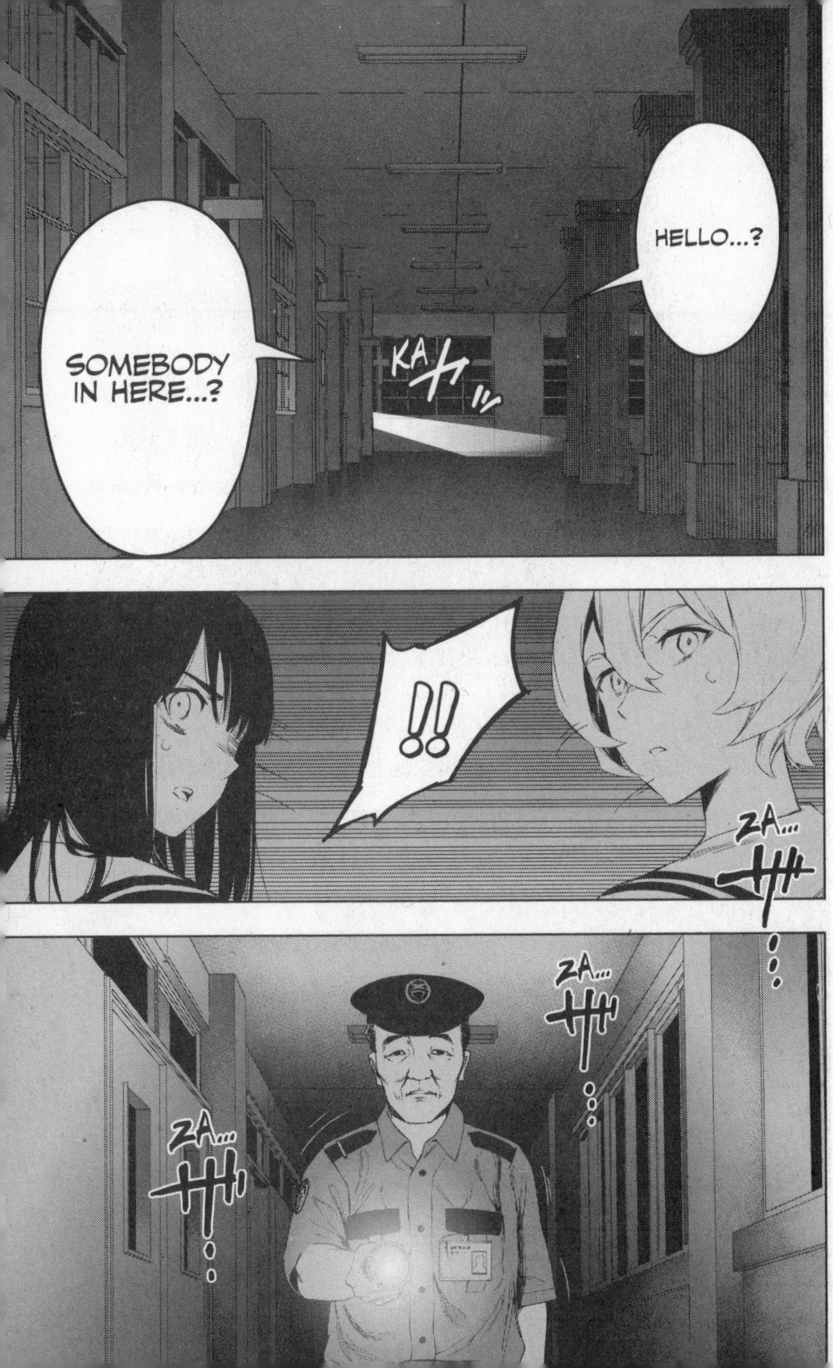
HELLO...?
KA
SOMEBODY IN HERE...?
!!
ZA...
ZA...
ZA...

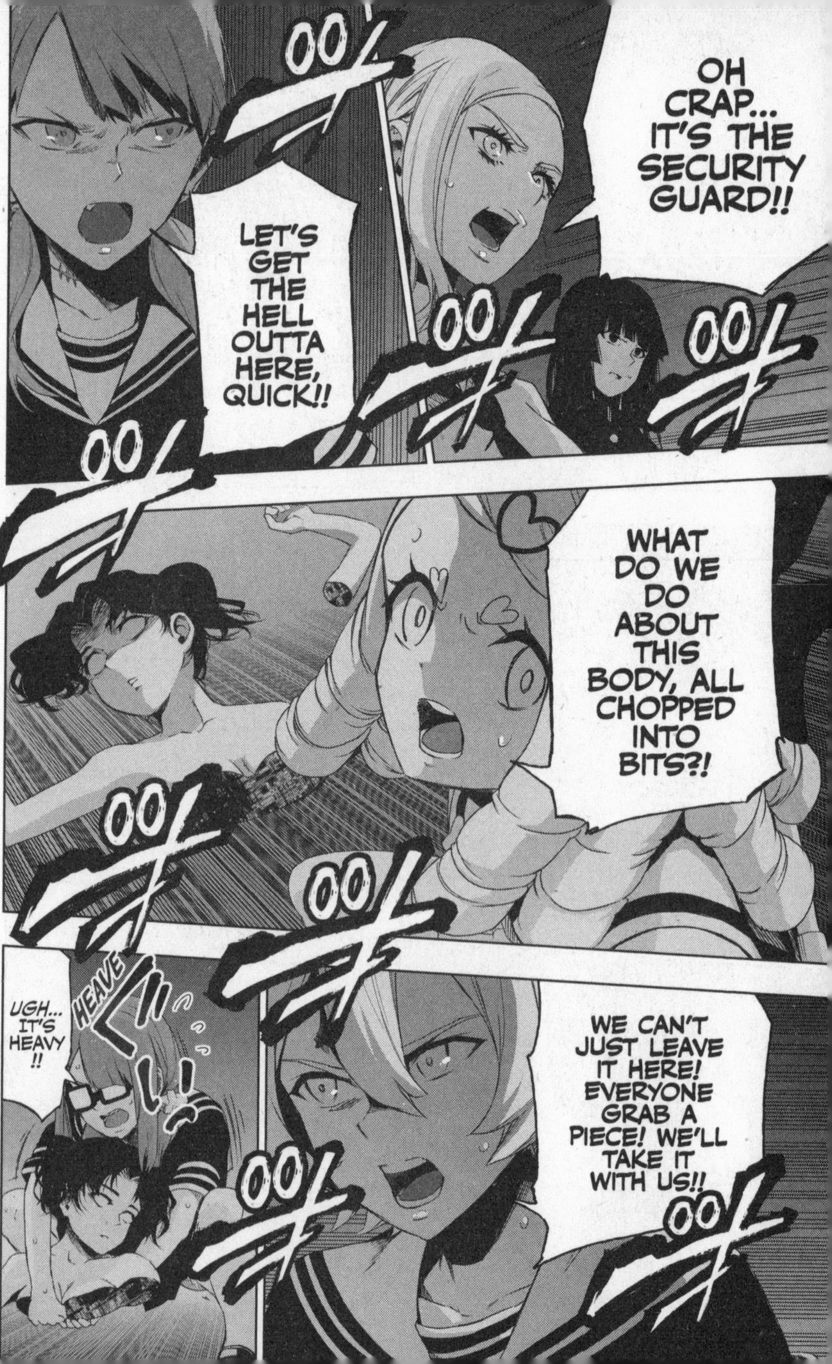
OH CRAP... IT'S THE SECURITY GUARD!!
LET'S GET THE HELL OUTTA HERE, QUICK!!
WHAT DO WE DO ABOUT THIS BODY, ALL CHOPPED INTO BITS?!
WE CAN'T JUST LEAVE IT HERE! EVERYONE GRAB A PIECE! WE'LL TAKE IT WITH US!!
HEAVE
UGH... IT'S HEAVY!!

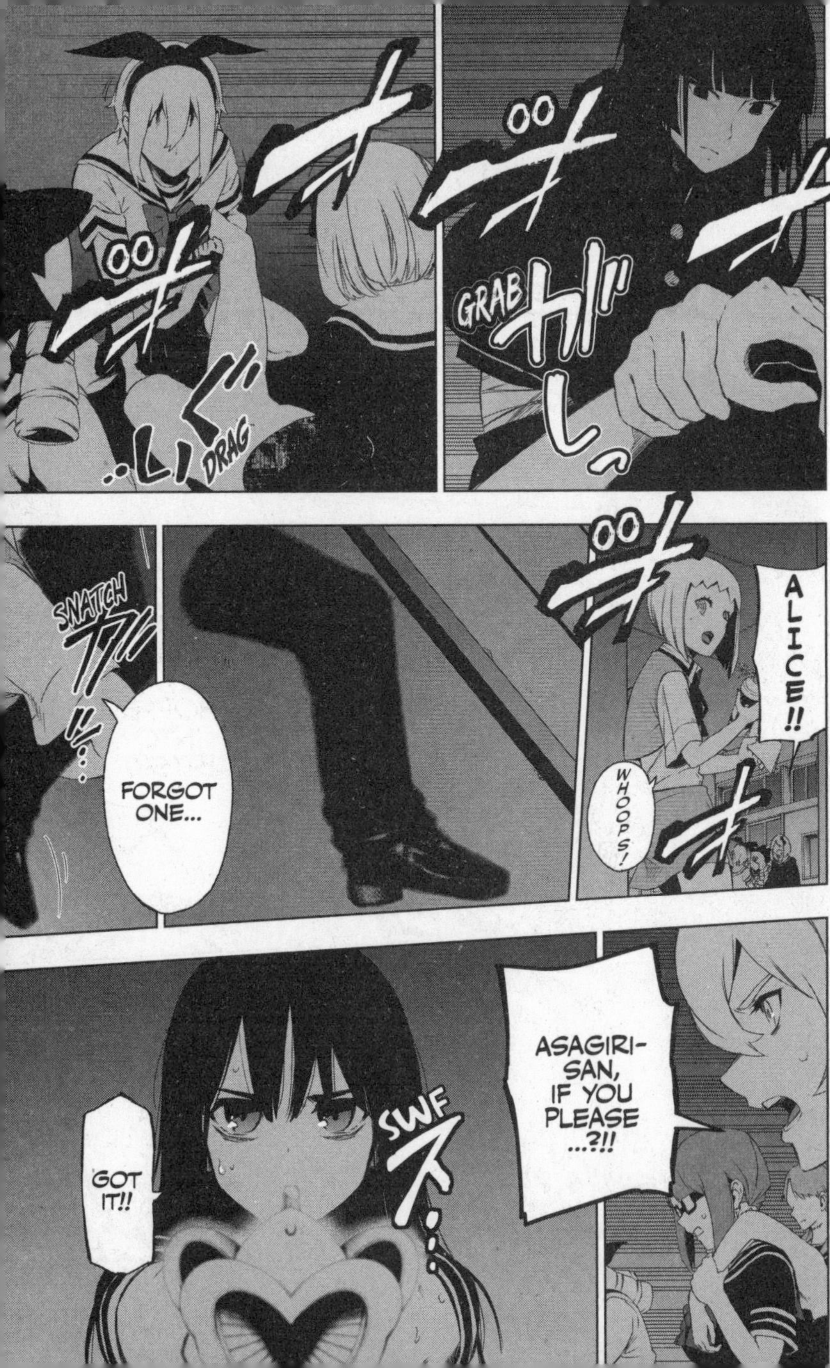
OO
GRAB
OO
DRAG
OO
ALICE!!
WHOOPS!
FORGOT ONE...
SNATCH
ASAGIRI-SAN, IF YOU PLEASE ...?!!
SWF
GOT IT!!

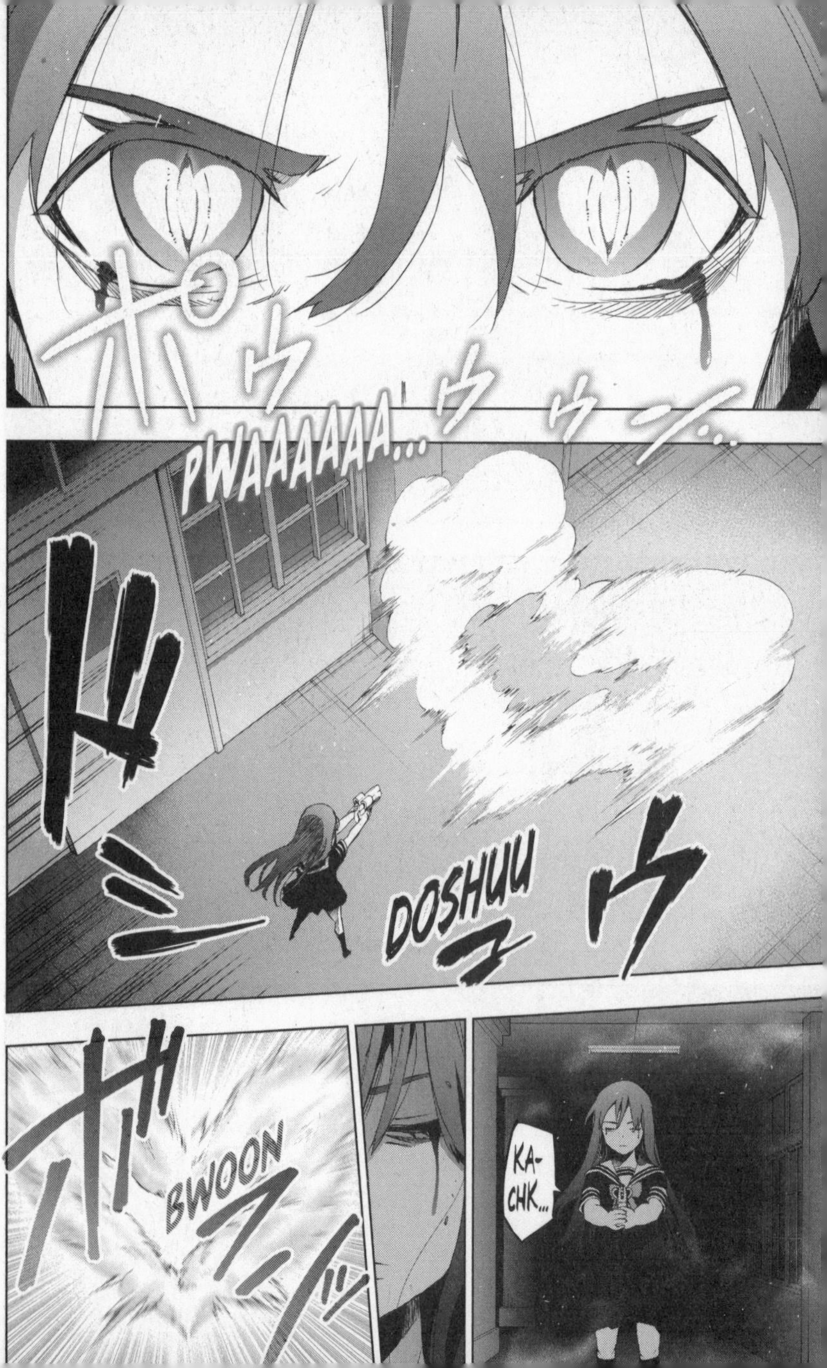
PWAAAAAA...
DOSHUU
KA-CHK...
BWOON

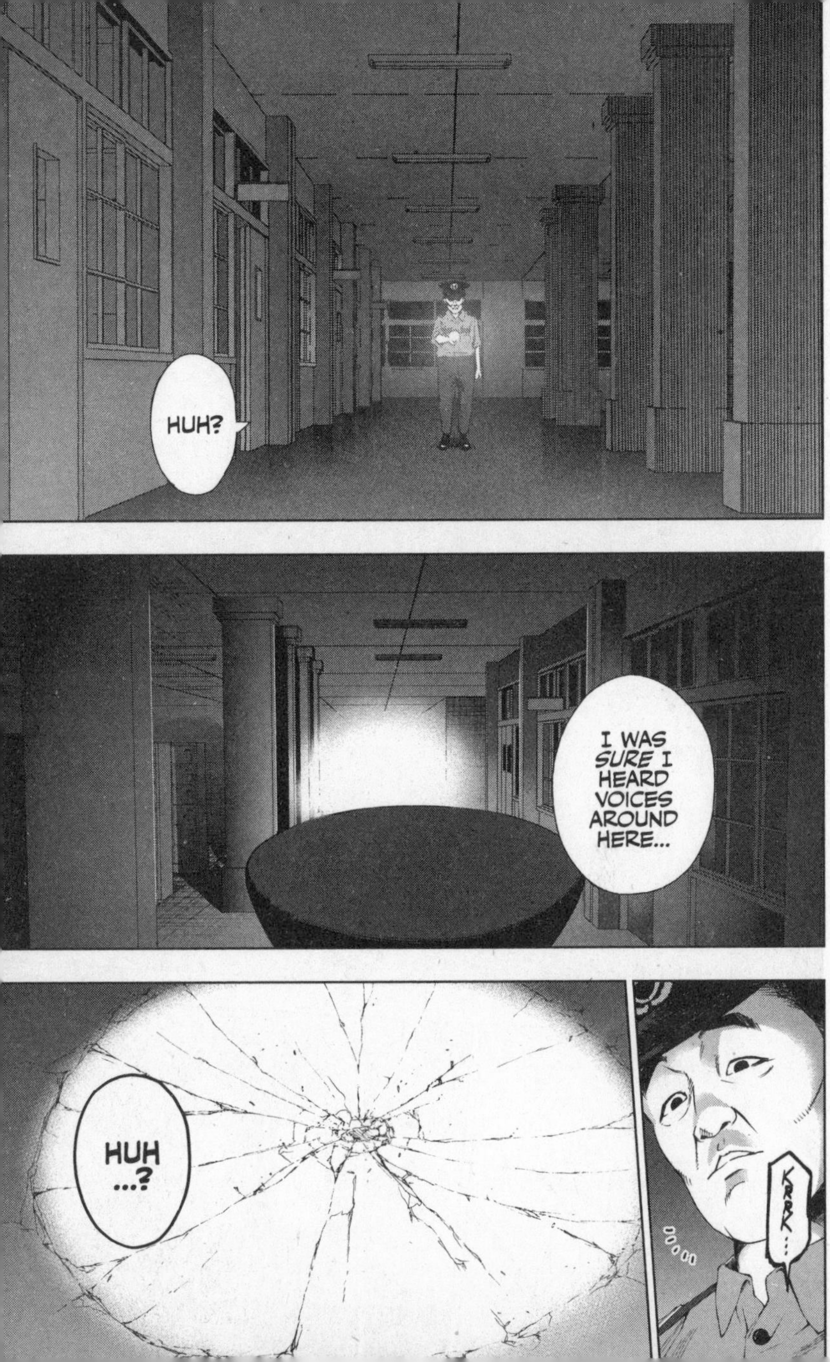
HUH?
I WAS SURE I HEARD VOICES AROUND HERE...
KRRK...
HUH ...?

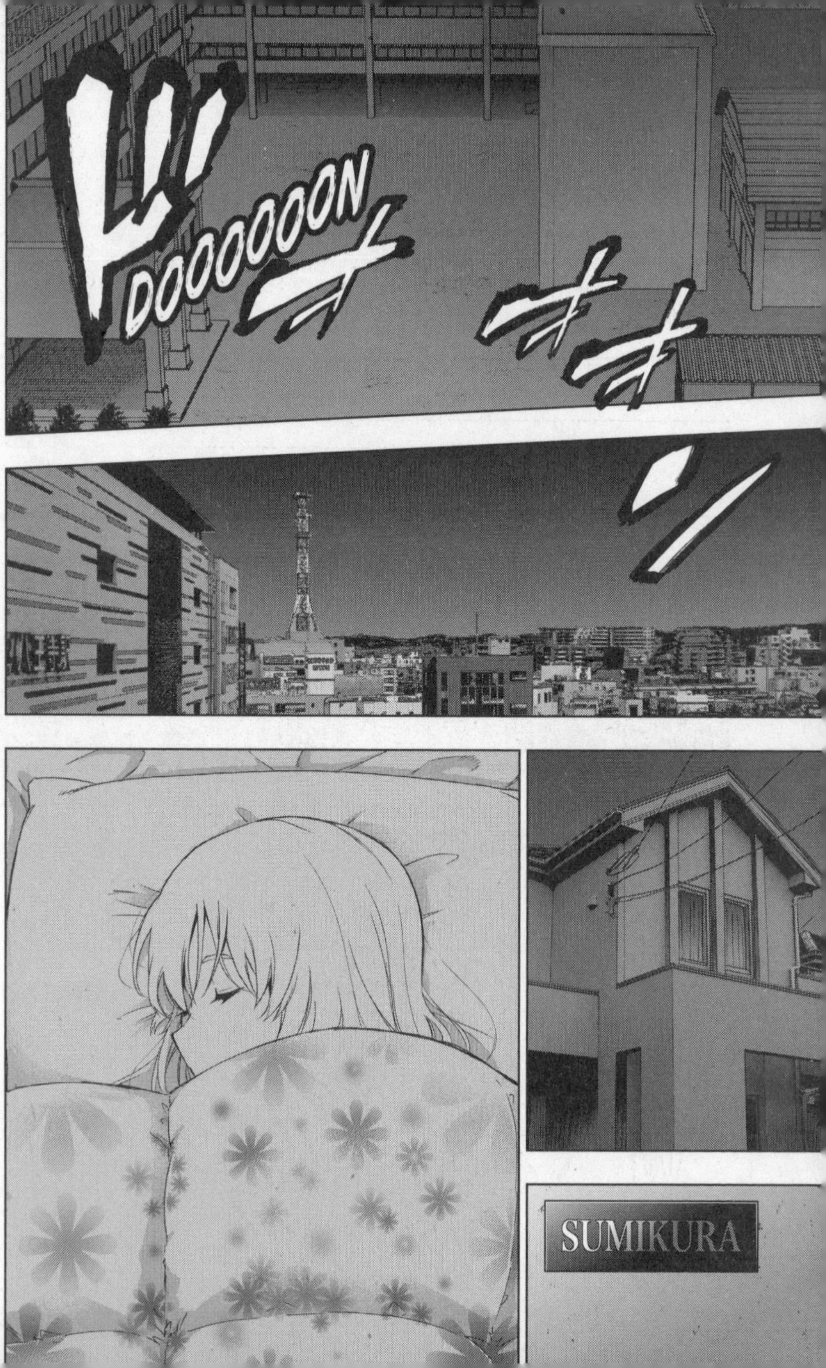
DOOOOOON
SUMIKURA

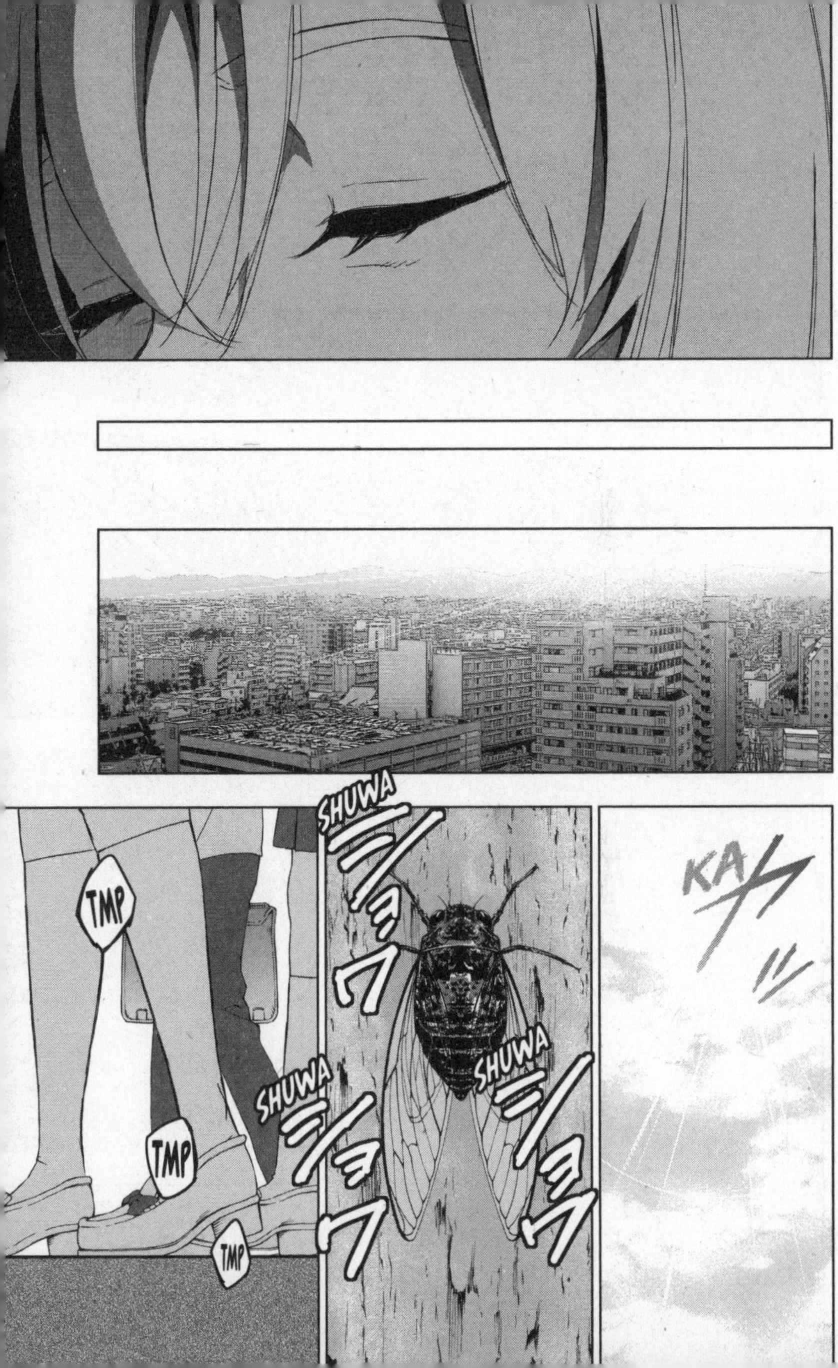
KA
SHUWA
SHUWA
SHUWA
TMP
TMP
TMP

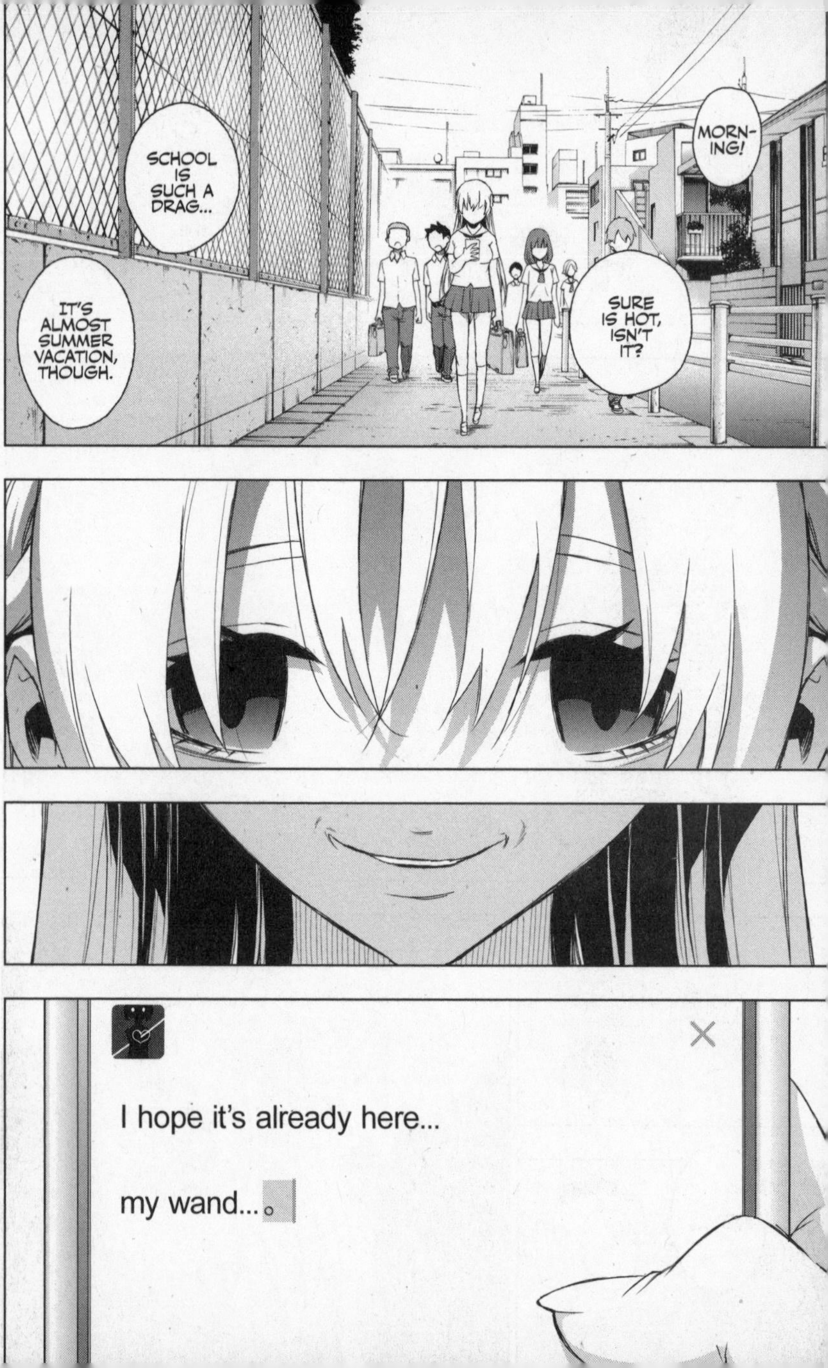
MORNING!
SURE IS HOT, ISN'T IT?
SCHOOL IS SUCH A DRAG...
IT'S ALMOST SUMMER VACATION, THOUGH.
I hope it's already here...
my wand...。

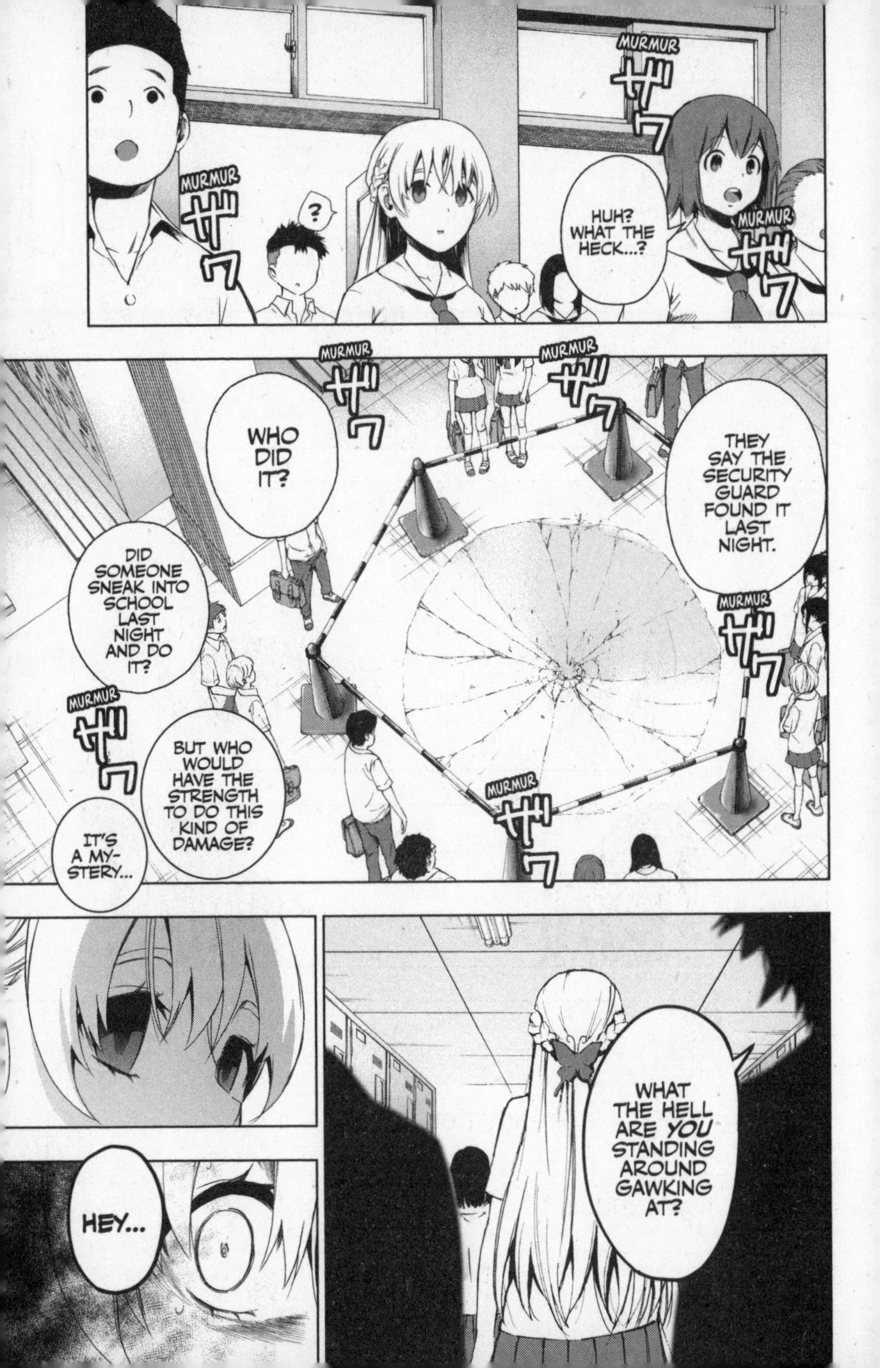
MURMUR
ザワ
MURMUR
ザワ
HUH? WHAT THE HECK...?
?
MURMUR
ザワ
MURMUR
ザワ
THEY SAY THE SECURITY GUARD FOUND IT LAST NIGHT.
MURMUR
ザワ
WHO DID IT?
MURMUR
ザワ
DID SOMEONE SNEAK INTO SCHOOL LAST NIGHT AND DO IT?
MURMUR
ザワ
MURMUR
ザワ
BUT WHO WOULD HAVE THE STRENGTH TO DO THIS KIND OF DAMAGE?
IT'S A MYSTERY...
WHAT THE HELL ARE *YOU* STANDING AROUND GAWKING AT?
HEY...

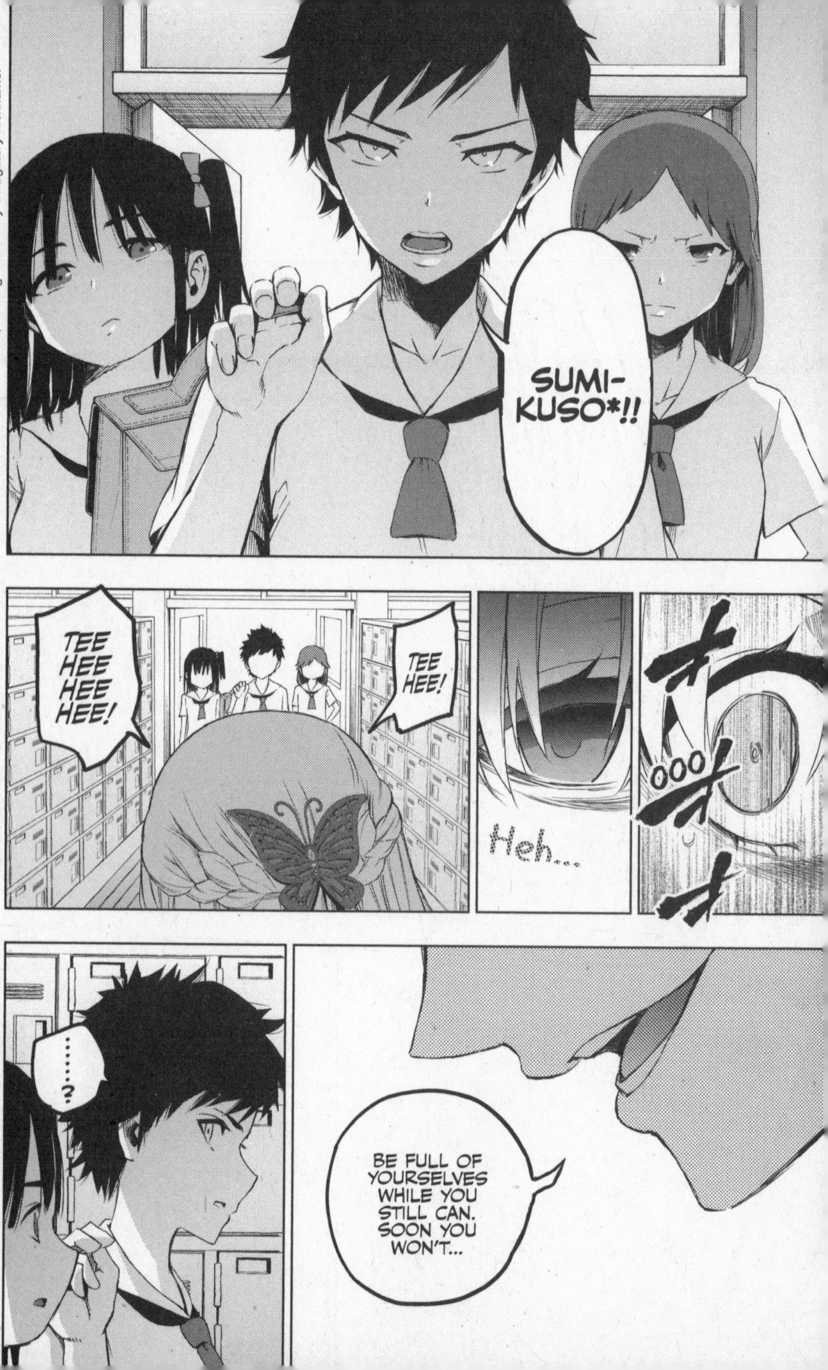
SUMI-KUSO*!!
OOO
Heh...
TEE HEE!
TEE HEE HEE HEE!
BE FULL OF YOURSELVES WHILE YOU STILL CAN. SOON YOU WON'T...
......?

*Sumikuso is a play on her name, Sumikura. "Kuso" means "shit" or "waste product" when combined with another word, making this a very derogatory nickname.

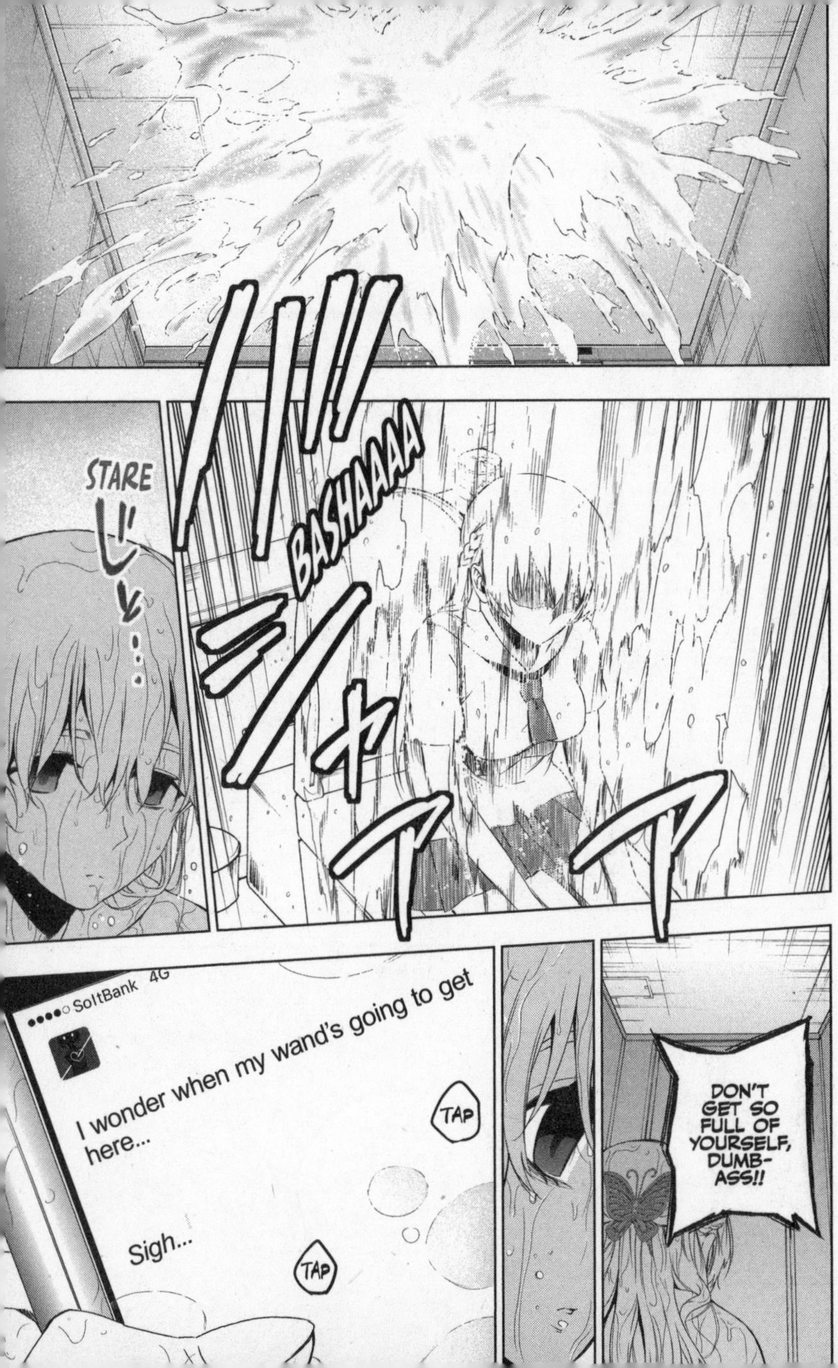
BASHAAAA
STARE
じと…
DON'T GET SO FULL OF YOURSELF, DUMB-ASS!!
●●●●○ SoltBank 4G
I wonder when my wand's going to get here...
TAP
Sigh...
TAP

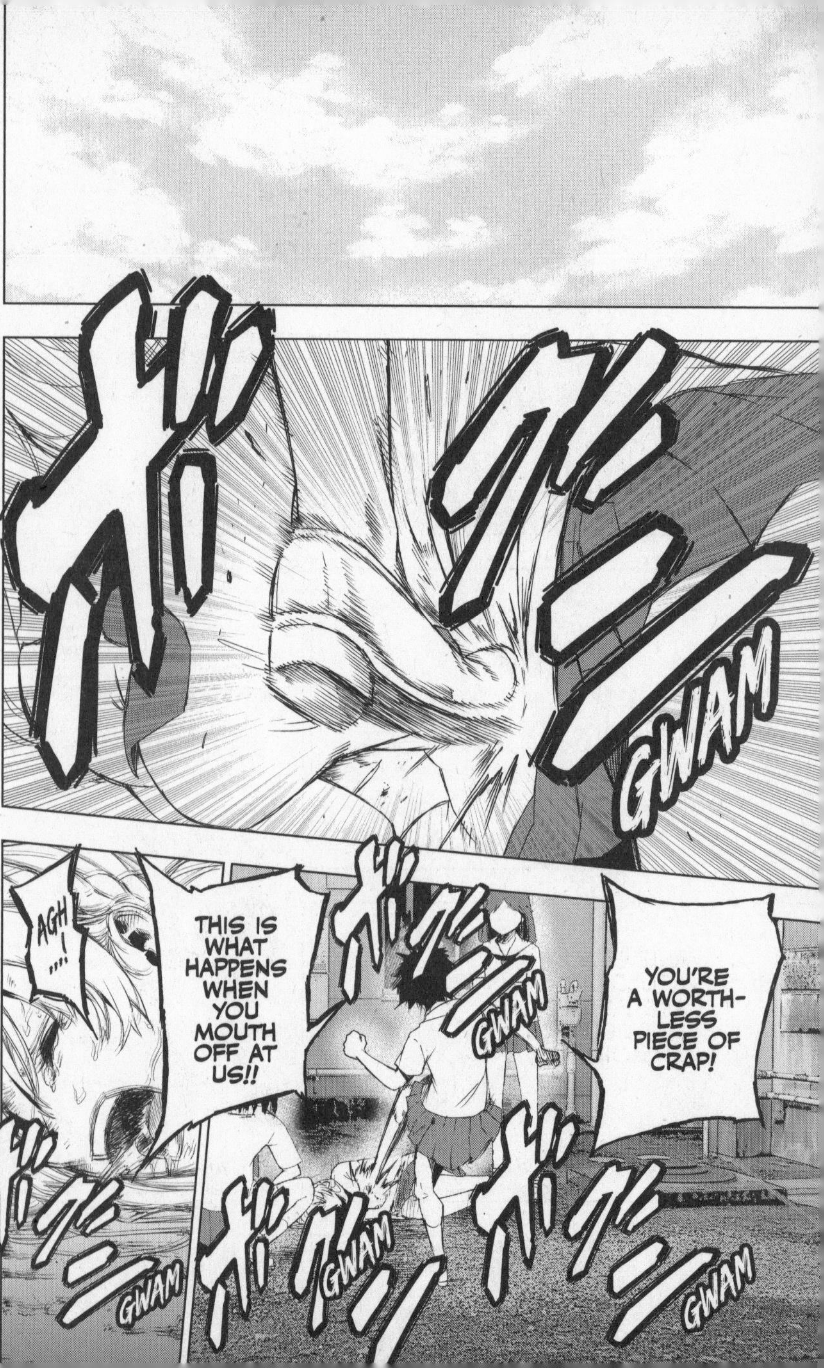
GWAM
YOU'RE A WORTH-LESS PIECE OF CRAP!
GWAM
THIS IS WHAT HAPPENS WHEN YOU MOUTH OFF AT US!!
GWAM
GWAM
AGH!
GWAM

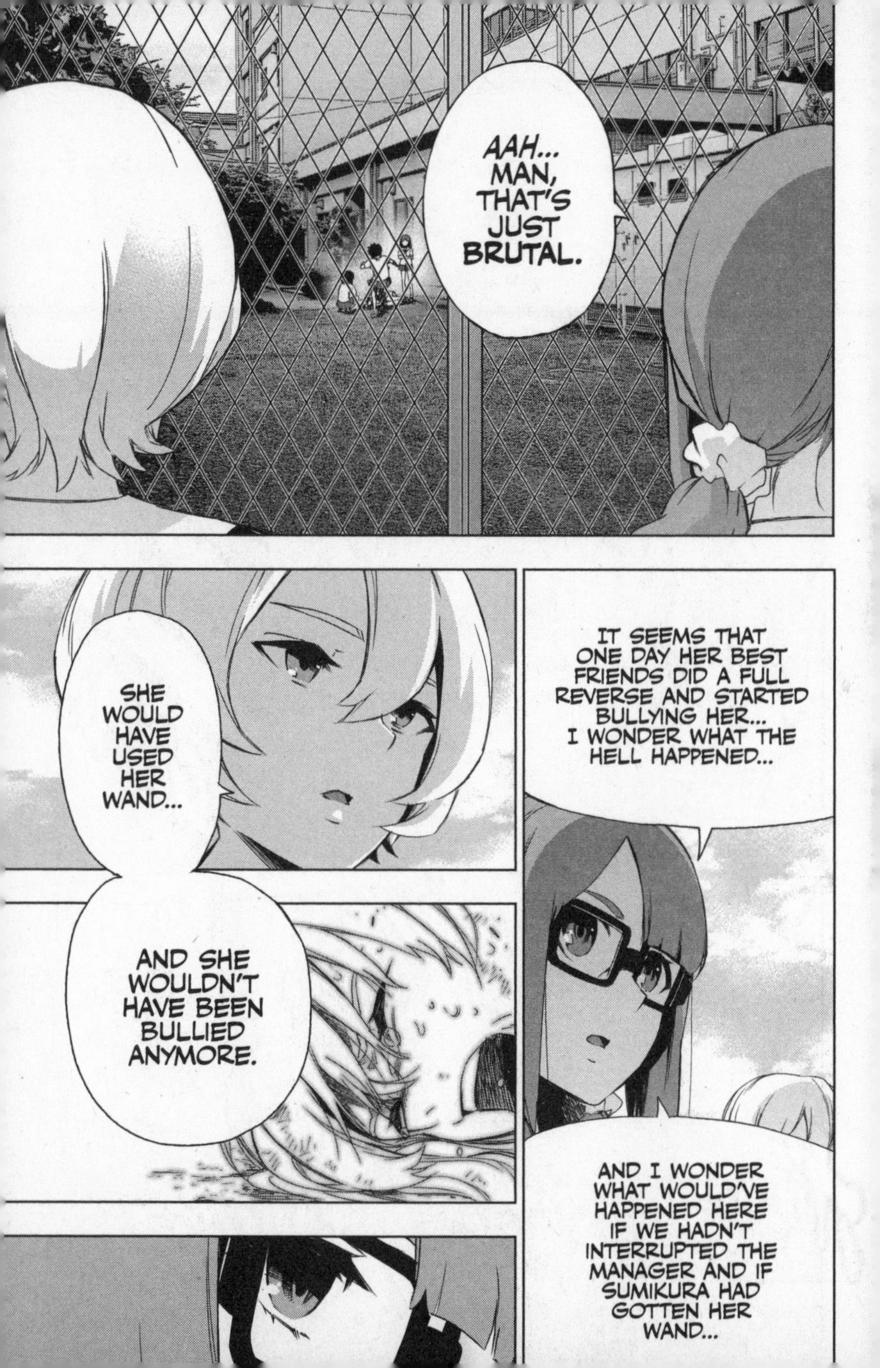
AAH... MAN, THAT'S JUST BRUTAL.
IT SEEMS THAT ONE DAY HER BEST FRIENDS DID A FULL REVERSE AND STARTED BULLYING HER... I WONDER WHAT THE HELL HAPPENED...
AND I WONDER WHAT WOULD'VE HAPPENED HERE IF WE HADN'T INTERRUPTED THE MANAGER AND IF SUMIKURA HAD GOTTEN HER WAND...
SHE WOULD HAVE USED HER WAND...
AND SHE WOULDN'T HAVE BEEN BULLIED ANYMORE.

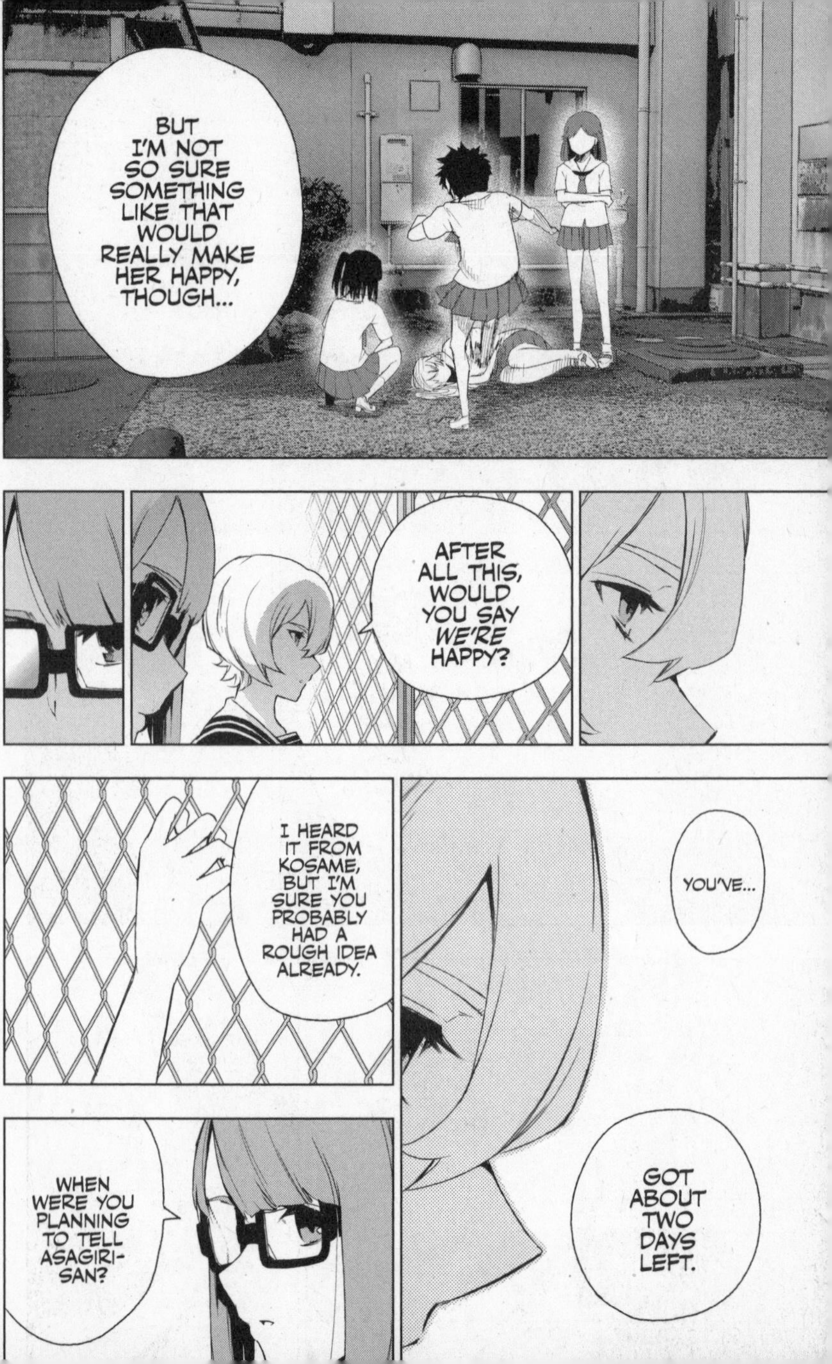
BUT I'M NOT SO SURE SOMETHING LIKE THAT WOULD REALLY MAKE HER HAPPY, THOUGH...
AFTER ALL THIS, WOULD YOU SAY *WE'RE* HAPPY?
YOU'VE...
GOT ABOUT TWO DAYS LEFT.
I HEARD IT FROM KOSAME, BUT I'M SURE YOU PROBABLY HAD A ROUGH IDEA ALREADY.
WHEN WERE YOU PLANNING TO TELL ASAGIRI-SAN?

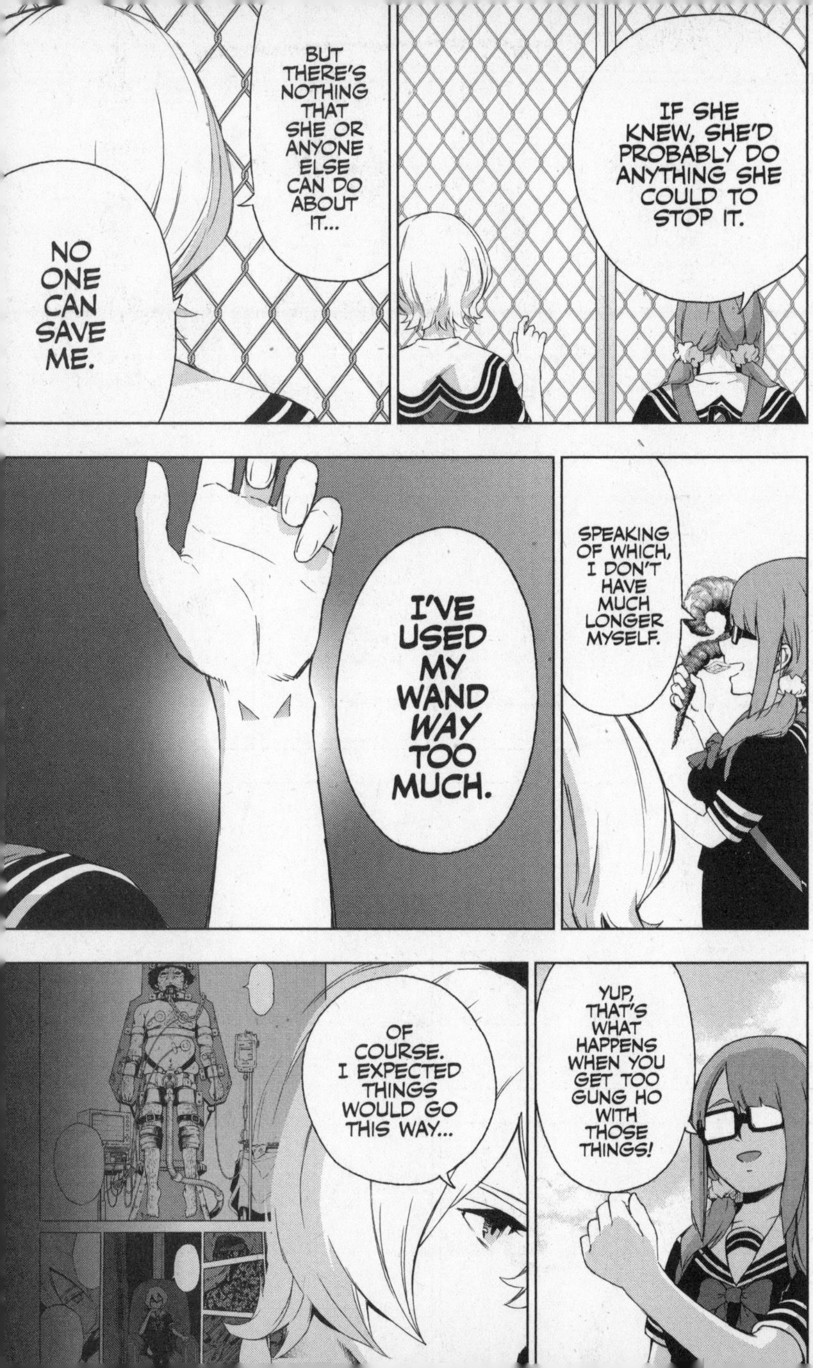
IF SHE KNEW, SHE'D PROBABLY DO ANYTHING SHE COULD TO STOP IT.
BUT THERE'S NOTHING THAT SHE OR ANYONE ELSE CAN DO ABOUT IT...
NO ONE CAN SAVE ME.
SPEAKING OF WHICH, I DON'T HAVE MUCH LONGER MYSELF.
I'VE USED MY WAND *WAY* TOO MUCH.
YUP, THAT'S WHAT HAPPENS WHEN YOU GET TOO GUNG HO WITH THOSE THINGS!
OF COURSE. I EXPECTED THINGS WOULD GO THIS WAY...
...

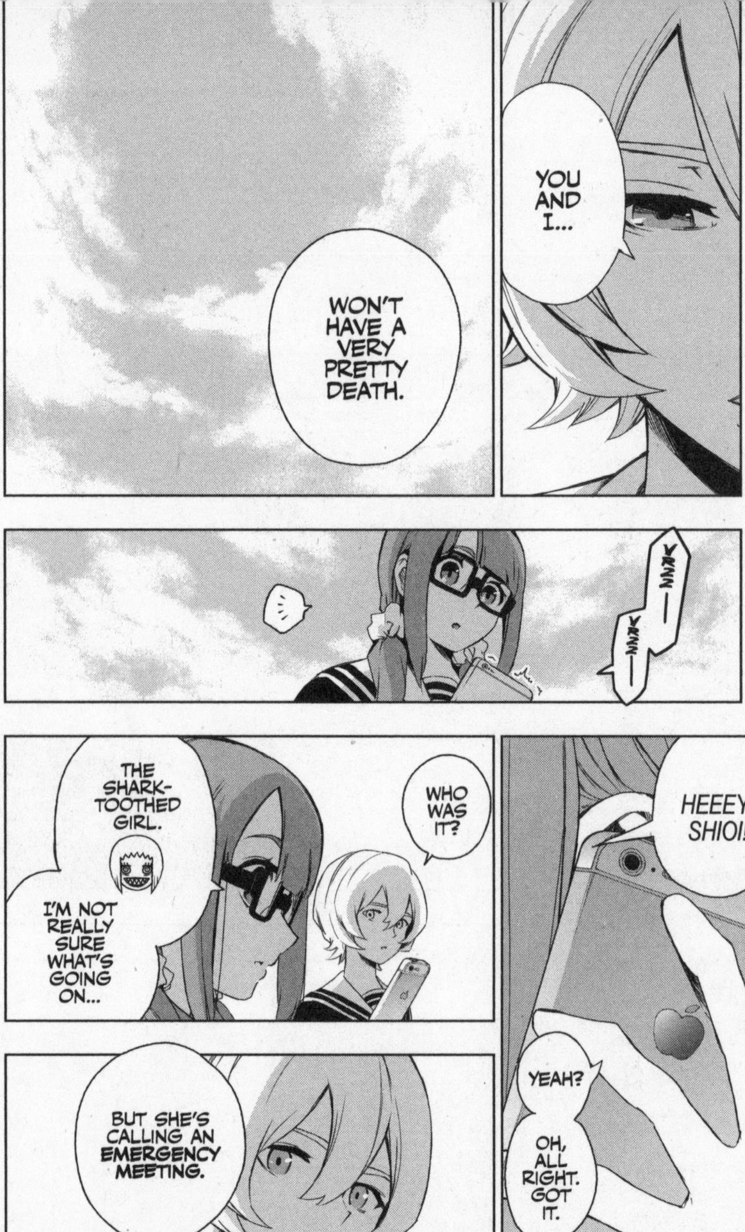
YOU AND I...
WON'T HAVE A VERY PRETTY DEATH.
VRZZ—
VRZZ—
HEEEY! SHIOI!
YEAH?
OH, ALL RIGHT. GOT IT.
WHO WAS IT?
THE SHARK-TOOTHED GIRL.
I'M NOT REALLY SURE WHAT'S GOING ON...
BUT SHE'S CALLING AN EMERGENCY MEETING.

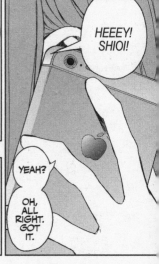

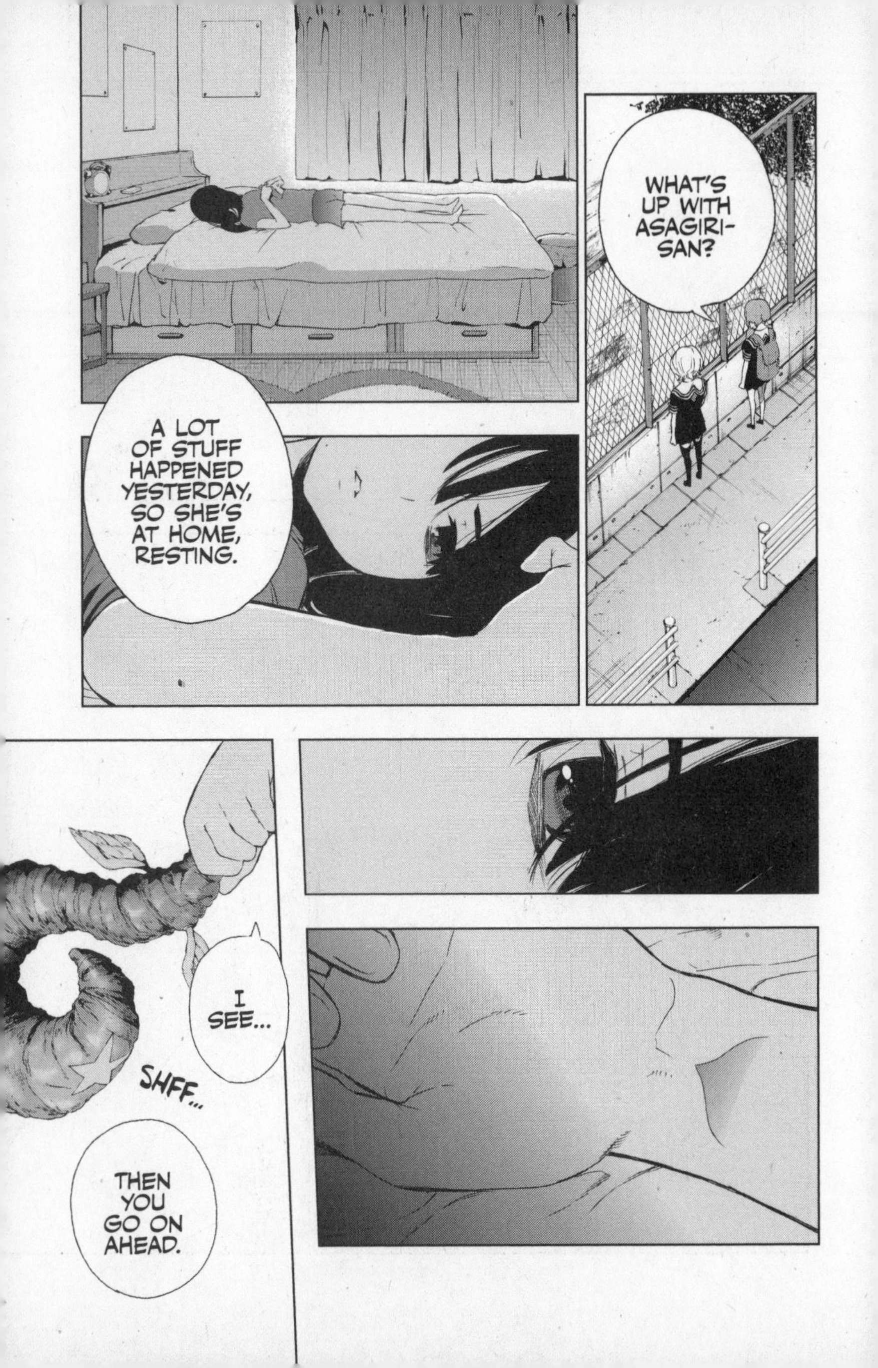
WHAT'S UP WITH ASAGIRI-SAN?
A LOT OF STUFF HAPPENED YESTERDAY, SO SHE'S AT HOME, RESTING.
I SEE...
SHFF...
THEN YOU GO ON AHEAD.

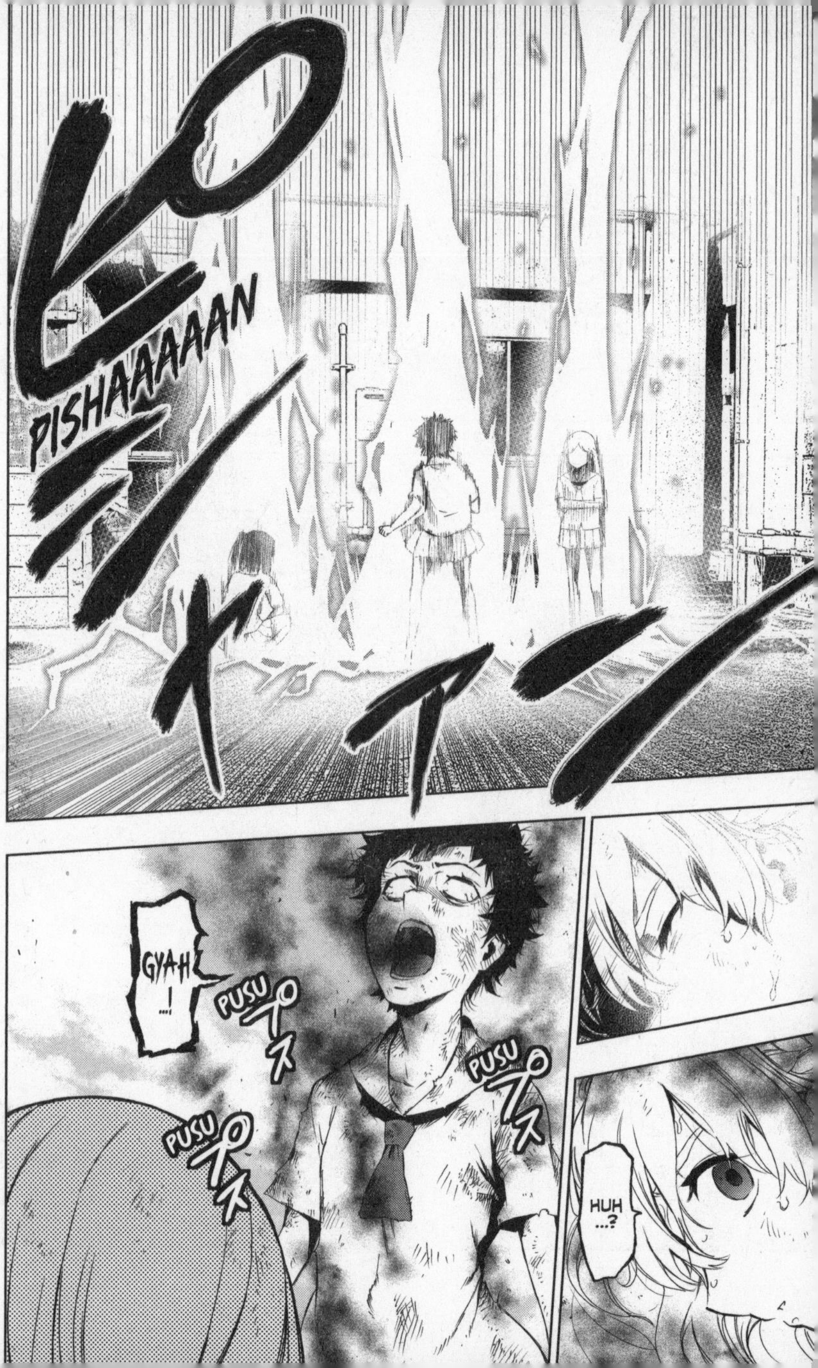

PISHAAAAAN
HUH ...?
GYAH ...!
PUSU
PUSU
PUSU

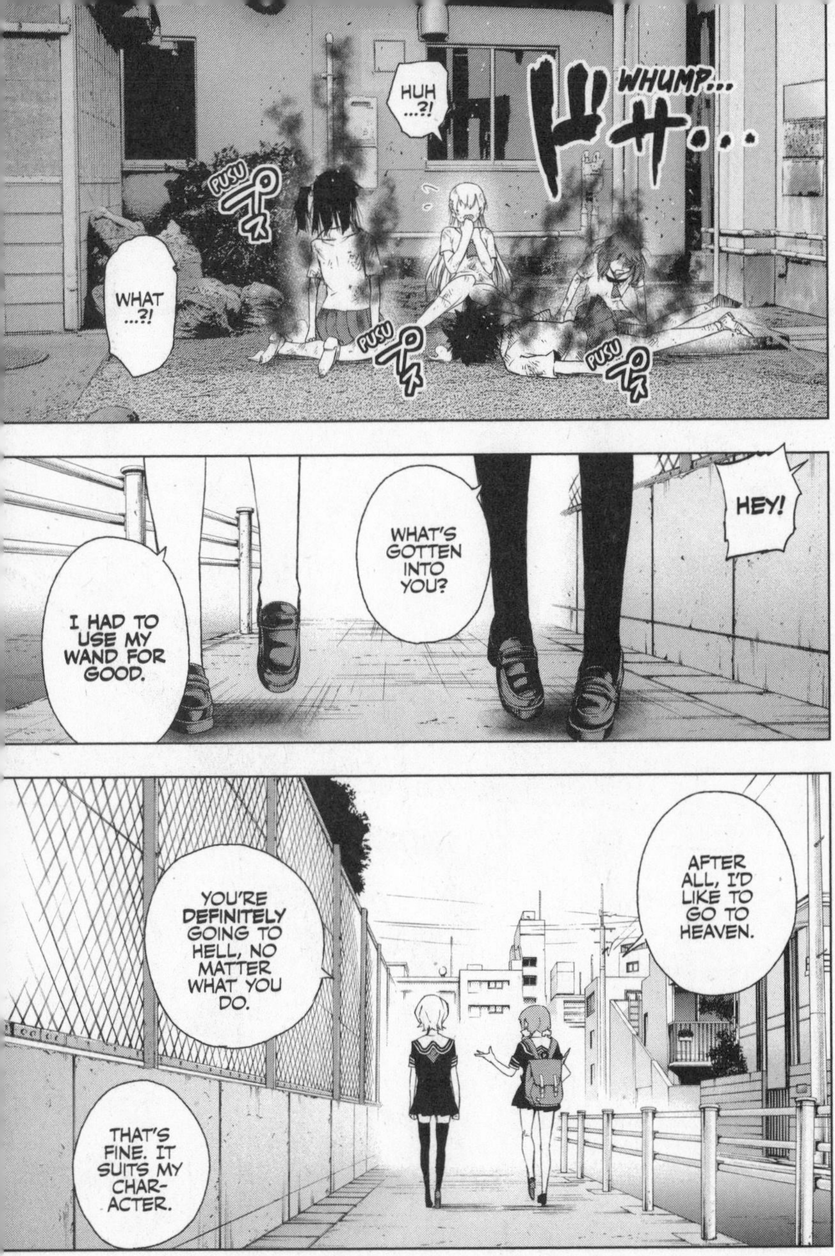

WHUMP...
ドサ...
HUH ...?!
PUSU
プス
WHAT ...?!
PUSU
プス
PUSU
プス
HEY!
WHAT'S GOTTEN INTO YOU?
I HAD TO USE MY WAND FOR GOOD.
AFTER ALL, I'D LIKE TO GO TO HEAVEN.
YOU'RE DEFINITELY GOING TO HELL, NO MATTER WHAT YOU DO.
THAT'S FINE. IT SUITS MY CHAR-ACTER.

Sumikura Yuka

Sex: Female
Age: 14
Date of Birth: June 19 (Gemini)
Height: 151cm
Weight: 46kg
Blood Type: A
Birthplace: Tokyo
Interests/Hobbies: Reading, studying, cooking, track and field

Strengths: Mental clarity; good athletic reflexes

Dislikes/Weakness: Spicy food, reptiles

Likes: Sweets

• Eighth Grader

• Yuka's best friend became jealous of her talent for both academics and sports, and began bullying her when the guy she liked began taking an interest in Yuka. Once a bright, cheerful girl, Yuka became very dark and gloomy after her friend turned on her.

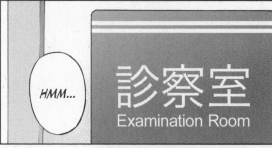

HMM...

診察室

Examination Room

THINGS HAVE REALLY TAKEN A SEVERE TURN FOR THE WORSE.

ENTER.51 VARIOUS PASTS, PART 1

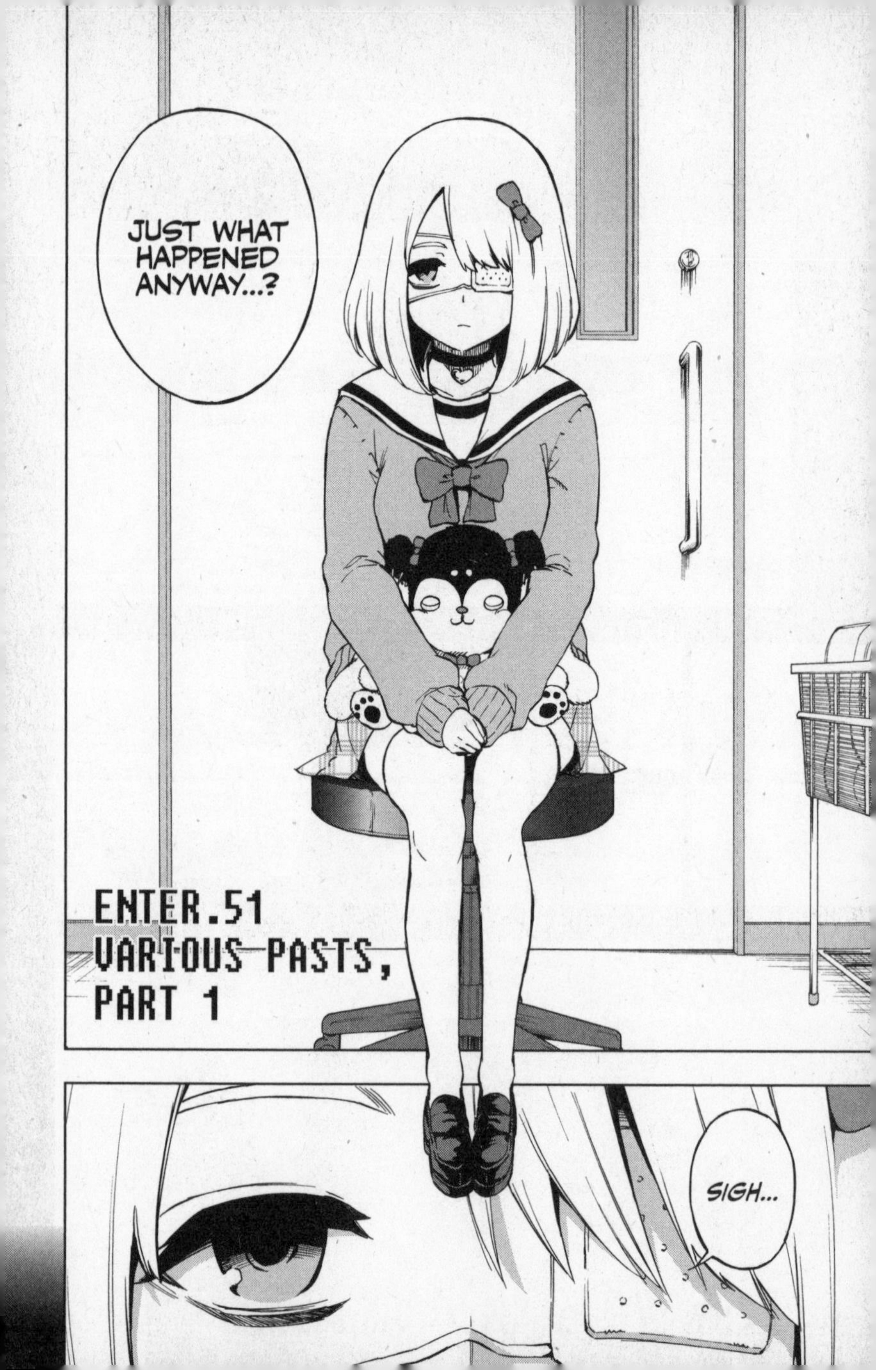
JUST WHAT HAPPENED ANYWAY...?
ENTER.51
VARIOUS PASTS, PART 1
SIGH...

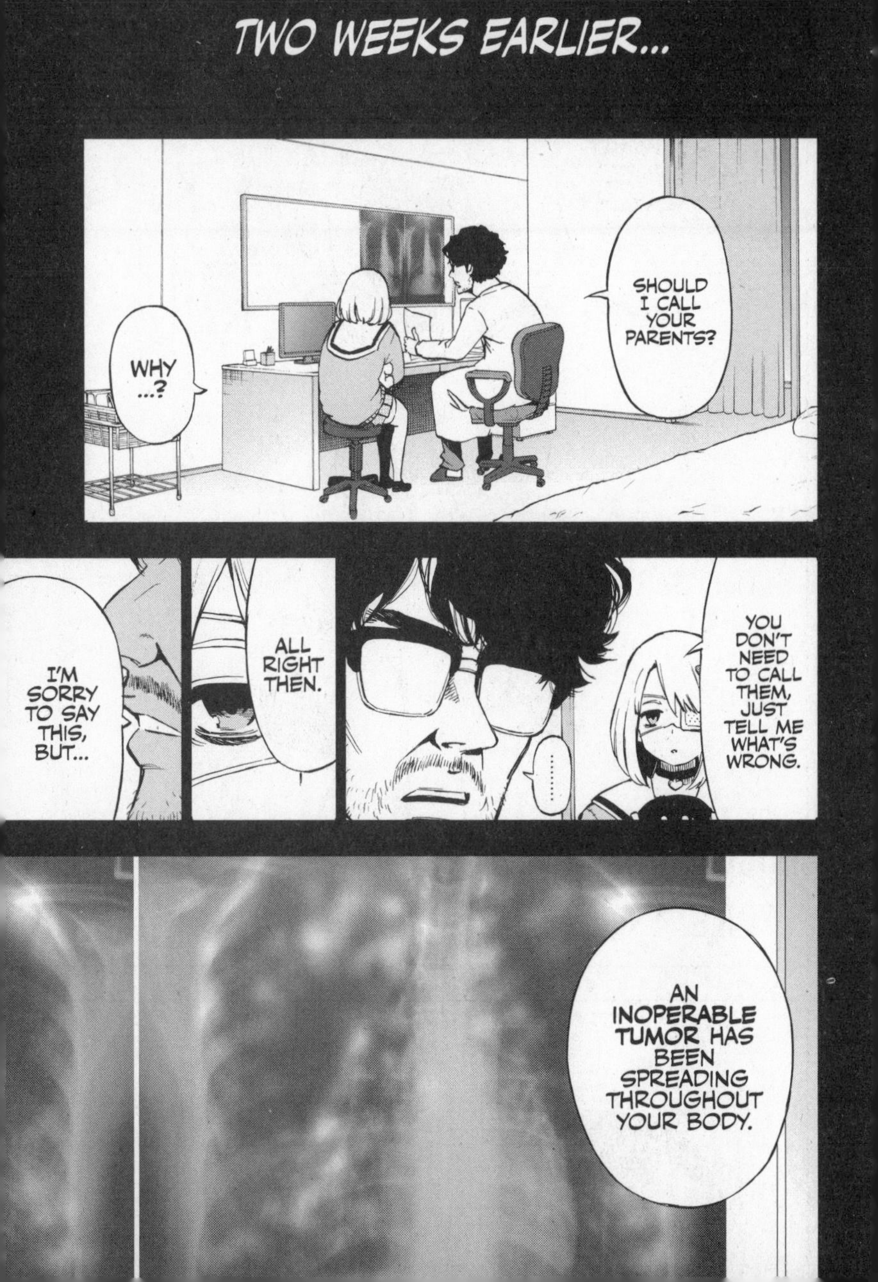
TWO WEEKS EARLIER...
SHOULD I CALL YOUR PARENTS?
WHY ...?
YOU DON'T NEED TO CALL THEM, JUST TELL ME WHAT'S WRONG.
......
ALL RIGHT THEN.
I'M SORRY TO SAY THIS, BUT...
AN INOPERABLE TUMOR HAS BEEN SPREADING THROUGHOUT YOUR BODY.

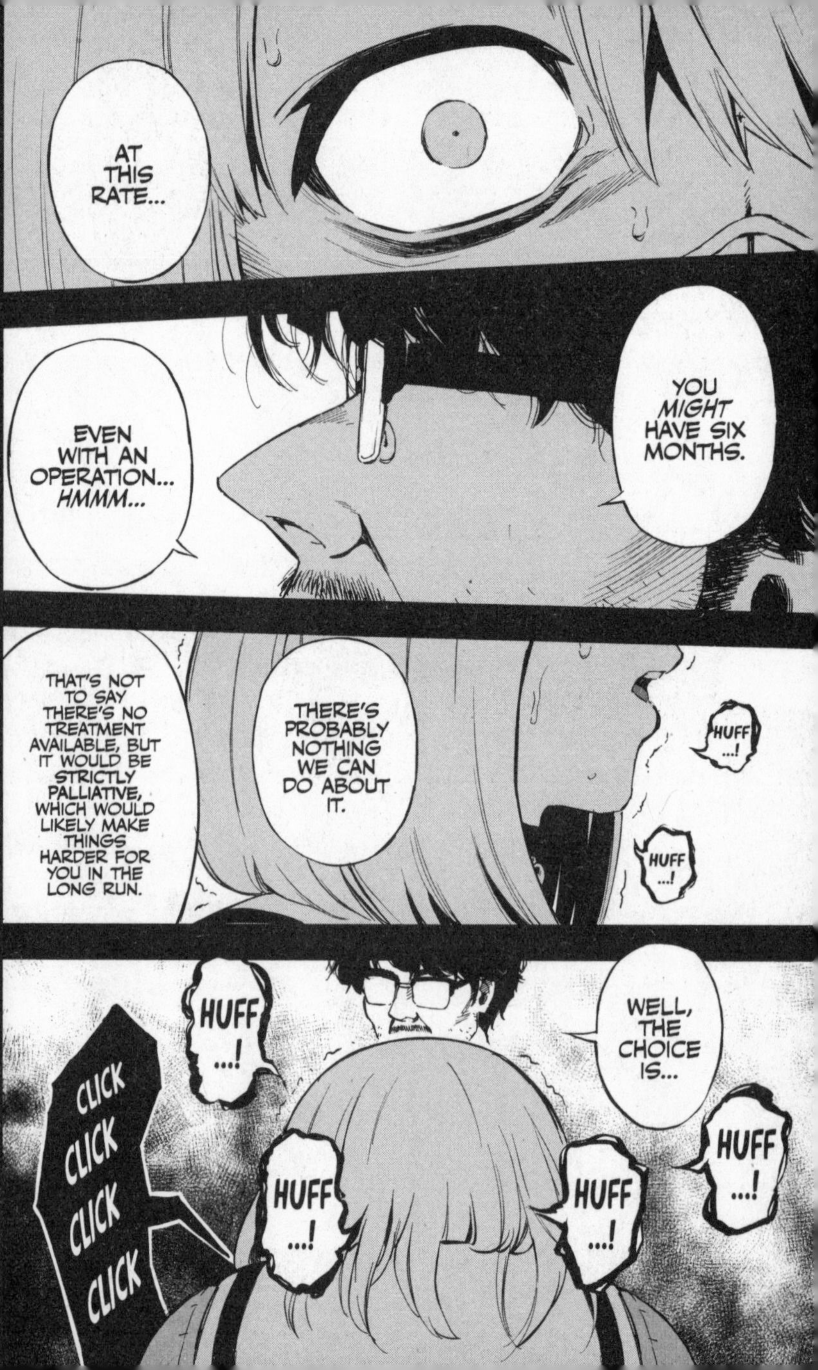
AT THIS RATE...
YOU *MIGHT* HAVE SIX MONTHS.
EVEN WITH AN OPERATION... *HMMM...*
HUFF ...!
HUFF ...!
THERE'S PROBABLY NOTHING WE CAN DO ABOUT IT.
THAT'S NOT TO SAY THERE'S NO TREATMENT AVAILABLE, BUT IT WOULD BE STRICTLY PALLIATIVE, WHICH WOULD LIKELY MAKE THINGS HARDER FOR YOU IN THE LONG RUN.
WELL, THE CHOICE IS...
HUFF ...!
HUFF ...!
HUFF ...!
HUFF ...!
CLICK CLICK CLICK CLICK

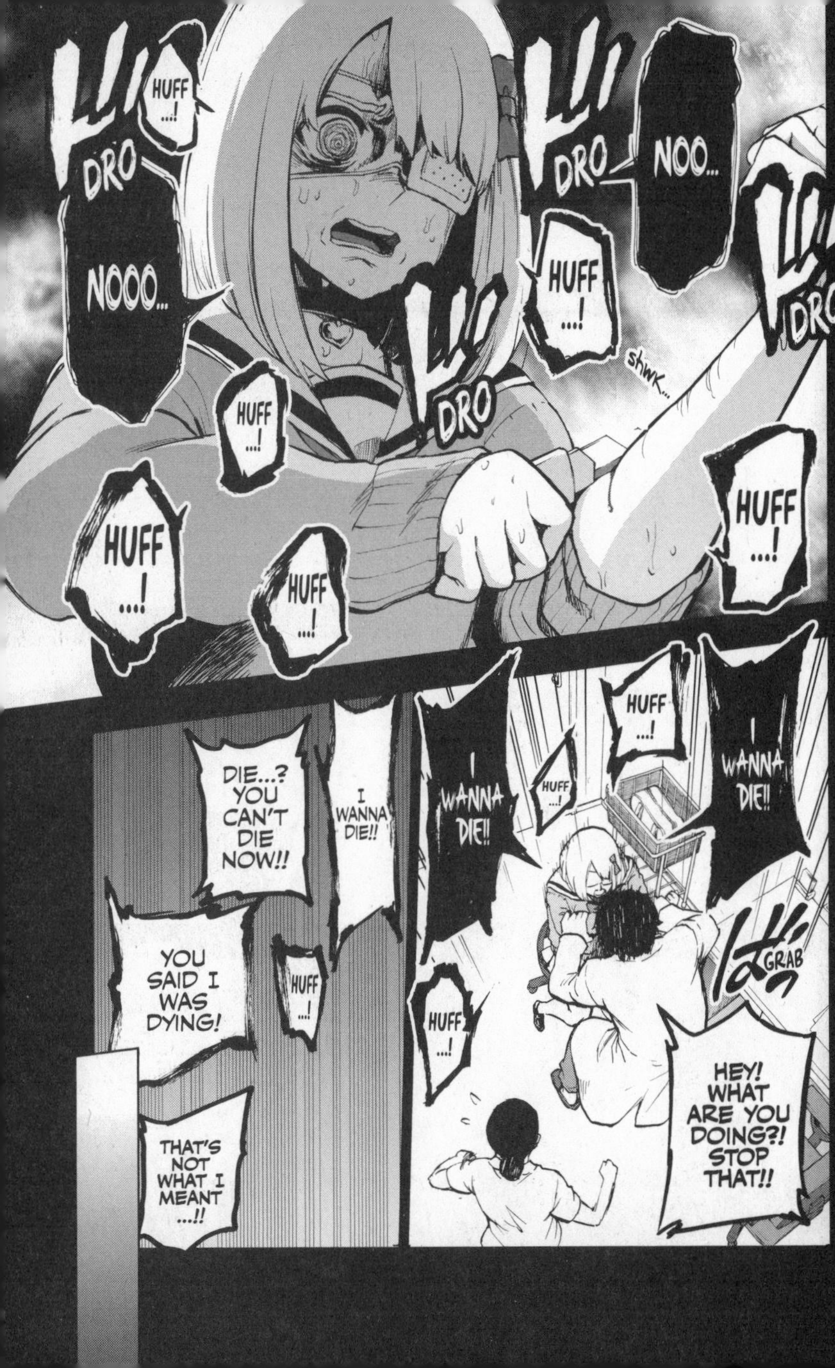
DRO
NOO...
DRO
HUFF ...!
shwk...
HUFF ...!
DRO
HUFF ...!
DRO
NOOO...
HUFF ...!
HUFF ...!
HUFF ...!
I WANNA DIE!!
HUFF ...!
HUFF ...!
I WANNA DIE!!
GRAB
HUFF ...!
HEY! WHAT ARE YOU DOING?! STOP THAT!!
I WANNA DIE!!
DIE...? YOU CAN'T DIE NOW!!
HUFF ...!
YOU SAID I WAS DYING!
THAT'S NOT WHAT I MEANT ...!!

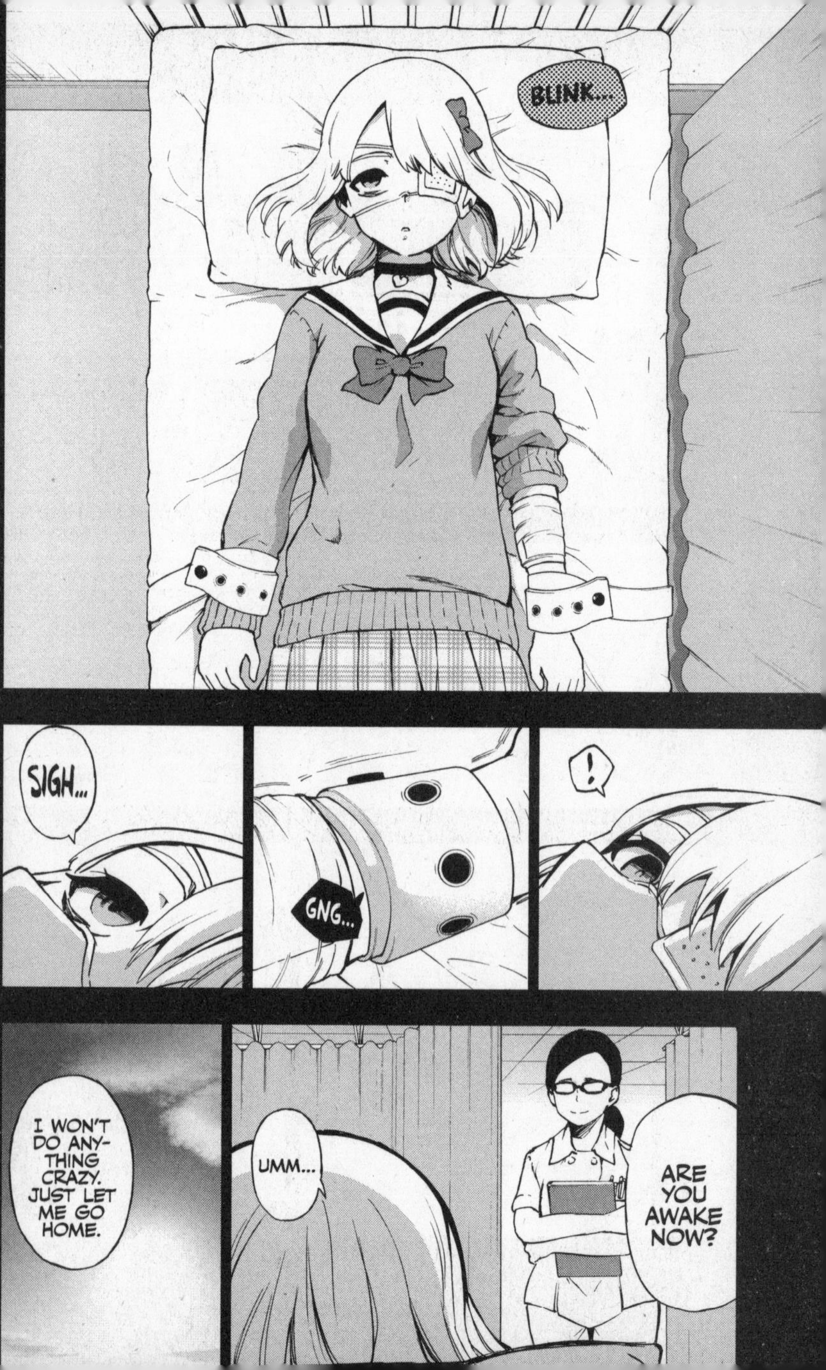
BLINK...
!
GNG...
SIGH...
ARE YOU AWAKE NOW?
UMM...
I WON'T DO ANY-
THING CRAZY.
JUST LET ME GO HOME.

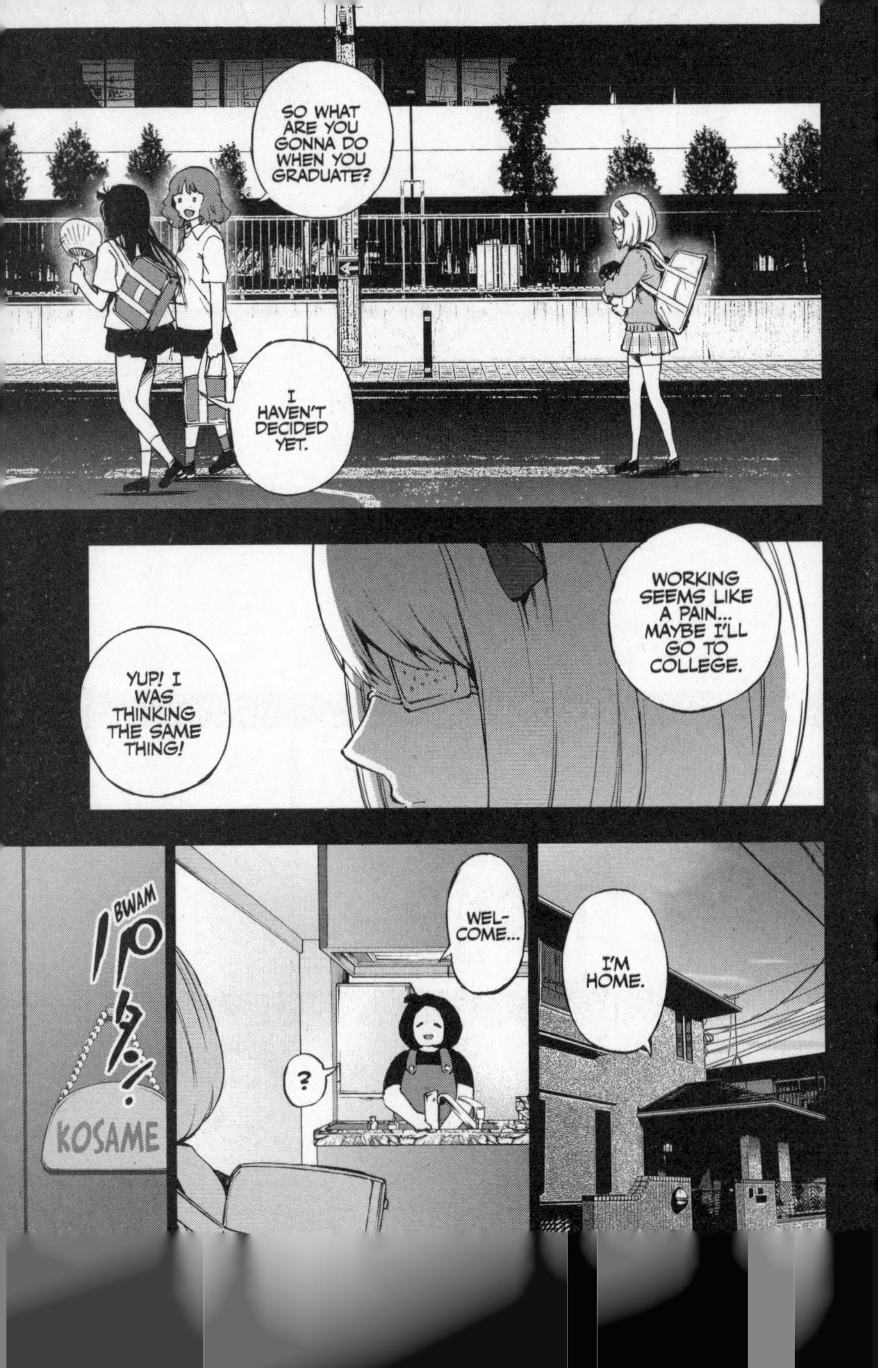
SO WHAT ARE YOU GONNA DO WHEN YOU GRADUATE?
I HAVEN'T DECIDED YET.
WORKING SEEMS LIKE A PAIN... MAYBE I'LL GO TO COLLEGE.
YUP! I WAS THINKING THE SAME THING!
I'M HOME.
WEL-COME...
?
BWAM
KOSAME

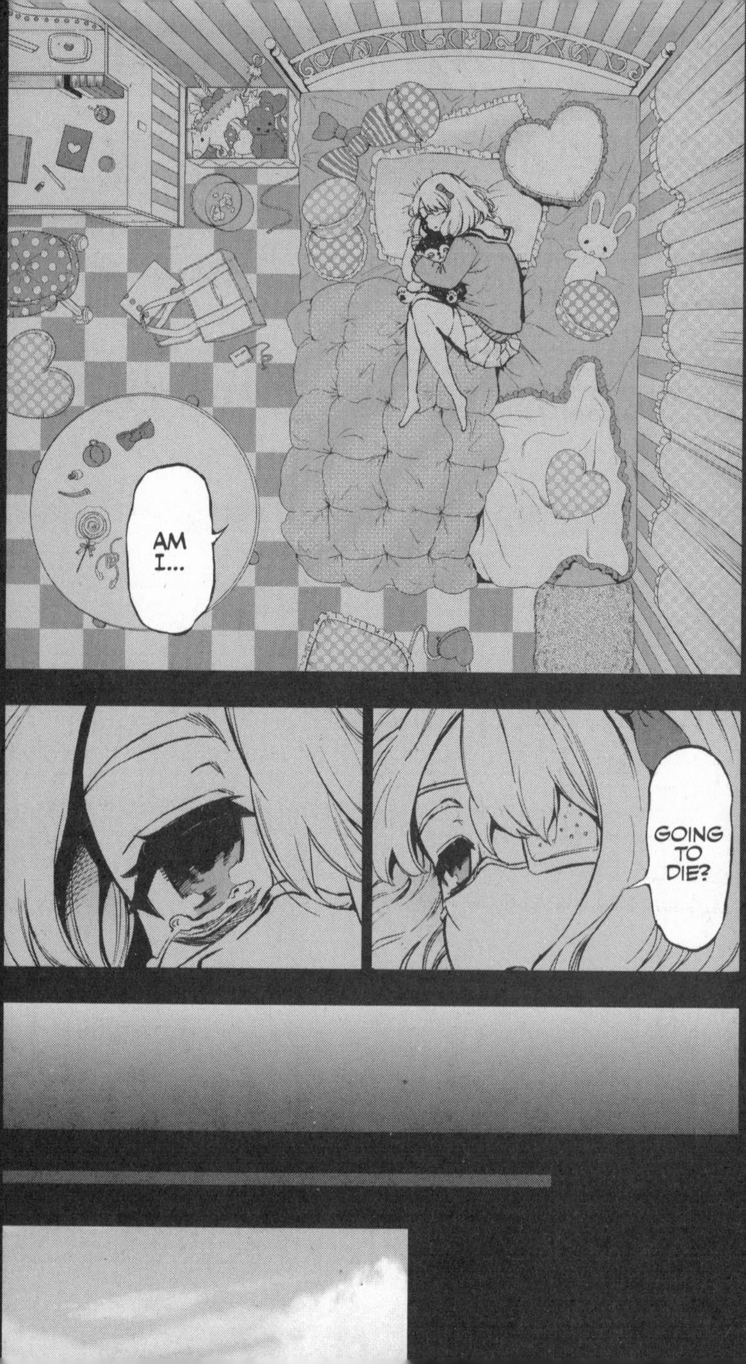
AM I...
GOING TO DIE?

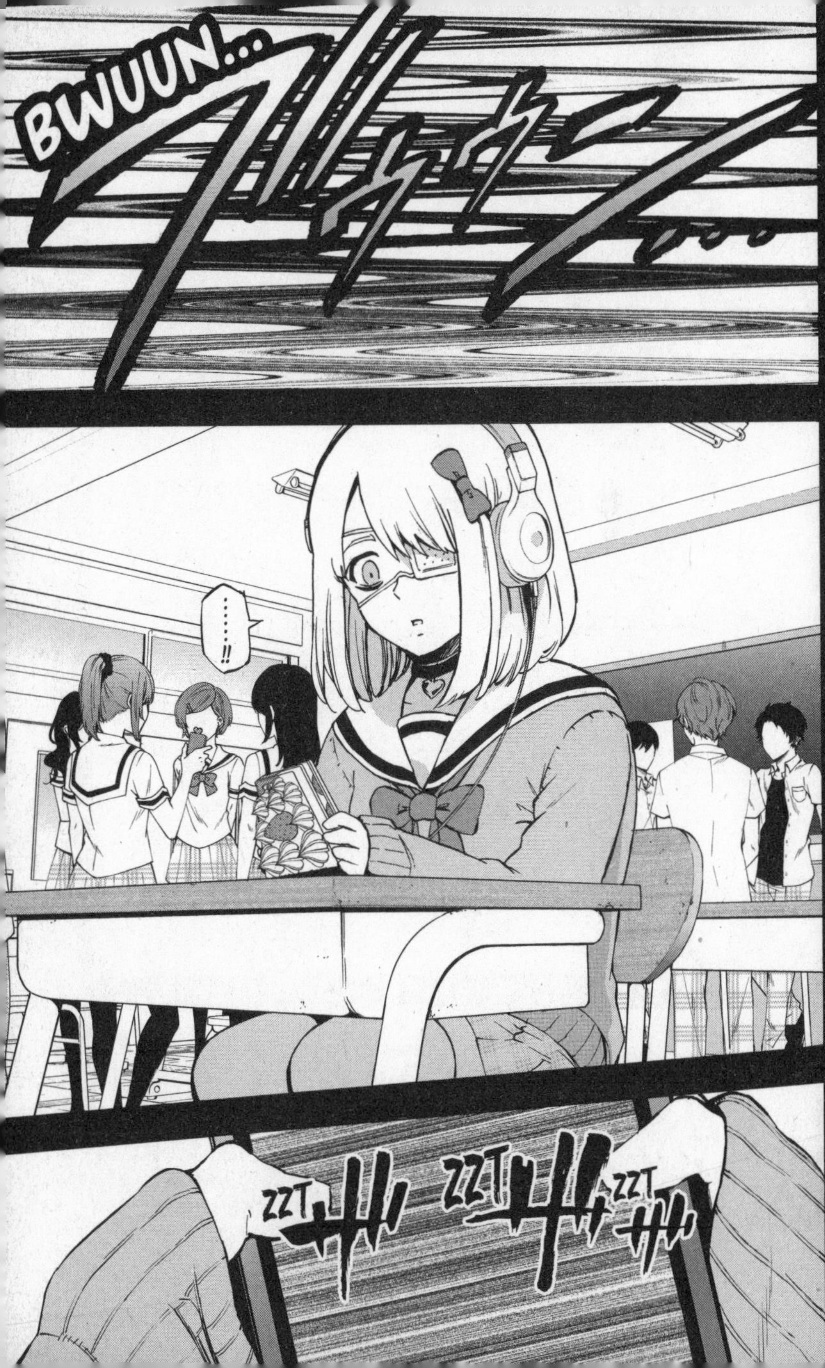
BWUUN...
......!!
ZZT
ZZT
ZZT

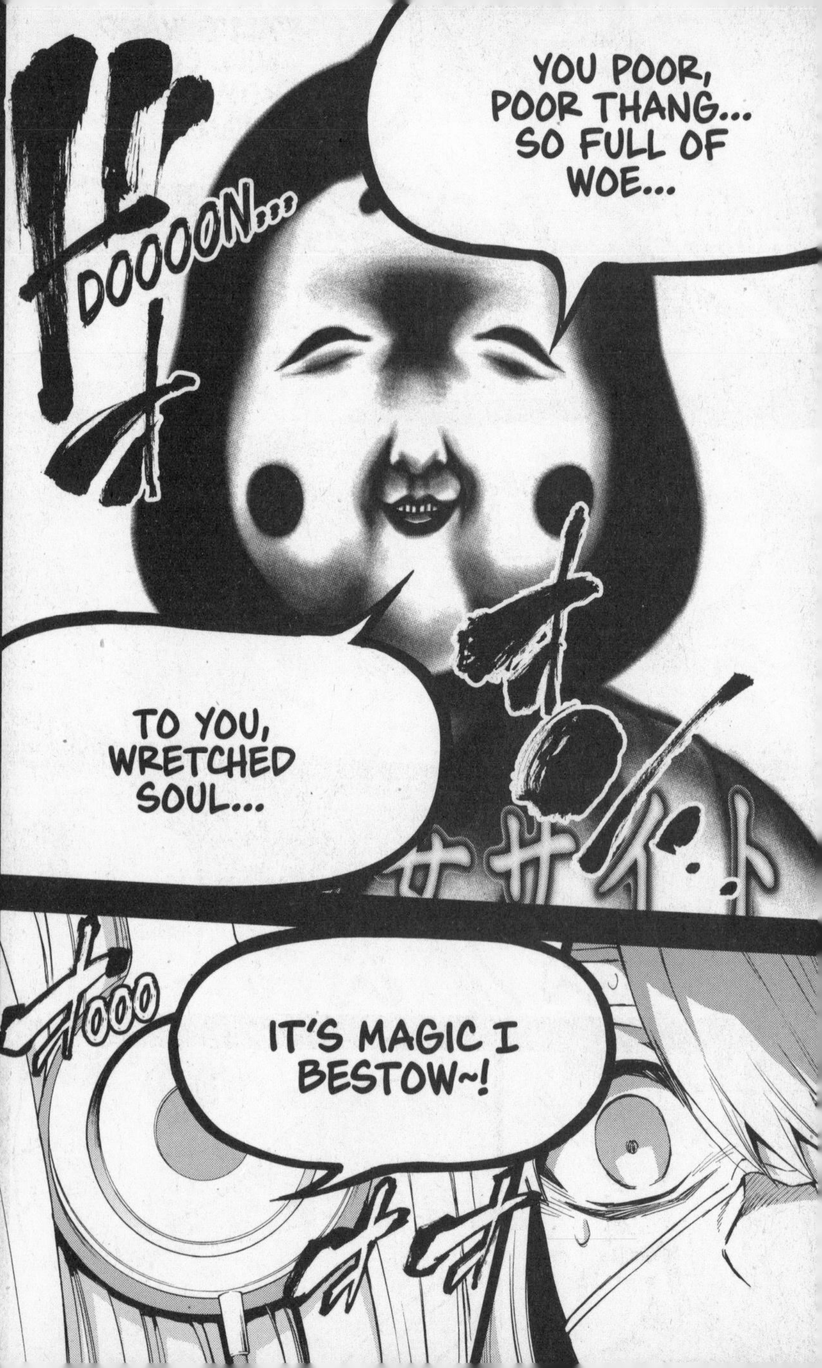
YOU POOR, POOR THANG... SO FULL OF WOE...
DOOOON...
TO YOU, WRETCHED SOUL...
IT'S MAGIC I BESTOW~!

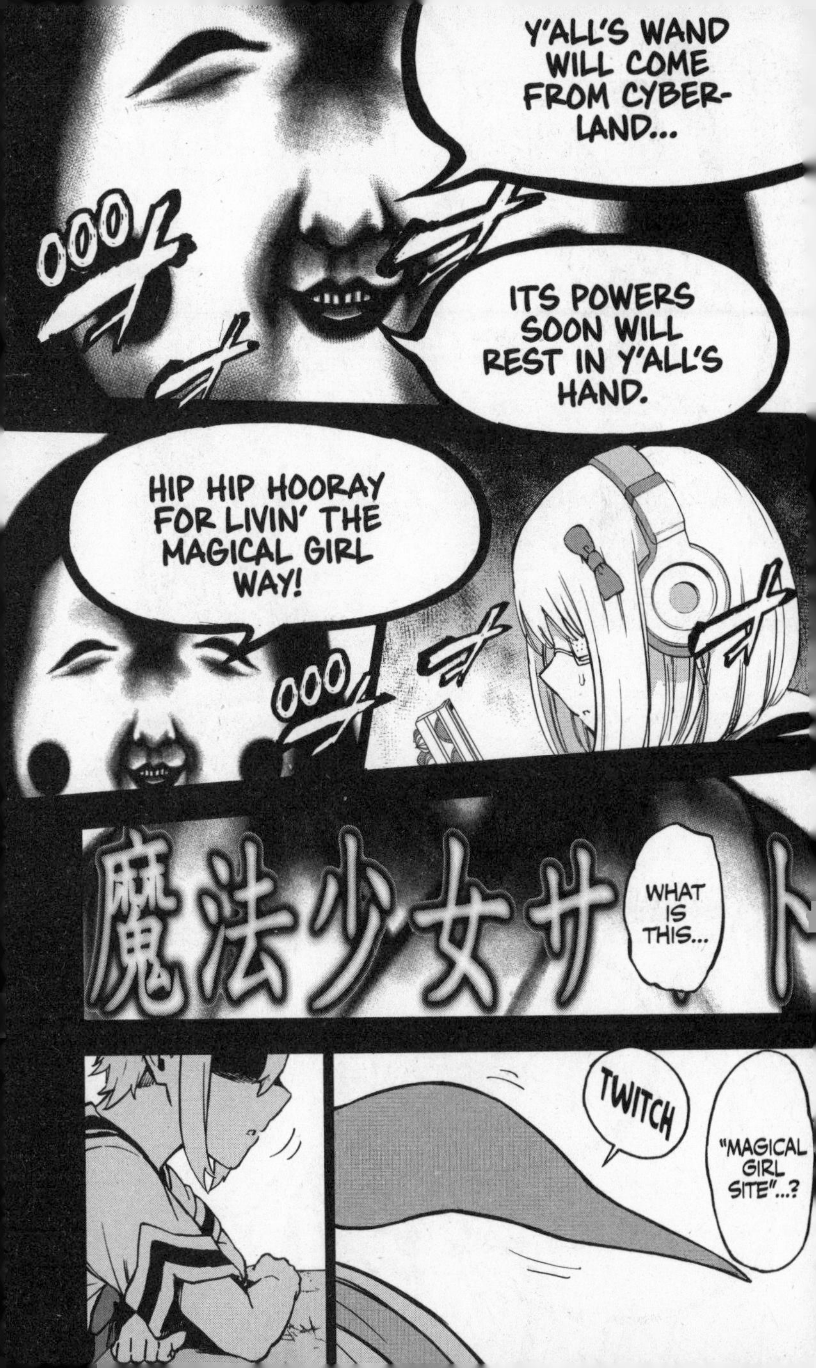
Y'ALL'S WAND WILL COME FROM CYBER-LAND...
ITS POWERS SOON WILL REST IN Y'ALL'S HAND.
HIP HIP HOORAY FOR LIVIN' THE MAGICAL GIRL WAY!
魔法少女サ ト
WHAT IS THIS...
TWITCH
"MAGICAL GIRL SITE"...?

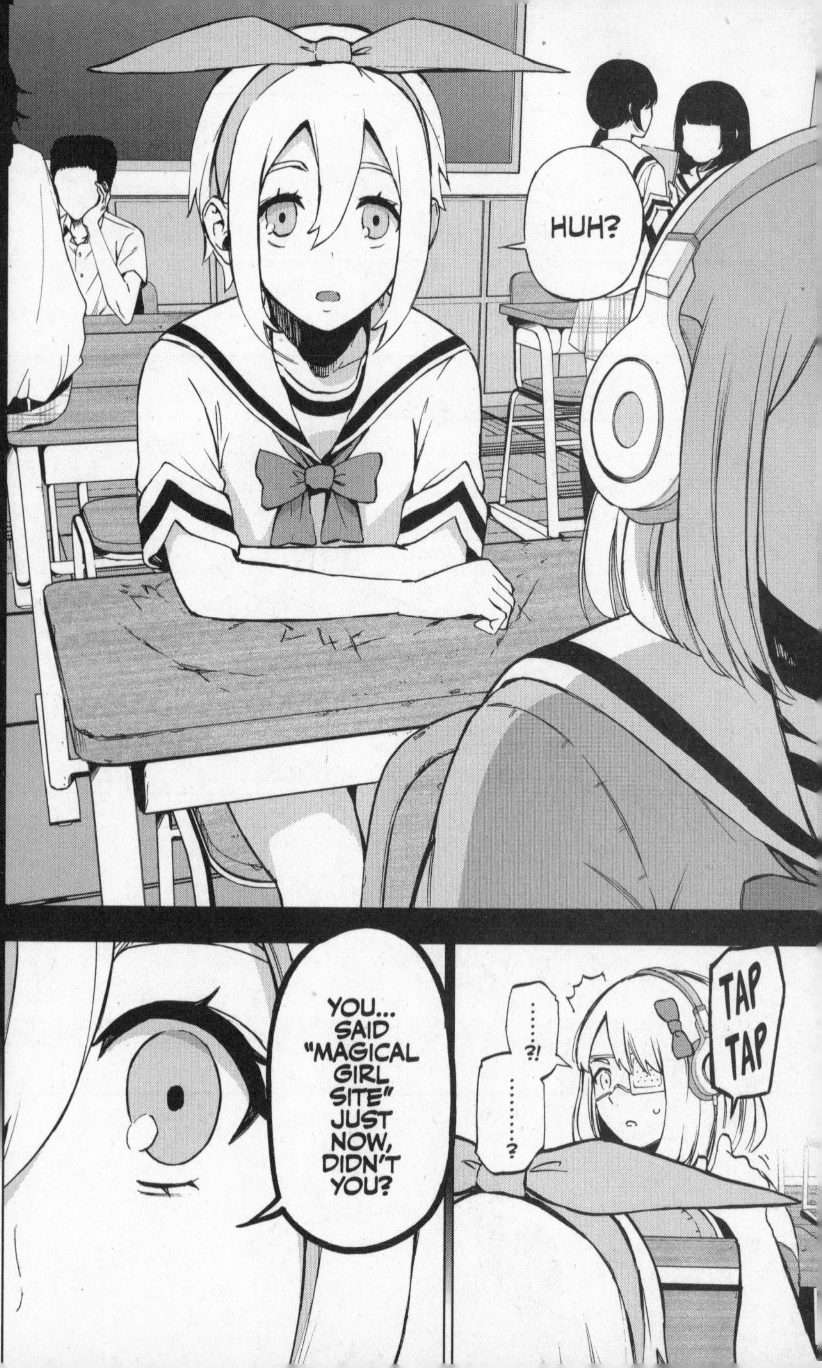
HUH?
TAP TAP
......?!
......?
YOU... SAID "MAGICAL GIRL SITE" JUST NOW, DIDN'T YOU?

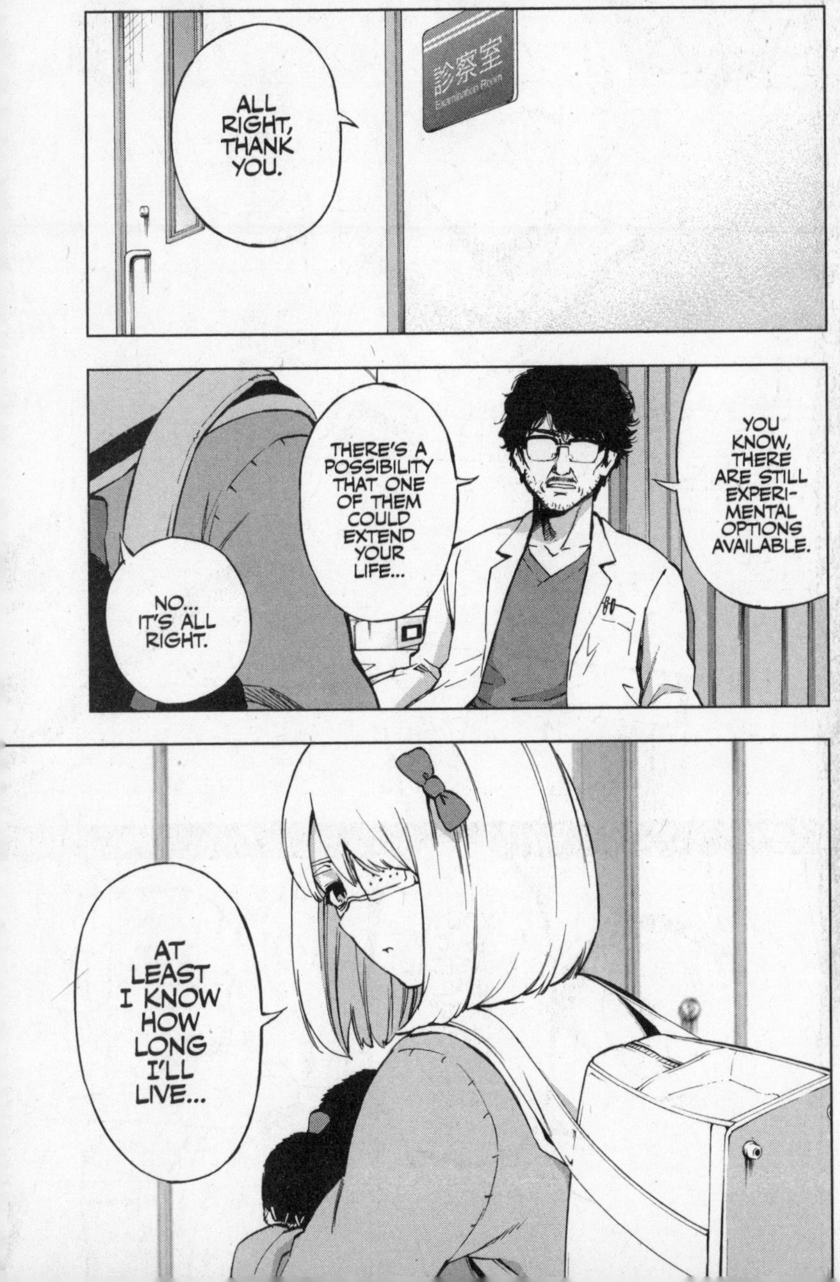
診察室
Examination Room
ALL RIGHT, THANK YOU.
YOU KNOW, THERE ARE STILL EXPERI-MENTAL OPTIONS AVAILABLE.
THERE'S A POSSIBILITY THAT ONE OF THEM COULD EXTEND YOUR LIFE...
NO... IT'S ALL RIGHT.
AT LEAST I KNOW HOW LONG I'LL LIVE...

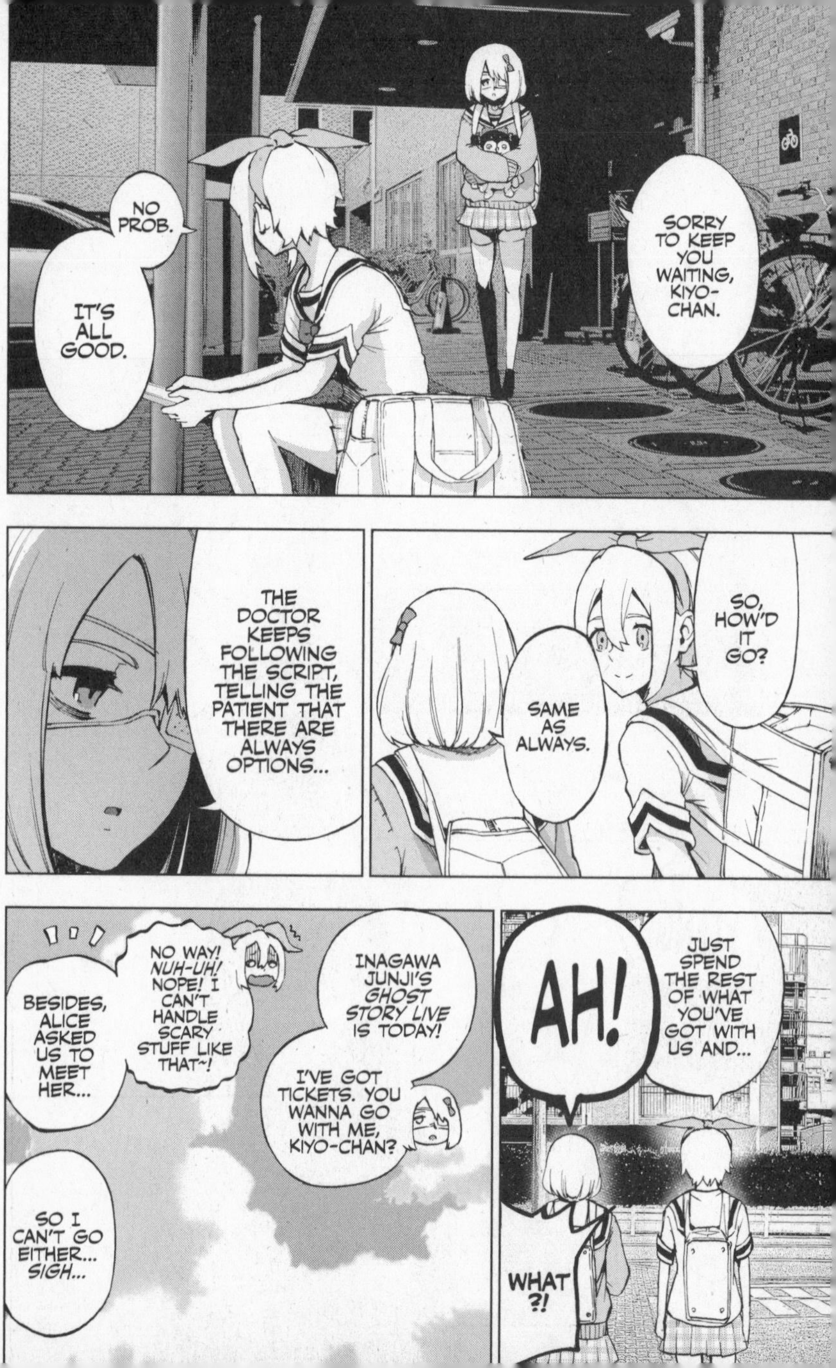
SORRY TO KEEP YOU WAITING, KIYO-CHAN.
NO PROB.
IT'S ALL GOOD.
SO, HOW'D IT GO?
SAME AS ALWAYS.
THE DOCTOR KEEPS FOLLOWING THE SCRIPT, TELLING THE PATIENT THAT THERE ARE ALWAYS OPTIONS...
JUST SPEND THE REST OF WHAT YOU'VE GOT WITH US AND...
AH!
WHAT ?!
INAGAWA JUNJI'S *GHOST STORY LIVE* IS TODAY!
I'VE GOT TICKETS. YOU WANNA GO WITH ME, KIYO-CHAN?
NO WAY! *NUH-UH!* NOPE! I CAN'T HANDLE SCARY STUFF LIKE THAT~!
BESIDES, ALICE ASKED US TO MEET HER...
SO I CAN'T GO EITHER... *SIGH...*

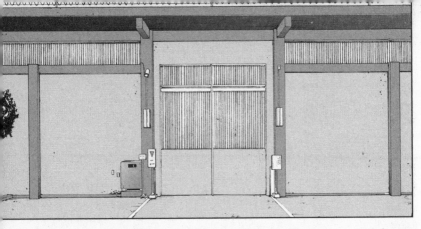

Renma Penitentiary

KLANG...

KNK...

KNK...

!

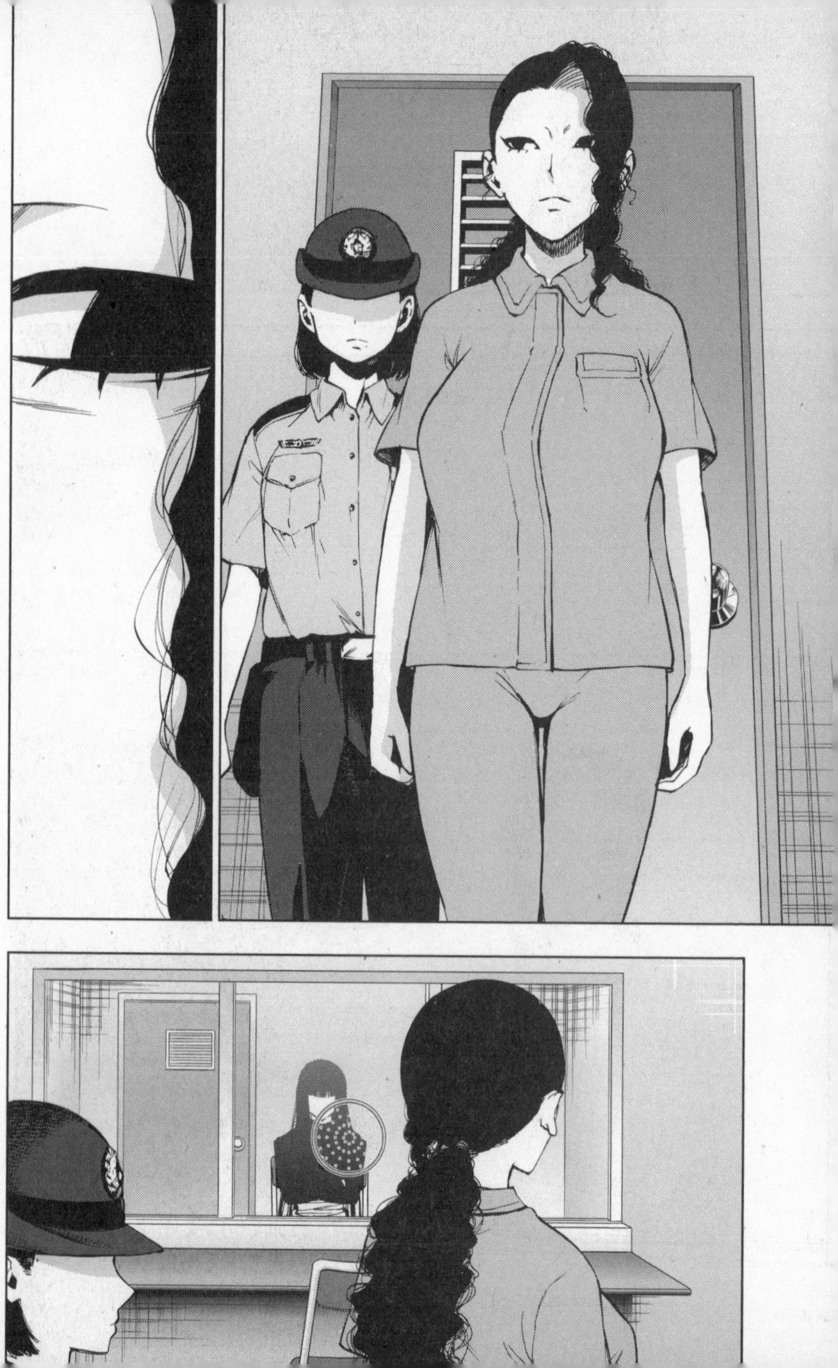

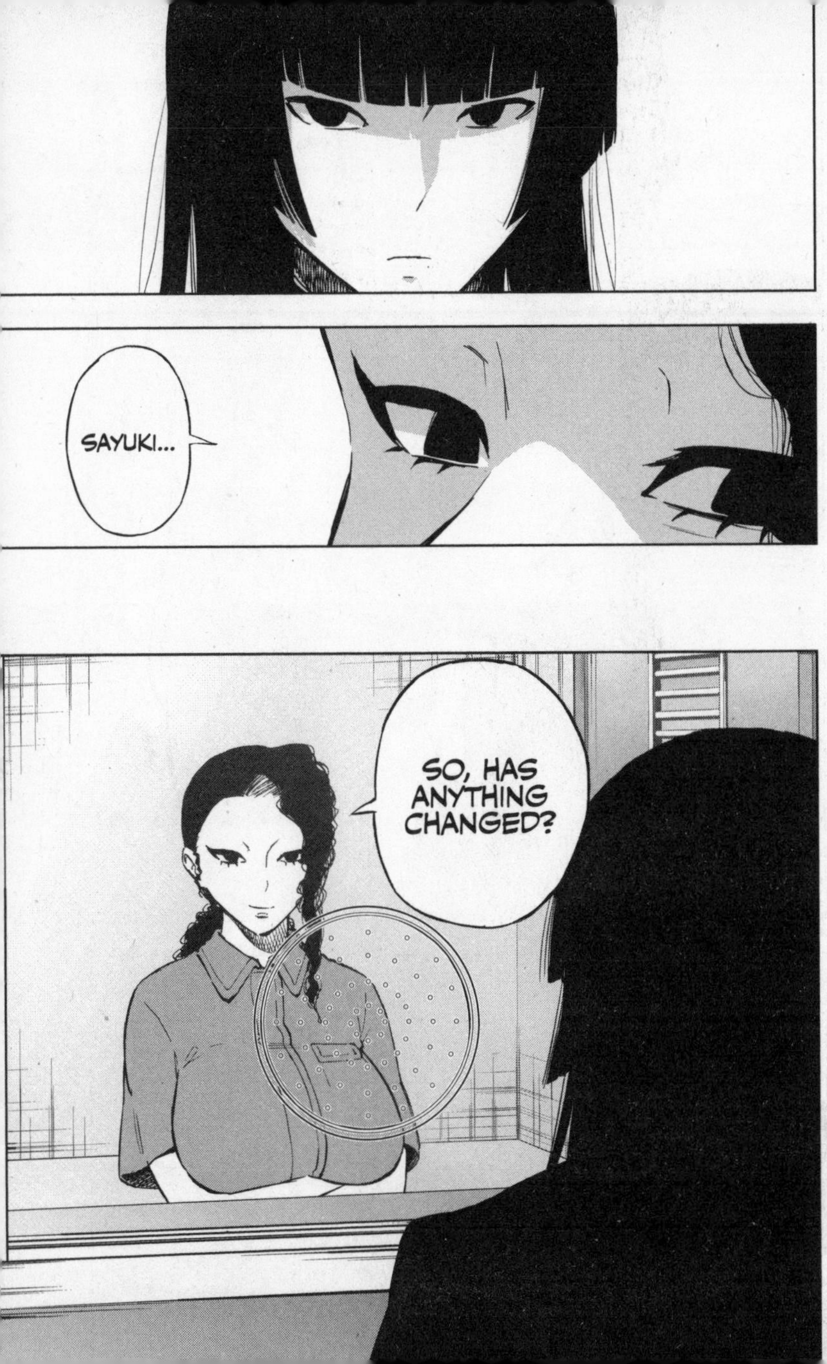
SAYUKI...
SO, HAS ANYTHING CHANGED?

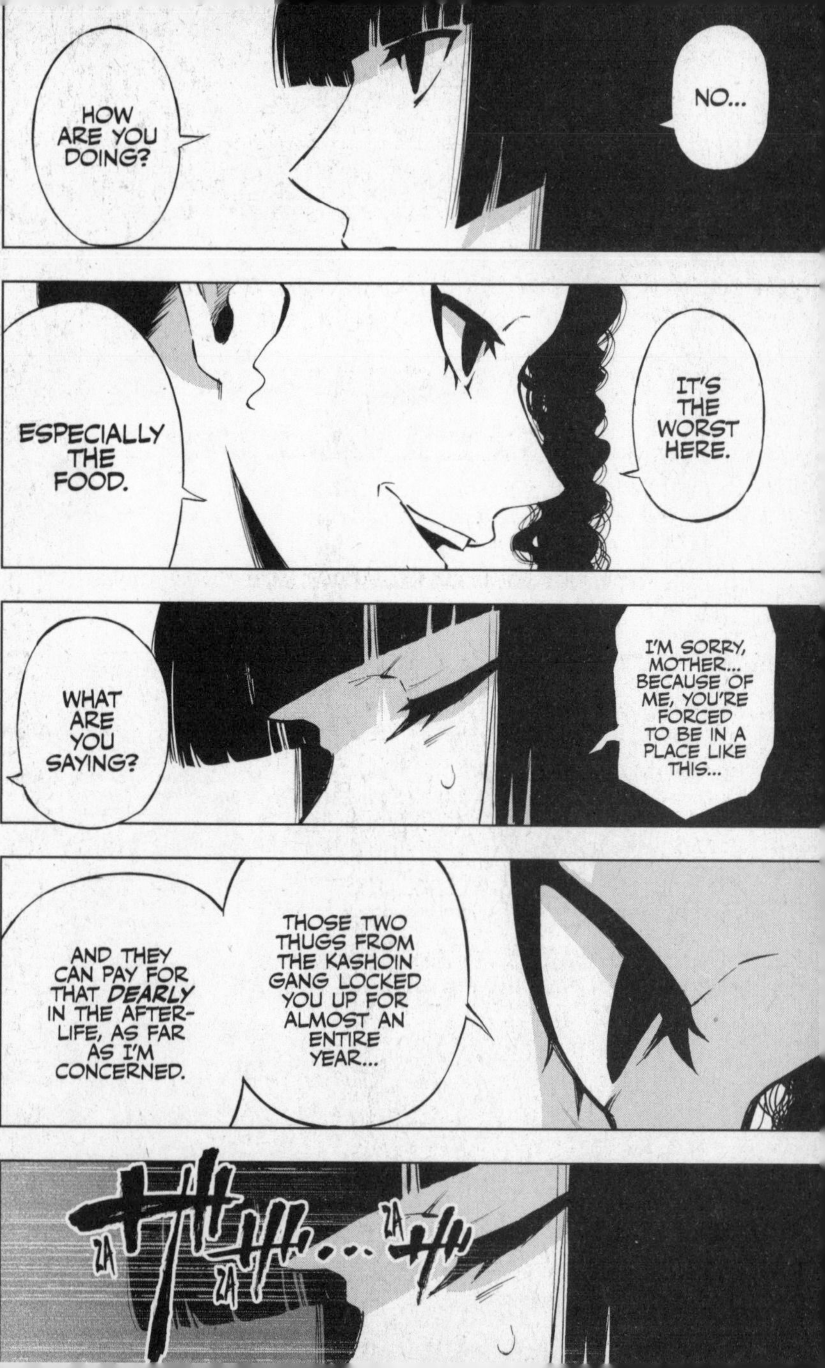
NO...
HOW ARE YOU DOING?
IT'S THE WORST HERE.
ESPECIALLY THE FOOD.
I'M SORRY, MOTHER... BECAUSE OF ME, YOU'RE FORCED TO BE IN A PLACE LIKE THIS...
WHAT ARE YOU SAYING?
THOSE TWO THUGS FROM THE KASHOIN GANG LOCKED YOU UP FOR ALMOST AN ENTIRE YEAR...
AND THEY CAN PAY FOR THAT *DEARLY* IN THE AFTER-LIFE, AS FAR AS I'M CONCERNED.
ZA ZA ZA

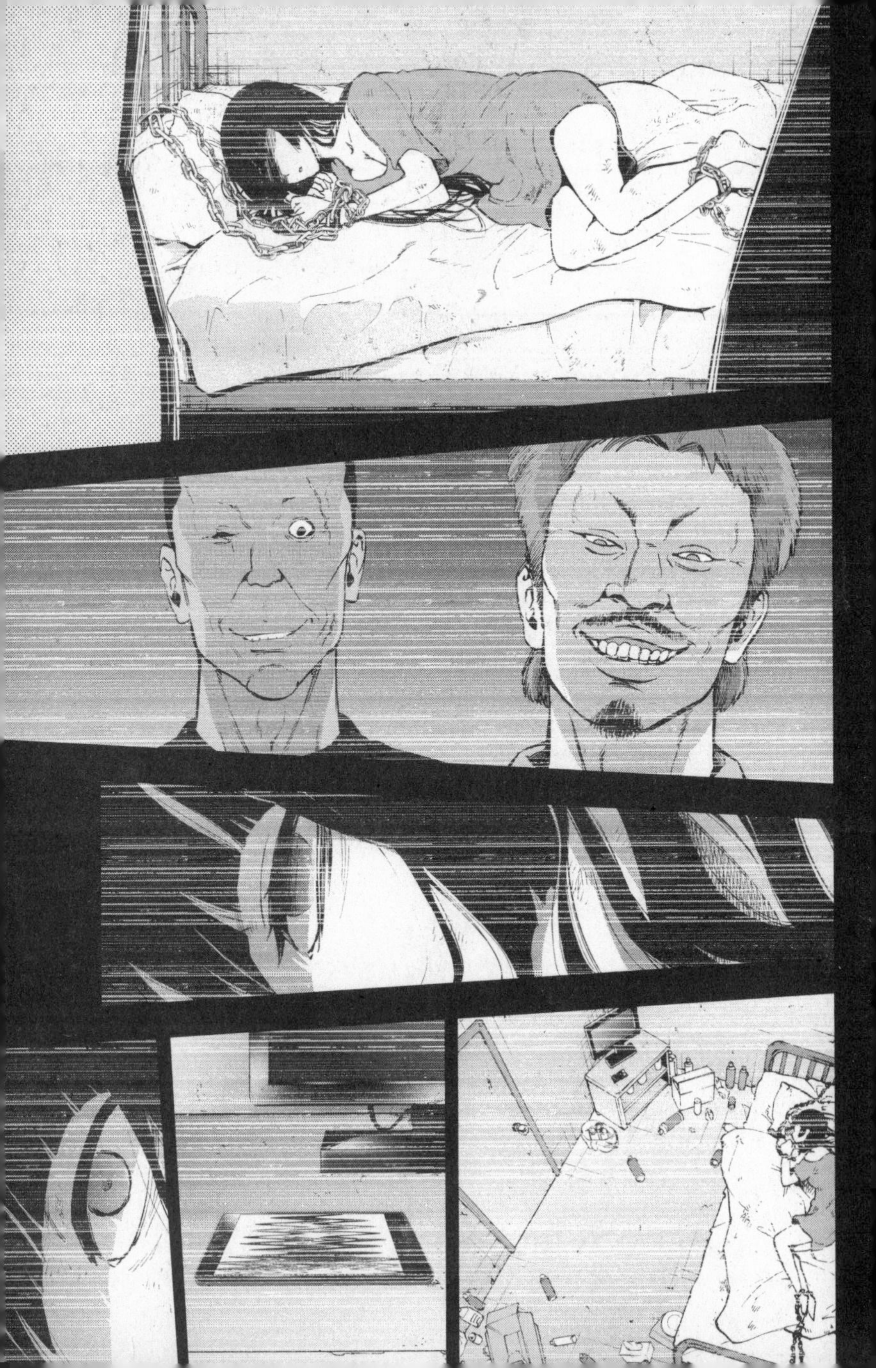

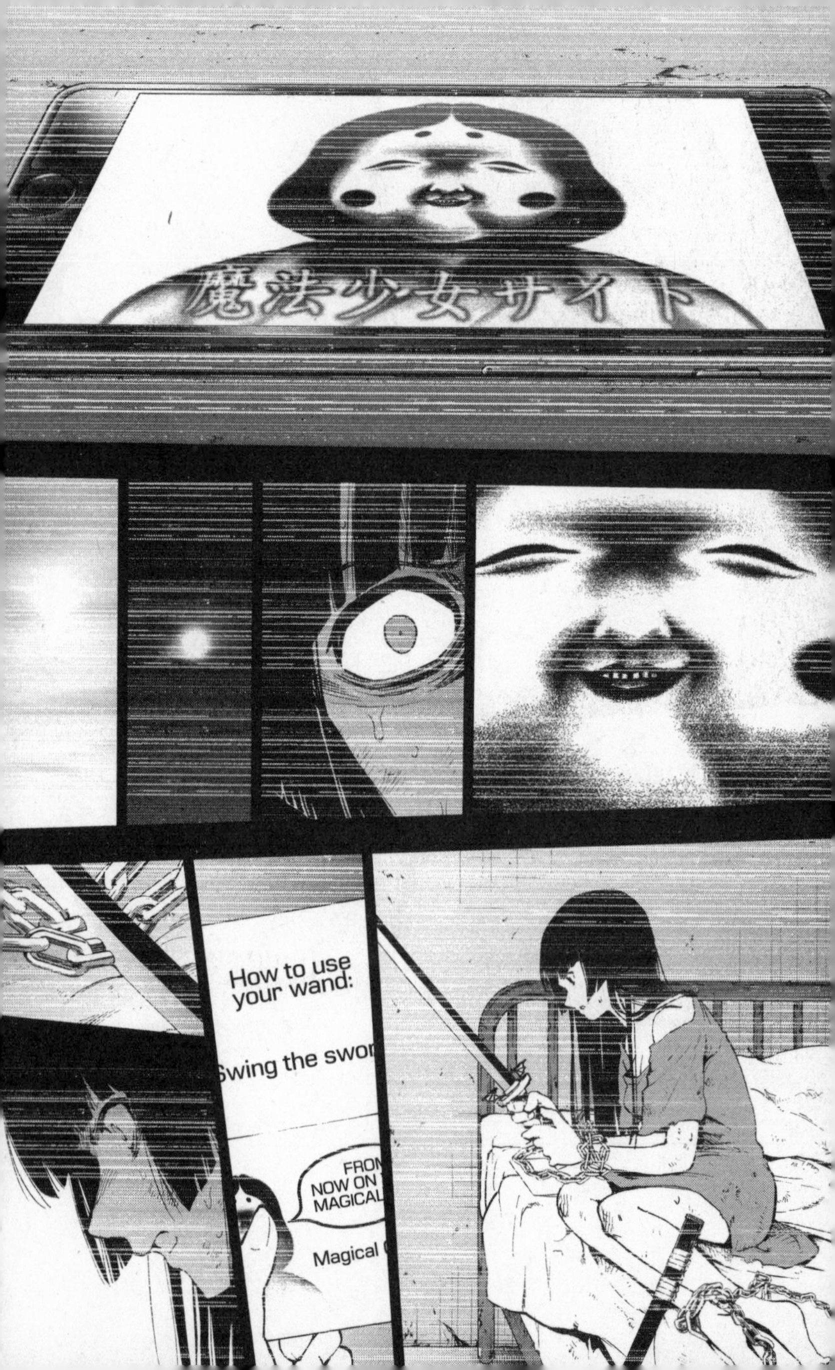
魔法少女サイト
How to use your wand:
Swing the swor
FROM NOW ON
MAGICAL
Magical

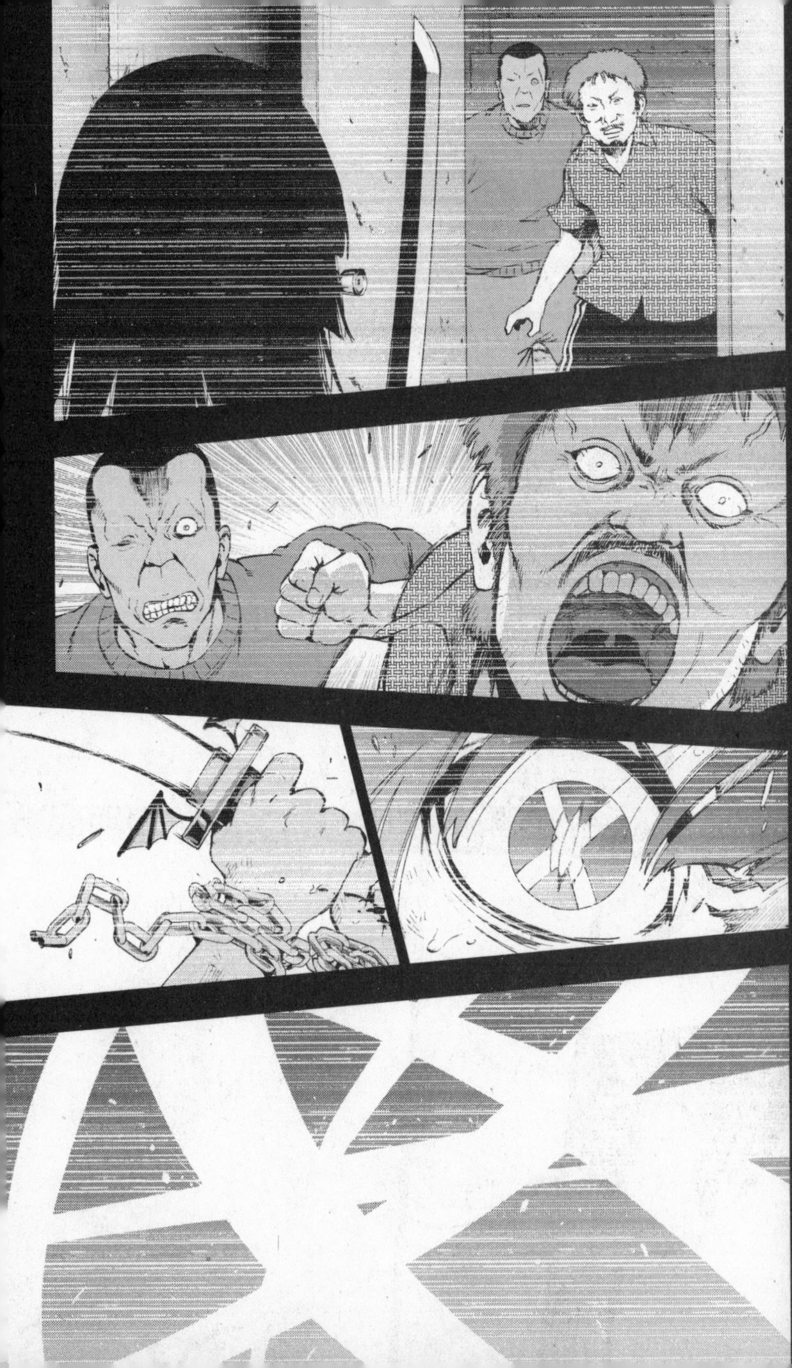

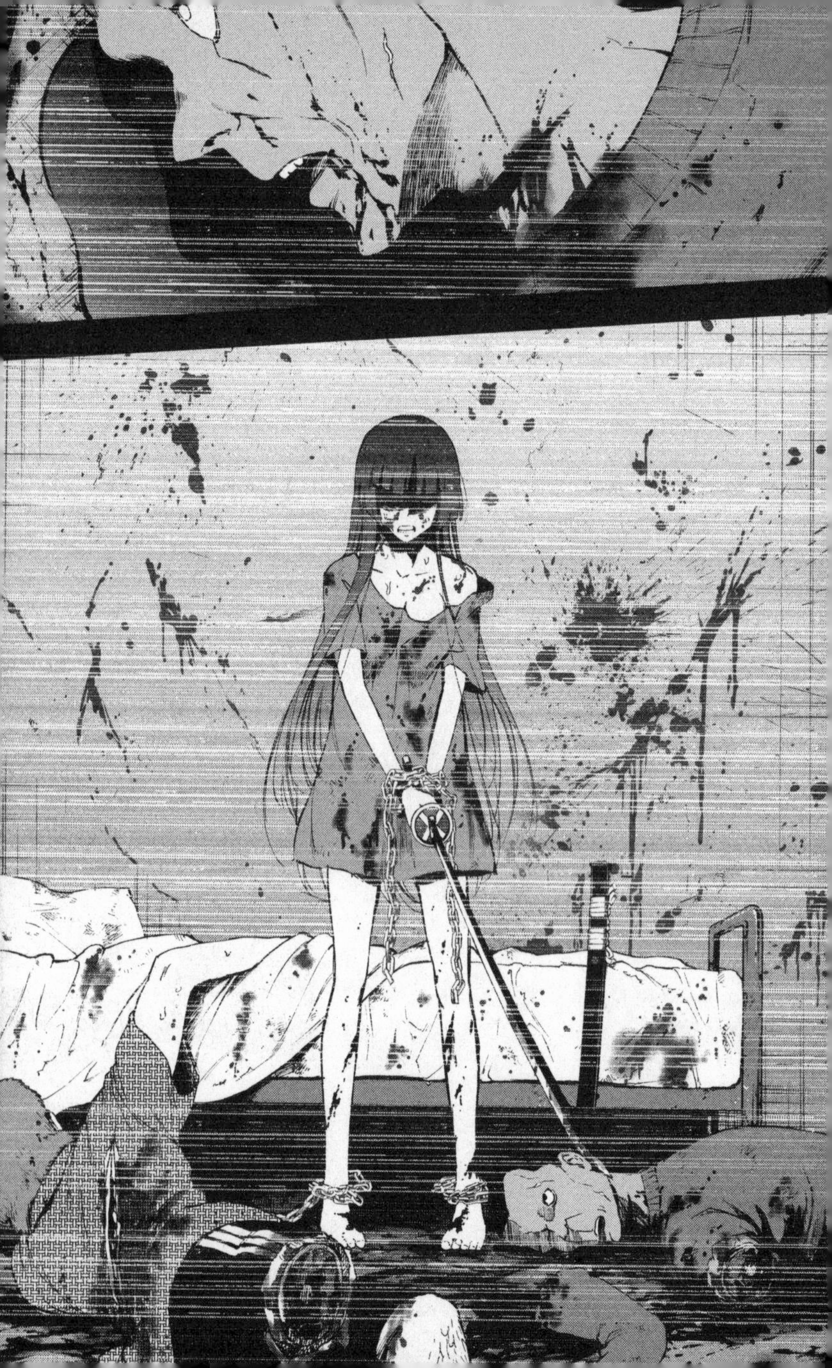

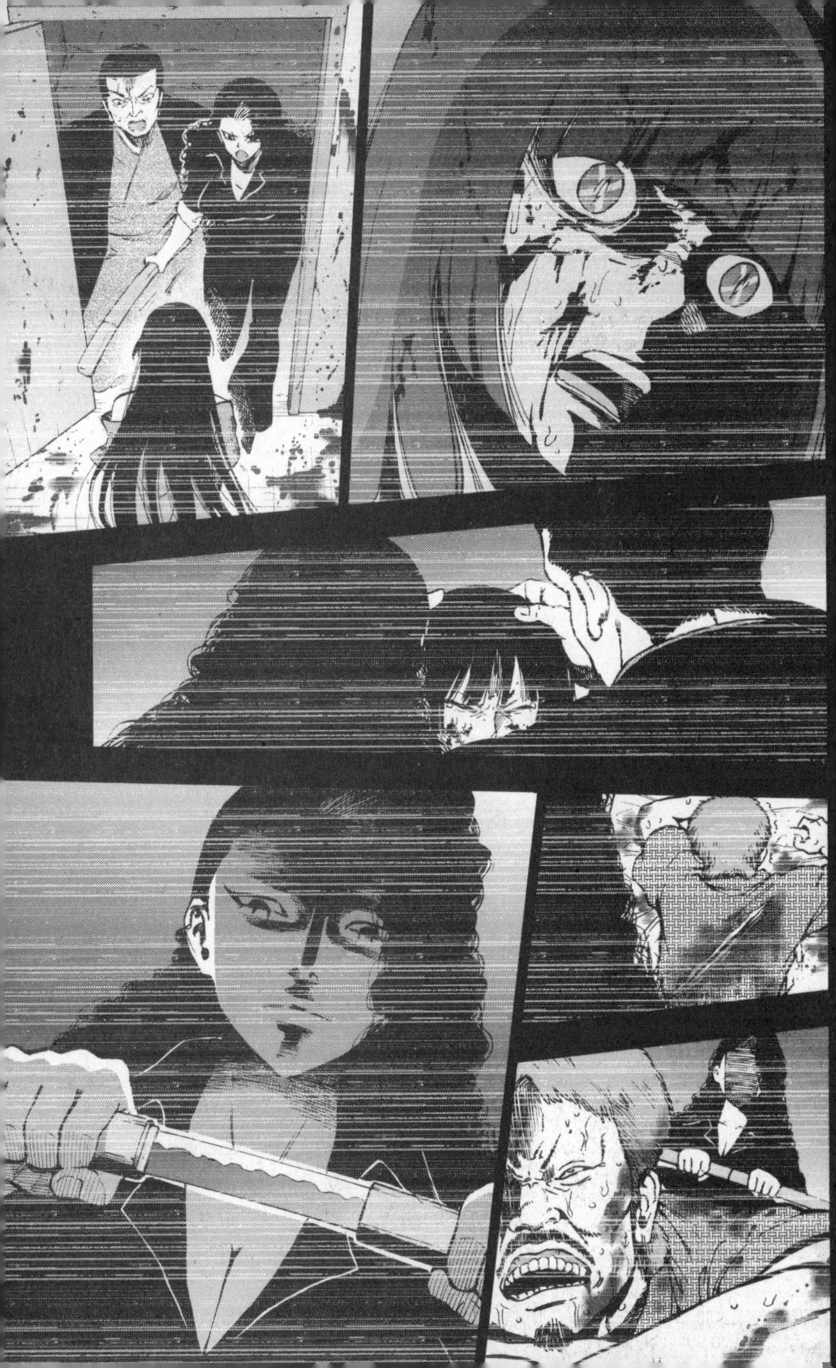

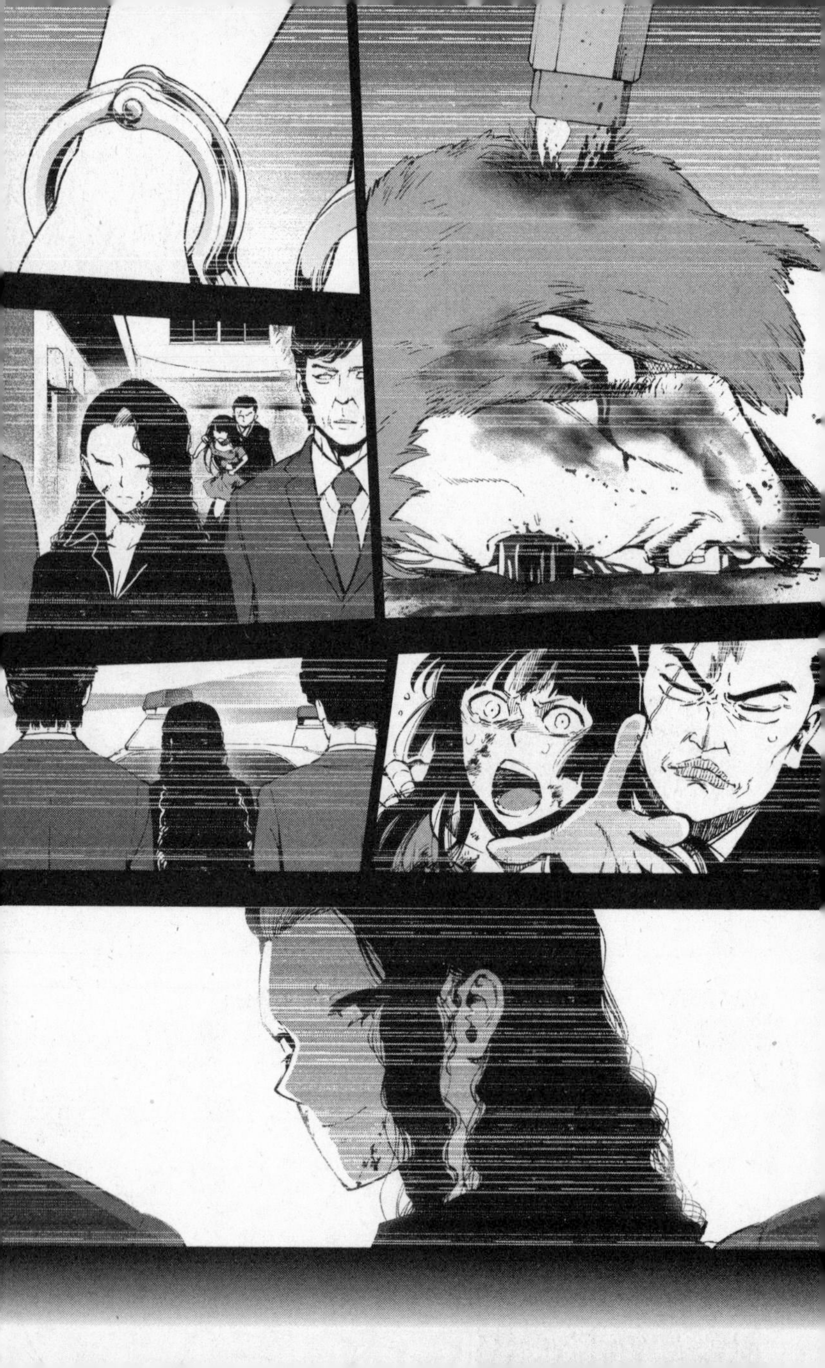

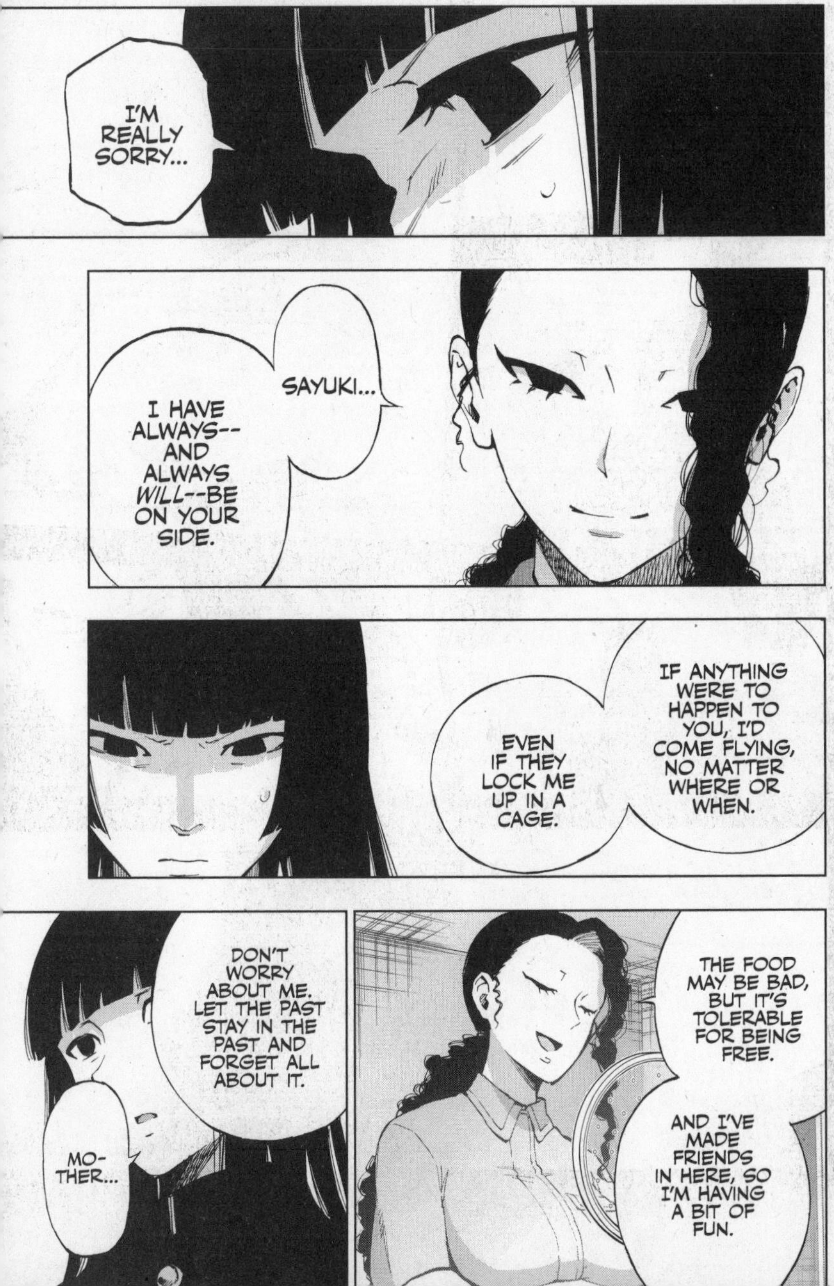
I'M REALLY SORRY...
SAYUKI...
I HAVE ALWAYS--AND ALWAYS *WILL*--BE ON YOUR SIDE.
IF ANYTHING WERE TO HAPPEN TO YOU, I'D COME FLYING, NO MATTER WHERE OR WHEN.
EVEN IF THEY LOCK ME UP IN A CAGE.
THE FOOD MAY BE BAD, BUT IT'S TOLERABLE FOR BEING FREE.
AND I'VE MADE FRIENDS IN HERE, SO I'M HAVING A BIT OF FUN.
DON'T WORRY ABOUT ME. LET THE PAST STAY IN THE PAST AND FORGET ALL ABOUT IT.
MO-THER...

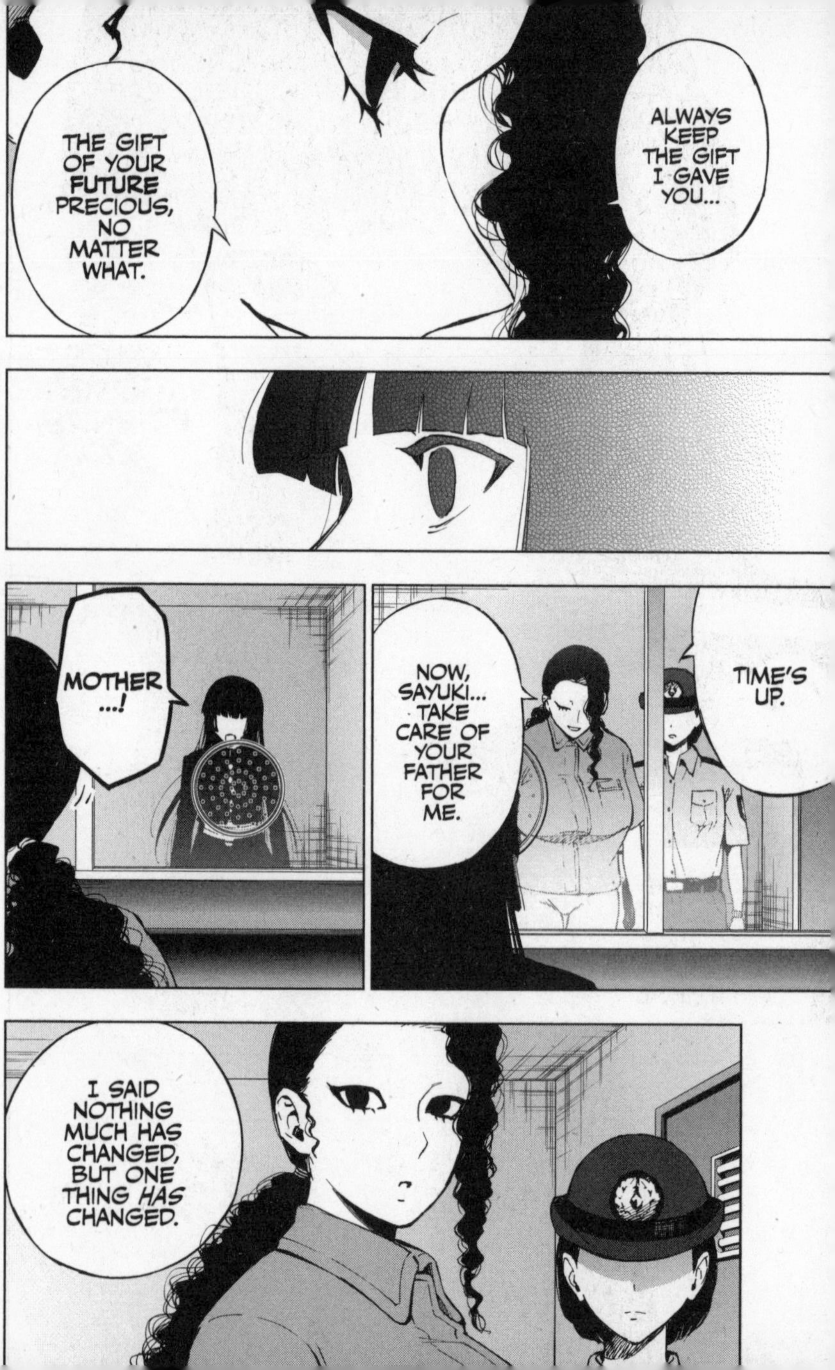
ALWAYS KEEP THE GIFT I GAVE YOU...
THE GIFT OF YOUR FUTURE PRECIOUS, NO MATTER WHAT.
TIME'S UP.
NOW, SAYUKI... TAKE CARE OF YOUR FATHER FOR ME.
MOTHER ...!
I SAID NOTHING MUCH HAS CHANGED, BUT ONE THING *HAS* CHANGED.

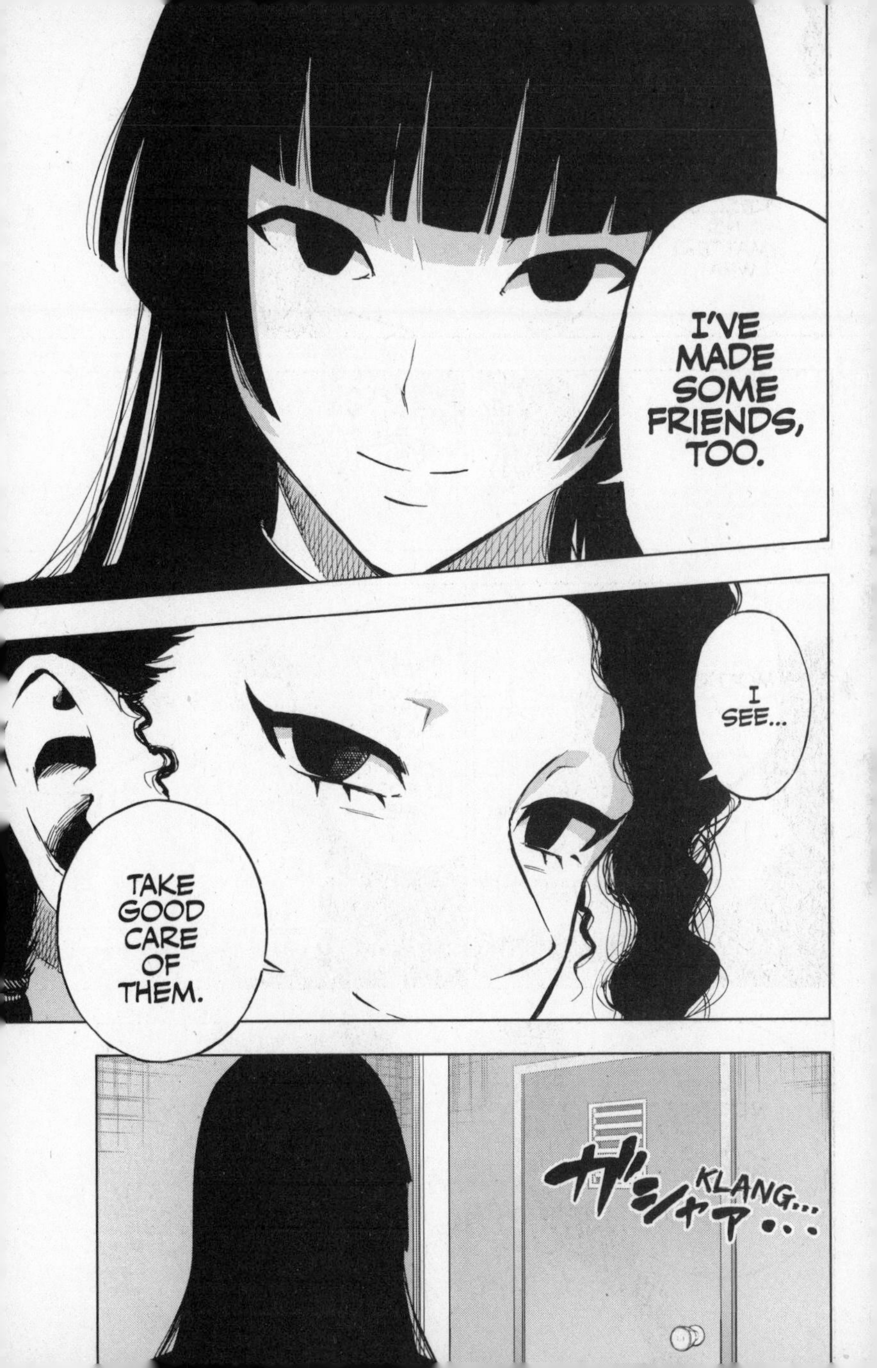
I'VE MADE SOME FRIENDS, TOO.
I SEE...
TAKE GOOD CARE OF THEM.
KLANG...

That doctor's a quack...

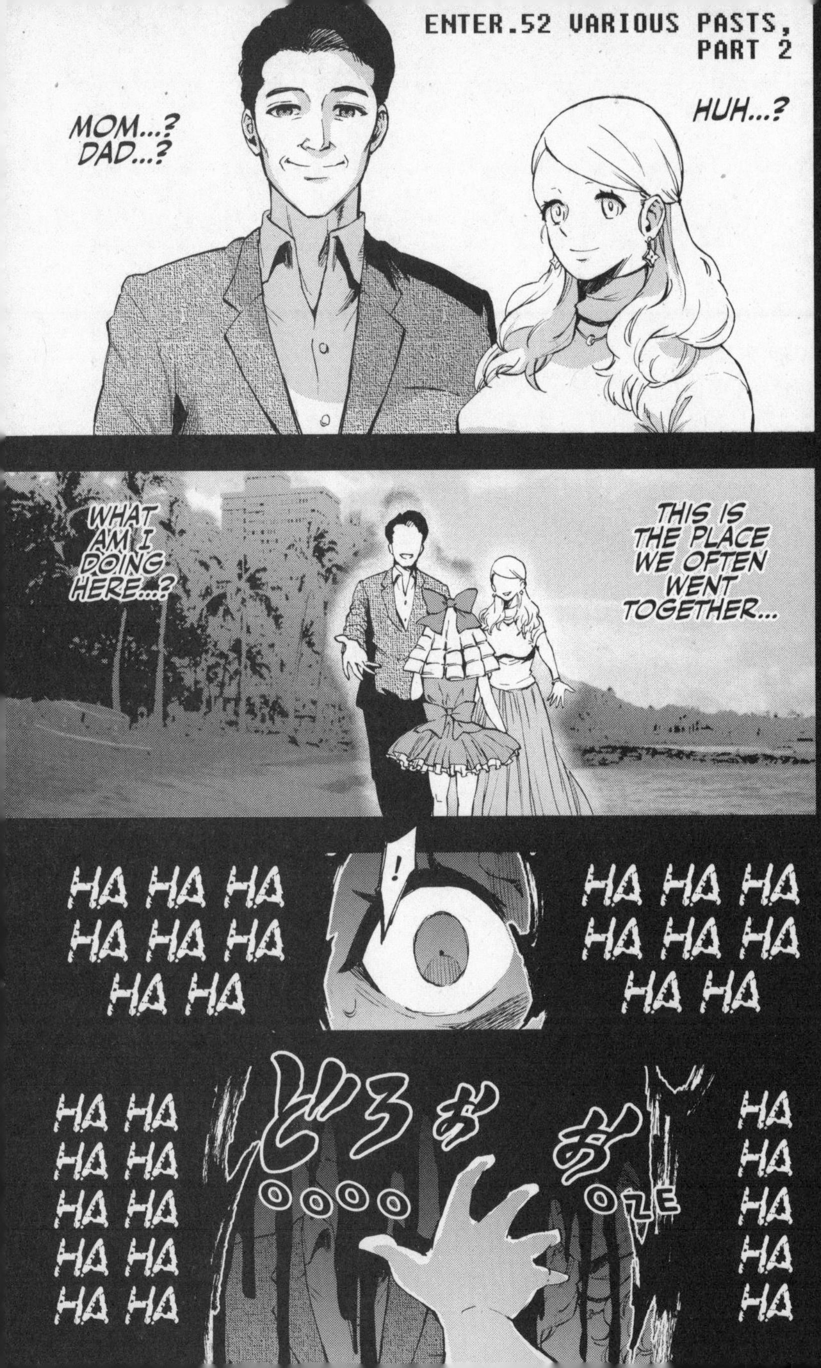
ENTER.52 VARIOUS PASTS, PART 2
HUH...?
MOM...? DAD...?
THIS IS THE PLACE WE OFTEN WENT TOGETHER...
WHAT AM I DOING HERE...?
HA HA HA HA HA HA HA HA
!
HA HA HA HA HA HA HA HA
HA HA HA HA HA
どろぉお
OOOOOOZE
HA HA HA HA HA HA HA HA HA HA

DON'T LEAVE ME...!!

BLINK...

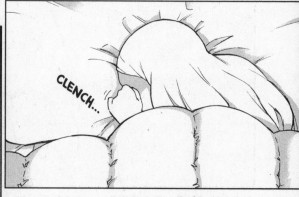

CLENCH...

A DREAM ...?

ENTER.52

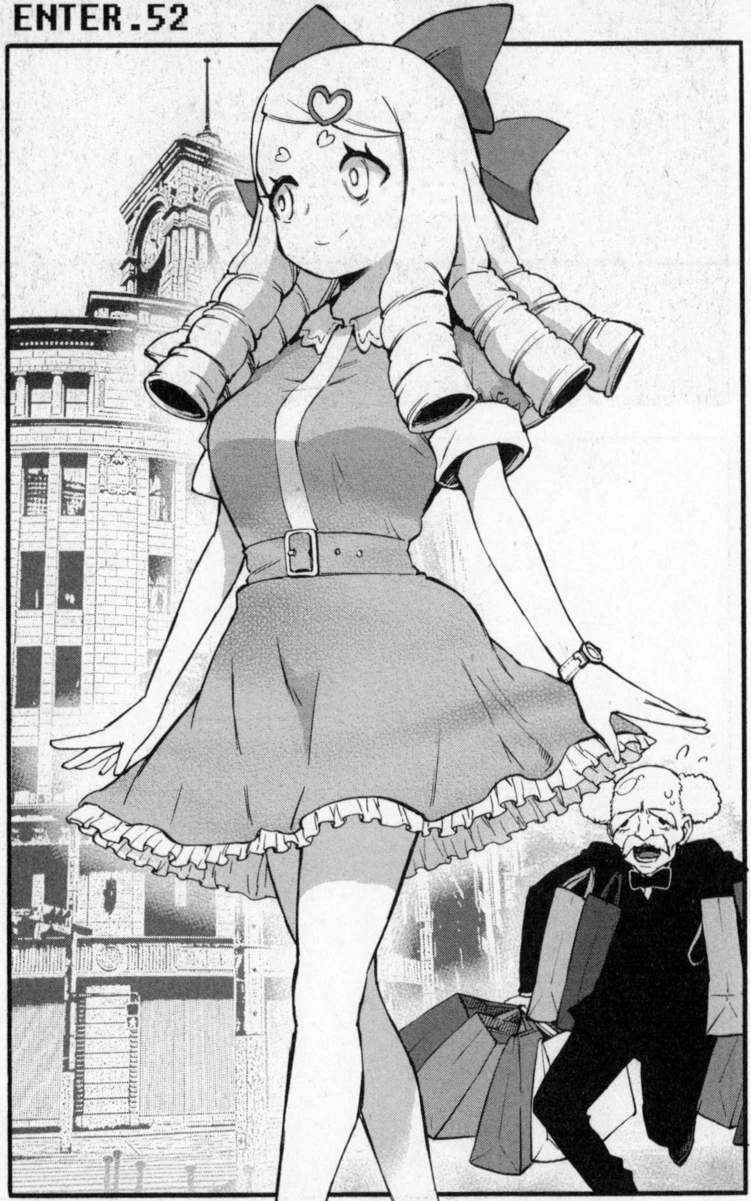

VARIOUS PASTS, PART 2

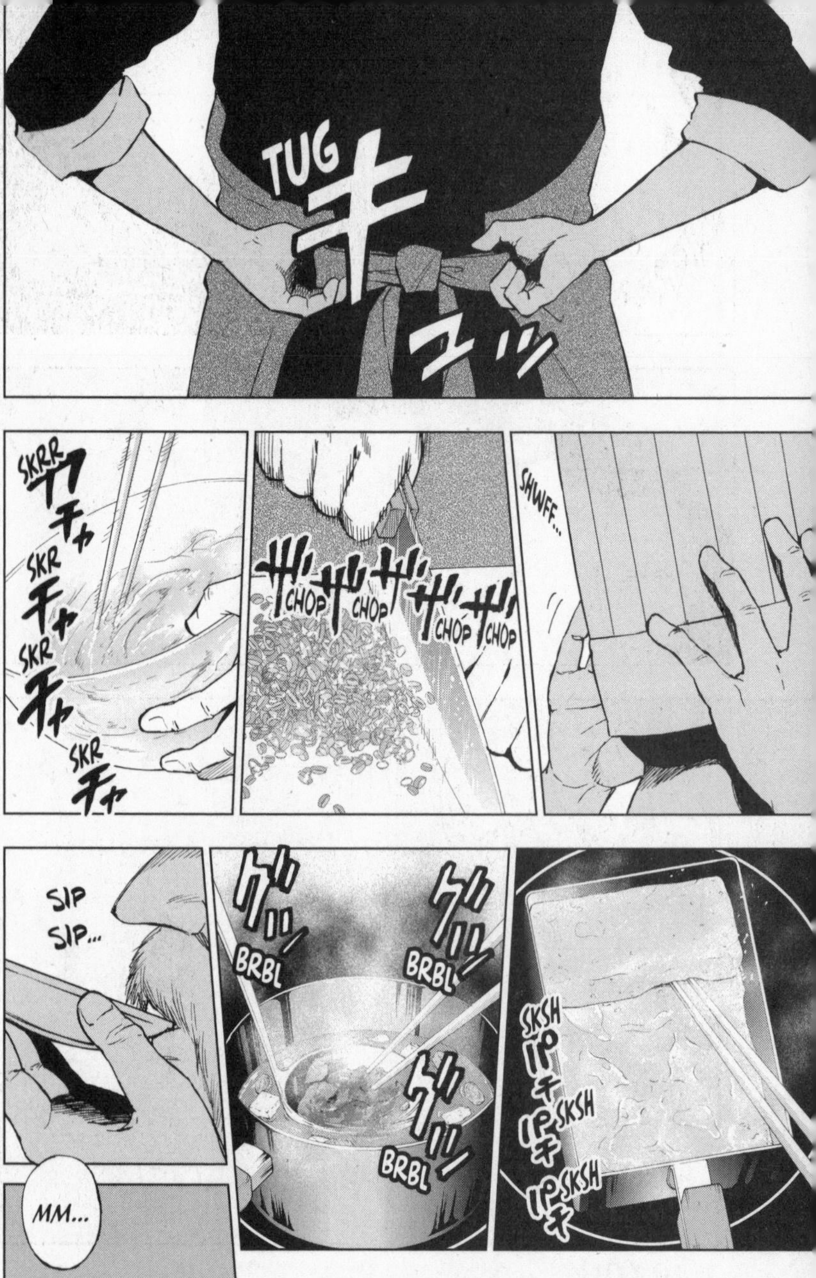
TUG
SHWFF...
CHOP CHOP CHOP CHOP
SKRR
SKR
SKR
SKR
SKSH
SKSH
SKSH
BRBL
BRBL
BRBL
SIP SIP...
MM...

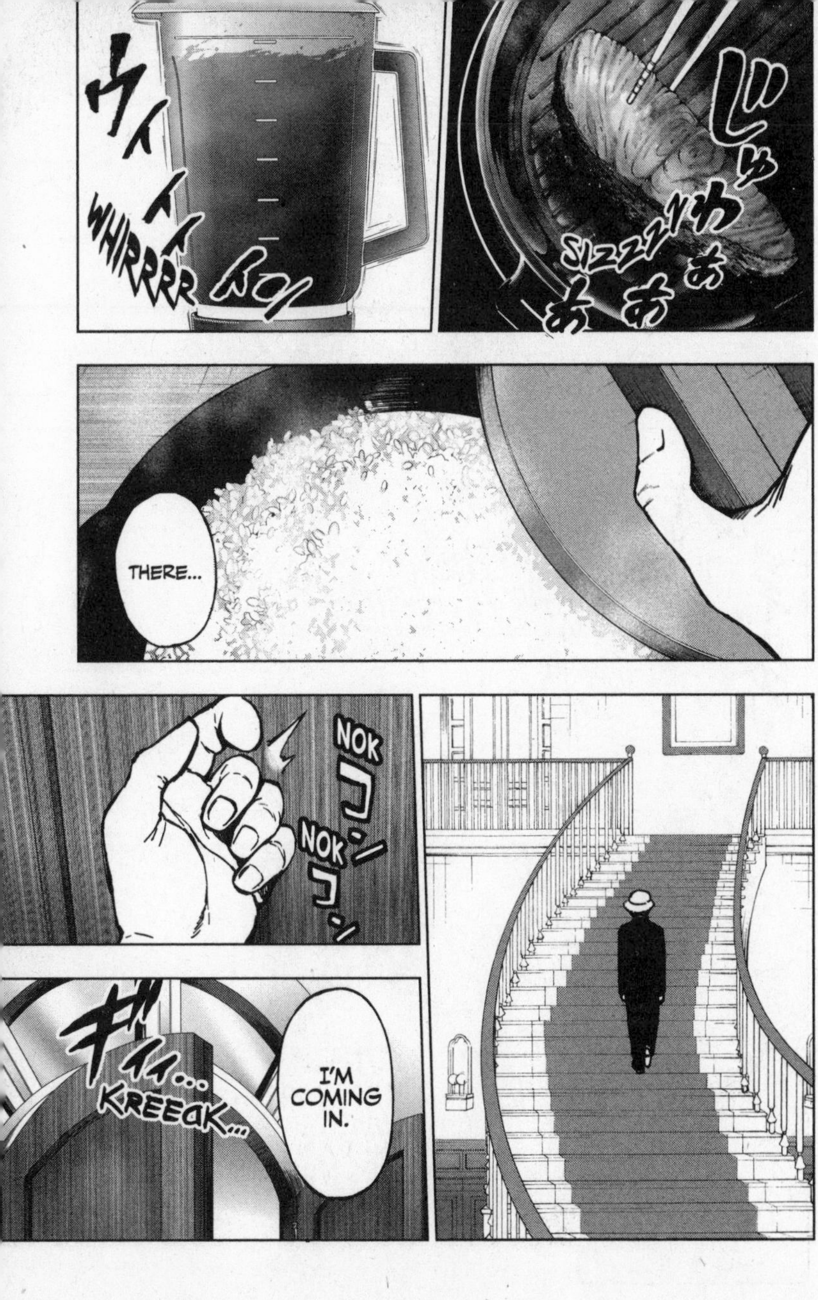
じゅわああ
SIZZZZ
ウイイイイン
WHIRRRR
THERE...
NOK
コン
NOK
コン
ギイイ...
KREEAK...
I'M COMING IN.

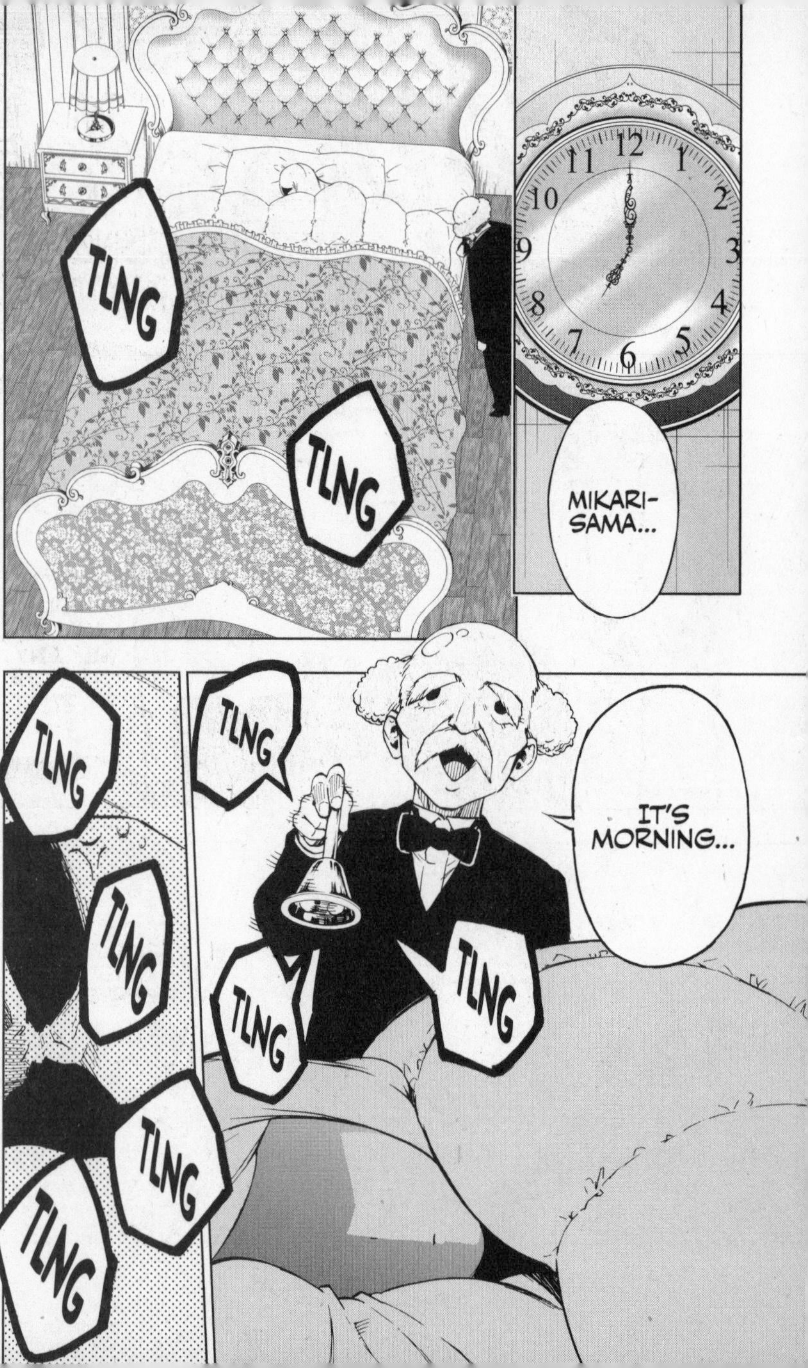
MIKARI-SAMA...
TLNG
TLNG
IT'S MORNING...
TLNG
TLNG
TLNG
TLNG
TLNG
TLNG
TLNG

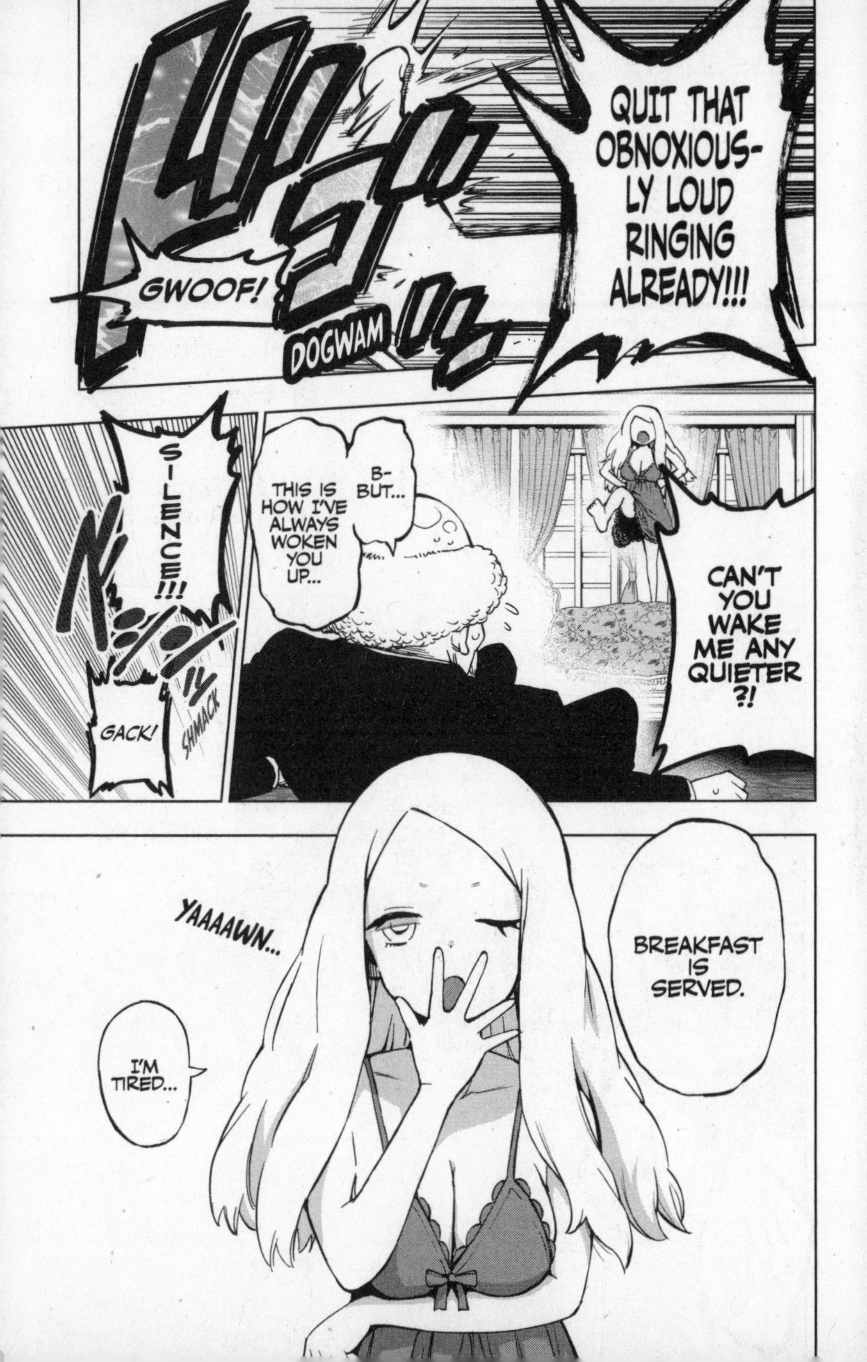
QUIT THAT OBNOXIOUSLY LOUD RINGING ALREADY!!!
GWOOF!
DOGWAM
CAN'T YOU WAKE ME ANY QUIETER?!
B-BUT...
THIS IS HOW I'VE ALWAYS WOKEN YOU UP...
SILENCE!!!
SHMACK
GACK!
BREAKFAST IS SERVED.
YAAAAWN...
I'M TIRED...

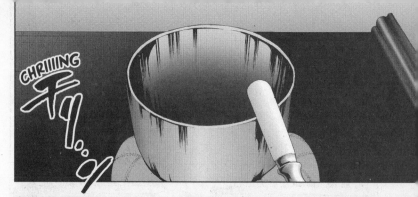

CHRIIIING

MOM... DAD.

GOOD MORNING...

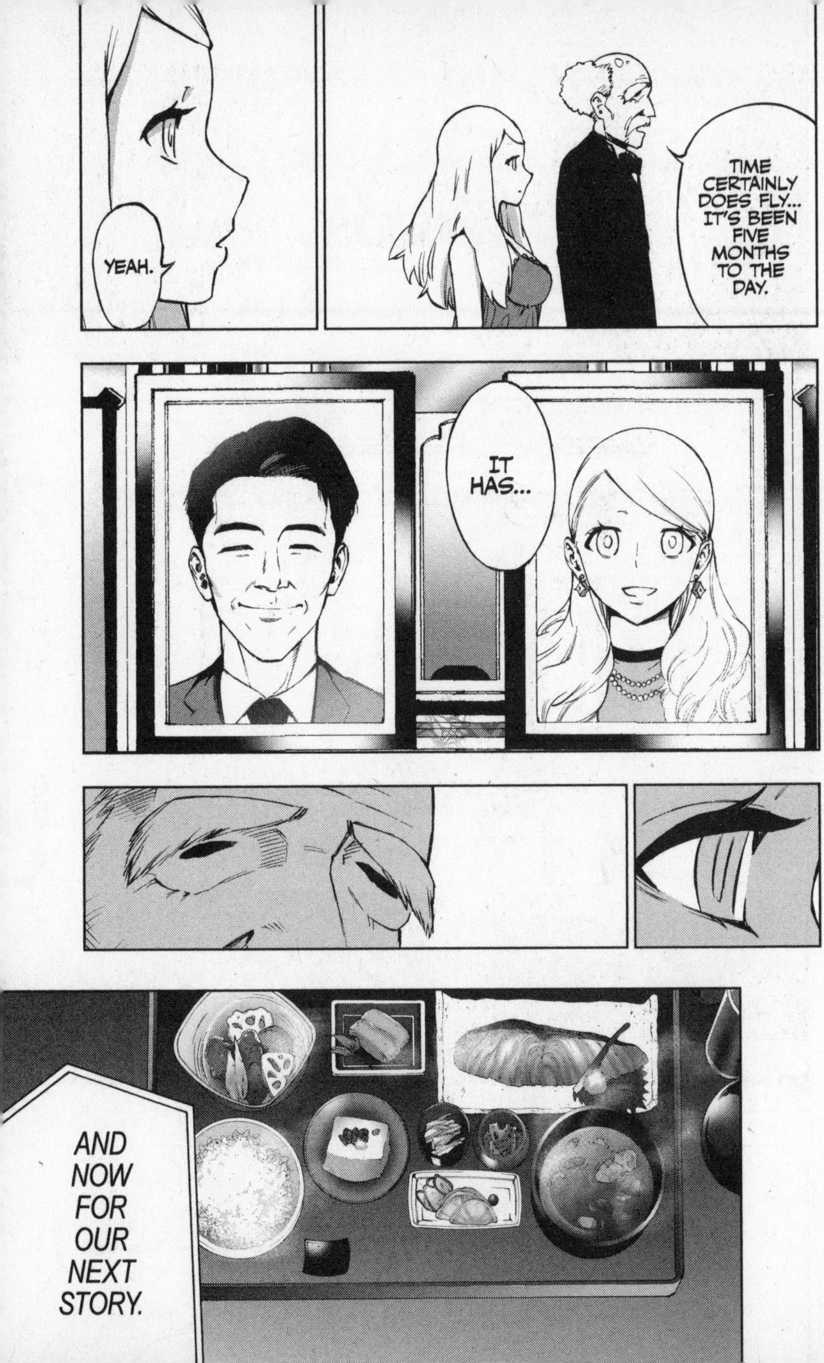
TIME CERTAINLY DOES FLY... IT'S BEEN FIVE MONTHS TO THE DAY.
YEAH.
IT HAS...
AND NOW FOR OUR NEXT STORY.

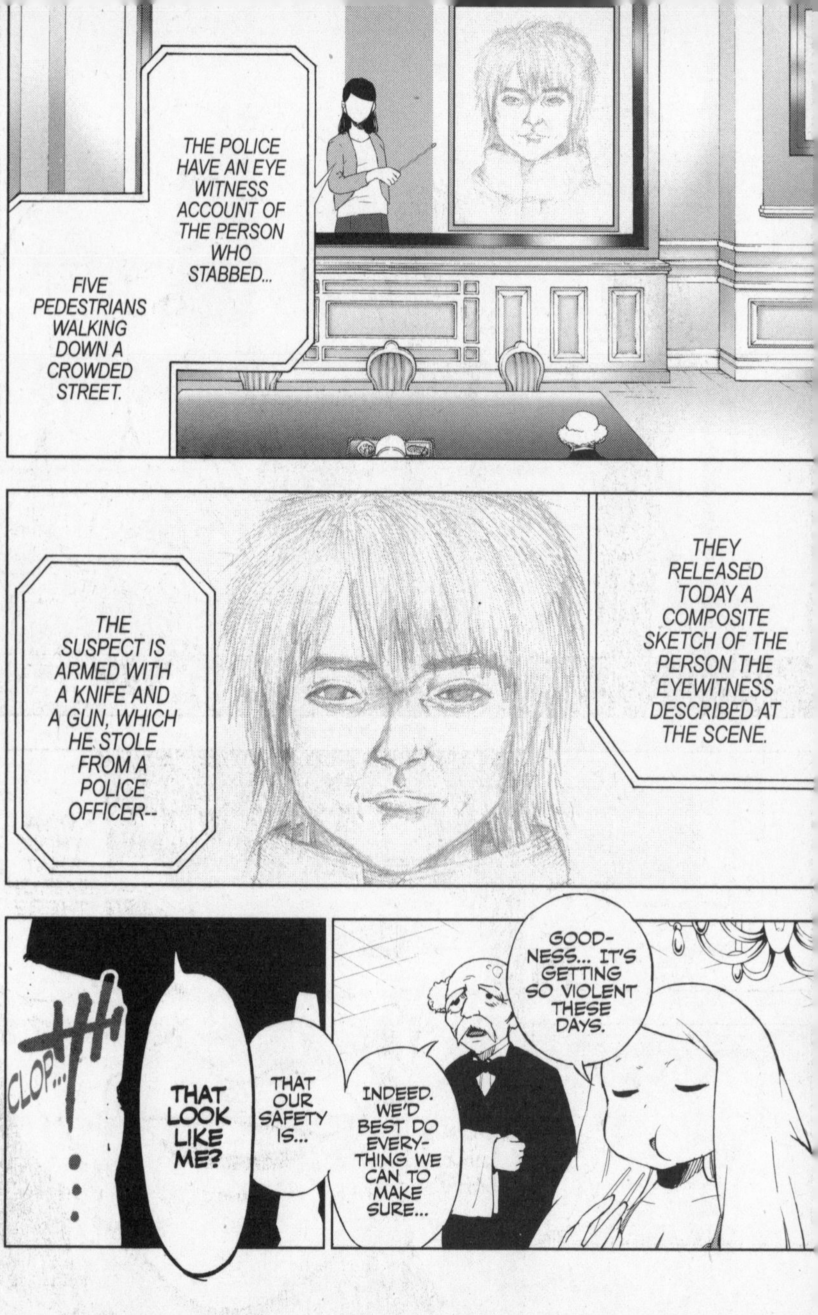
THE POLICE HAVE AN EYE WITNESS ACCOUNT OF THE PERSON WHO STABBED...
FIVE PEDESTRIANS WALKING DOWN A CROWDED STREET.
THEY RELEASED TODAY A COMPOSITE SKETCH OF THE PERSON THE EYEWITNESS DESCRIBED AT THE SCENE.
THE SUSPECT IS ARMED WITH A KNIFE AND A GUN, WHICH HE STOLE FROM A POLICE OFFICER--
GOOD-NESS... IT'S GETTING SO VIOLENT THESE DAYS.
INDEED. WE'D BEST DO EVERY-THING WE CAN TO MAKE SURE...
THAT OUR SAFETY IS...
THAT LOOK LIKE ME?
CLOP...
...

SAY...

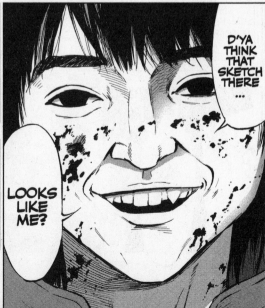

D'YA THINK THAT SKETCH THERE ...

LOOKS LIKE ME?

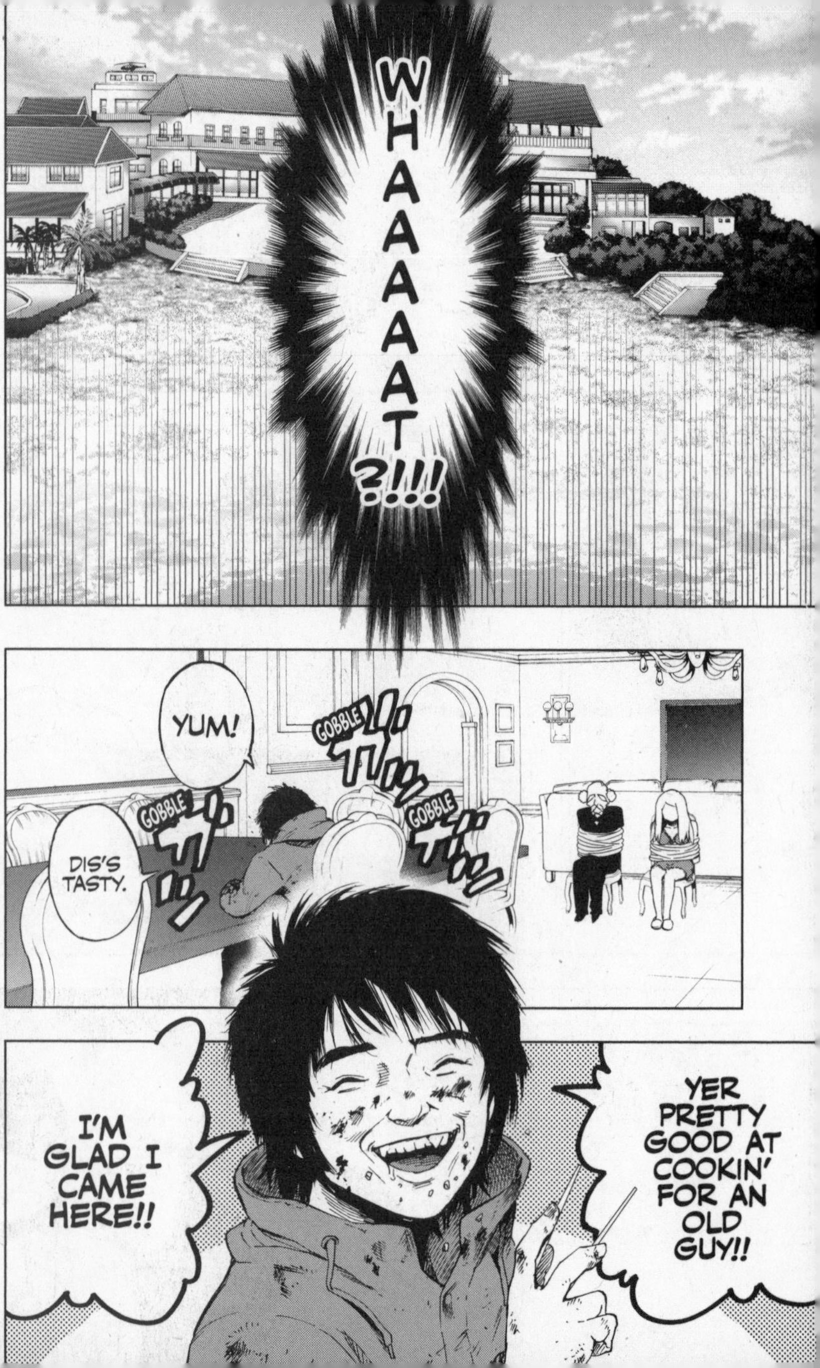
WHAAAAAT?!!!
GOBBLE
YUM!
GOBBLE
GOBBLE
DIS'S TASTY.
YER PRETTY GOOD AT COOKIN' FOR AN OLD GUY!!
I'M GLAD I CAME HERE!!

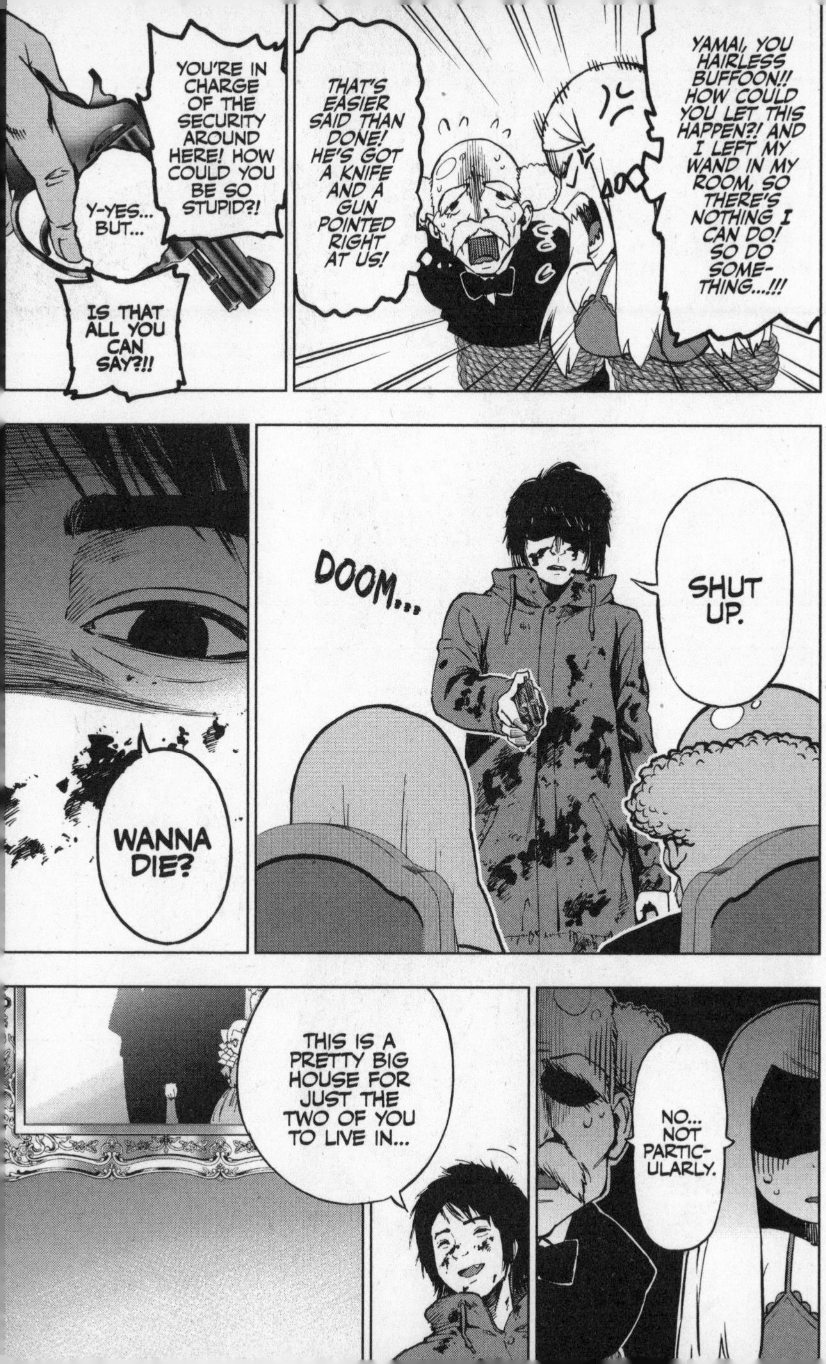
YAMAI, YOU HAIRLESS BUFFOON!! HOW COULD YOU LET THIS HAPPEN?! AND I LEFT MY WAND IN MY ROOM, SO THERE'S NOTHING I CAN DO! SO DO SOME-THING...!!!
THAT'S EASIER SAID THAN DONE! HE'S GOT A KNIFE AND A GUN POINTED RIGHT AT US!
YOU'RE IN CHARGE OF THE SECURITY AROUND HERE! HOW COULD YOU BE SO STUPID?!
Y-YES... BUT...
IS THAT ALL YOU CAN SAY?!!
SHUT UP.
DOOM...
WANNA DIE?
NO... NOT PARTIC-ULARLY.
THIS IS A PRETTY BIG HOUSE FOR JUST THE TWO OF YOU TO LIVE IN...

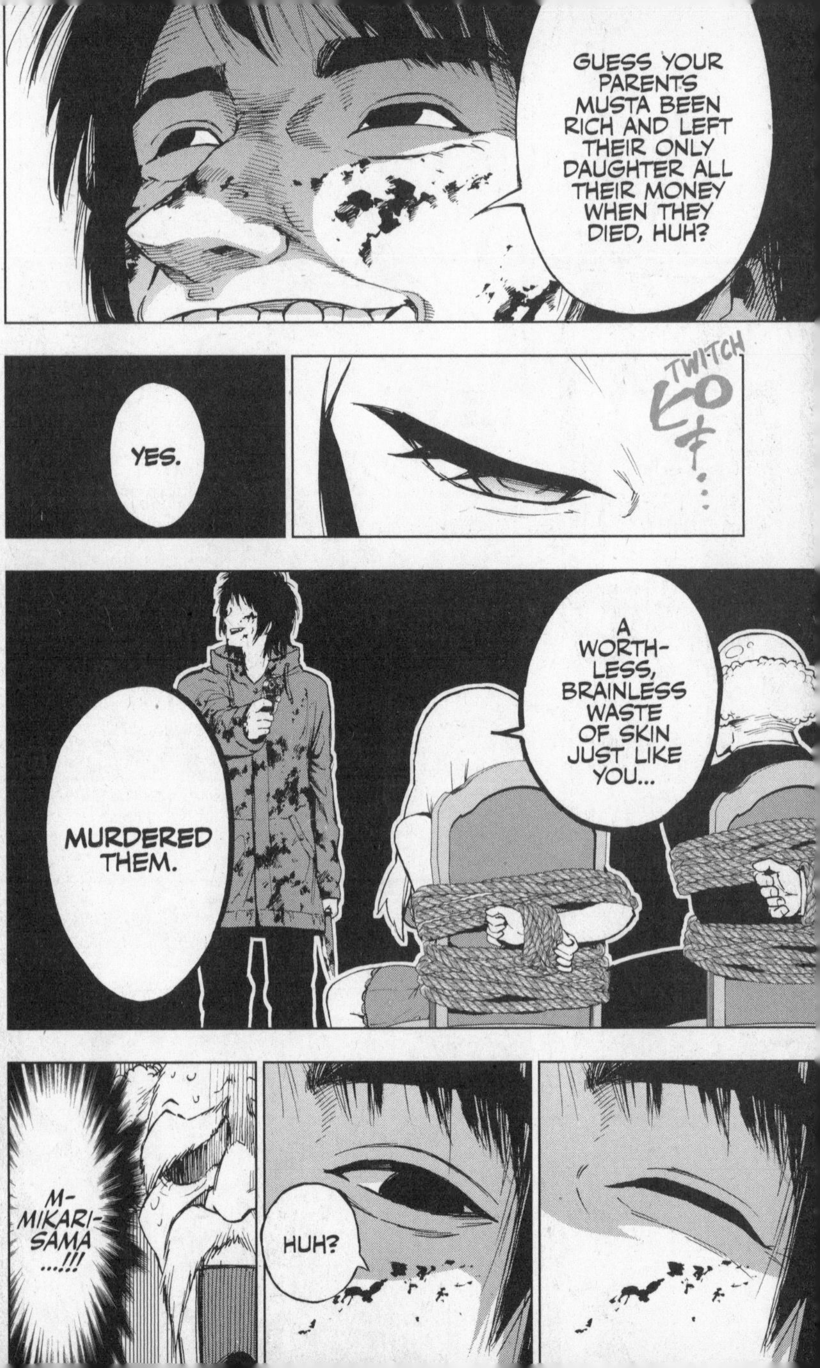
GUESS YOUR PARENTS MUSTA BEEN RICH AND LEFT THEIR ONLY DAUGHTER ALL THEIR MONEY WHEN THEY DIED, HUH?
TWITCH
YES.
A WORTH-LESS, BRAINLESS WASTE OF SKIN JUST LIKE YOU...
MURDERED THEM.
HUH?
M-MIKARI-SAMA ...!!!

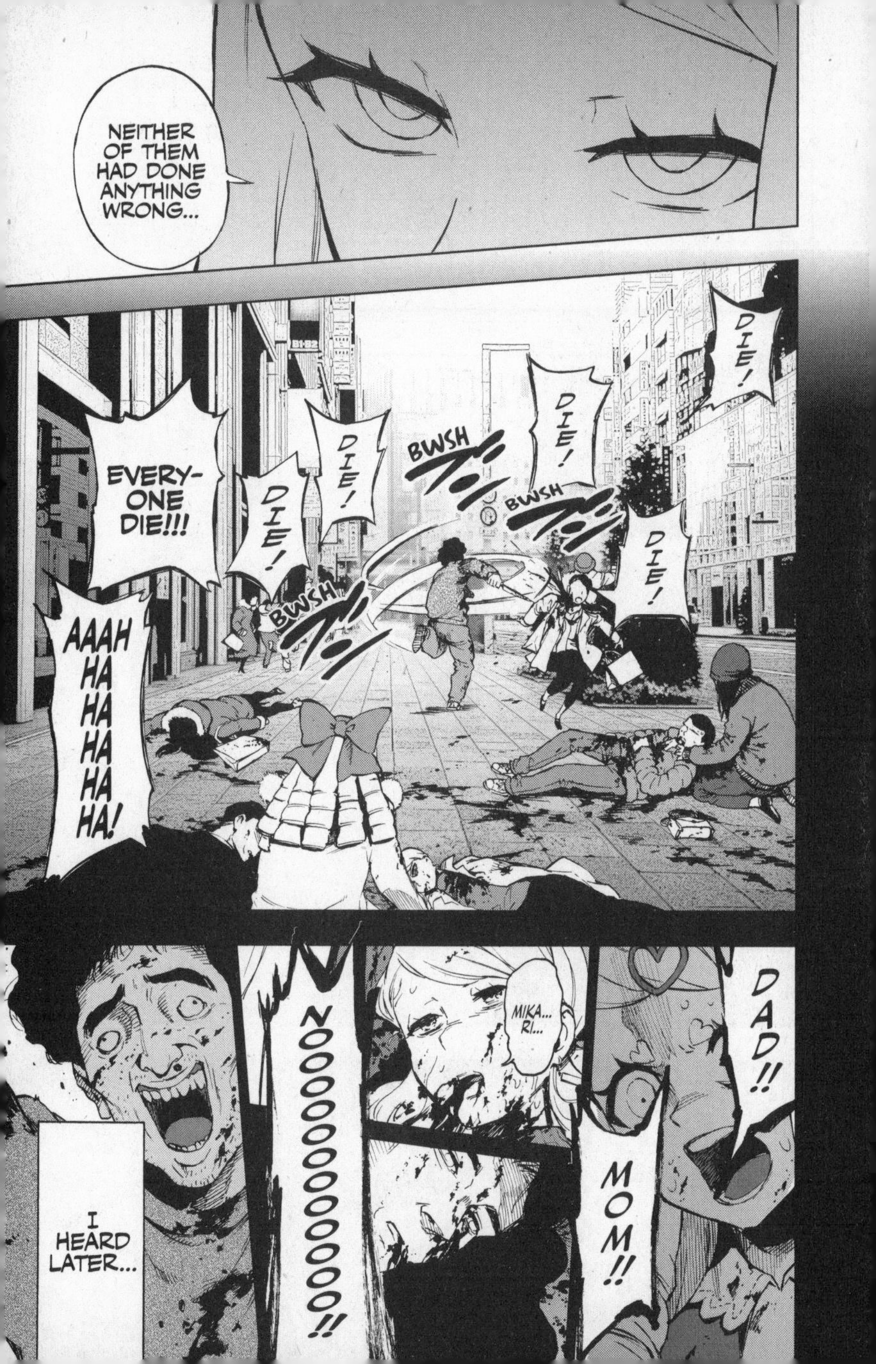
NEITHER OF THEM HAD DONE ANYTHING WRONG...
DIE!
DIE!
BWSH
DIE!
BWSH
DIE!
DIE!
EVERY-ONE DIE!!!
BWSH
AAAH HA HA HA HA HA HA!
DAD!!
MOM!!
MIKA... RI...
NOOOOOOOOOOOOO!!
I HEARD LATER...

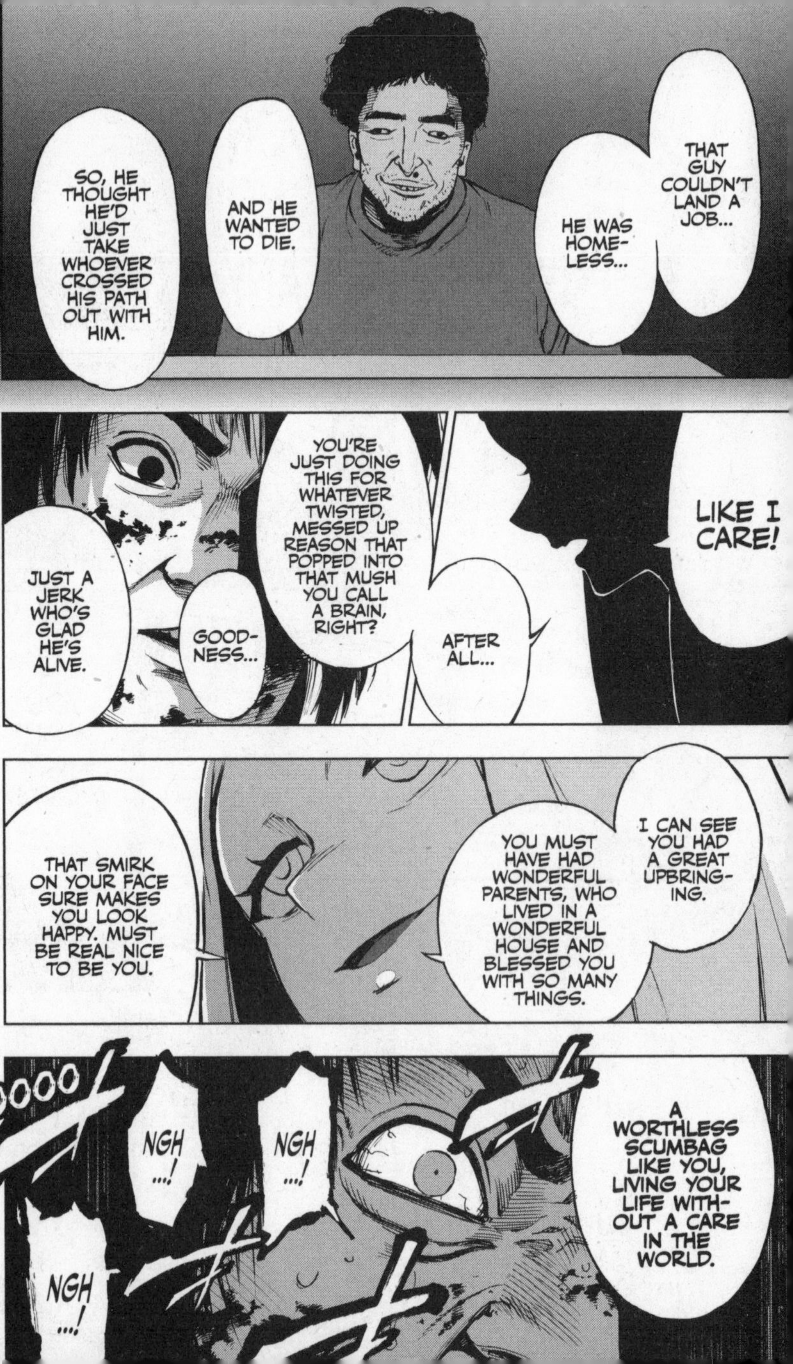
THAT GUY COULDN'T LAND A JOB...
HE WAS HOME-LESS...
AND HE WANTED TO DIE.
SO, HE THOUGHT HE'D JUST TAKE WHOEVER CROSSED HIS PATH OUT WITH HIM.
LIKE I CARE!
AFTER ALL...
YOU'RE JUST DOING THIS FOR WHATEVER TWISTED, MESSED UP REASON THAT POPPED INTO THAT MUSH YOU CALL A BRAIN, RIGHT?
GOOD-NESS...
JUST A JERK WHO'S GLAD HE'S ALIVE.
I CAN SEE YOU HAD A GREAT UPBRING-ING.
YOU MUST HAVE HAD WONDERFUL PARENTS, WHO LIVED IN A WONDERFUL HOUSE AND BLESSED YOU WITH SO MANY THINGS.
THAT SMIRK ON YOUR FACE SURE MAKES YOU LOOK HAPPY. MUST BE REAL NICE TO BE YOU.
A WORTHLESS SCUMBAG LIKE YOU, LIVING YOUR LIFE WITH-OUT A CARE IN THE WORLD.
NGH ...!
NGH ...!
OOOO
NGH ...!

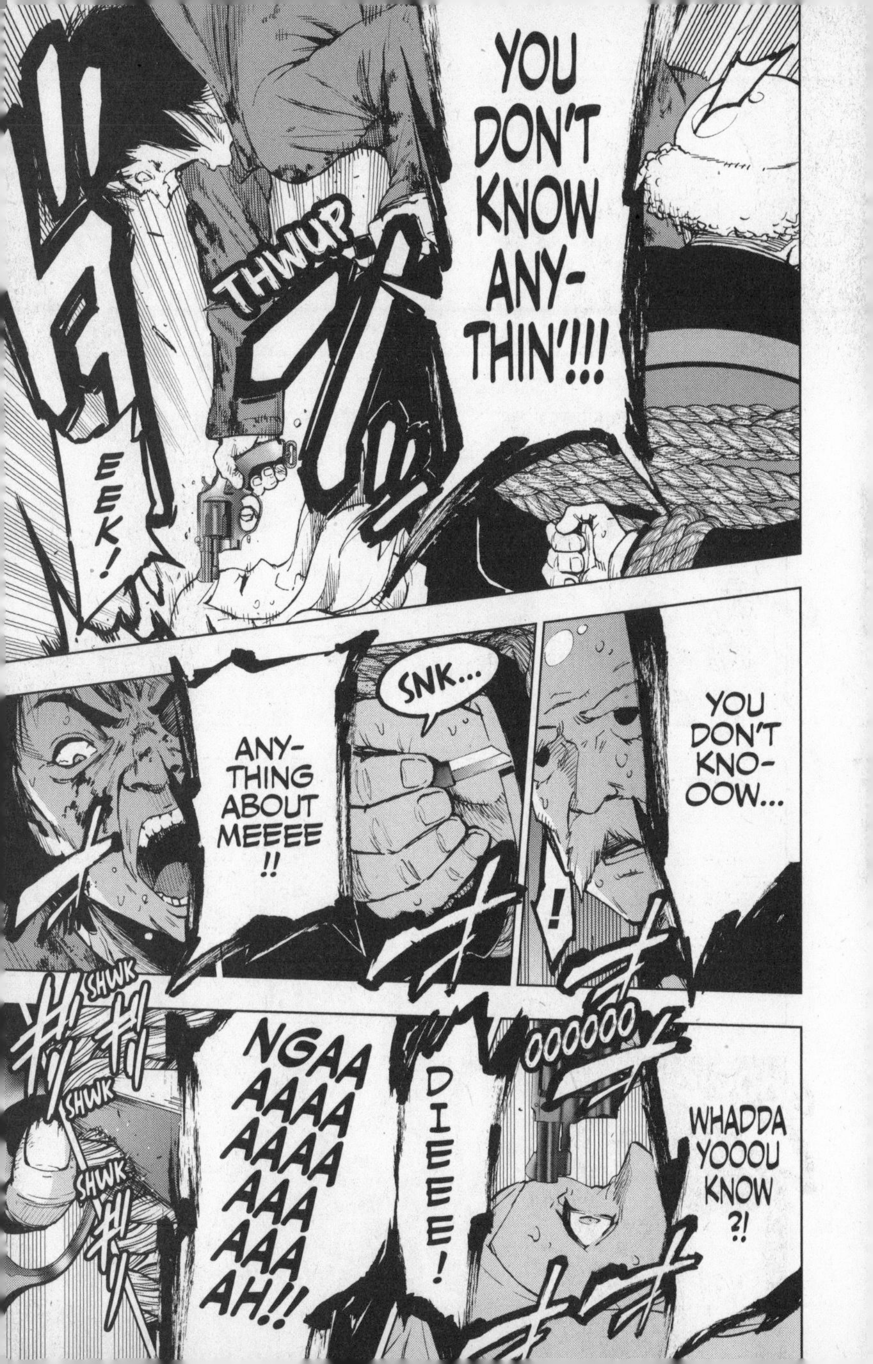
YOU DON'T KNOW ANY-THIN'!!!
THWUP
EEK!
YOU DON'T KNO-OOW...
!
SNK...
ANY-THING ABOUT MEEEE !!
WHADDA YOOOU KNOW ?!
OOOOOO
DIEEE!
NGAAAAAAAAAAAAAAAAAAAAAAH!!
SHWK
SHWK
SHWK

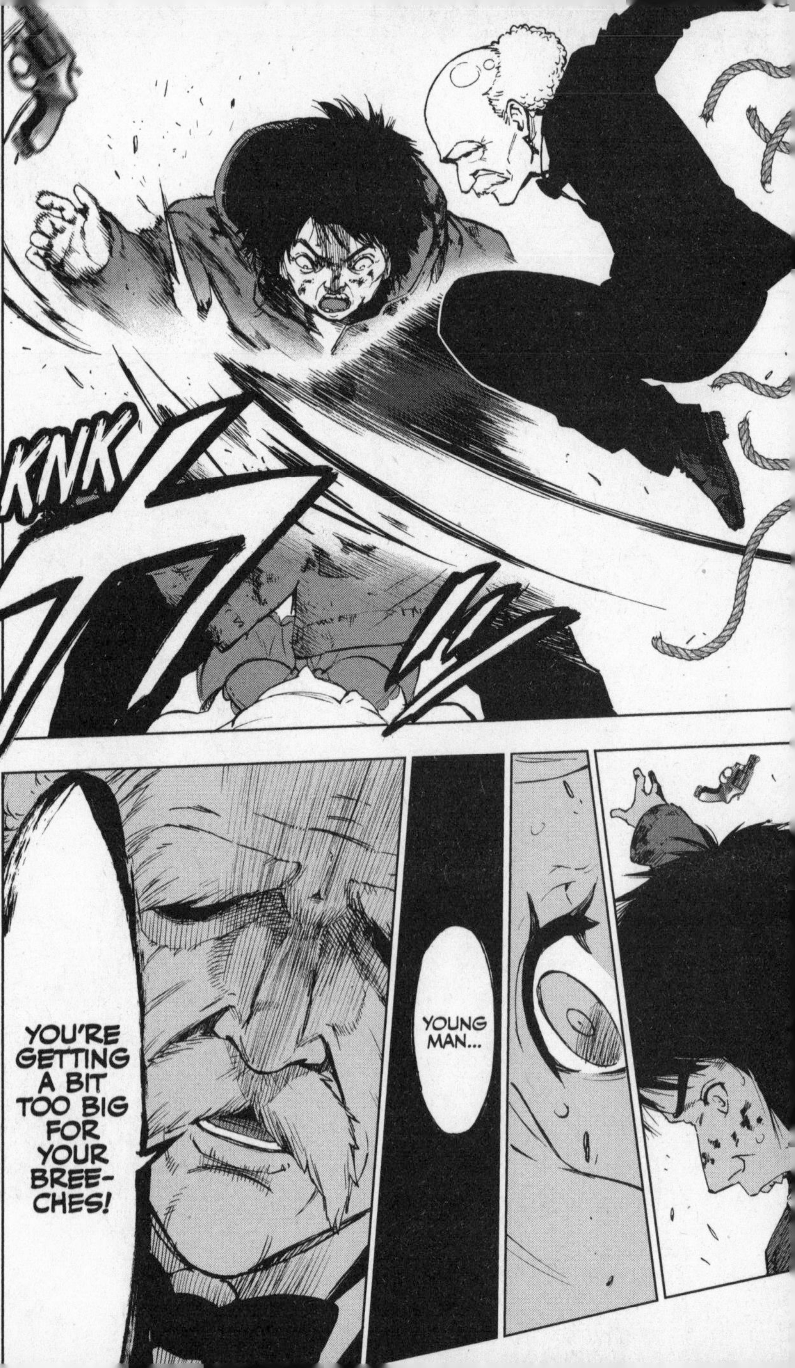
KNK
YOUNG MAN...
YOU'RE GETTING A BIT TOO BIG FOR YOUR BREE-CHES!

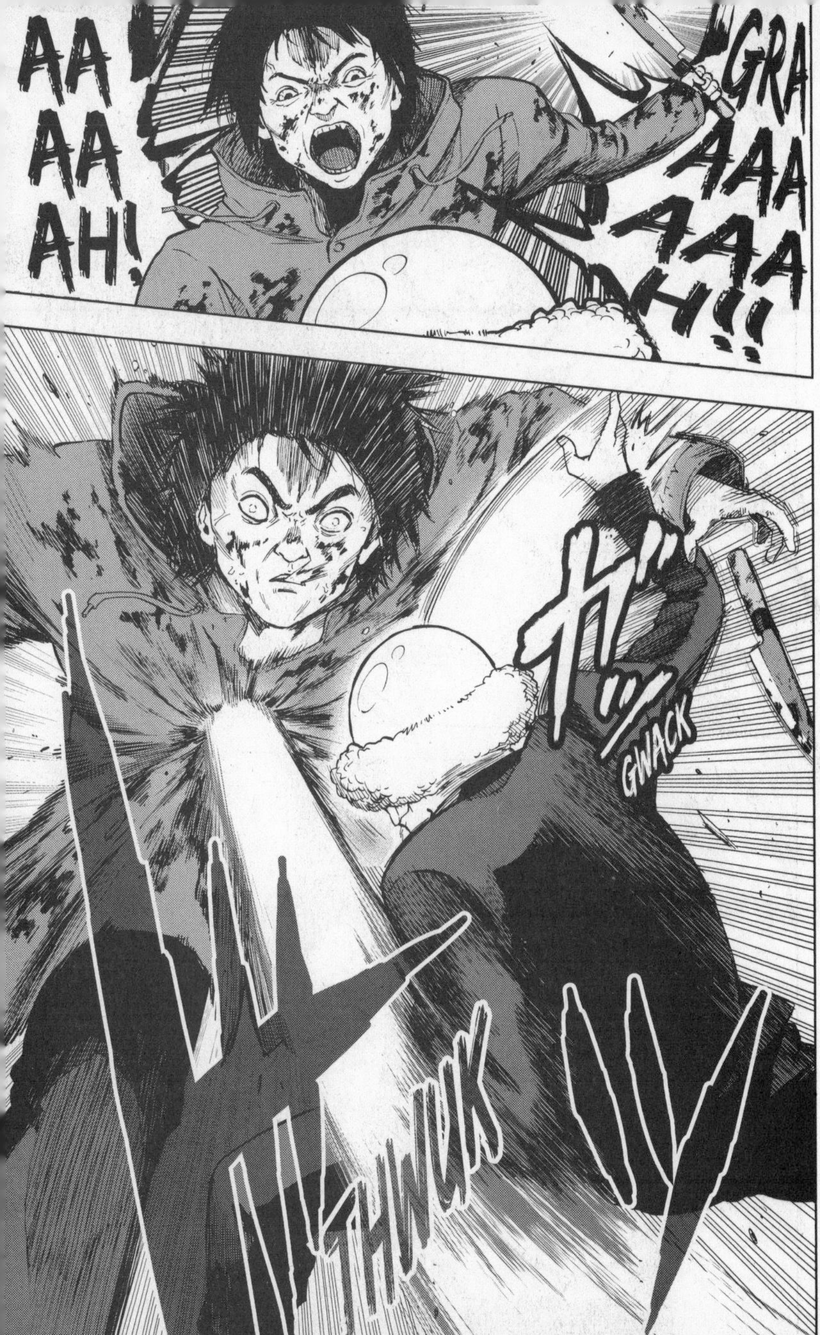
GRAAAAAAAH!!
AAAAAAH!
ガッ
GWACK
THWACK

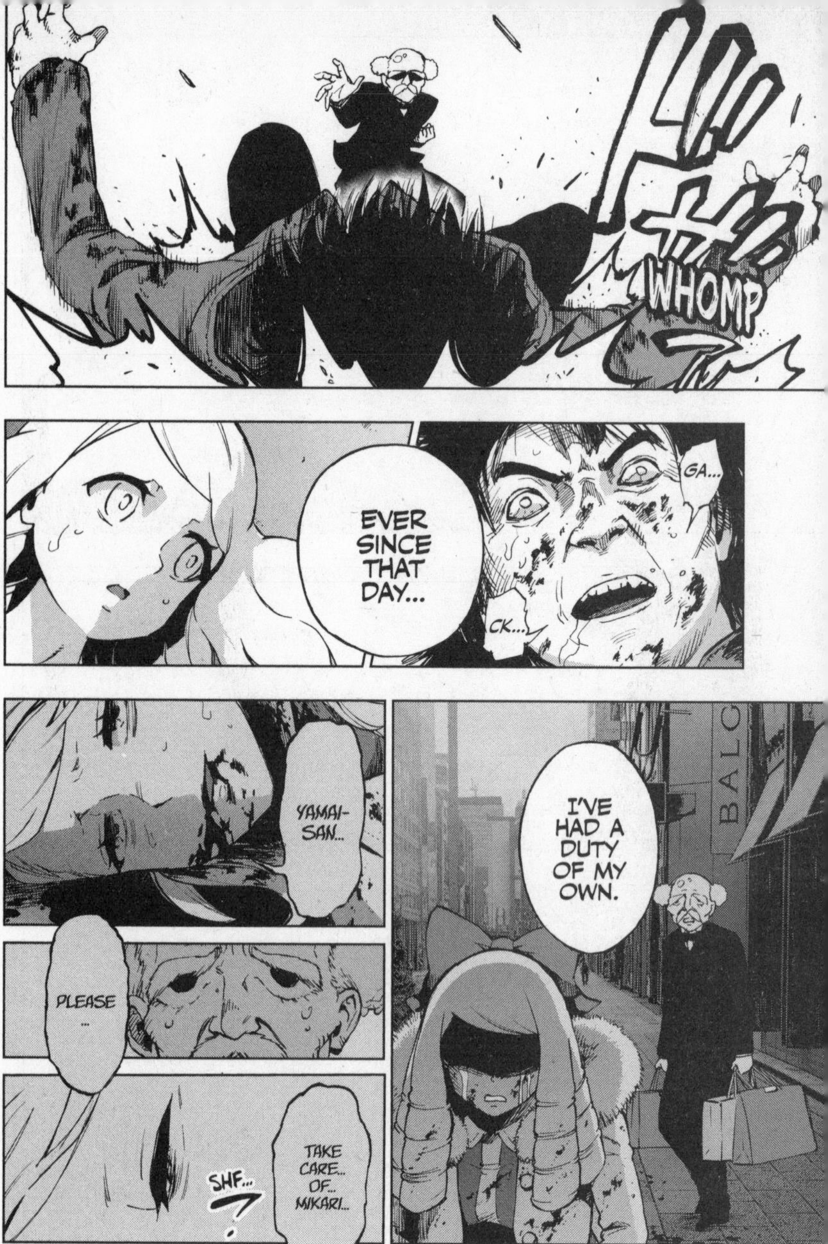
WHOMP
GA...
CK...
EVER SINCE THAT DAY...
BALC
I'VE HAD A DUTY OF MY OWN.
YAMAI-SAN...
PLEASE...
SHF...
TAKE CARE... OF... MIKARI...

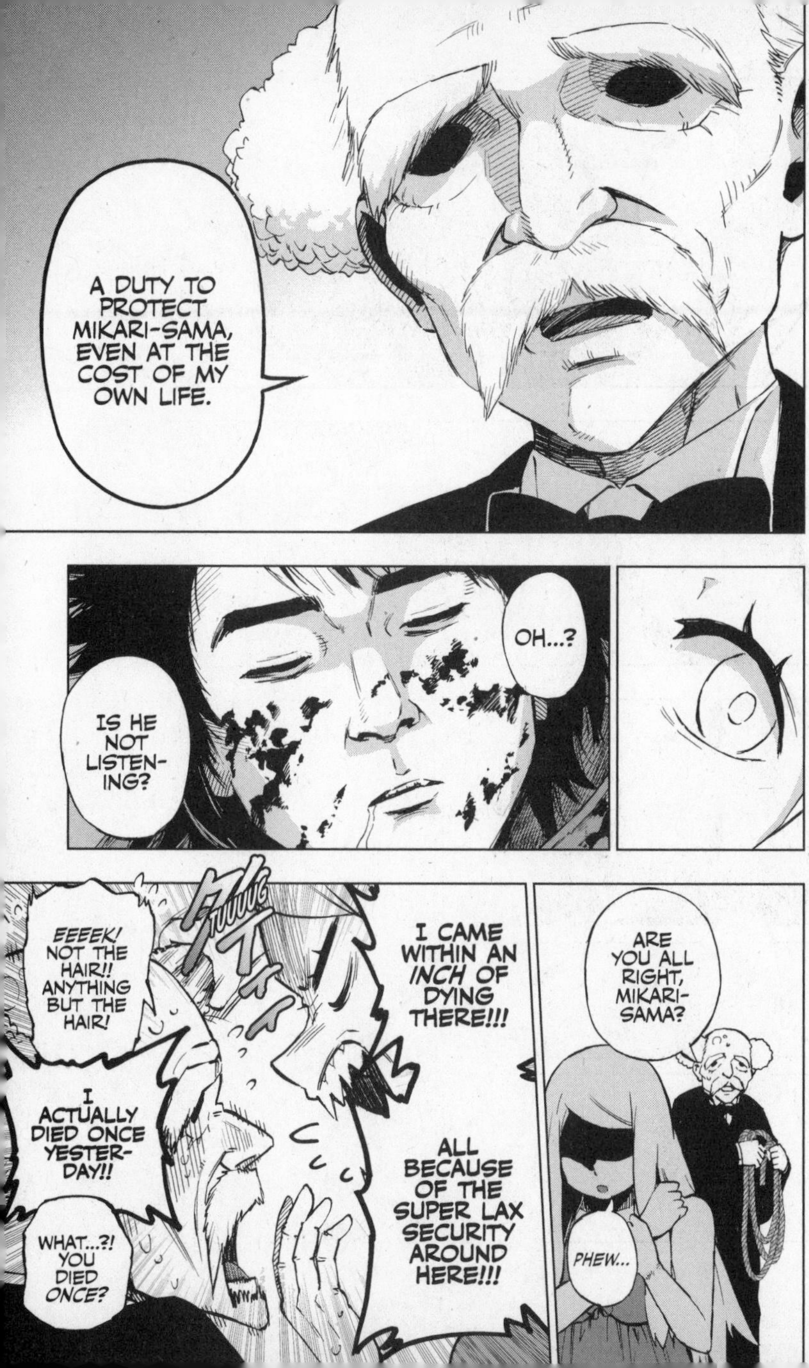
A DUTY TO PROTECT MIKARI-SAMA, EVEN AT THE COST OF MY OWN LIFE.
OH...?
IS HE NOT LISTENING?
ARE YOU ALL RIGHT, MIKARI-SAMA?
PHEW...
I CAME WITHIN AN *INCH* OF DYING THERE!!!
ALL BECAUSE OF THE SUPER LAX SECURITY AROUND HERE!!!
EEEEK! NOT THE HAIR!! ANYTHING BUT THE HAIR!
I ACTUALLY DIED ONCE YESTER-DAY!!
WHAT...?! YOU DIED *ONCE?*

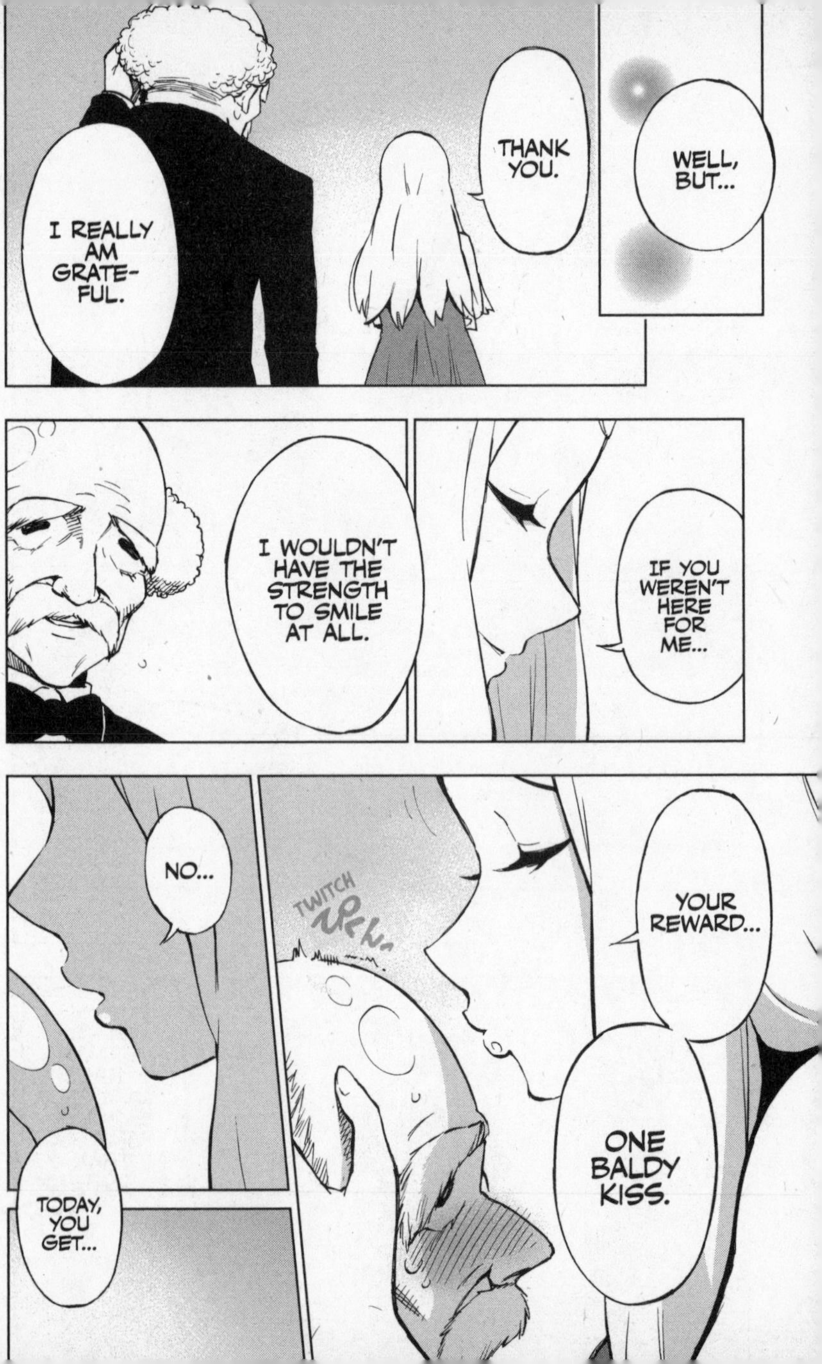
WELL, BUT...
THANK YOU.
I REALLY AM GRATE-FUL.
IF YOU WEREN'T HERE FOR ME...
I WOULDN'T HAVE THE STRENGTH TO SMILE AT ALL.
YOUR REWARD...
TWITCH
ONE BALDY KISS.
NO...
TODAY, YOU GET...

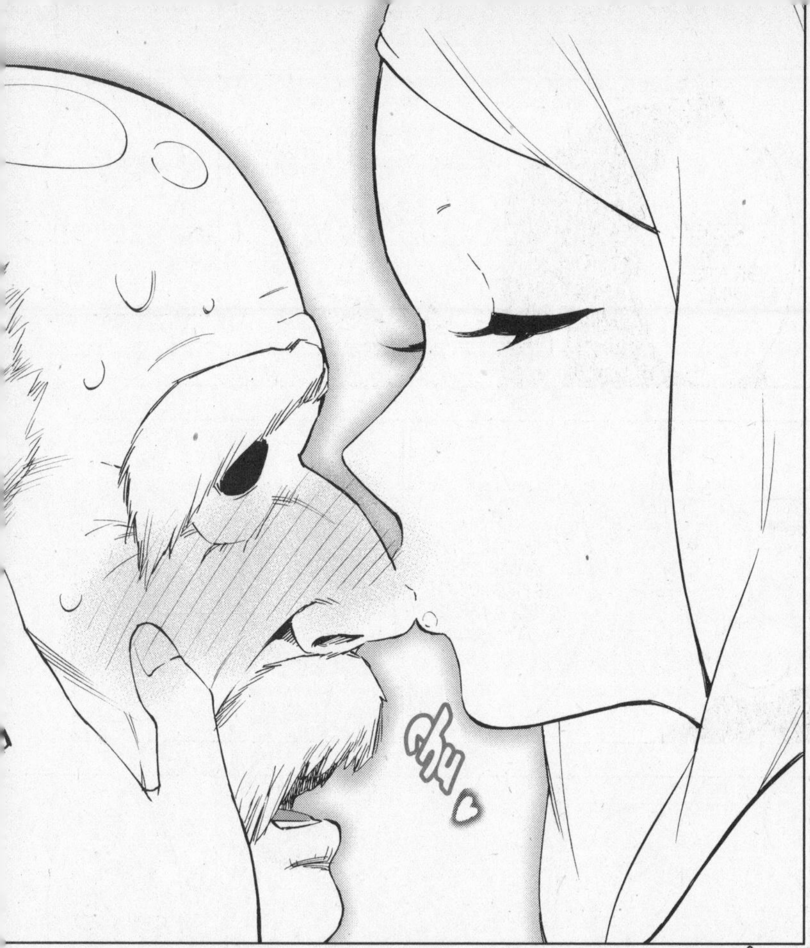
chu
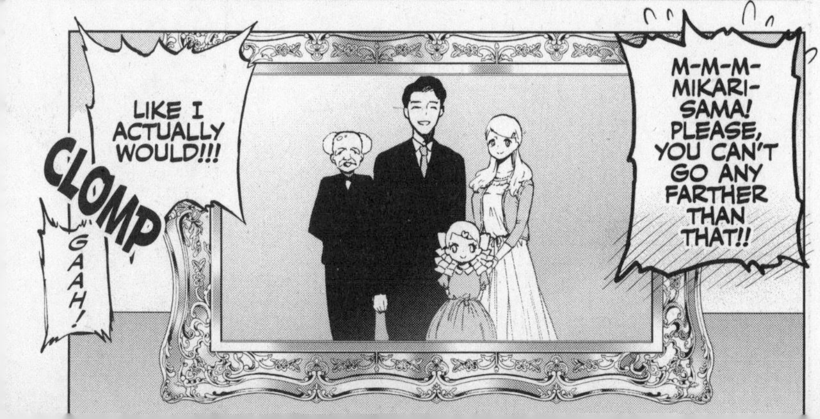
M-M-M-MIKARI-SAMA! PLEASE, YOU CAN'T GO ANY FARTHER THAN THAT!!
LIKE I ACTUALLY WOULD!!!
CLOMP
GAAH!

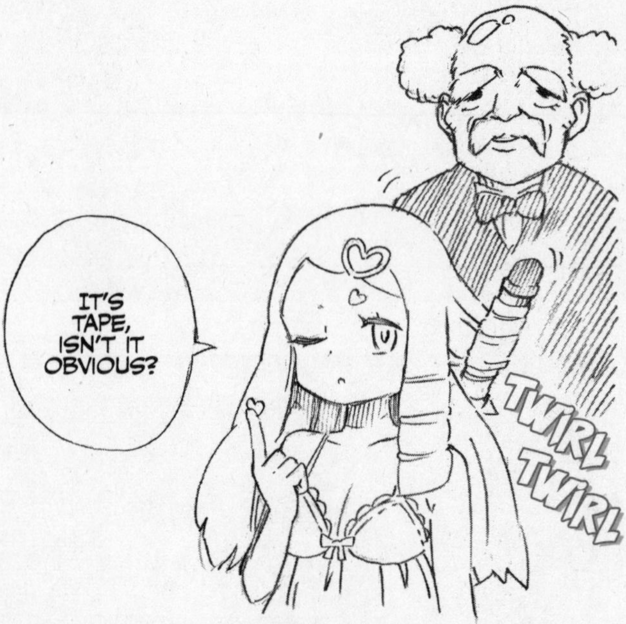
IT'S TAPE, ISN'T IT OBVIOUS?
TWIRL TWIRL

ENTER.53 PLAN

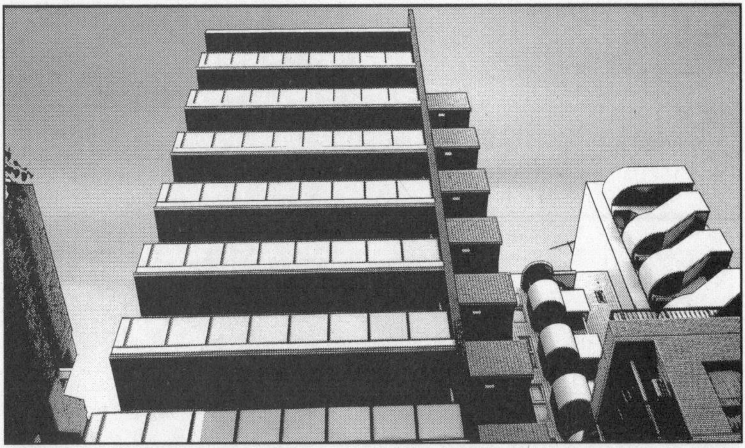

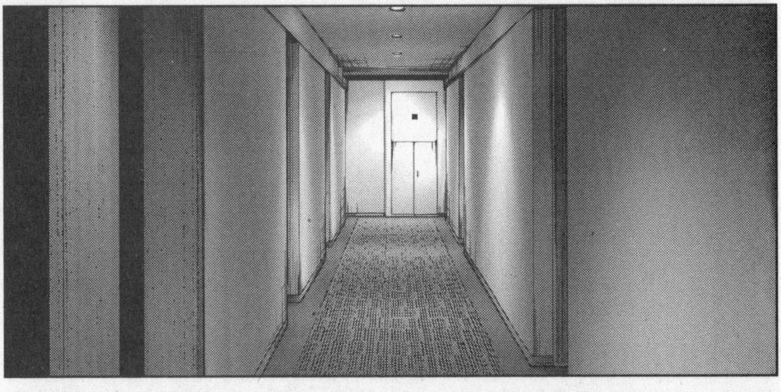

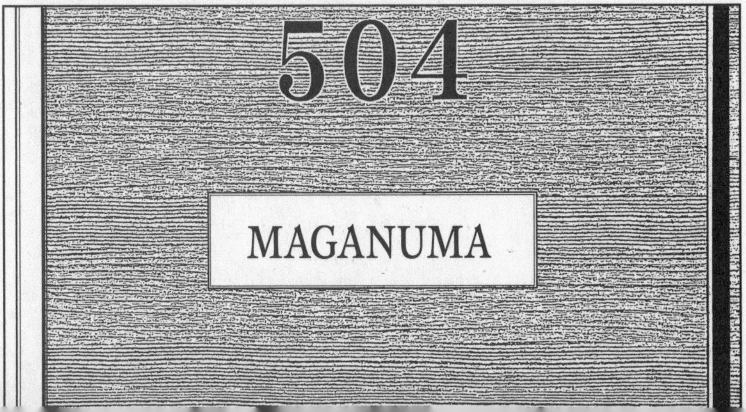
504
MAGANUMA

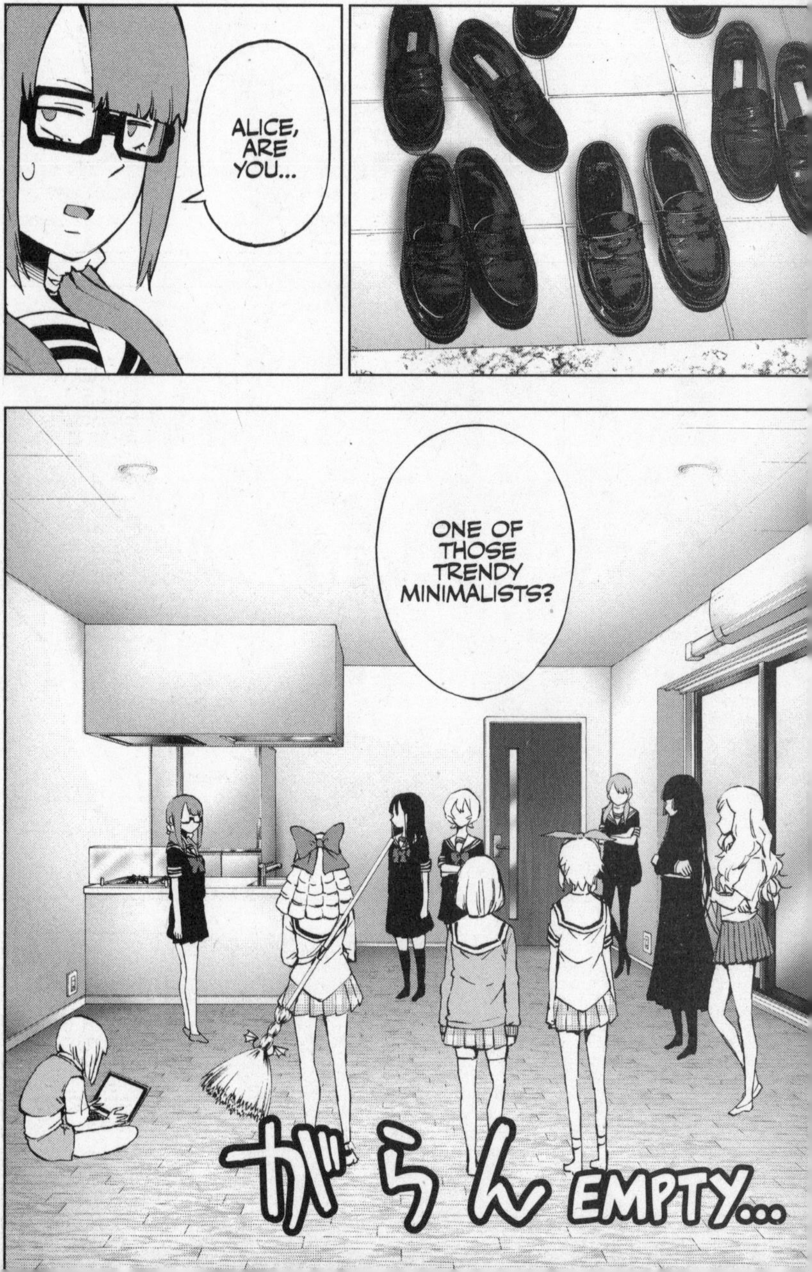
ALICE, ARE YOU...
ONE OF THOSE TRENDY MINIMALISTS?
がらん EMPTY...

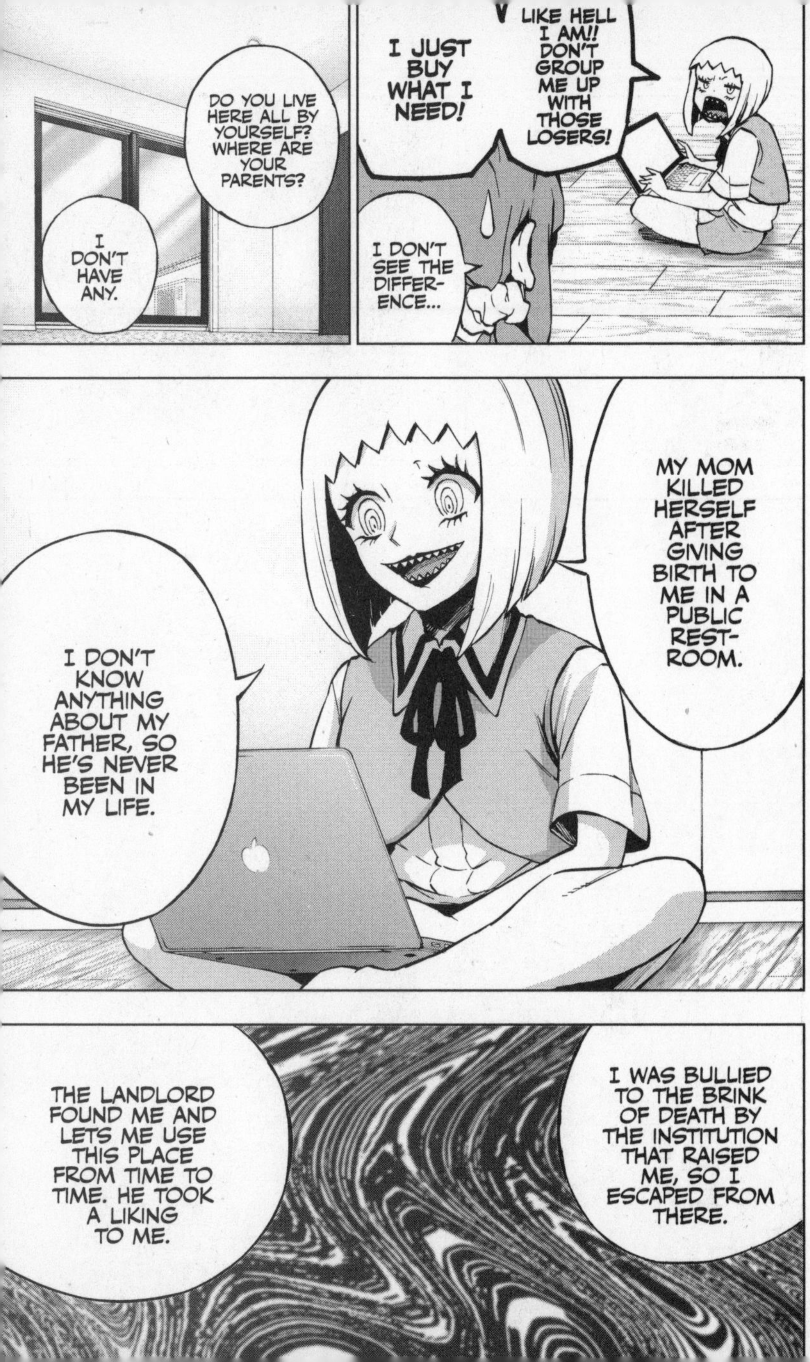
LIKE HELL I AM!! DON'T GROUP ME UP WITH THOSE LOSERS!
I JUST BUY WHAT I NEED!
I DON'T SEE THE DIFFERENCE...
DO YOU LIVE HERE ALL BY YOURSELF? WHERE ARE YOUR PARENTS?
I DON'T HAVE ANY.
MY MOM KILLED HERSELF AFTER GIVING BIRTH TO ME IN A PUBLIC REST-ROOM.
I DON'T KNOW ANYTHING ABOUT MY FATHER, SO HE'S NEVER BEEN IN MY LIFE.
I WAS BULLIED TO THE BRINK OF DEATH BY THE INSTITUTION THAT RAISED ME, SO I ESCAPED FROM THERE.
THE LANDLORD FOUND ME AND LETS ME USE THIS PLACE FROM TIME TO TIME. HE TOOK A LIKING TO ME.

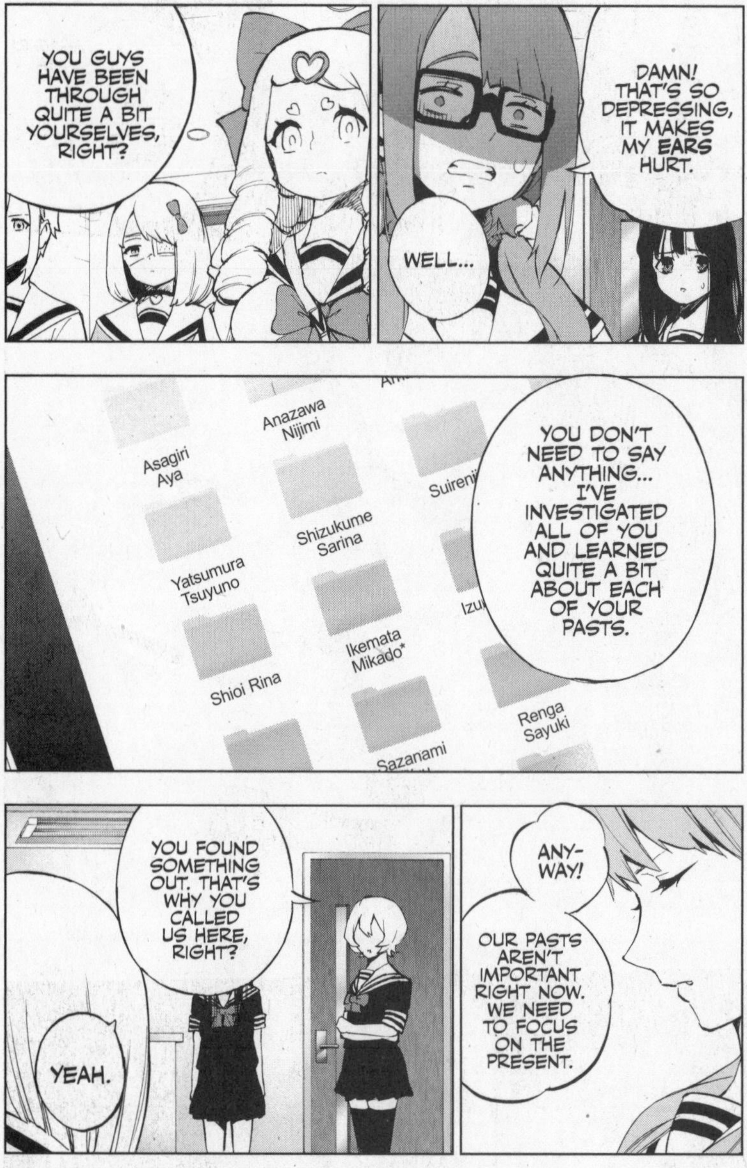
DAMN! THAT'S SO DEPRESSING, IT MAKES MY EARS HURT.
WELL...
YOU GUYS HAVE BEEN THROUGH QUITE A BIT YOURSELVES, RIGHT?
YOU DON'T NEED TO SAY ANYTHING... I'VE INVESTIGATED ALL OF YOU AND LEARNED QUITE A BIT ABOUT EACH OF YOUR PASTS.
Anazawa Nijimi
Asagiri Aya
Shizukume Sarina
Yatsumura Tsuyuno
Ikemata Mikado*
Shioi Rina
Renga Sayuki
Sazanami
ANY-WAY!
OUR PASTS AREN'T IMPORTANT RIGHT NOW. WE NEED TO FOCUS ON THE PRESENT.
YOU FOUND SOMETHING OUT. THAT'S WHY YOU CALLED US HERE, RIGHT?
YEAH.

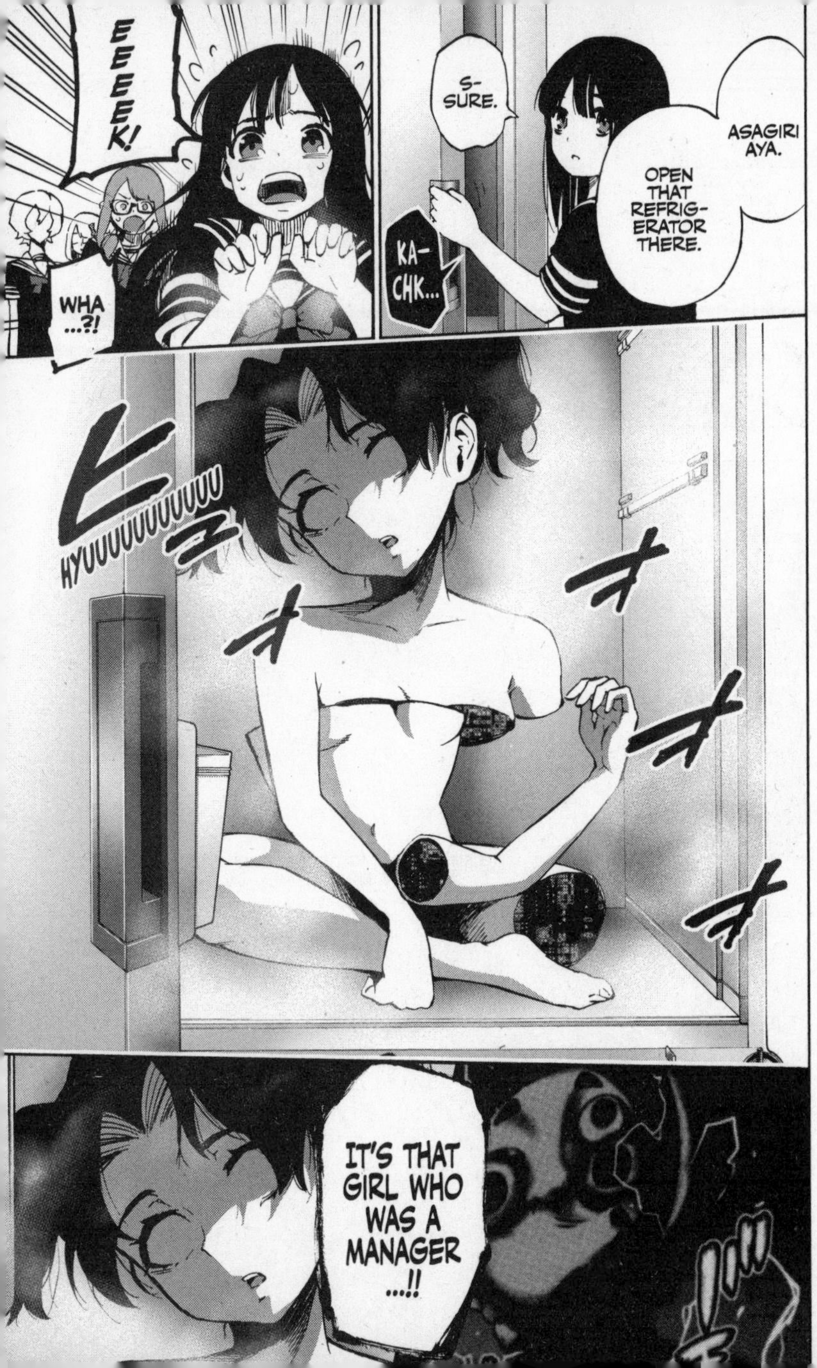
ASAGIRI AYA.
OPEN THAT REFRIGERATOR THERE.
S-SURE.
KA-CHK...
EEEEEK!
WHA ...?!
HYUUUUUUUUUUU
IT'S THAT GIRL WHO WAS A MANAGER ...!!

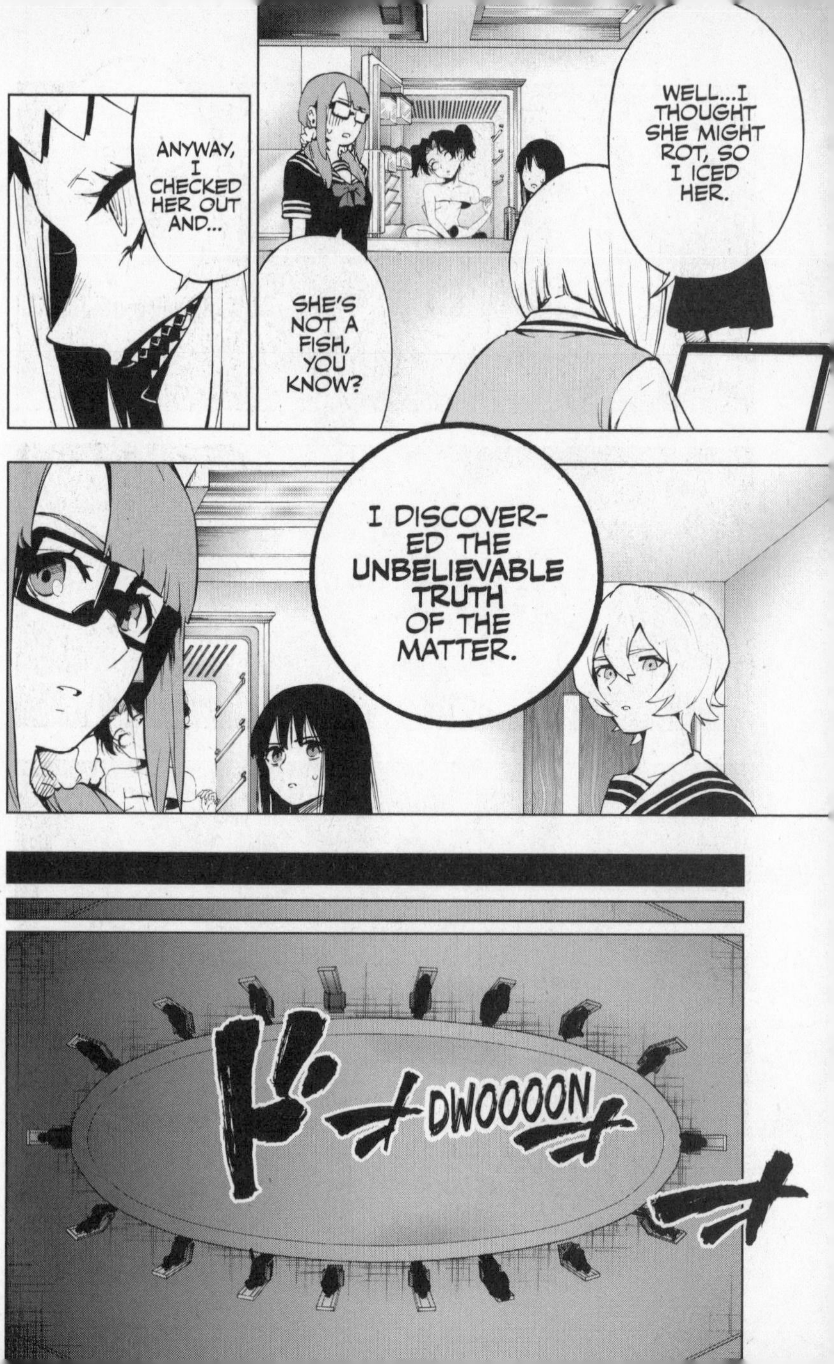
WELL...I THOUGHT SHE MIGHT ROT, SO I ICED HER.
SHE'S NOT A FISH, YOU KNOW?
ANYWAY, I CHECKED HER OUT AND...
I DISCOVER-ED THE UNBELIEVABLE TRUTH OF THE MATTER.
DWOOOON

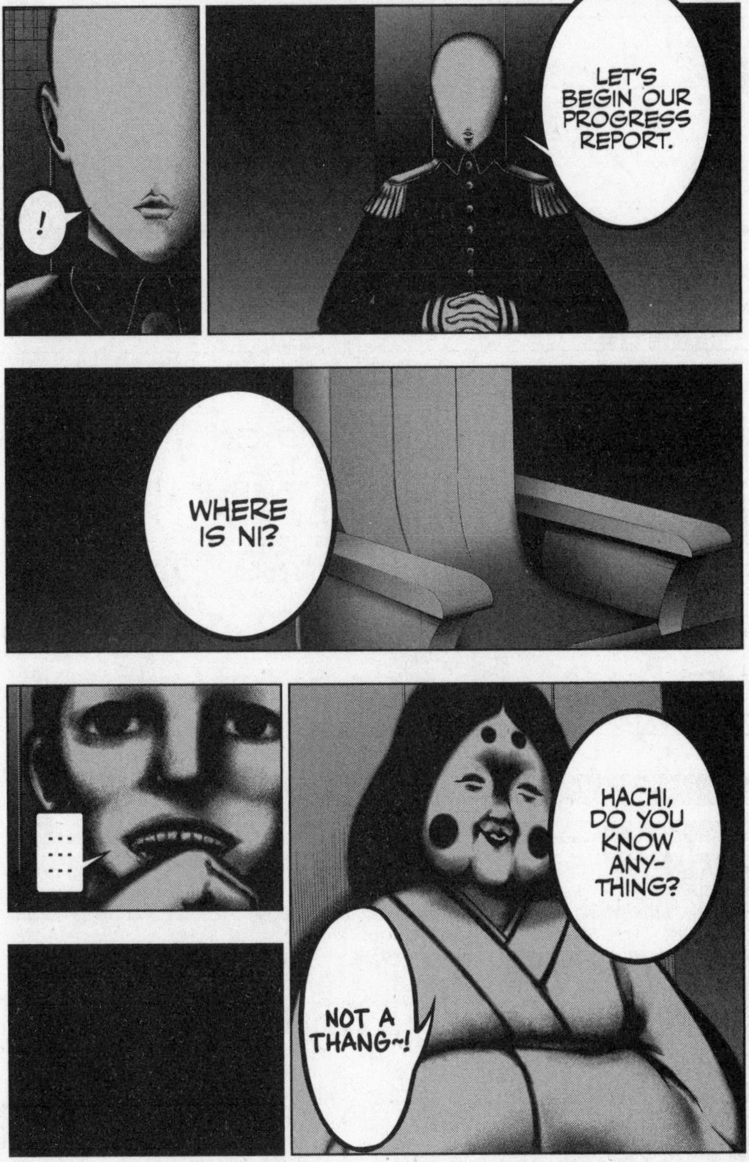
LET'S BEGIN OUR PROGRESS REPORT.
!
WHERE IS NI?
HACHI, DO YOU KNOW ANY-THING?
NOT A THANG~!
......

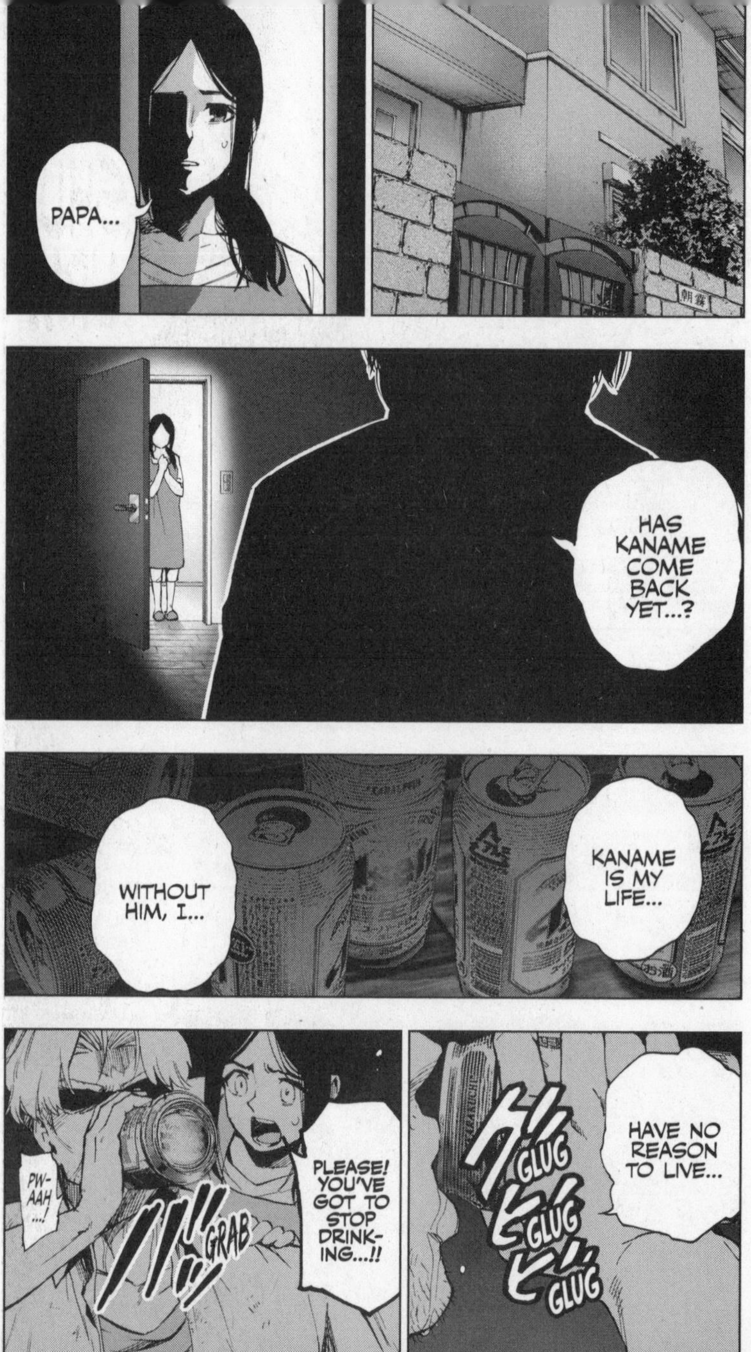
朝霧
PAPA...
HAS KANAME COME BACK YET...?
KANAME IS MY LIFE...
WITHOUT HIM, I...
HAVE NO REASON TO LIVE...
GLUG
GLUG
GLUG
PLEASE! YOU'VE GOT TO STOP DRINK-ING...!!
GRAB
PW-AAH...!

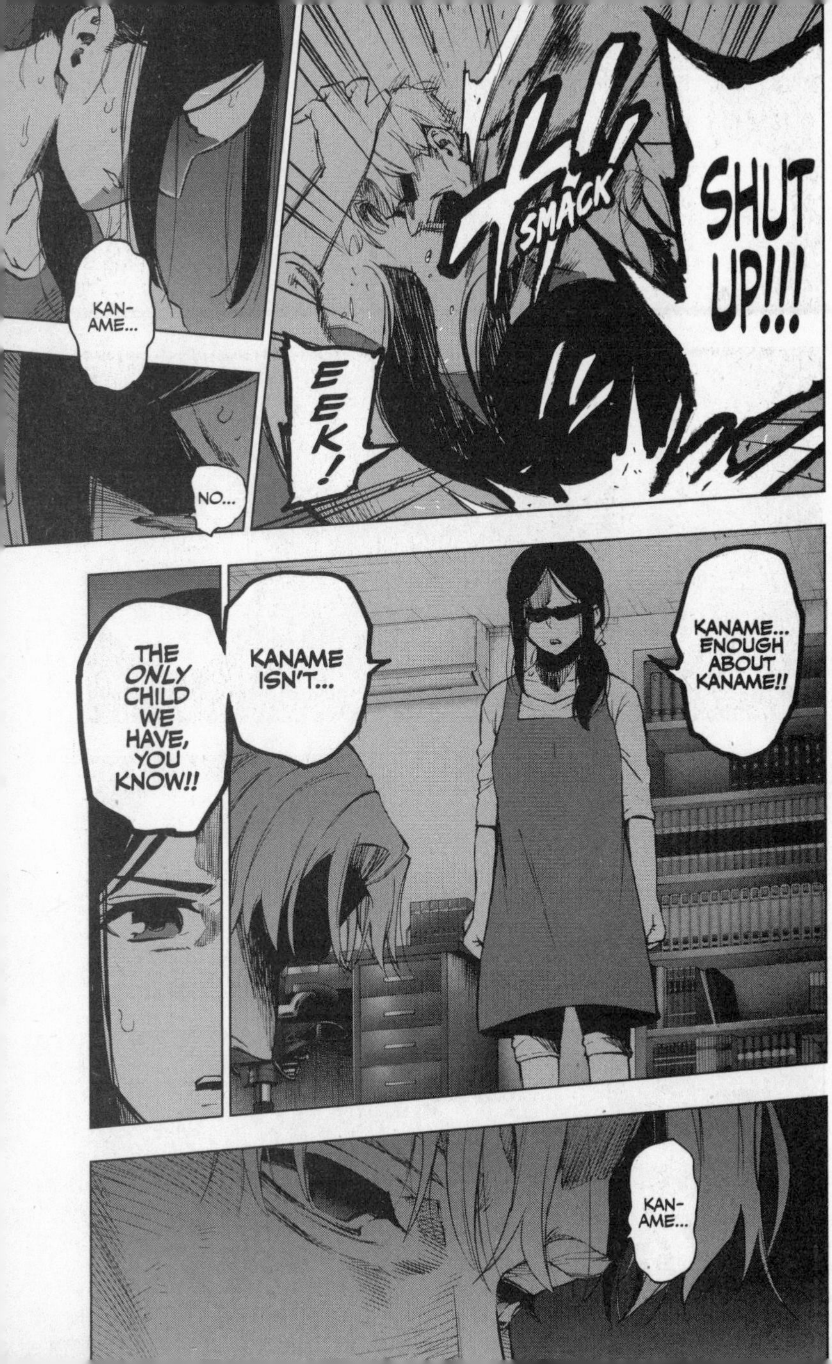
SHUT UP!!!
SMACK
EEK!
KAN-AME...
NO...
KANAME... ENOUGH ABOUT KANAME!!
KANAME ISN'T...
THE ONLY CHILD WE HAVE, YOU KNOW!!
KAN-AME...

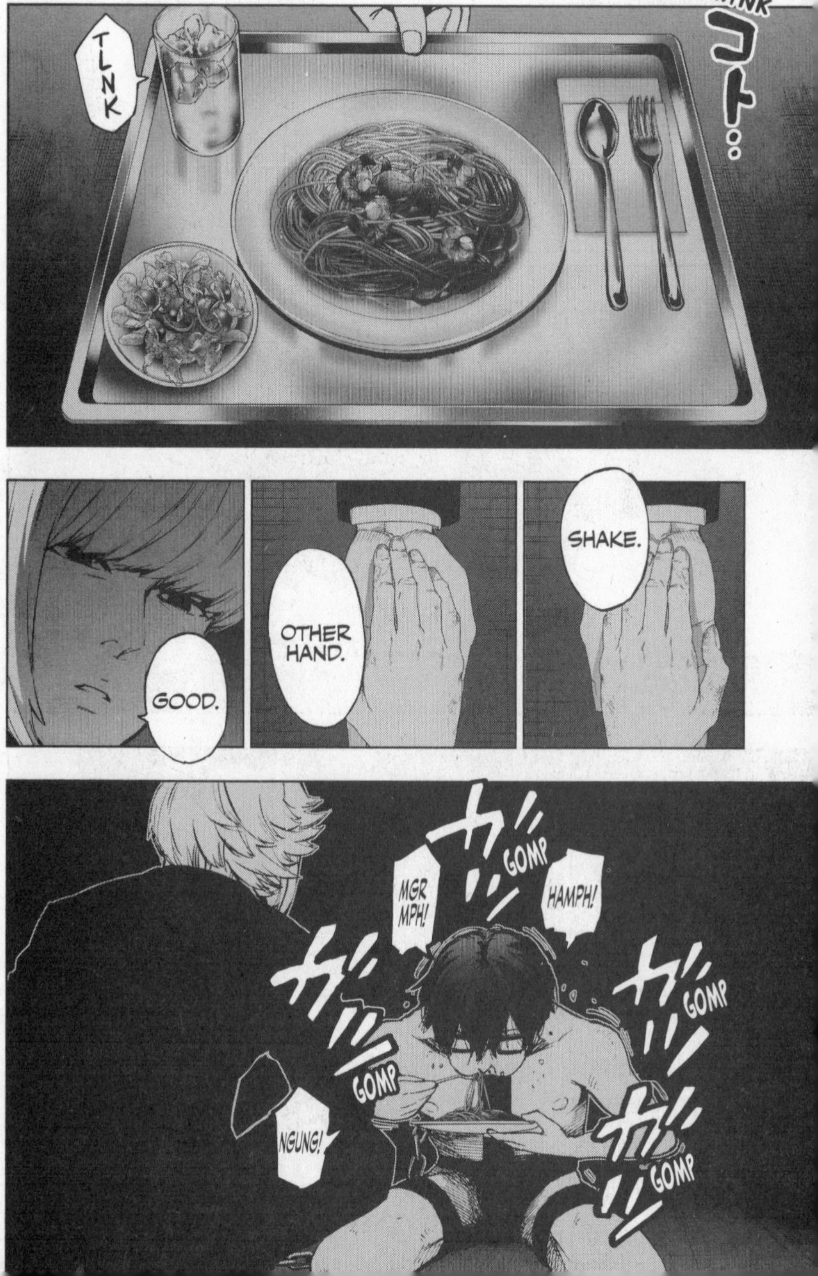
KTNK
コト‥
TLNK
SHAKE.
OTHER HAND.
GOOD.
HAMPH!
GOMP
MGR MPH!
GOMP
GOMP
GOMP
NGUNG!

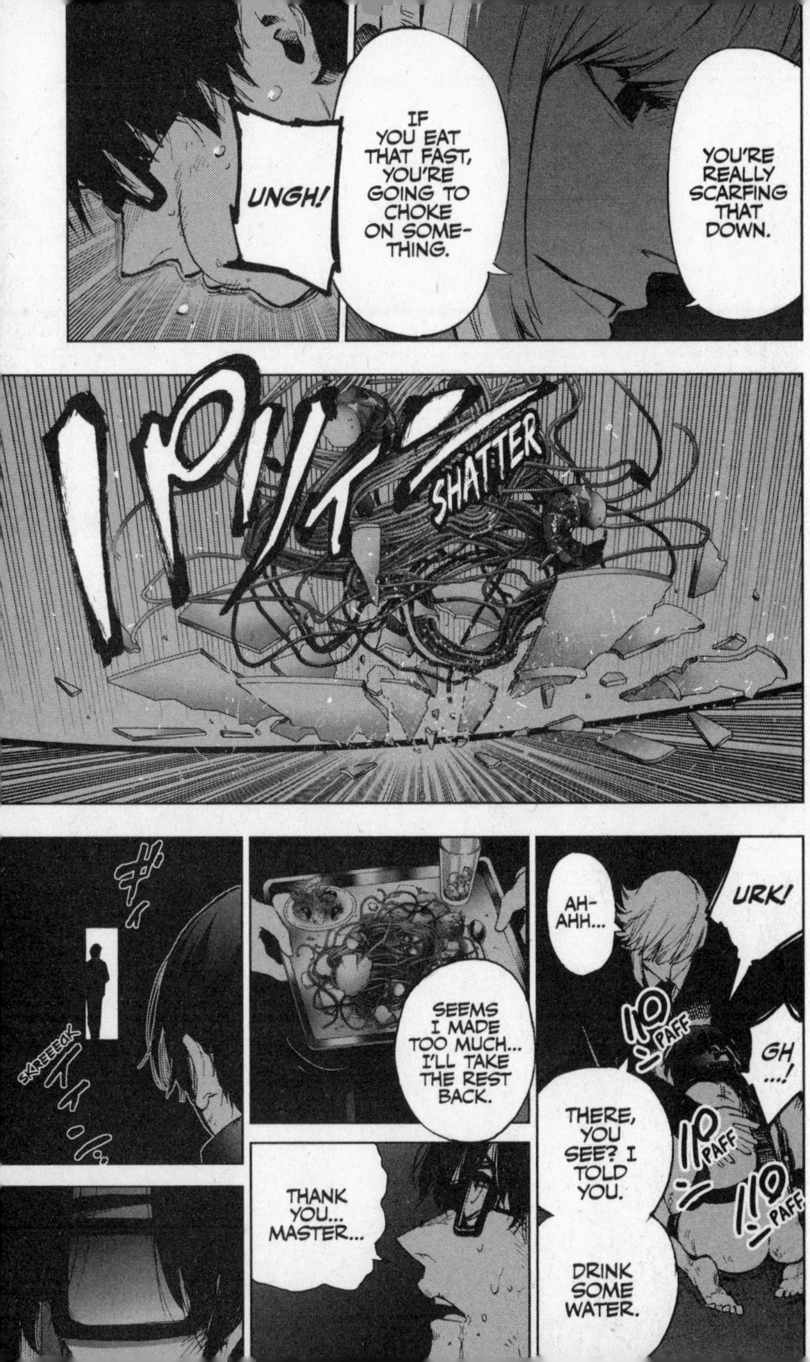
YOU'RE REALLY SCARFING THAT DOWN.
IF YOU EAT THAT FAST, YOU'RE GOING TO CHOKE ON SOME-THING.
UNGH!
SHATTER
URK!
AH-AHH...
PAFF
GH...!
PAFF
PAFF
THERE, YOU SEE? I TOLD YOU.
DRINK SOME WATER.
SEEMS I MADE TOO MUCH... I'LL TAKE THE REST BACK.
THANK YOU... MASTER...
SKREEEEK

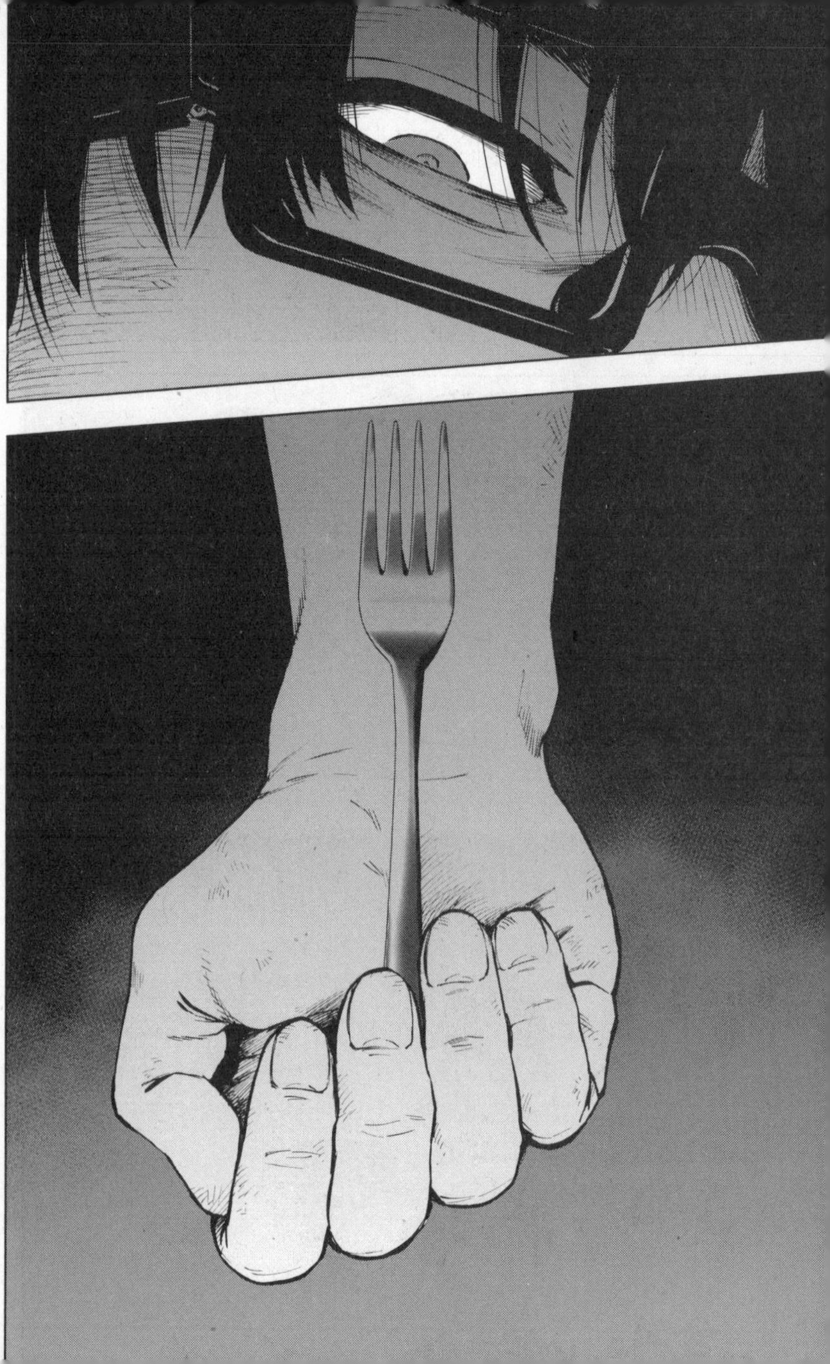

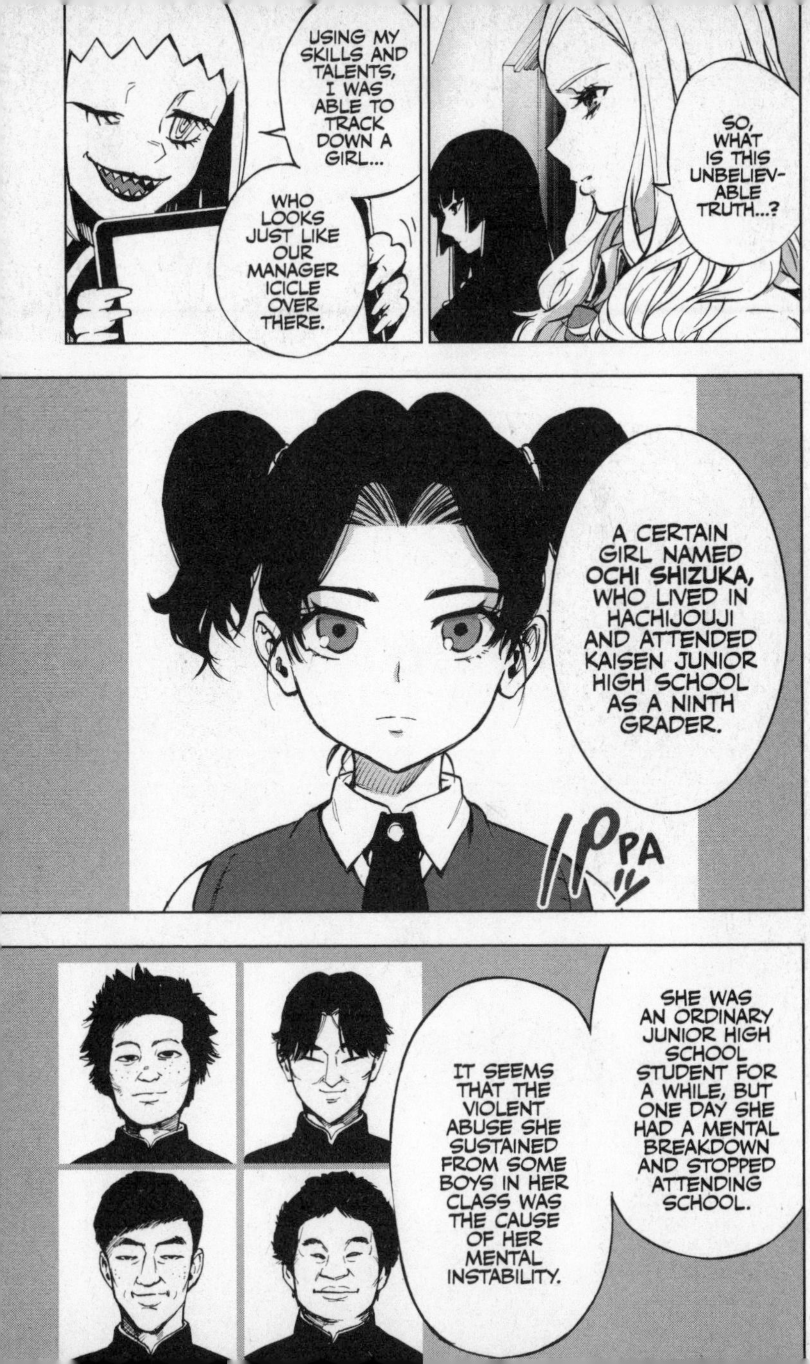
SO, WHAT IS THIS UNBELIEV-ABLE TRUTH...?
USING MY SKILLS AND TALENTS, I WAS ABLE TO TRACK DOWN A GIRL...
WHO LOOKS JUST LIKE OUR MANAGER ICICLE OVER THERE.
A CERTAIN GIRL NAMED OCHI SHIZUKA, WHO LIVED IN HACHIJOUJI AND ATTENDED KAISEN JUNIOR HIGH SCHOOL AS A NINTH GRADER.
PA
SHE WAS AN ORDINARY JUNIOR HIGH SCHOOL STUDENT FOR A WHILE, BUT ONE DAY SHE HAD A MENTAL BREAKDOWN AND STOPPED ATTENDING SCHOOL.
IT SEEMS THAT THE VIOLENT ABUSE SHE SUSTAINED FROM SOME BOYS IN HER CLASS WAS THE CAUSE OF HER MENTAL INSTABILITY.

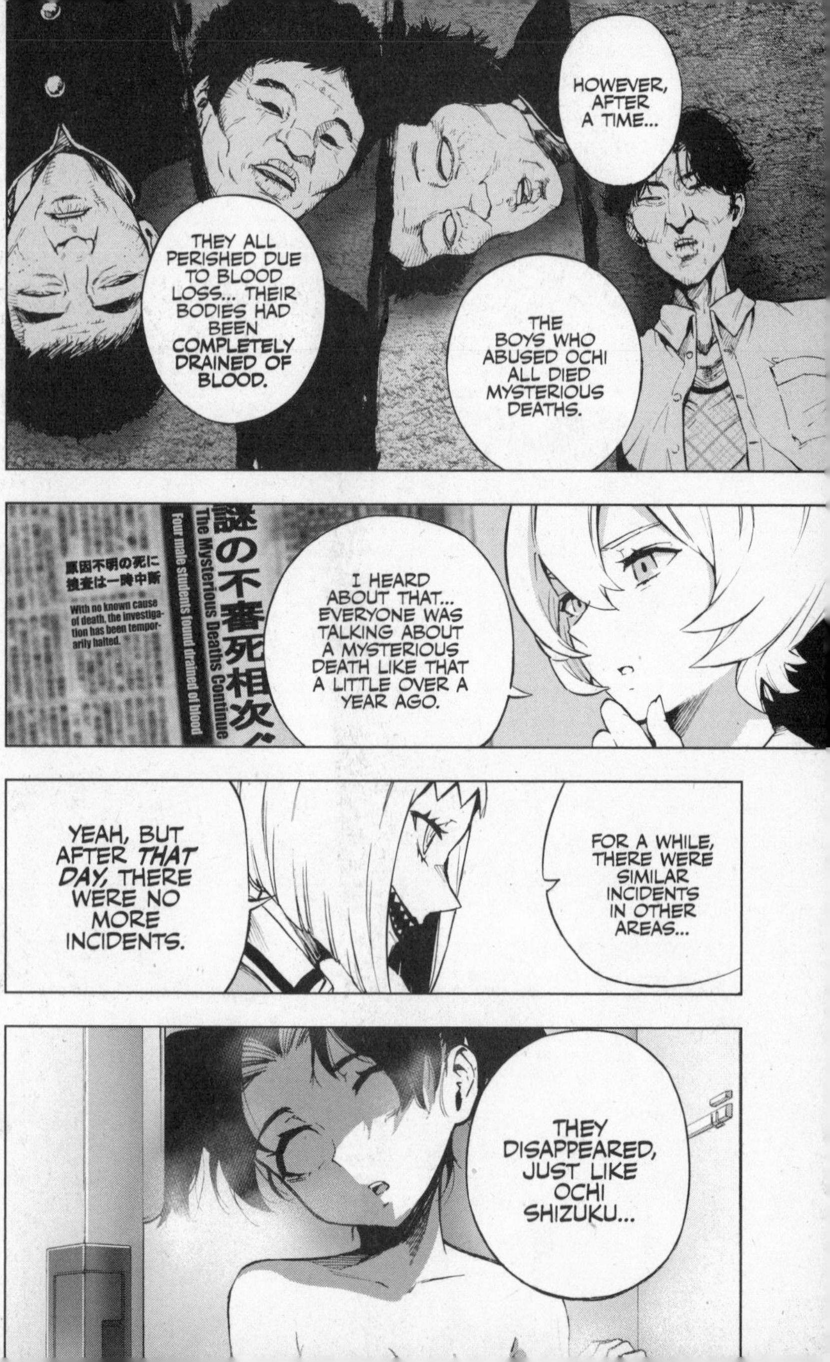
HOWEVER, AFTER A TIME...
THE BOYS WHO ABUSED OCHI ALL DIED MYSTERIOUS DEATHS.
THEY ALL PERISHED DUE TO BLOOD LOSS... THEIR BODIES HAD BEEN COMPLETELY DRAINED OF BLOOD.
I HEARD ABOUT THAT... EVERYONE WAS TALKING ABOUT A MYSTERIOUS DEATH LIKE THAT A LITTLE OVER A YEAR AGO.
謎の不審死相次ぐ
The Mysterious Deaths Continue
Four male students found drained of blood
原因不明の死に捜査は一時中断
With no known cause of death, the investigation has been temporarily halted.
FOR A WHILE, THERE WERE SIMILAR INCIDENTS IN OTHER AREAS...
YEAH, BUT AFTER *THAT DAY,* THERE WERE NO MORE INCIDENTS.
THEY DISAPPEARED, JUST LIKE OCHI SHIZUKU...

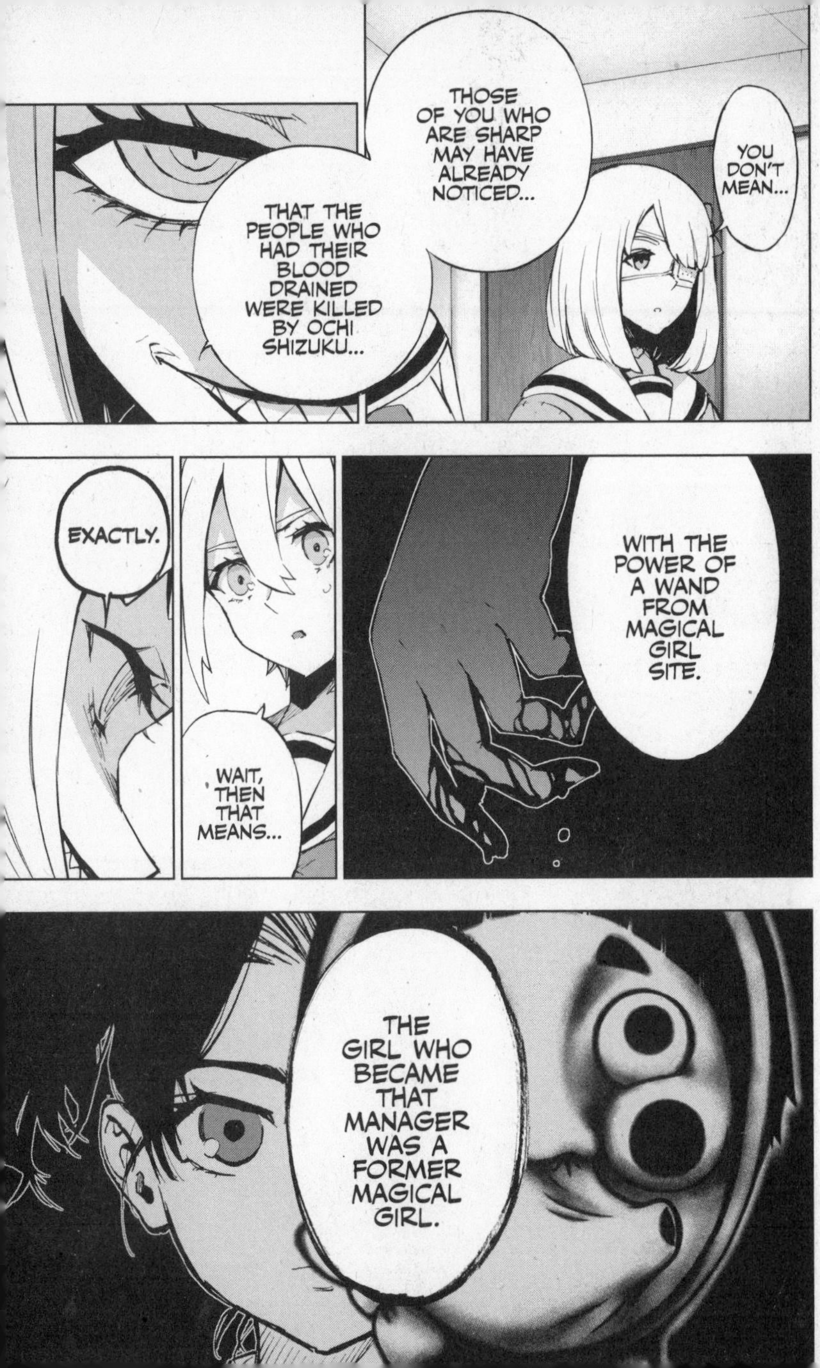
YOU DON'T MEAN...
THOSE OF YOU WHO ARE SHARP MAY HAVE ALREADY NOTICED...
THAT THE PEOPLE WHO HAD THEIR BLOOD DRAINED WERE KILLED BY OCHI SHIZUKU...
WITH THE POWER OF A WAND FROM MAGICAL GIRL SITE.
WAIT, THEN THAT MEANS...
EXACTLY.
THE GIRL WHO BECAME THAT MANAGER WAS A FORMER MAGICAL GIRL.

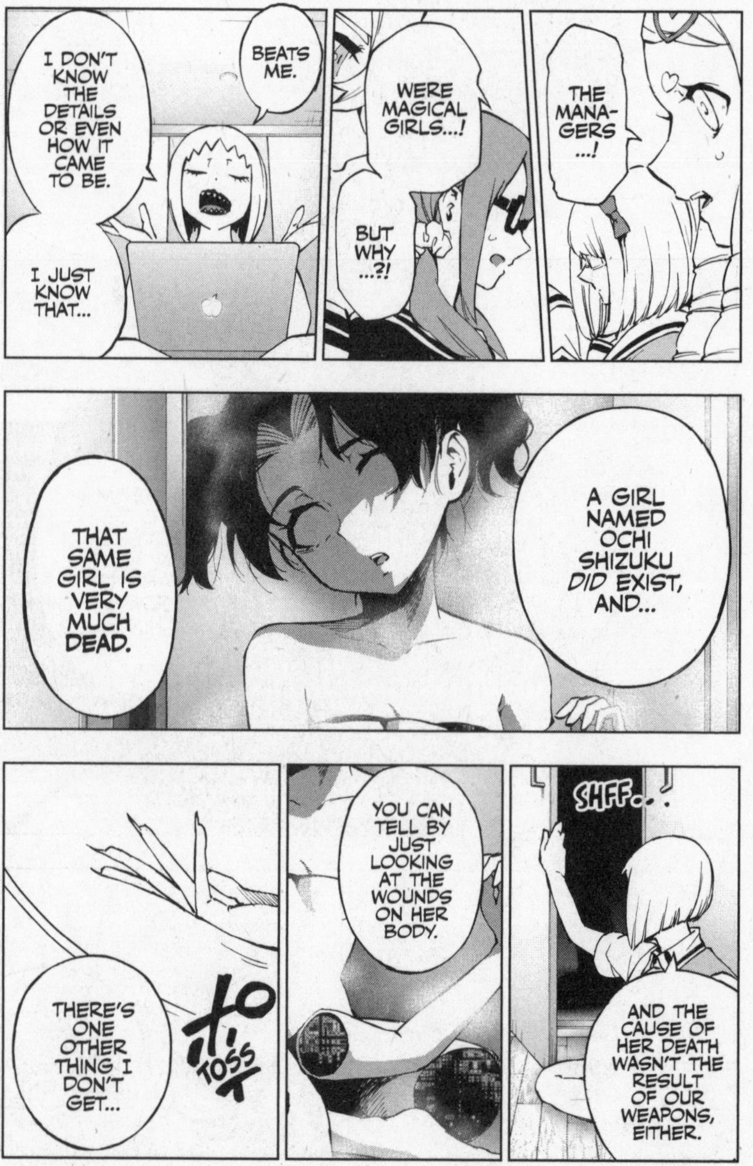
THE MANA-GERS ...!
WERE MAGICAL GIRLS...!
BUT WHY ...?!
BEATS ME.
I DON'T KNOW THE DETAILS OR EVEN HOW IT CAME TO BE.
I JUST KNOW THAT...
A GIRL NAMED OCHI SHIZUKU *DID* EXIST, AND...
THAT SAME GIRL IS VERY MUCH DEAD.
SHFF...
AND THE CAUSE OF HER DEATH WASN'T THE RESULT OF OUR WEAPONS, EITHER.
YOU CAN TELL BY JUST LOOKING AT THE WOUNDS ON HER BODY.
TOSS
THERE'S ONE OTHER THING I DON'T GET...

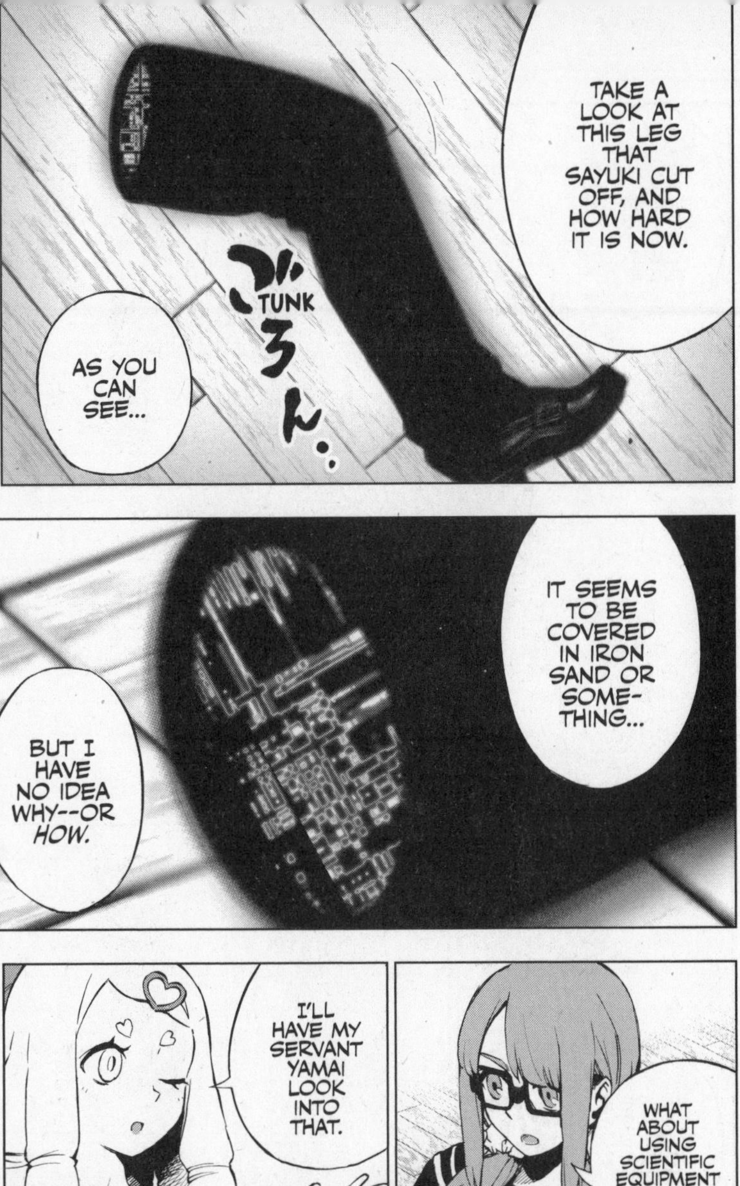
TAKE A LOOK AT THIS LEG THAT SAYUKI CUT OFF, AND HOW HARD IT IS NOW.
ごろん..
TUNK
AS YOU CAN SEE...
IT SEEMS TO BE COVERED IN IRON SAND OR SOME-THING...
BUT I HAVE NO IDEA WHY--OR *HOW.*
WHAT ABOUT USING SCIENTIFIC EQUIPMENT TO ANALYZE IT?
I'LL HAVE MY SERVANT YAMAI LOOK INTO THAT.

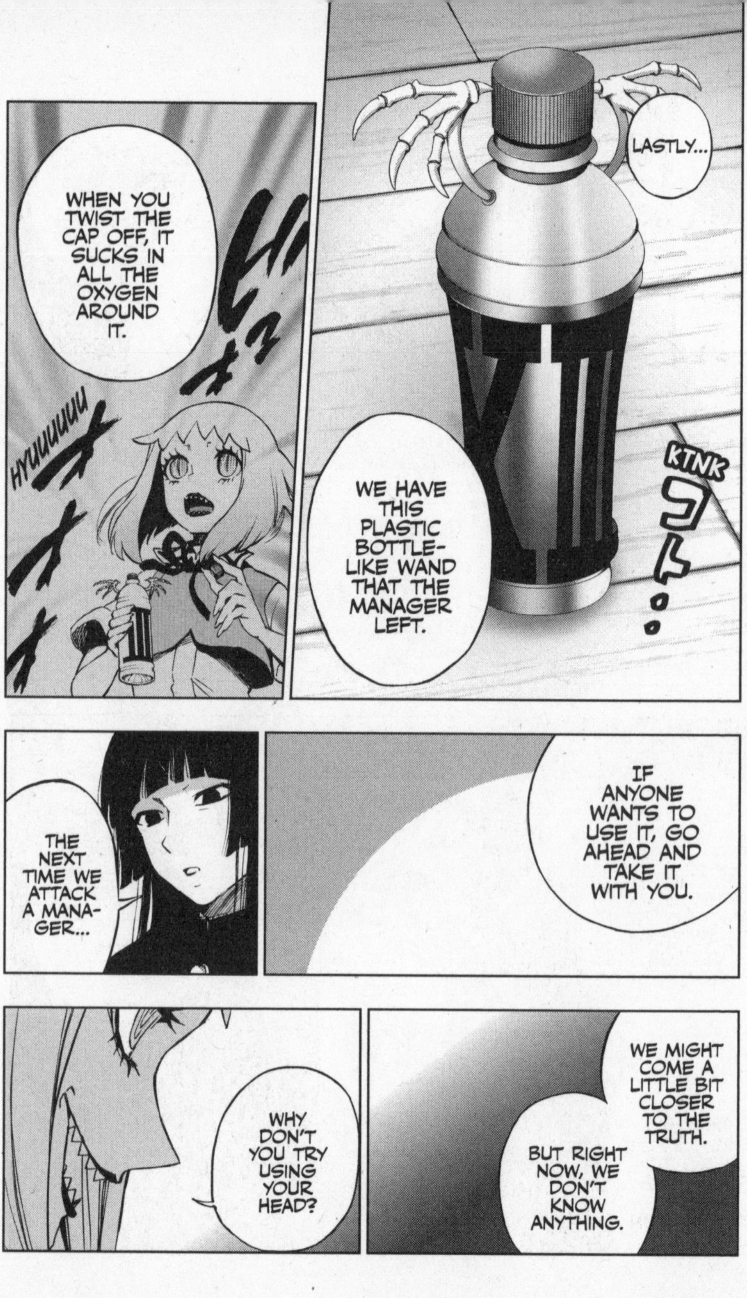
LASTLY...
WE HAVE THIS PLASTIC BOTTLE-LIKE WAND THAT THE MANAGER LEFT.
KTNK
WHEN YOU TWIST THE CAP OFF, IT SUCKS IN ALL THE OXYGEN AROUND IT.
HYUUUUUU
IF ANYONE WANTS TO USE IT, GO AHEAD AND TAKE IT WITH YOU.
THE NEXT TIME WE ATTACK A MANA-GER...
WE MIGHT COME A LITTLE BIT CLOSER TO THE TRUTH.
BUT RIGHT NOW, WE DON'T KNOW ANYTHING.
WHY DON'T YOU TRY USING YOUR HEAD?

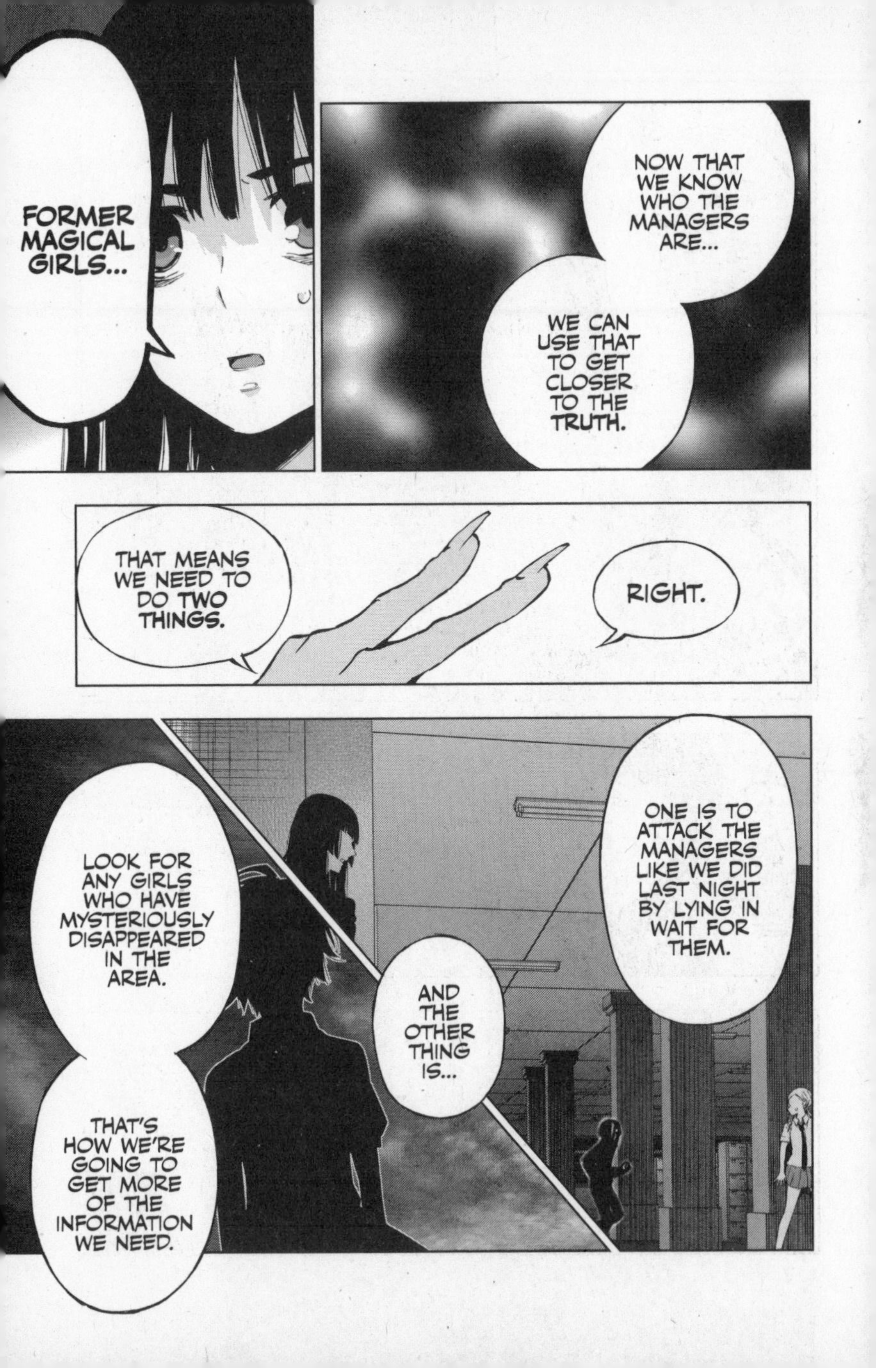
NOW THAT WE KNOW WHO THE MANAGERS ARE...
WE CAN USE THAT TO GET CLOSER TO THE TRUTH.
FORMER MAGICAL GIRLS...
THAT MEANS WE NEED TO DO TWO THINGS.
RIGHT.
ONE IS TO ATTACK THE MANAGERS LIKE WE DID LAST NIGHT BY LYING IN WAIT FOR THEM.
AND THE OTHER THING IS...
LOOK FOR ANY GIRLS WHO HAVE MYSTERIOUSLY DISAPPEARED IN THE AREA.
THAT'S HOW WE'RE GOING TO GET MORE OF THE INFORMATION WE NEED.

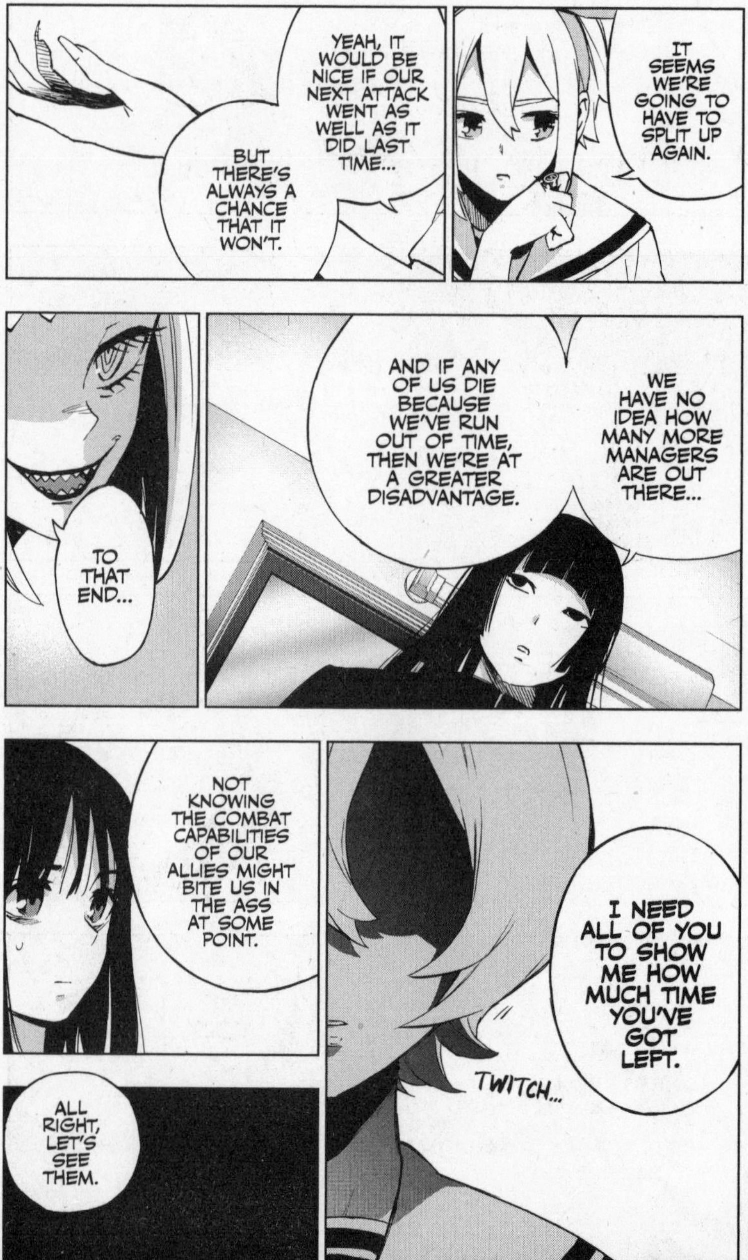
IT SEEMS WE'RE GOING TO HAVE TO SPLIT UP AGAIN.
YEAH, IT WOULD BE NICE IF OUR NEXT ATTACK WENT AS WELL AS IT DID LAST TIME...
BUT THERE'S ALWAYS A CHANCE THAT IT WON'T.
WE HAVE NO IDEA HOW MANY MORE MANAGERS ARE OUT THERE...
AND IF ANY OF US DIE BECAUSE WE'VE RUN OUT OF TIME, THEN WE'RE AT A GREATER DISADVANTAGE.
TO THAT END...
I NEED ALL OF YOU TO SHOW ME HOW MUCH TIME YOU'VE GOT LEFT.
TWITCH...
NOT KNOWING THE COMBAT CAPABILITIES OF OUR ALLIES MIGHT BITE US IN THE ASS AT SOME POINT.
ALL RIGHT, LET'S SEE THEM.

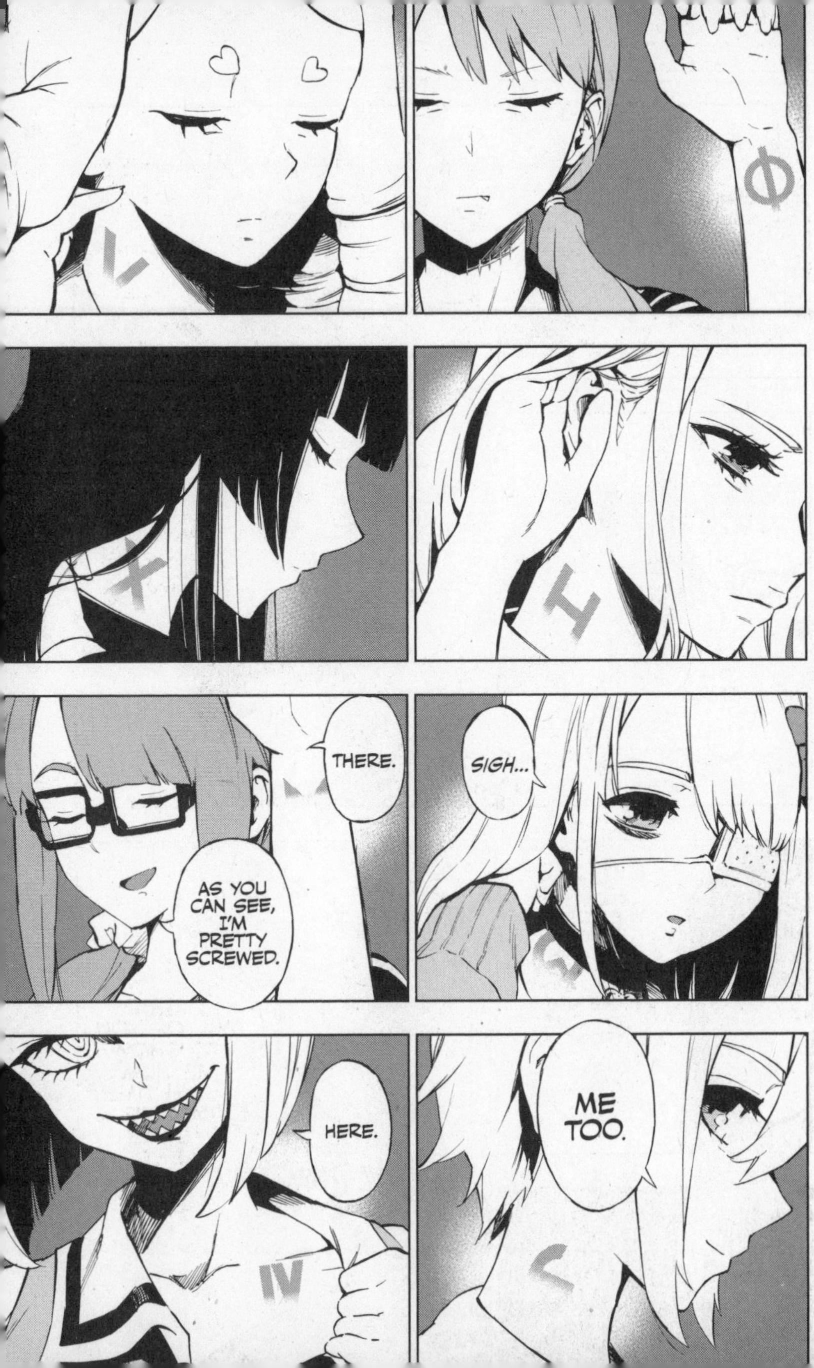
SIGH...
THERE.
AS YOU CAN SEE, I'M PRETTY SCREWED.
ME TOO.
HERE.

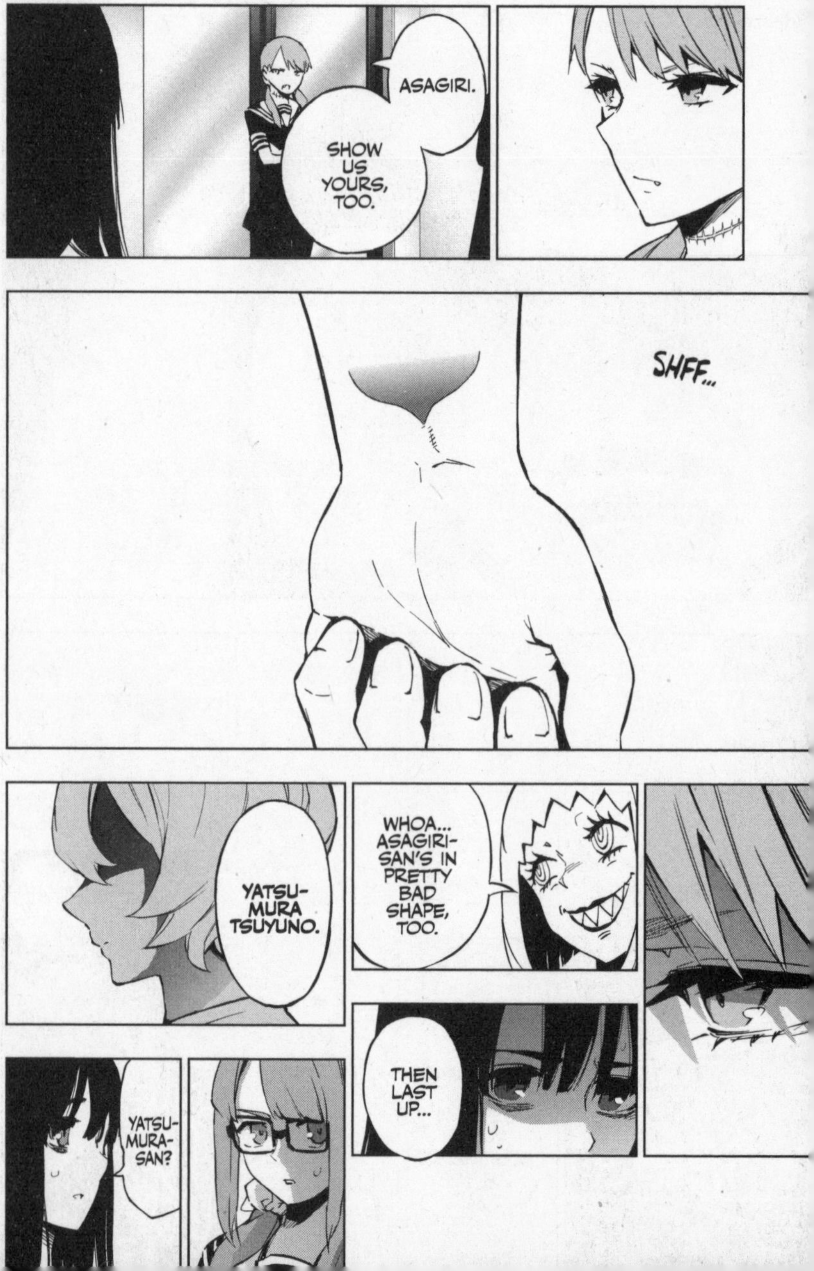
ASAGIRI.
SHOW US YOURS, TOO.
SHFF...
WHOA... ASAGIRI-SAN'S IN PRETTY BAD SHAPE, TOO.
THEN LAST UP...
YATSU-MURA TSUYUNO.
YATSU-MURA-SAN?

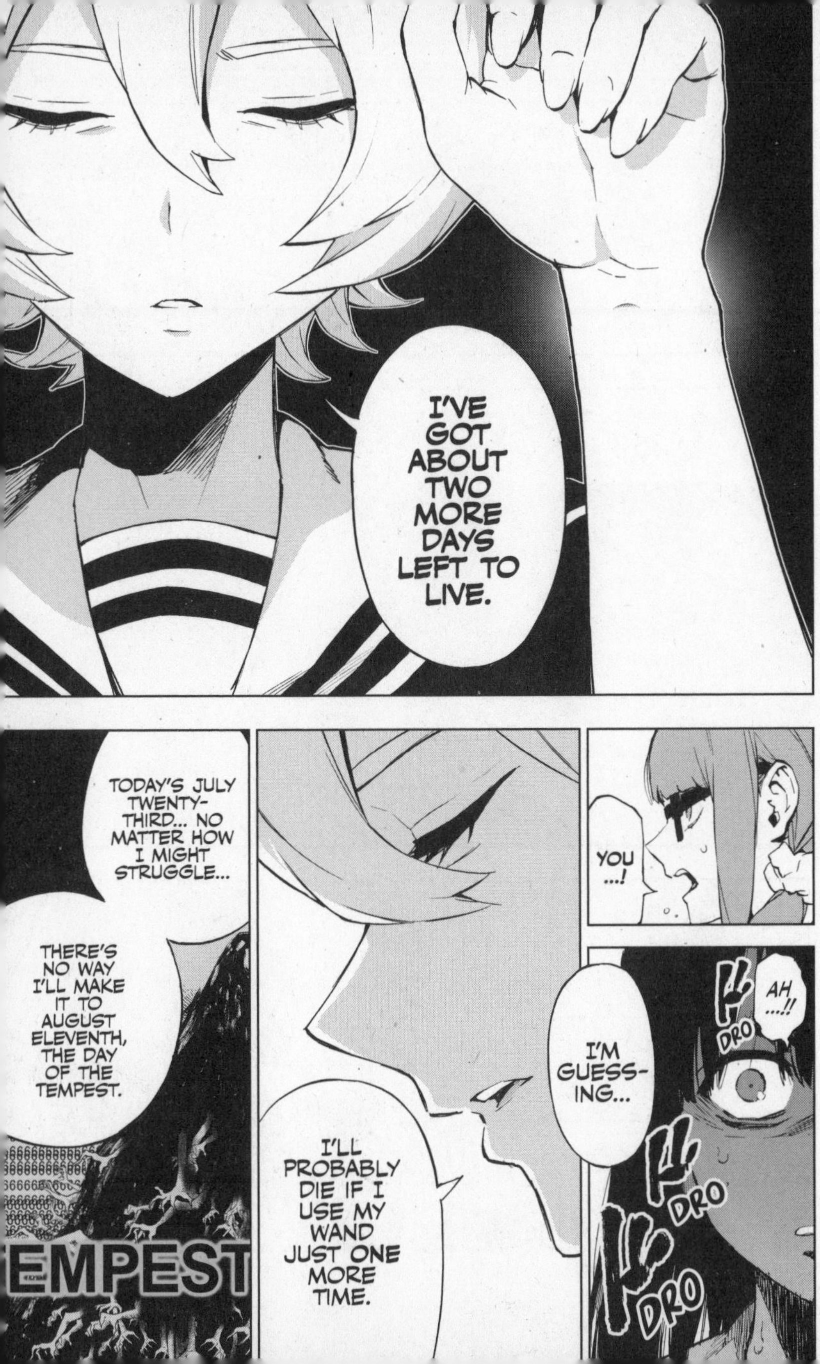
I'VE GOT ABOUT TWO MORE DAYS LEFT TO LIVE.
YOU ...!
AH ...!!
DRO
I'M GUESS-ING...
DRO
DRO
I'LL PROBABLY DIE IF I USE MY WAND JUST ONE MORE TIME.
TODAY'S JULY TWENTY-THIRD... NO MATTER HOW I MIGHT STRUGGLE...
THERE'S NO WAY I'LL MAKE IT TO AUGUST ELEVENTH, THE DAY OF THE TEMPEST.
TEMPEST

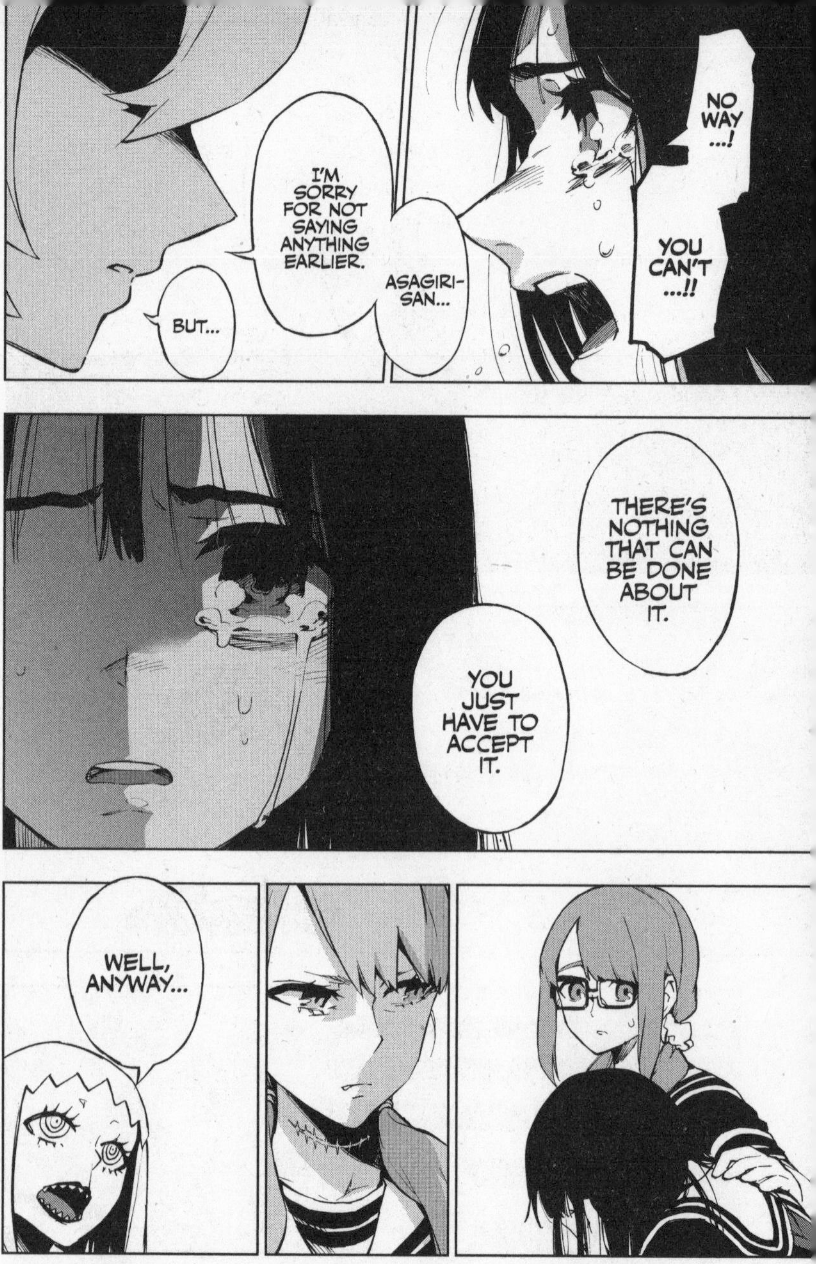
NO WAY ...!
YOU CAN'T ...!!
ASAGIRI-SAN...
I'M SORRY FOR NOT SAYING ANYTHING EARLIER.
BUT...
THERE'S NOTHING THAT CAN BE DONE ABOUT IT.
YOU JUST HAVE TO ACCEPT IT.
WELL, ANYWAY...

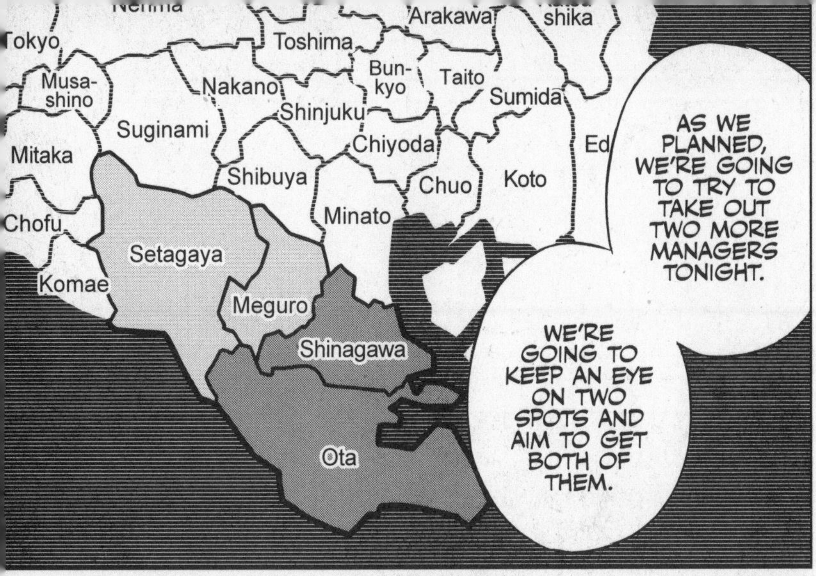
AS WE PLANNED, WE'RE GOING TO TRY TO TAKE OUT TWO MORE MANAGERS TONIGHT.
WE'RE GOING TO KEEP AN EYE ON TWO SPOTS AND AIM TO GET BOTH OF THEM.
Arakawa
Tokyo
Toshima
Musa-shino
Bun-kyo
Taito
Nakano
Sumida
Shinjuku
Suginami
Chiyoda
Mitaka
Shibuya
Chuo
Koto
Minato
Chofu
Setagaya
Komae
Meguro
Shinagawa
Ota
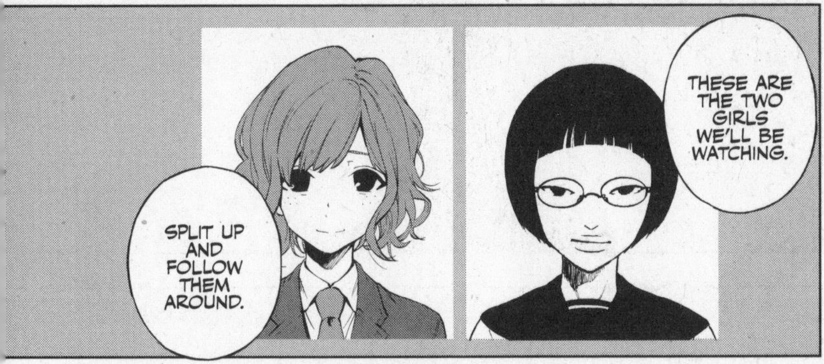
THESE ARE THE TWO GIRLS WE'LL BE WATCHING.
SPLIT UP AND FOLLOW THEM AROUND.
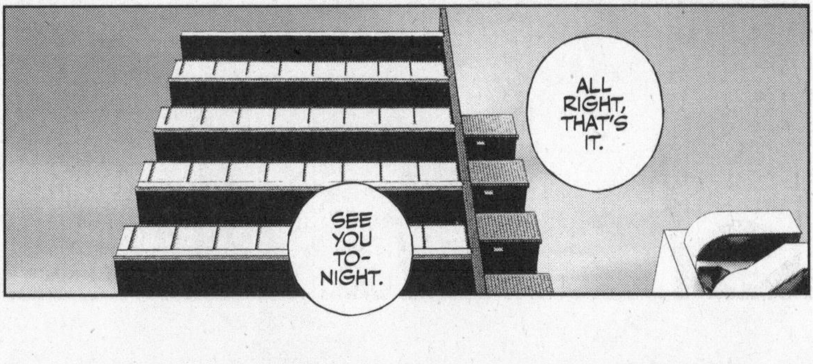
ALL RIGHT, THAT'S IT.
SEE YOU TO-NIGHT.

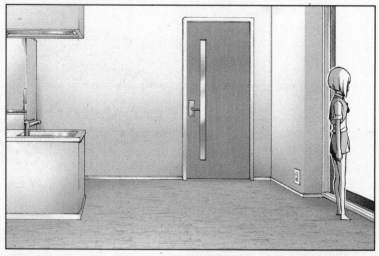

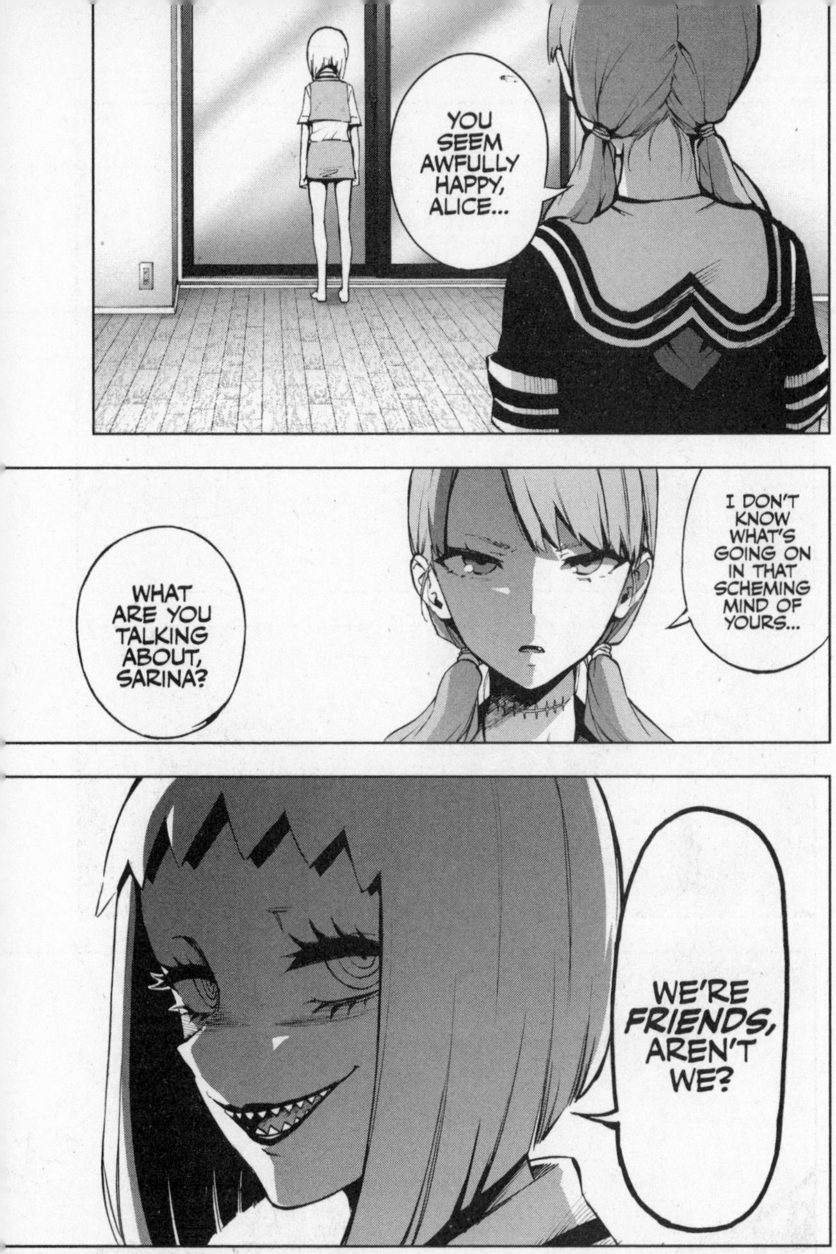
YOU SEEM AWFULLY HAPPY, ALICE...
I DON'T KNOW WHAT'S GOING ON IN THAT SCHEMING MIND OF YOURS...
WHAT ARE YOU TALKING ABOUT, SARINA?
WE'RE *FRIENDS,* AREN'T WE?

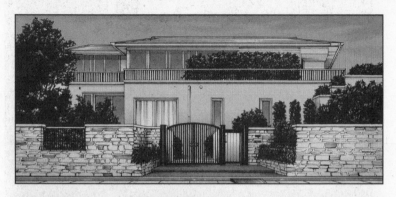

SKREEEEL

TAK

TAK

KANAME-
KUN...

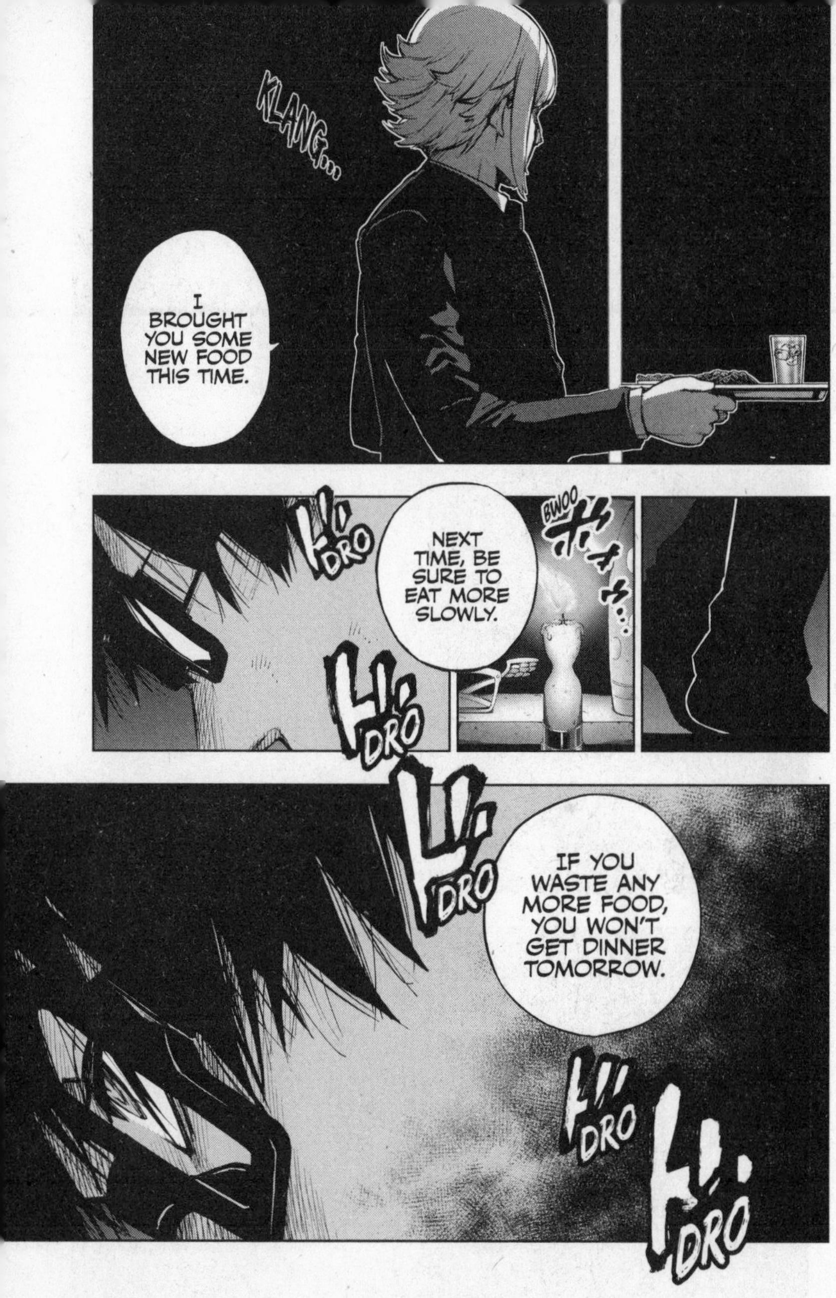
KLANG...
I BROUGHT YOU SOME NEW FOOD THIS TIME.
BWOO
DRO
NEXT TIME, BE SURE TO EAT MORE SLOWLY.
DRO
DRO
IF YOU WASTE ANY MORE FOOD, YOU WON'T GET DINNER TOMORROW.
DRO
DRO

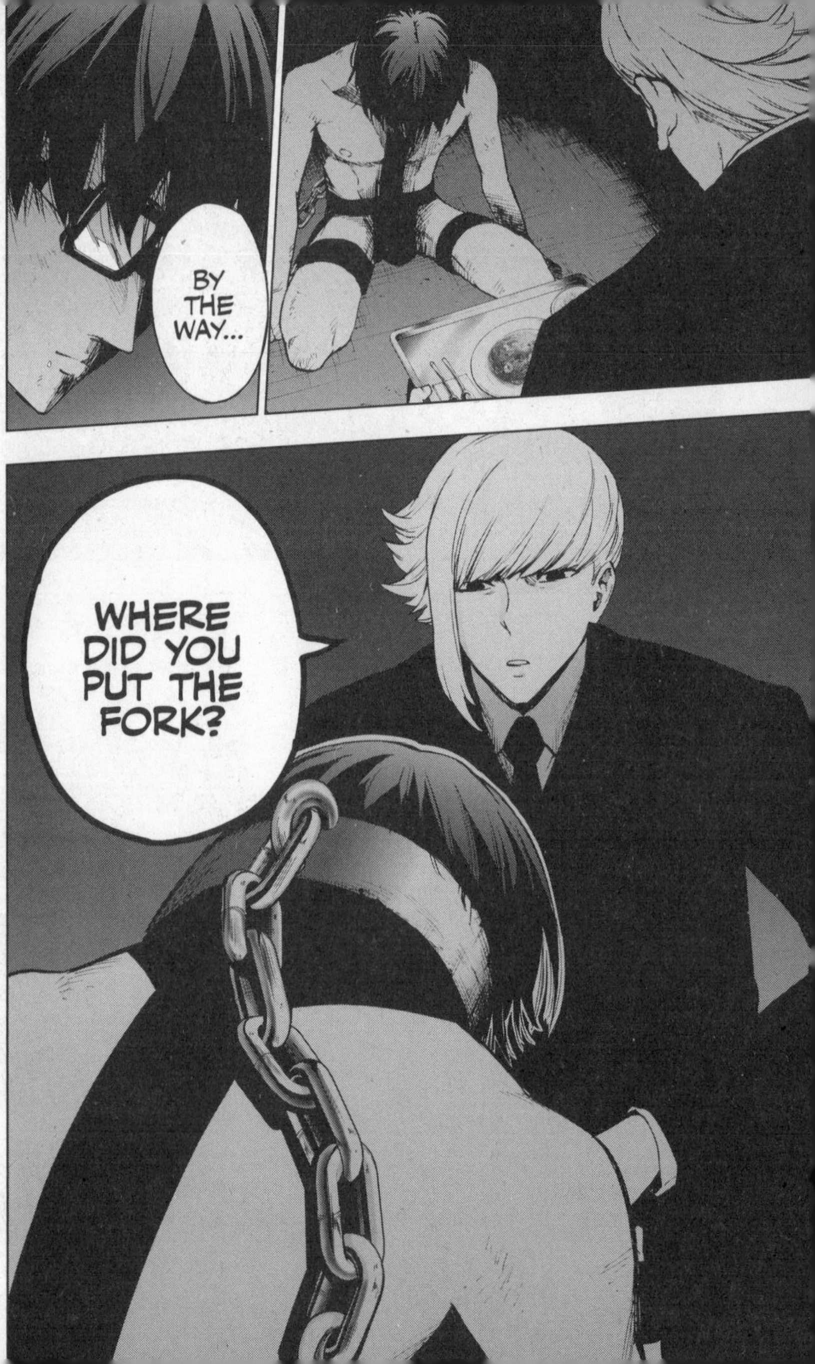
BY THE WAY...
WHERE DID YOU PUT THE FORK?

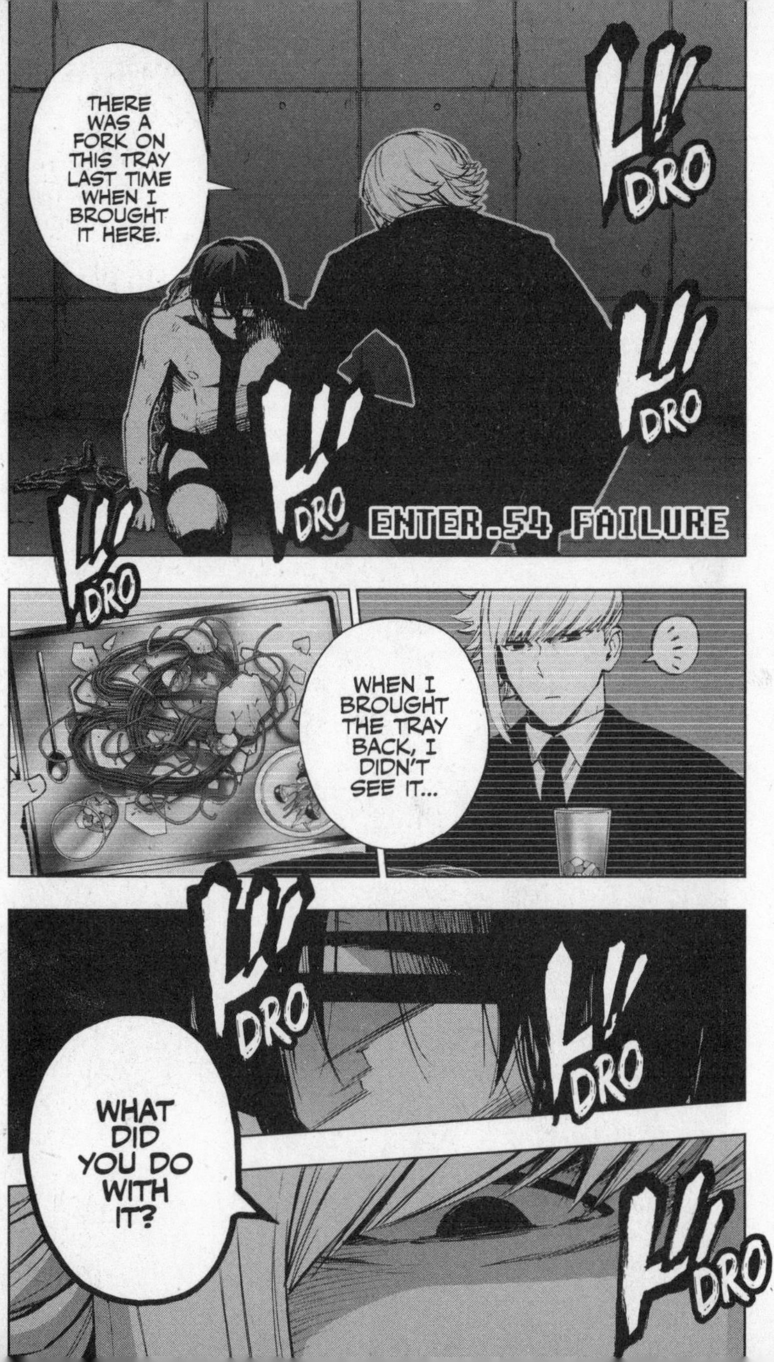
DRO
DRO
THERE WAS A FORK ON THIS TRAY LAST TIME WHEN I BROUGHT IT HERE.
DRO
DRO
ENTER.54 FAILURE
...
WHEN I BROUGHT THE TRAY BACK, I DIDN'T SEE IT...
DRO
DRO
DRO
WHAT DID YOU DO WITH IT?
DRO

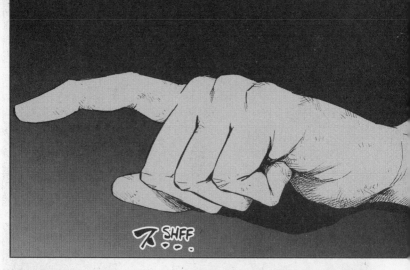

SHFF

SO IT FELL OFF OVER THERE.

OH...

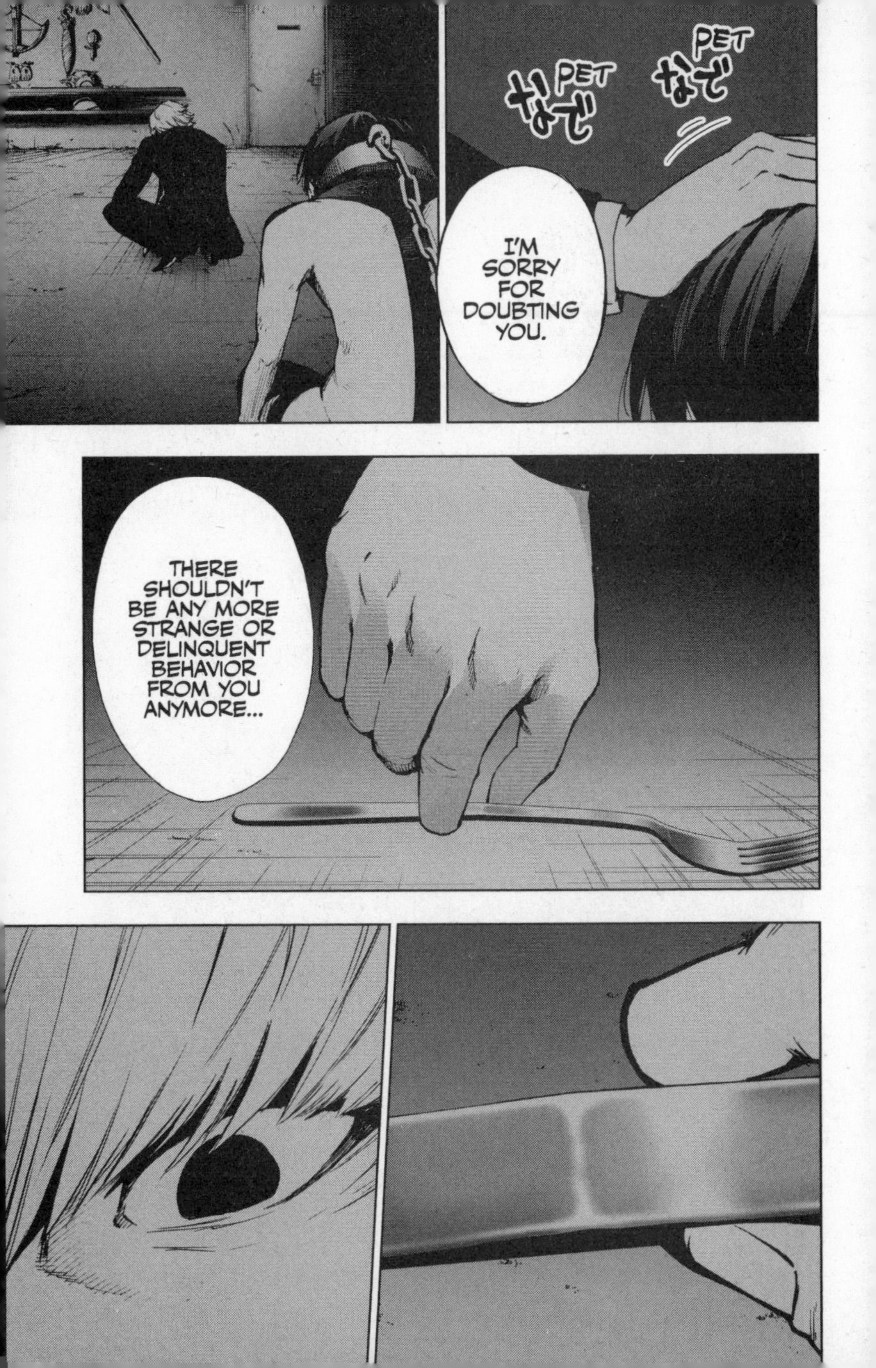
PET
なで
PET
なで
I'M SORRY FOR DOUBTING YOU.
THERE SHOULDN'T BE ANY MORE STRANGE OR DELINQUENT BEHAVIOR FROM YOU ANYMORE...

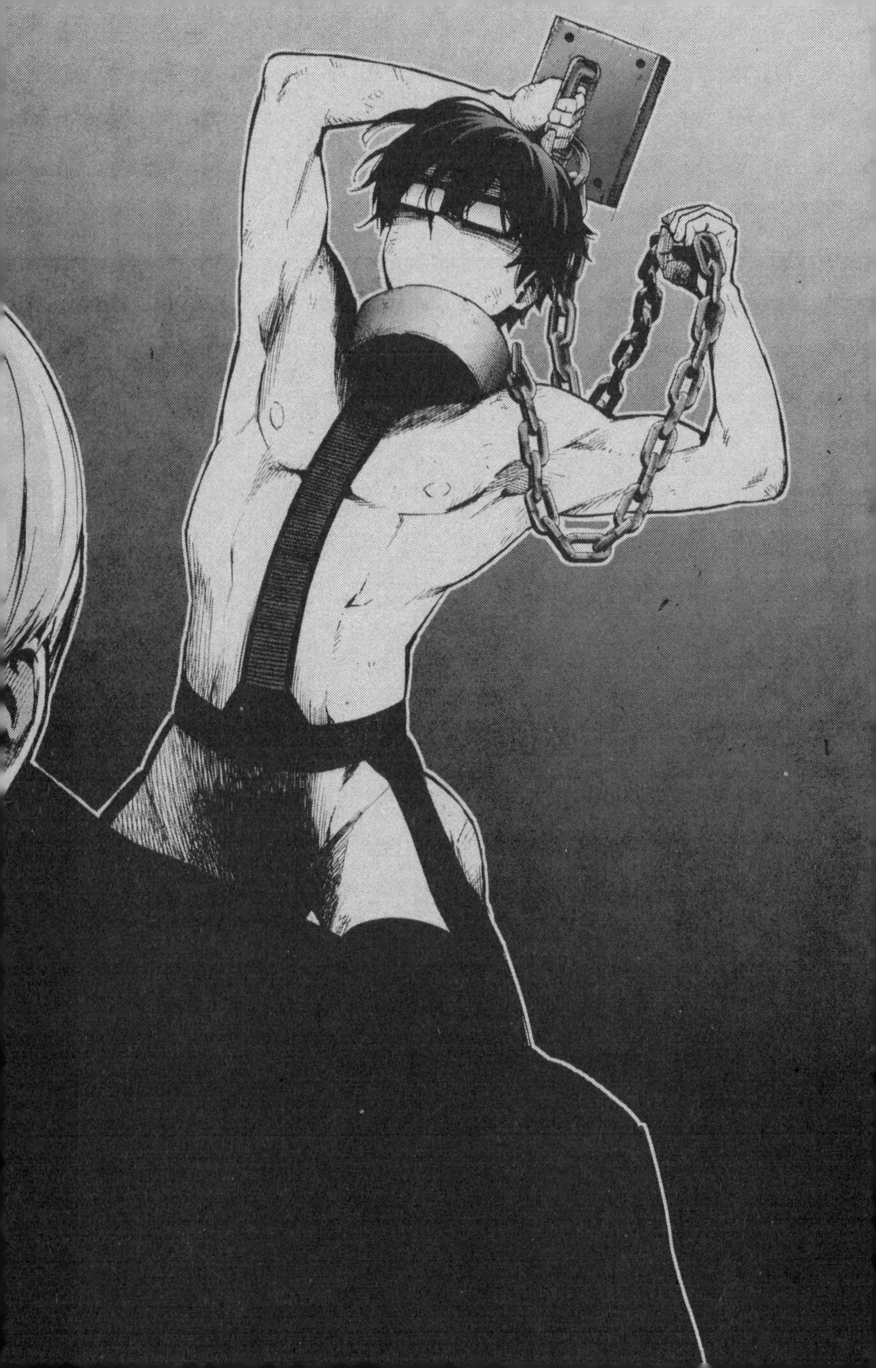

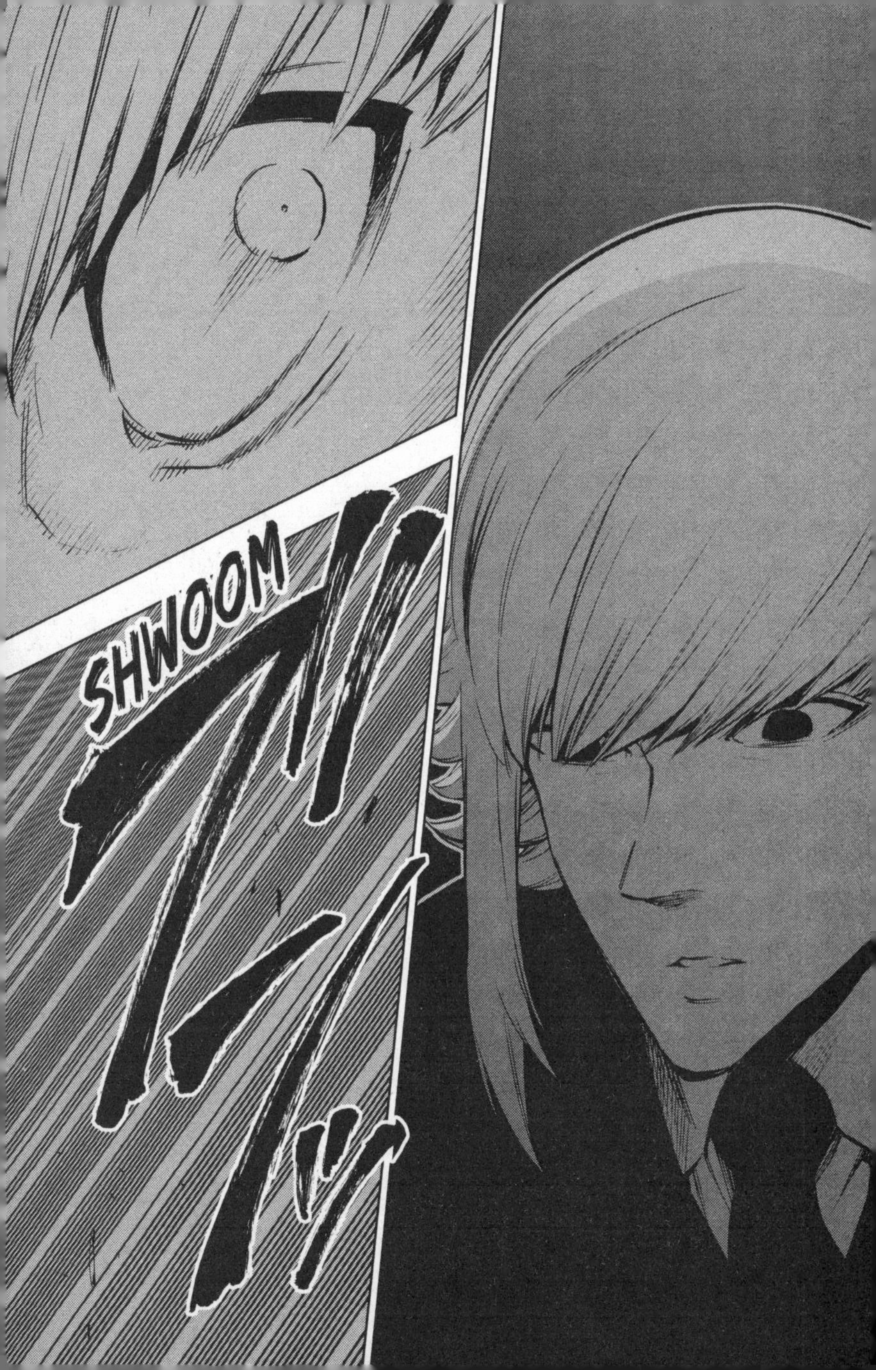
SHWOOM

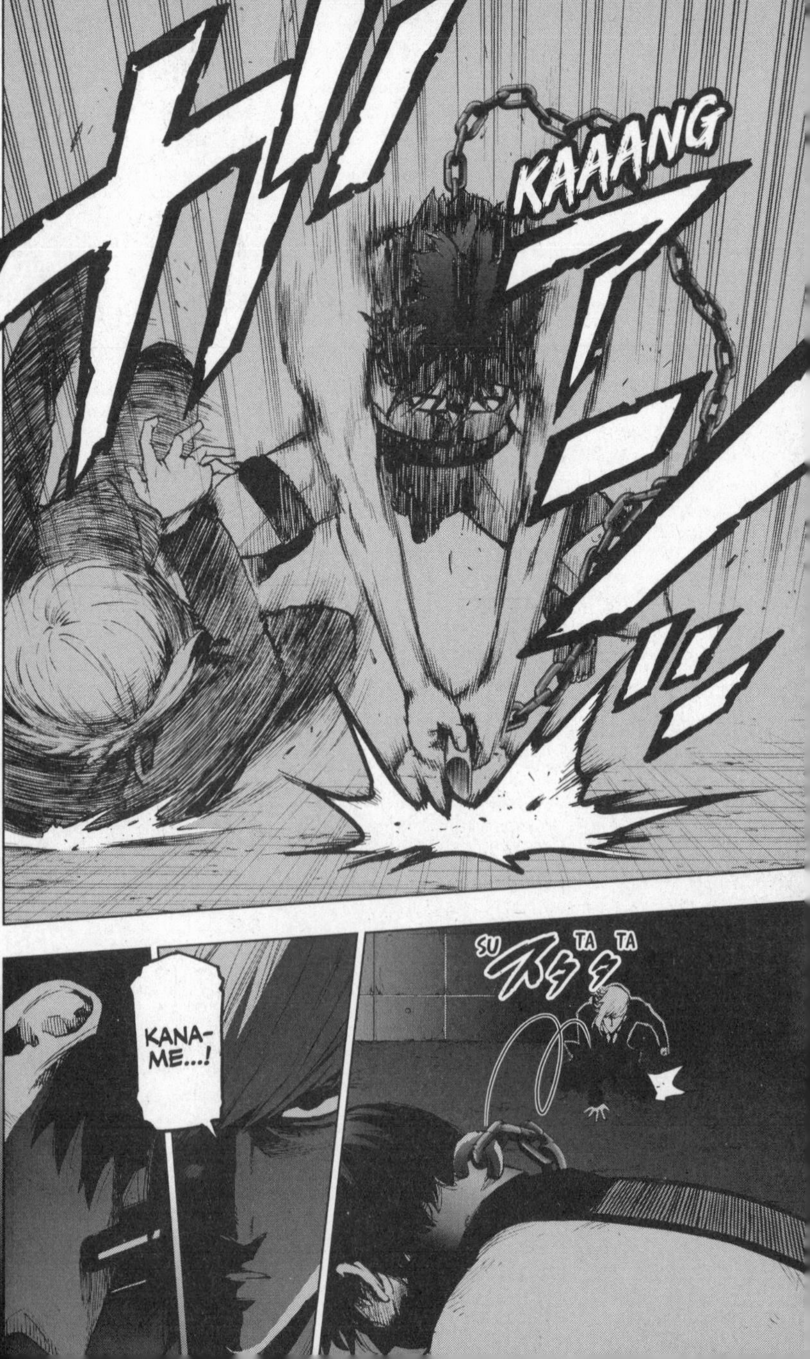
KAAANG
SU TA TA
KANA-ME...!

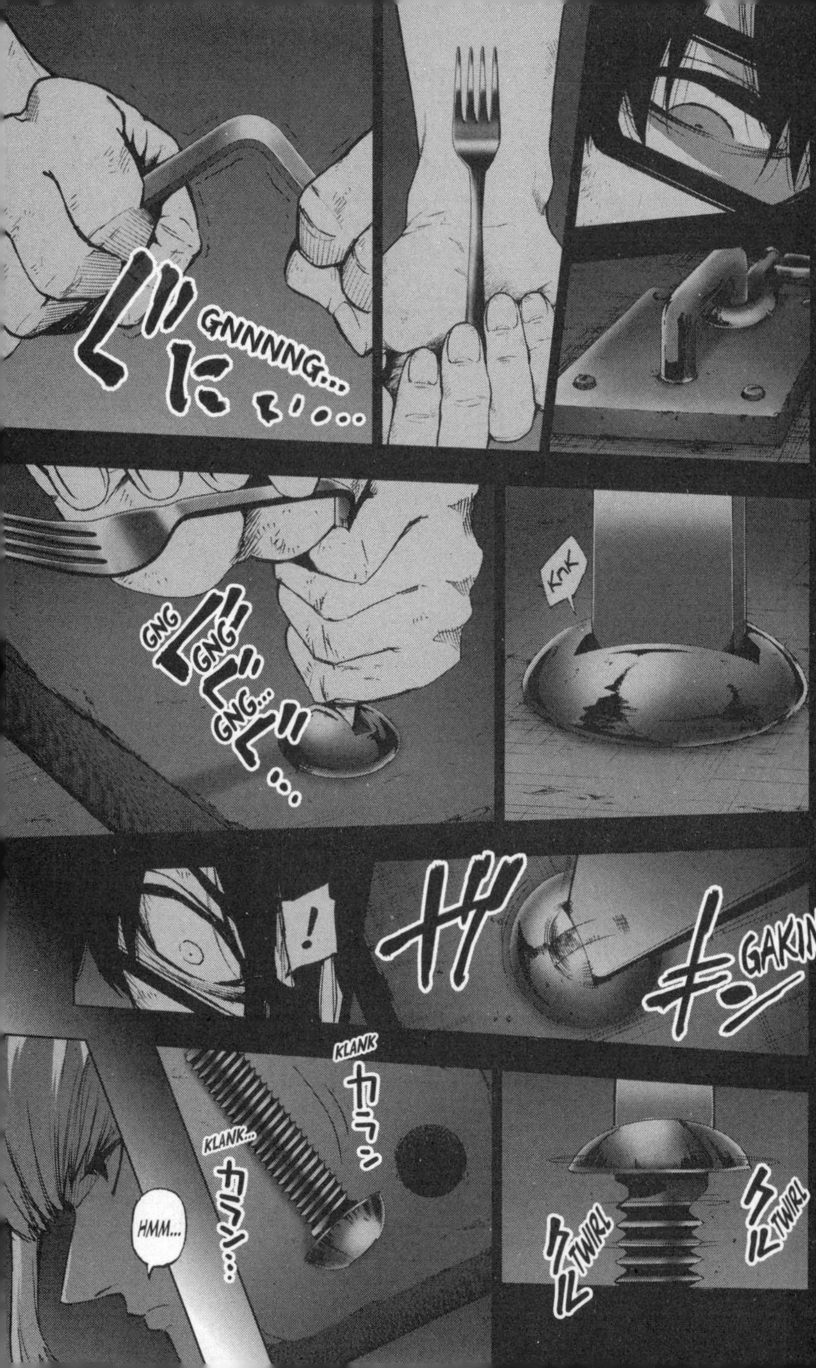
GNNNNG...
KnK
GNG
GNG
GNG...
GAKIN
!
TWIRL
TWIRL
KLANK
KLANK...
HMM...

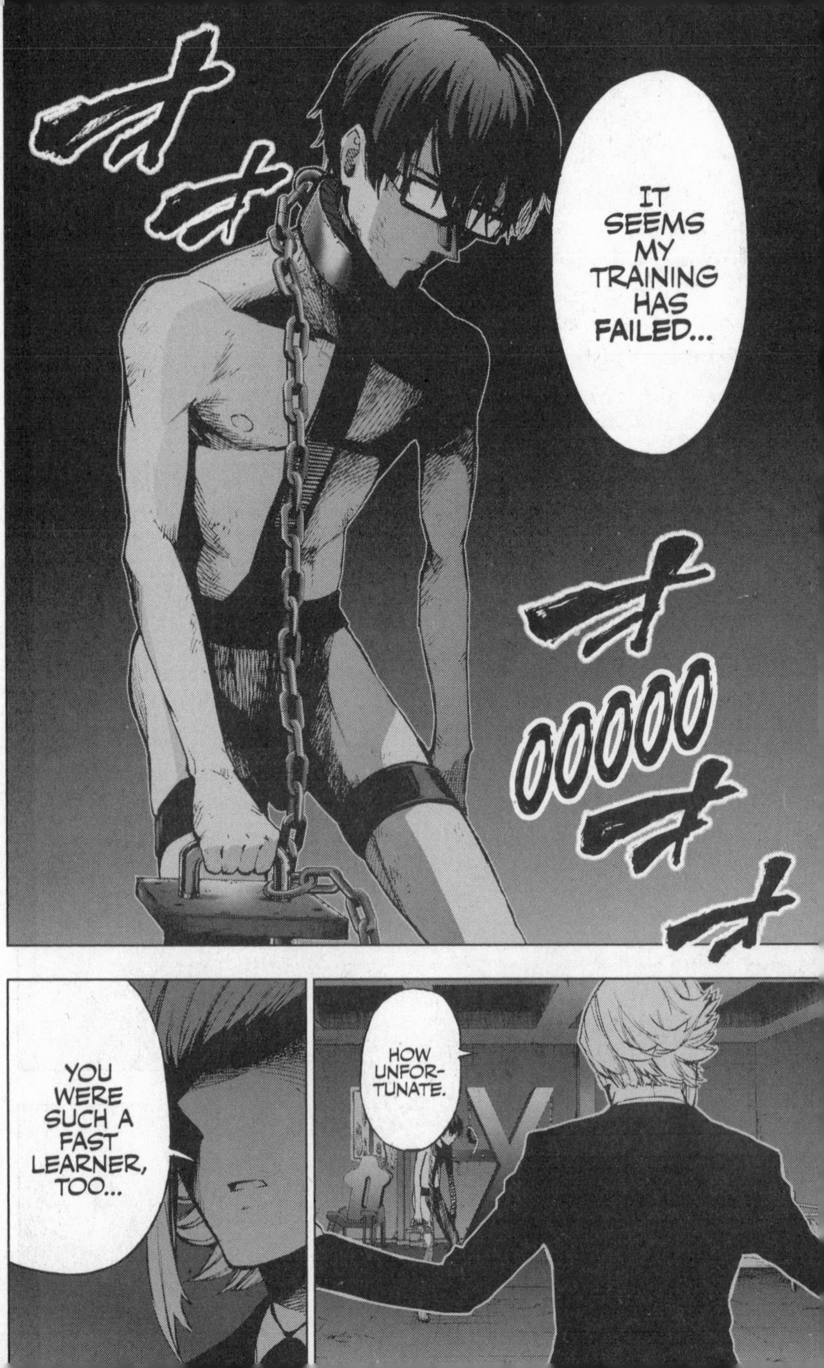
IT SEEMS MY TRAINING HAS FAILED...
OOOOO
HOW UNFOR-TUNATE.
YOU WERE SUCH A FAST LEARNER, TOO...

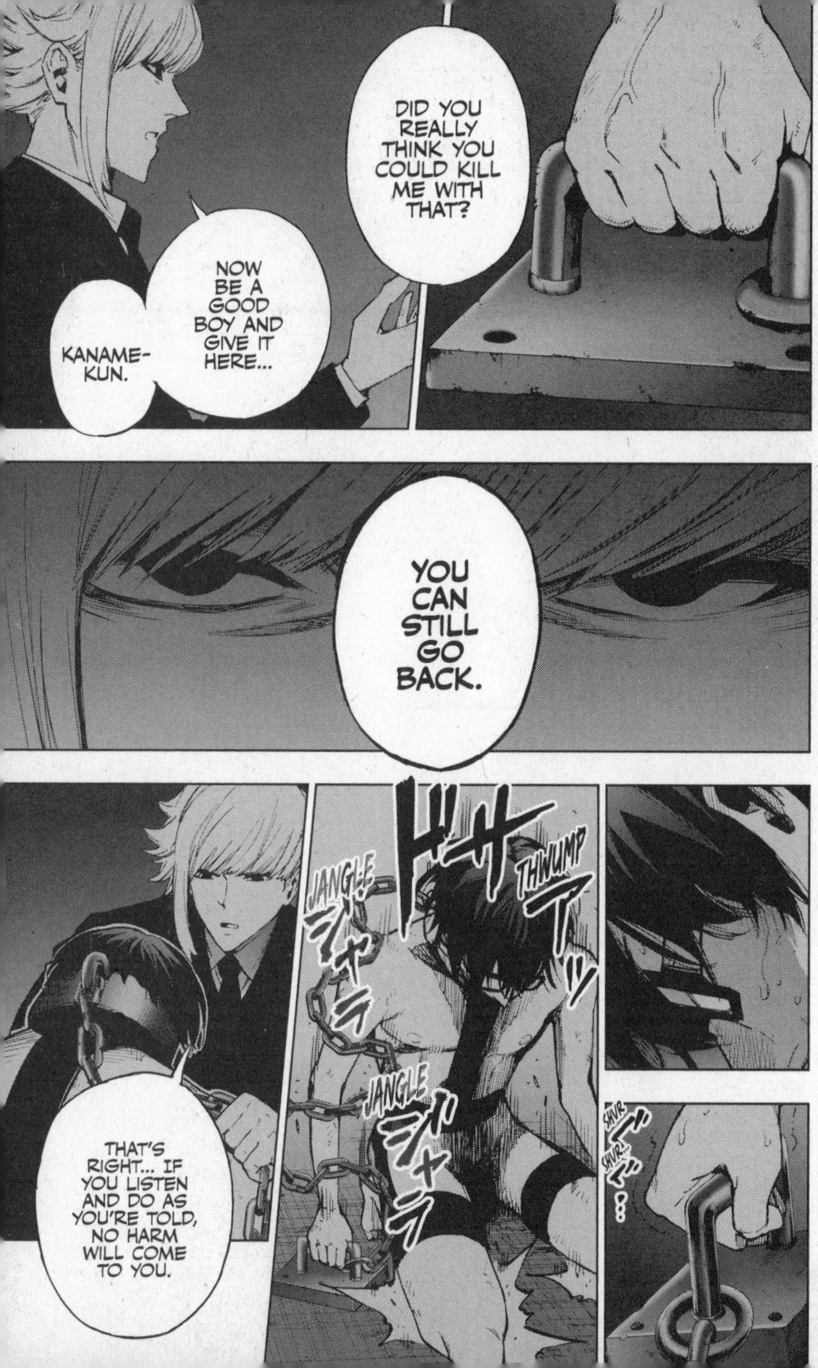
DID YOU REALLY THINK YOU COULD KILL ME WITH THAT?
NOW BE A GOOD BOY AND GIVE IT HERE...
KANAME-KUN.
YOU CAN STILL GO BACK.
SHVR... SHVR...
THWUMP
JANGLE
JANGLE
THAT'S RIGHT... IF YOU LISTEN AND DO AS YOU'RE TOLD, NO HARM WILL COME TO YOU.

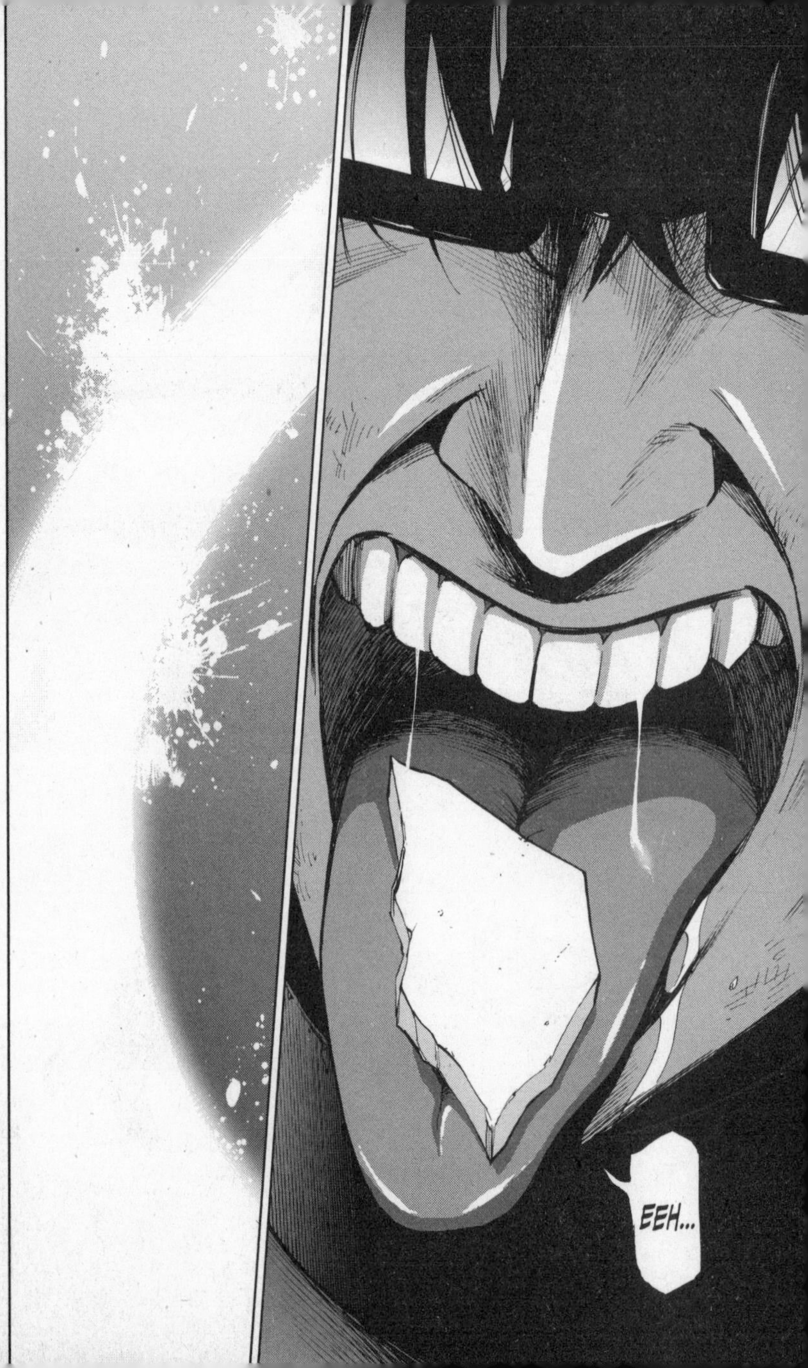
EEH...

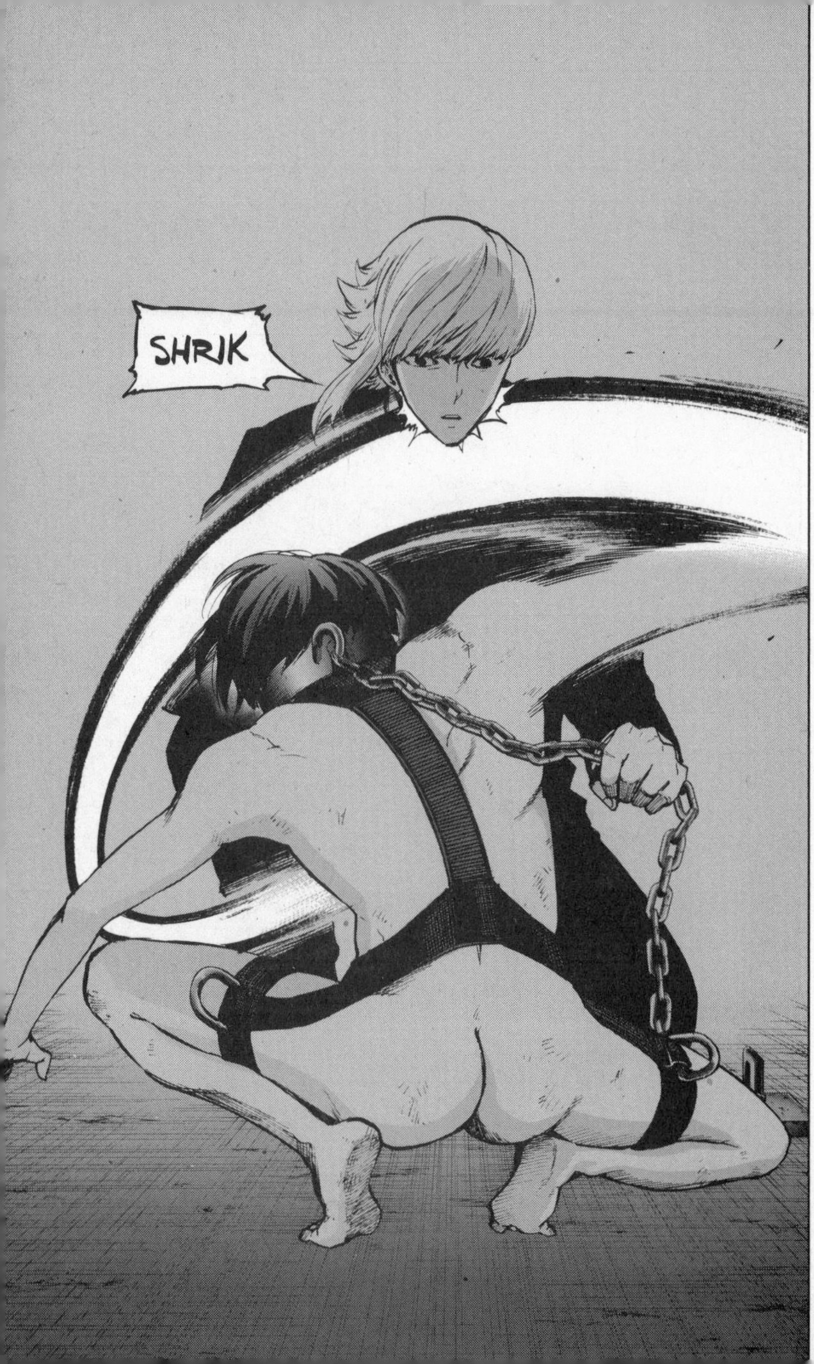
SHRIK

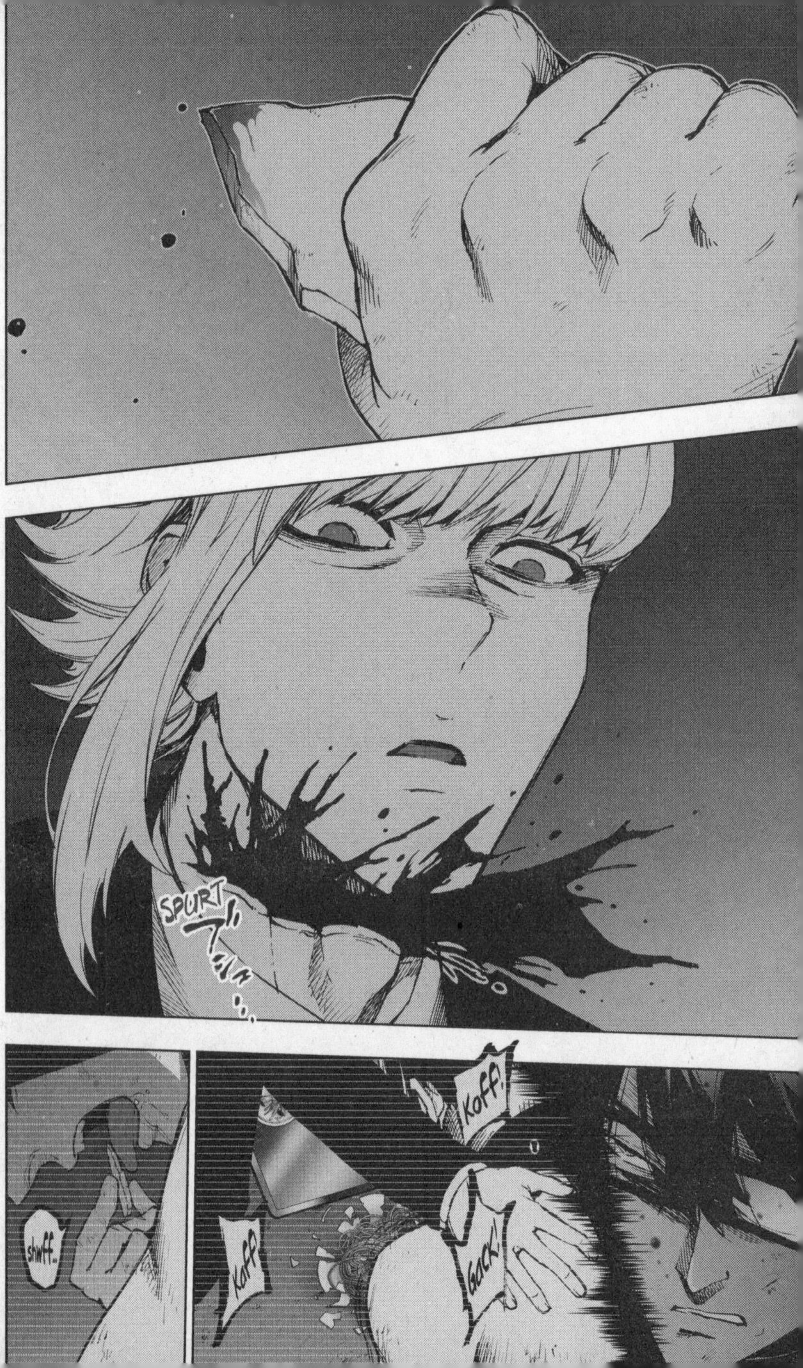
SPURT
Koff!
Gack!
Koff!
shwff...

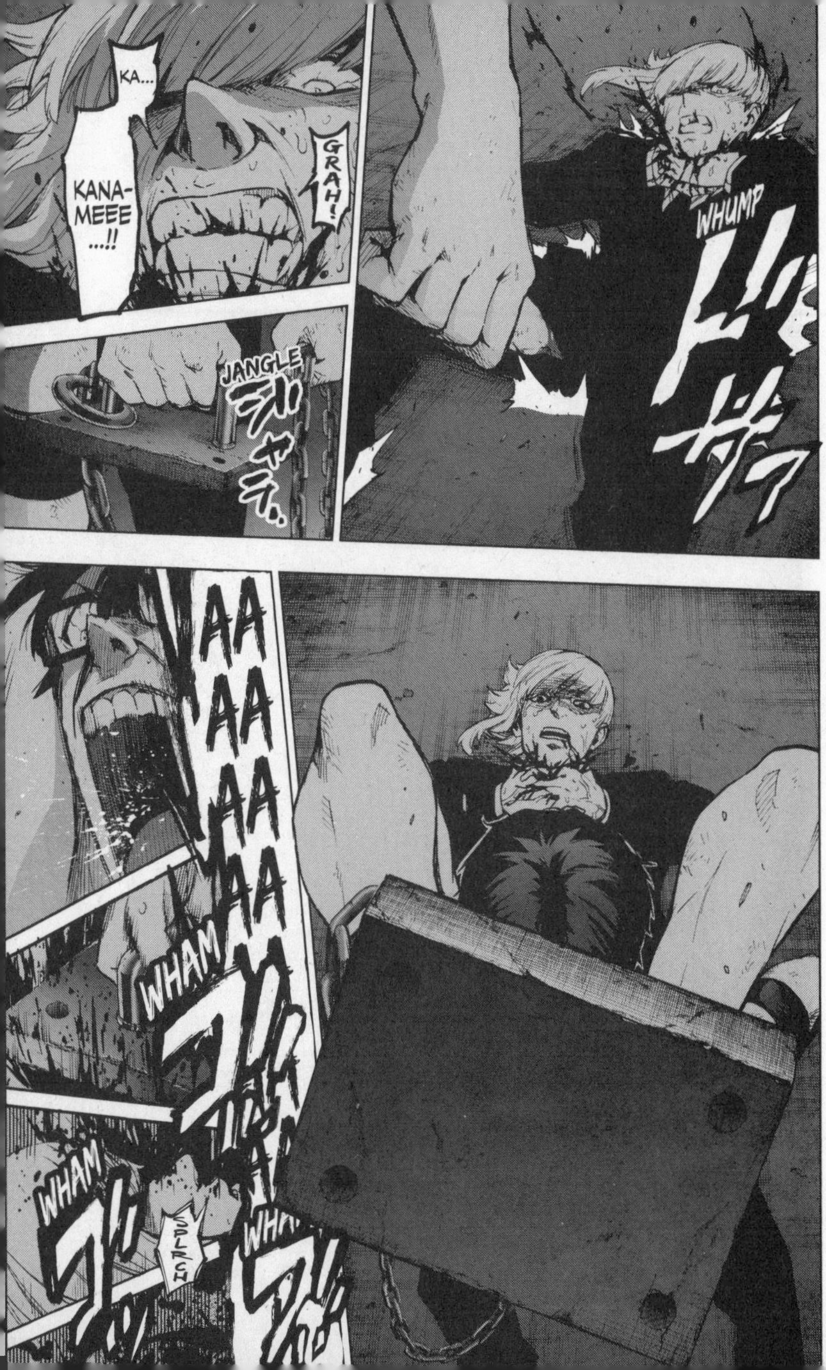
WHUMP
GRAH!
KA...
KANA-MEEE ...!!
JANGLE
AAAAAAAAAAAA
WHAM
WHAM
SPLRCH
WHA

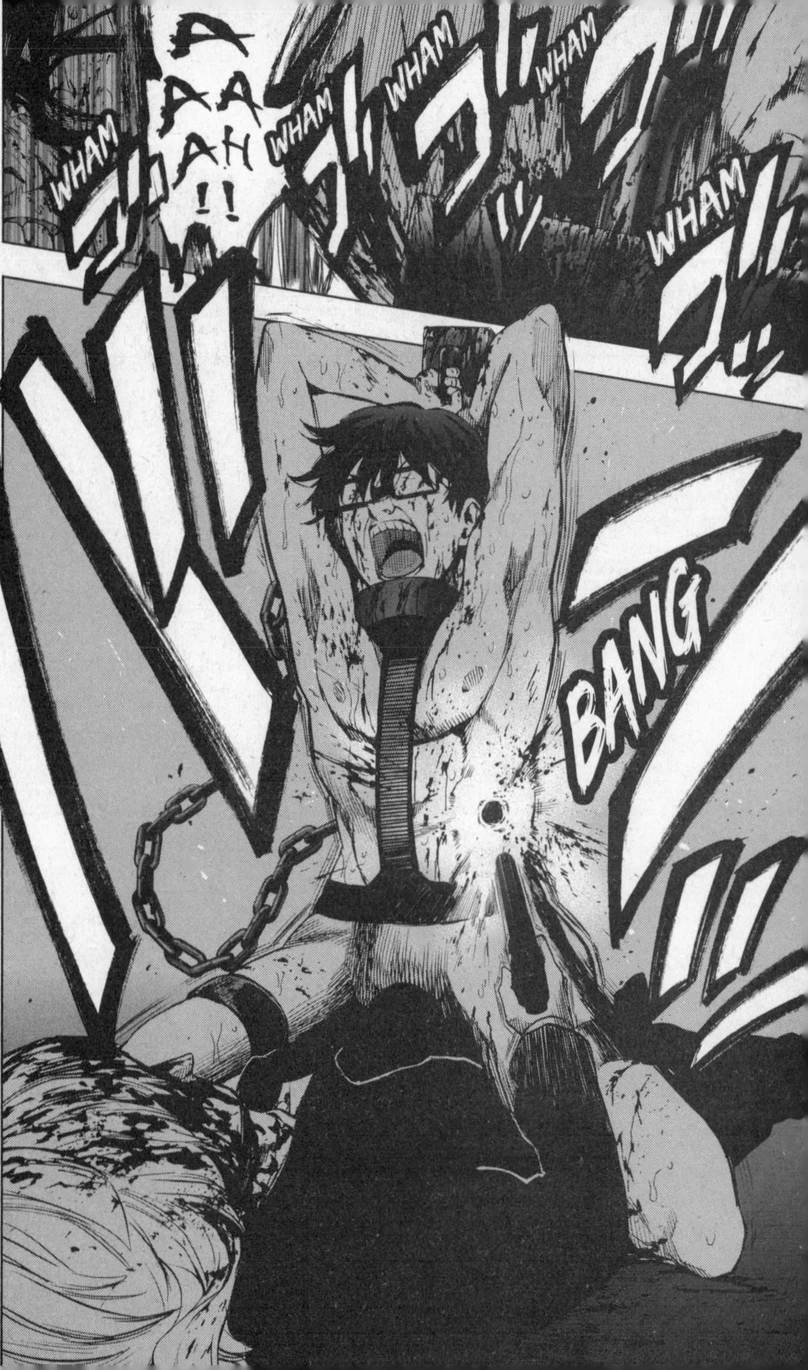
WHAM
WHAM
WHAM
WHAM
WHAM
AAAAH!!
WHAM
BANG

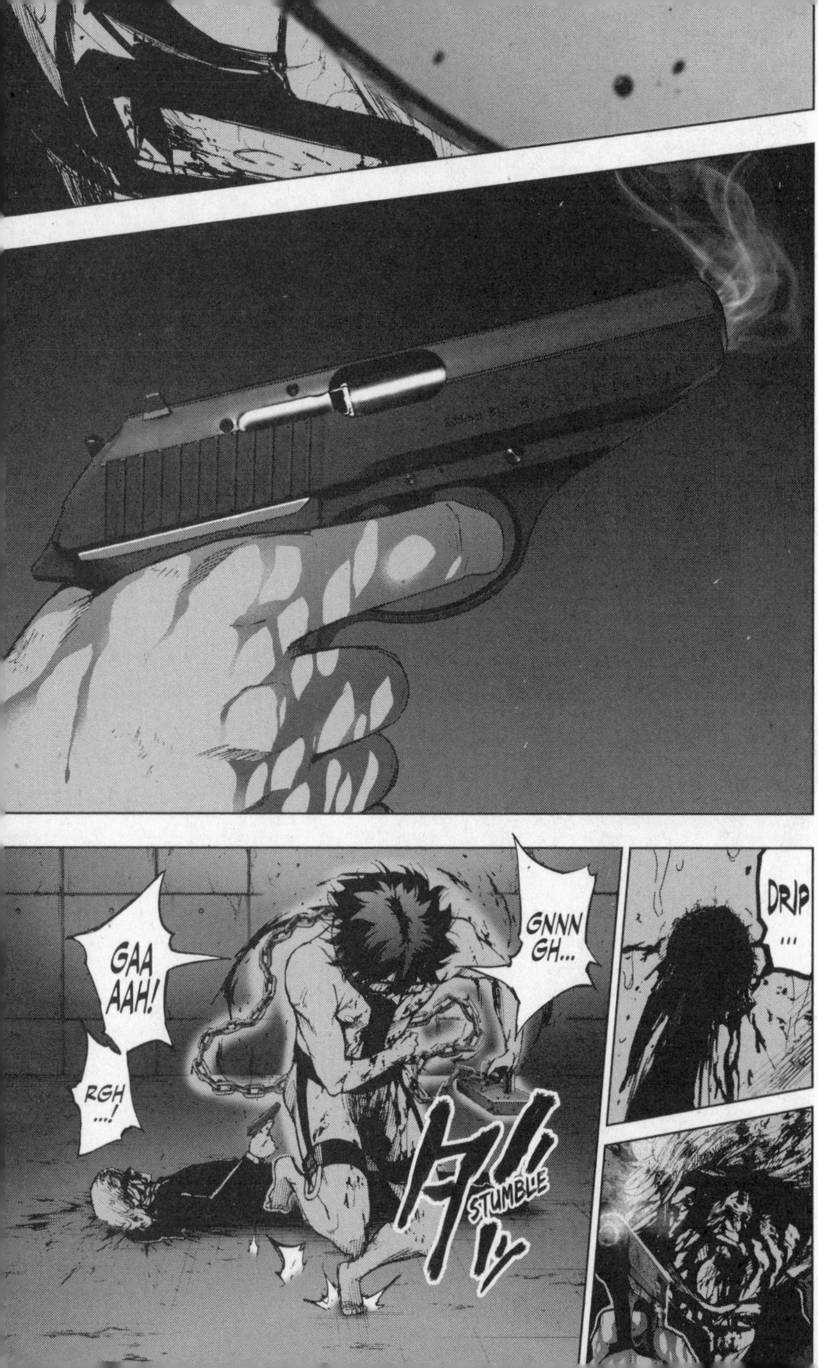
DRIP ...
GNNN GH...
GAA AAH!
RGH ...!
STUMBLE

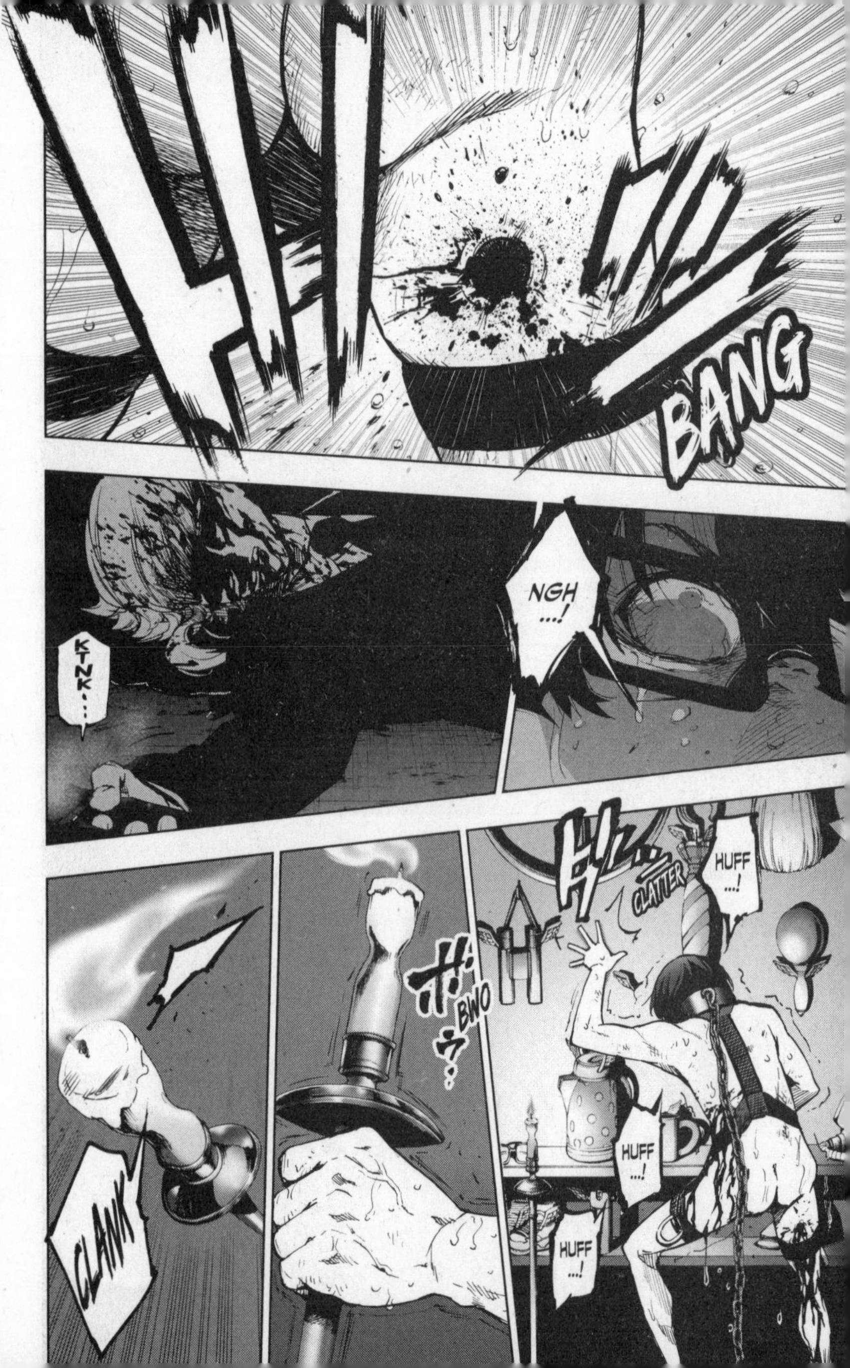
BANG
NGH ...!
KTNK...
HUFF ...!
CLATTER
HUFF ...!
HUFF ...!
BWO
CLANK

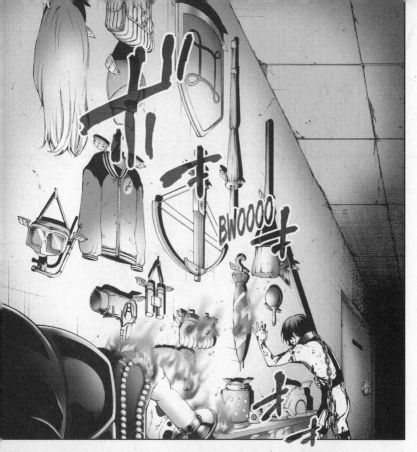

BWOOOO

STAGGER

WOULD YOU LET ME DO YOU...?

SHUT UP!!

I'M SORRY, KANAME...

JUST ONCE MORE, I...

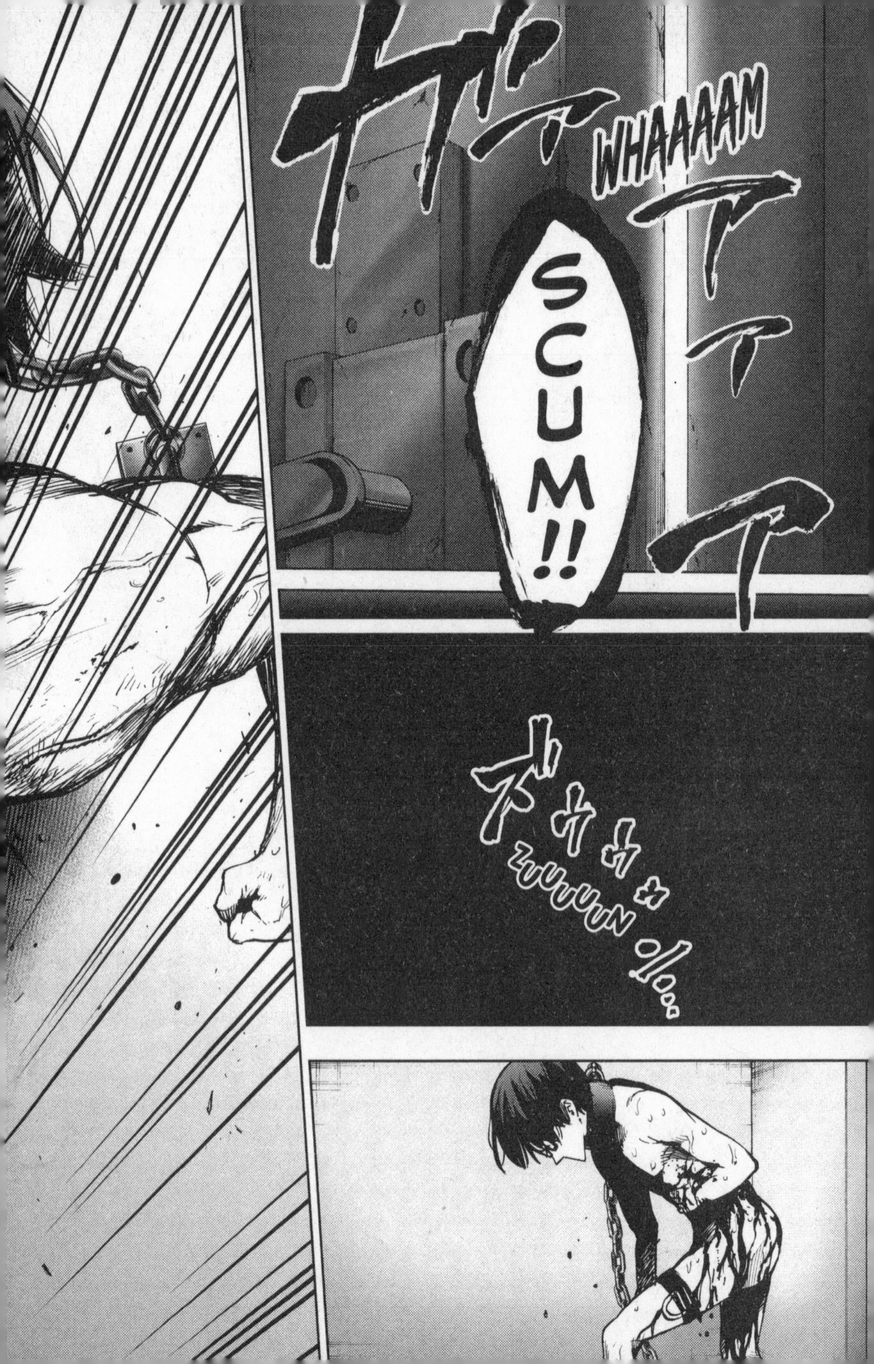
WHAAAAM
SCUM!!
ZUUUUUN

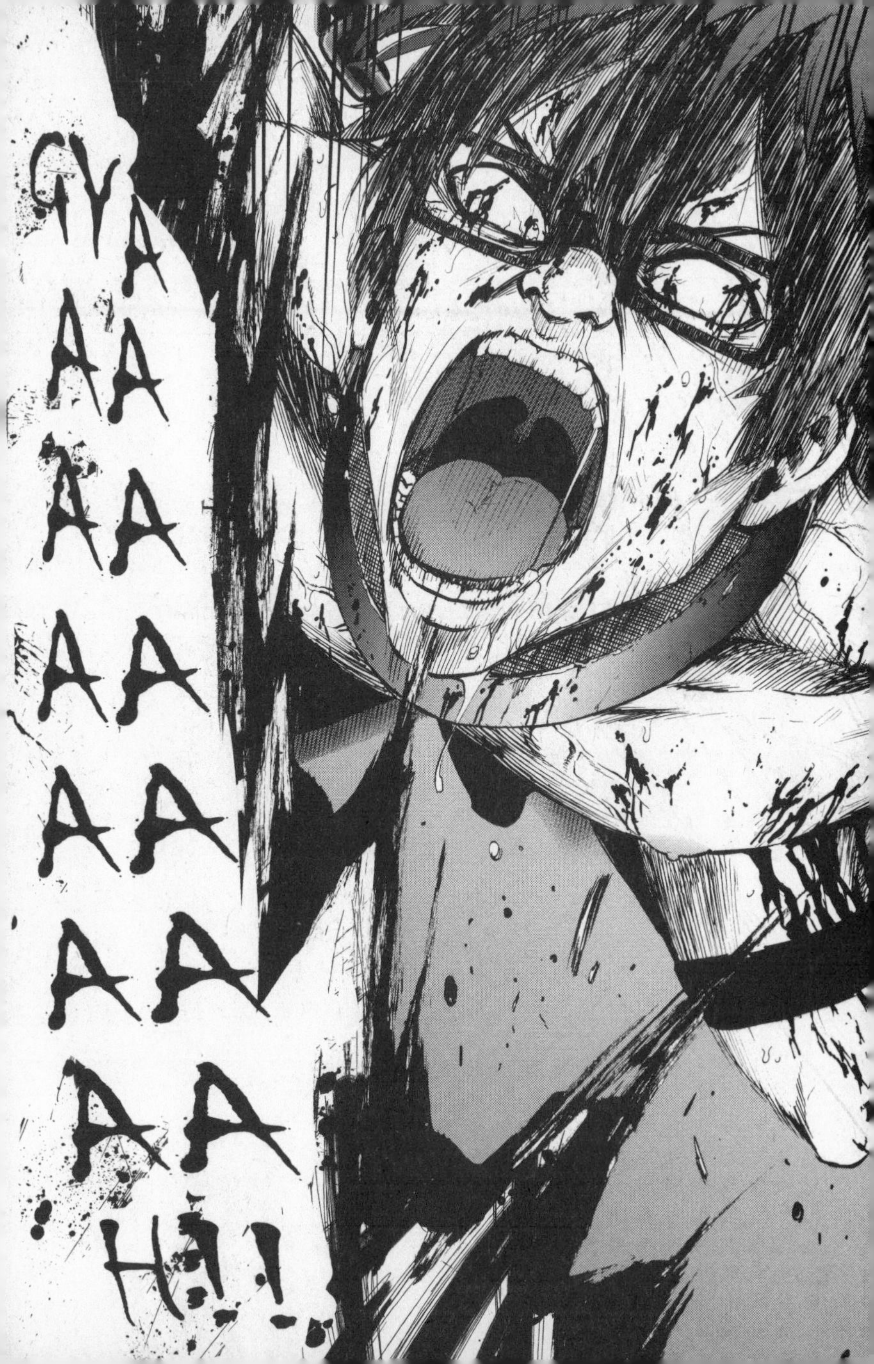
GYAAAAAAAAAAAAAAAH!!

ASAGIRI-SAN.

I'M SORRY...

FOR NOT TELLING YOU ANY- THING.

I THOUGHT IF I TOLD YOU, YOU'D ONLY GET DEPRESSED AGAIN...

．．．．．．

CLOP

CLOP

I'M REALLY SORRY...

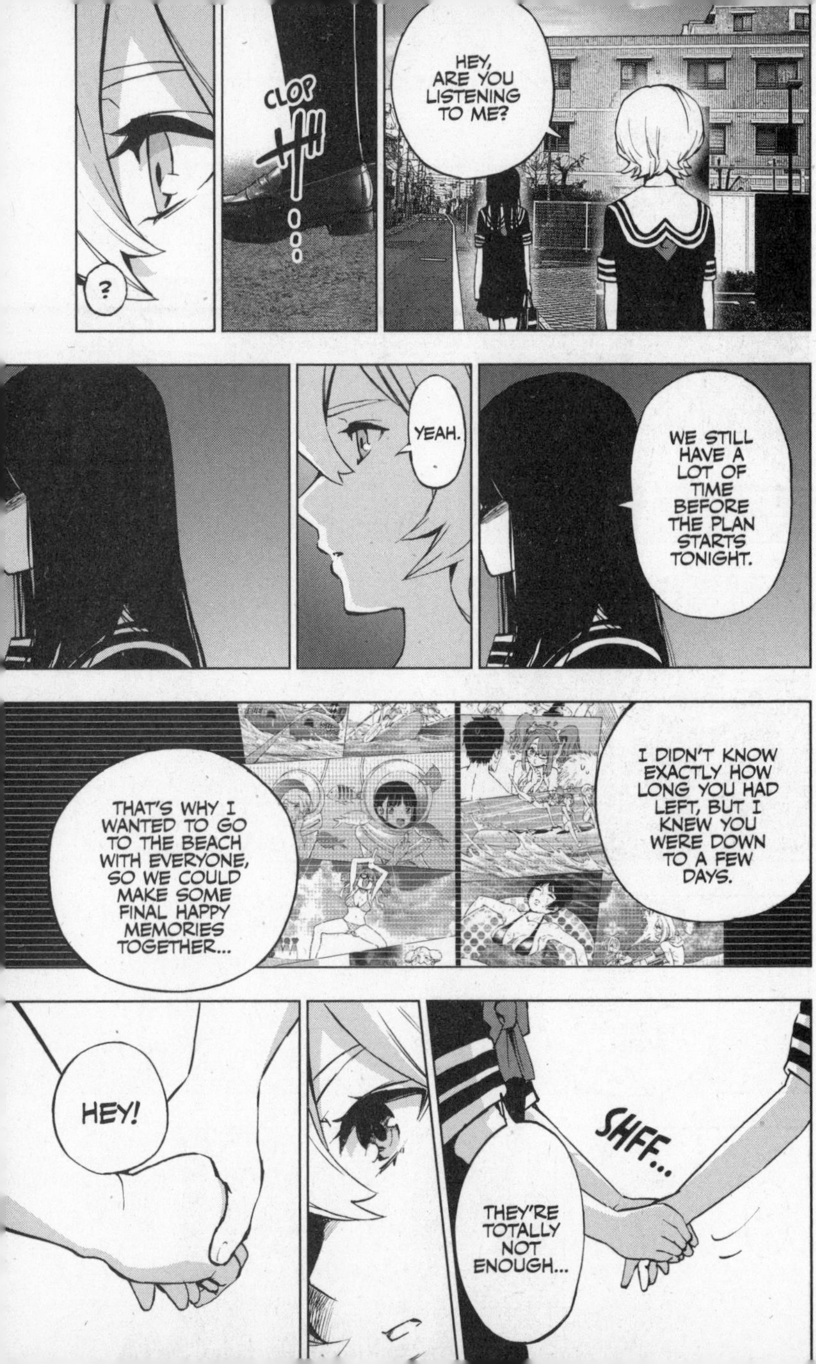
HEY, ARE YOU LISTENING TO ME?
CLOP
?
WE STILL HAVE A LOT OF TIME BEFORE THE PLAN STARTS TONIGHT.
YEAH.
I DIDN'T KNOW EXACTLY HOW LONG YOU HAD LEFT, BUT I KNEW YOU WERE DOWN TO A FEW DAYS.
THAT'S WHY I WANTED TO GO TO THE BEACH WITH EVERYONE, SO WE COULD MAKE SOME FINAL HAPPY MEMORIES TOGETHER...
SHFF...
THEY'RE TOTALLY NOT ENOUGH...
HEY!

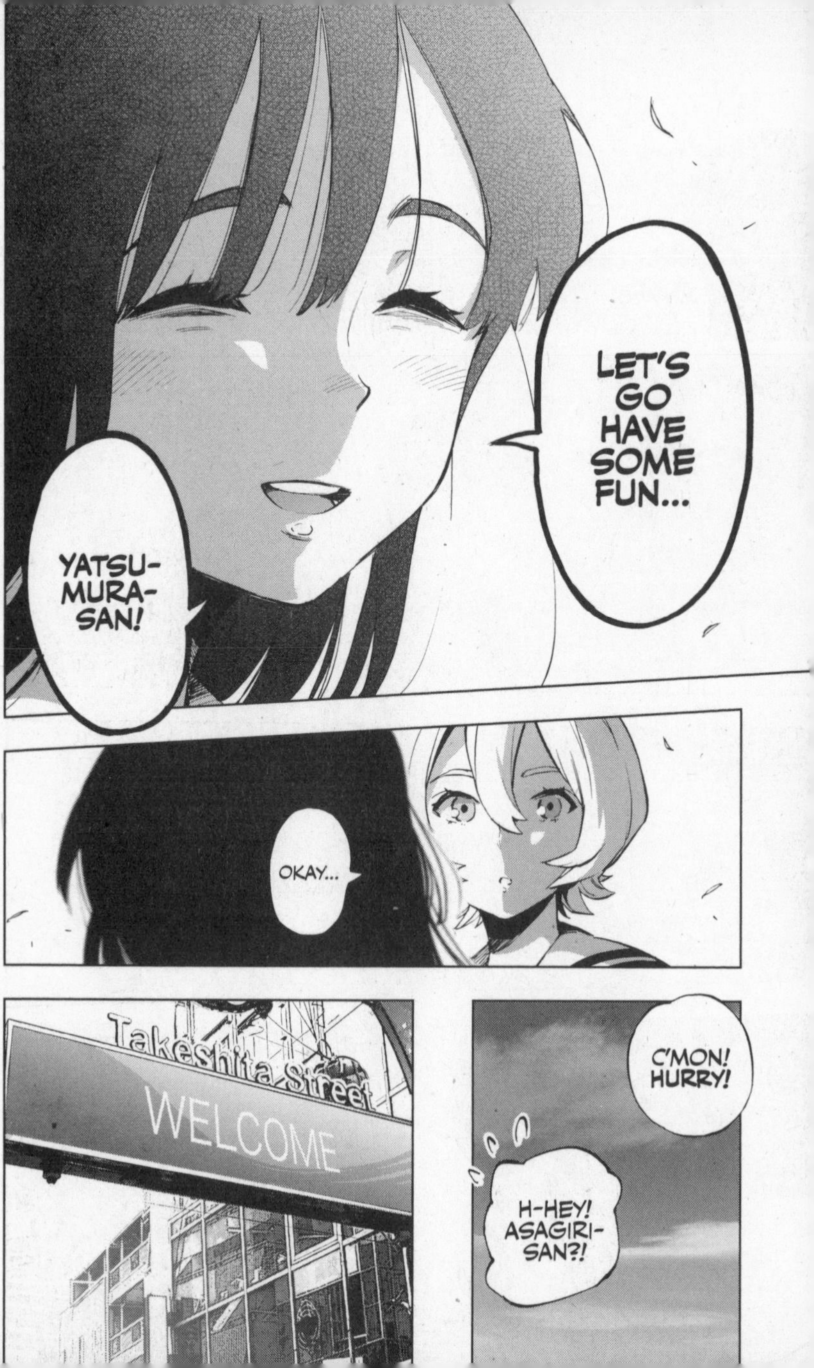
LET'S GO HAVE SOME FUN...
YATSU-MURA-SAN!
OKAY...
C'MON! HURRY!
H-HEY! ASAGIRI-SAN?!
Takeshita Street
WELCOME

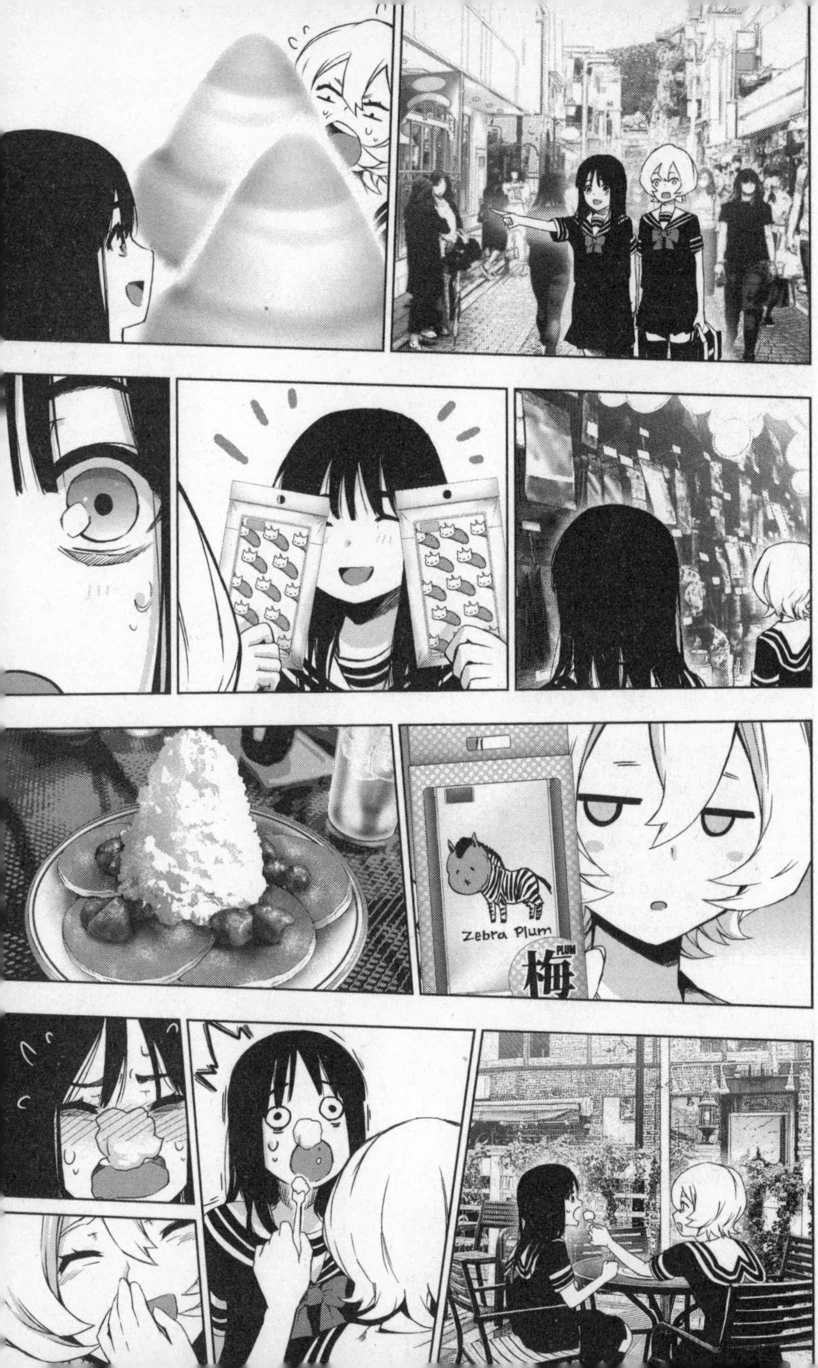
Zebra Plum
PLUM
梅

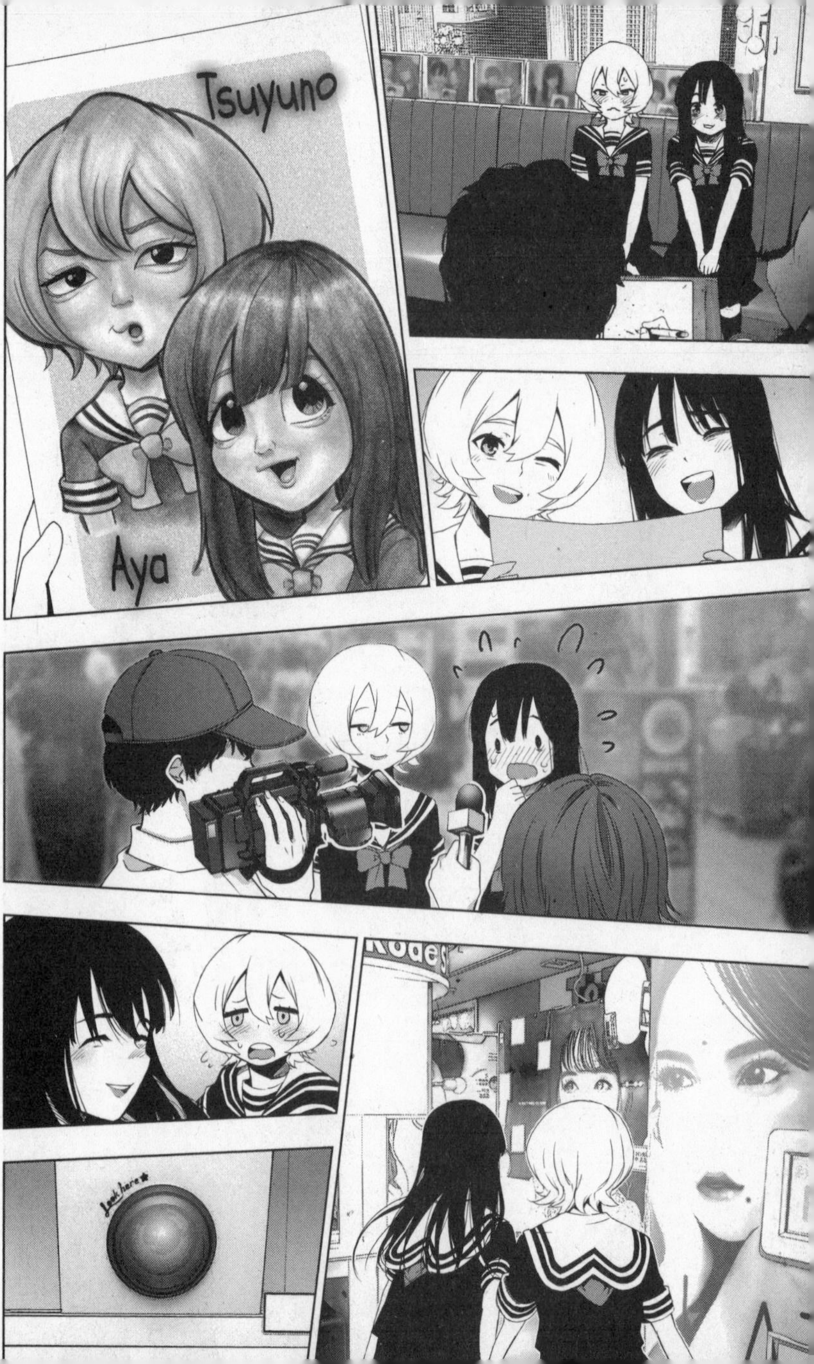
Tsuyuno
Aya
Look here★

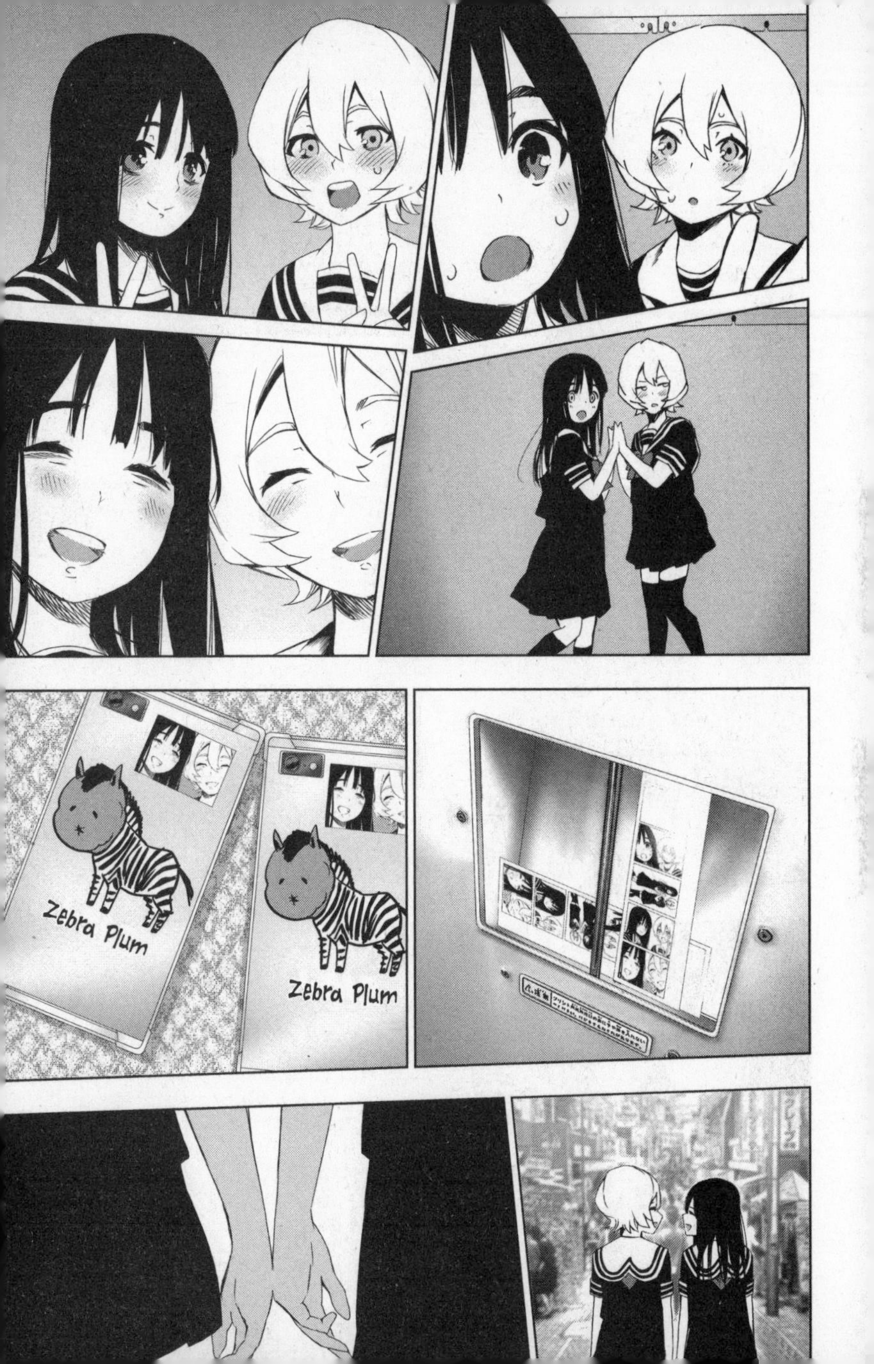
Zebra Plum
Zebra Plum

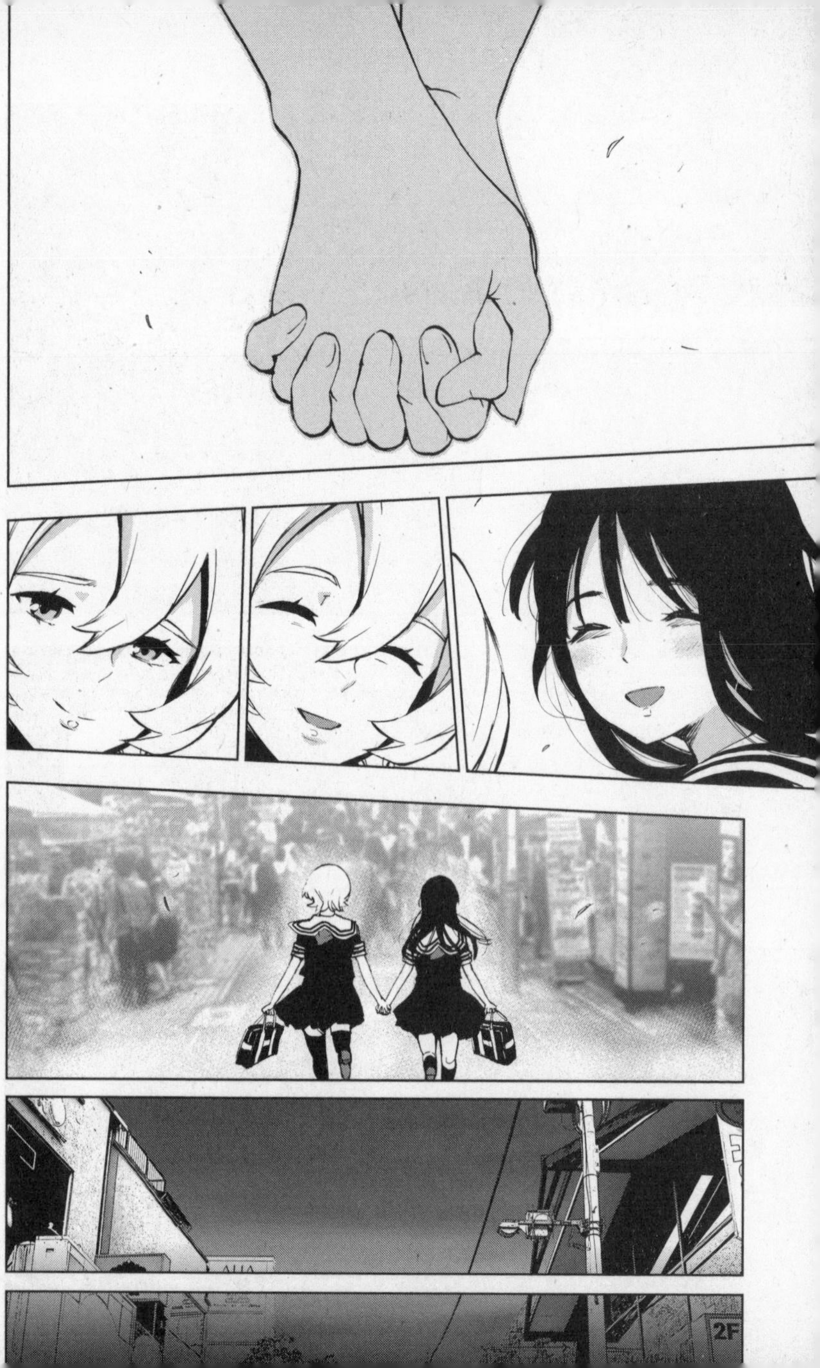
2F

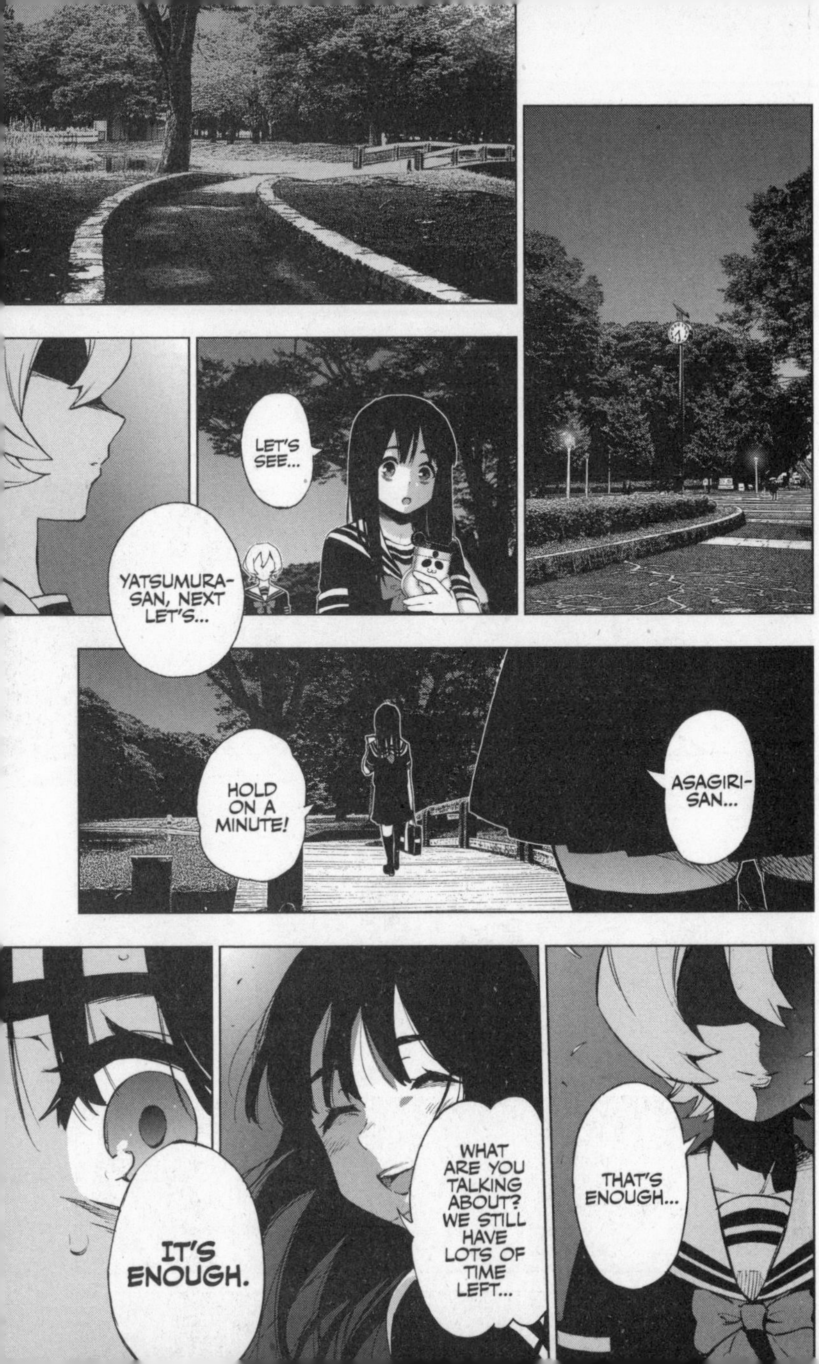
LET'S SEE...
YATSUMURA-SAN, NEXT LET'S...
ASAGIRI-SAN...
HOLD ON A MINUTE!
THAT'S ENOUGH...
WHAT ARE YOU TALKING ABOUT? WE STILL HAVE LOTS OF TIME LEFT...
IT'S ENOUGH.

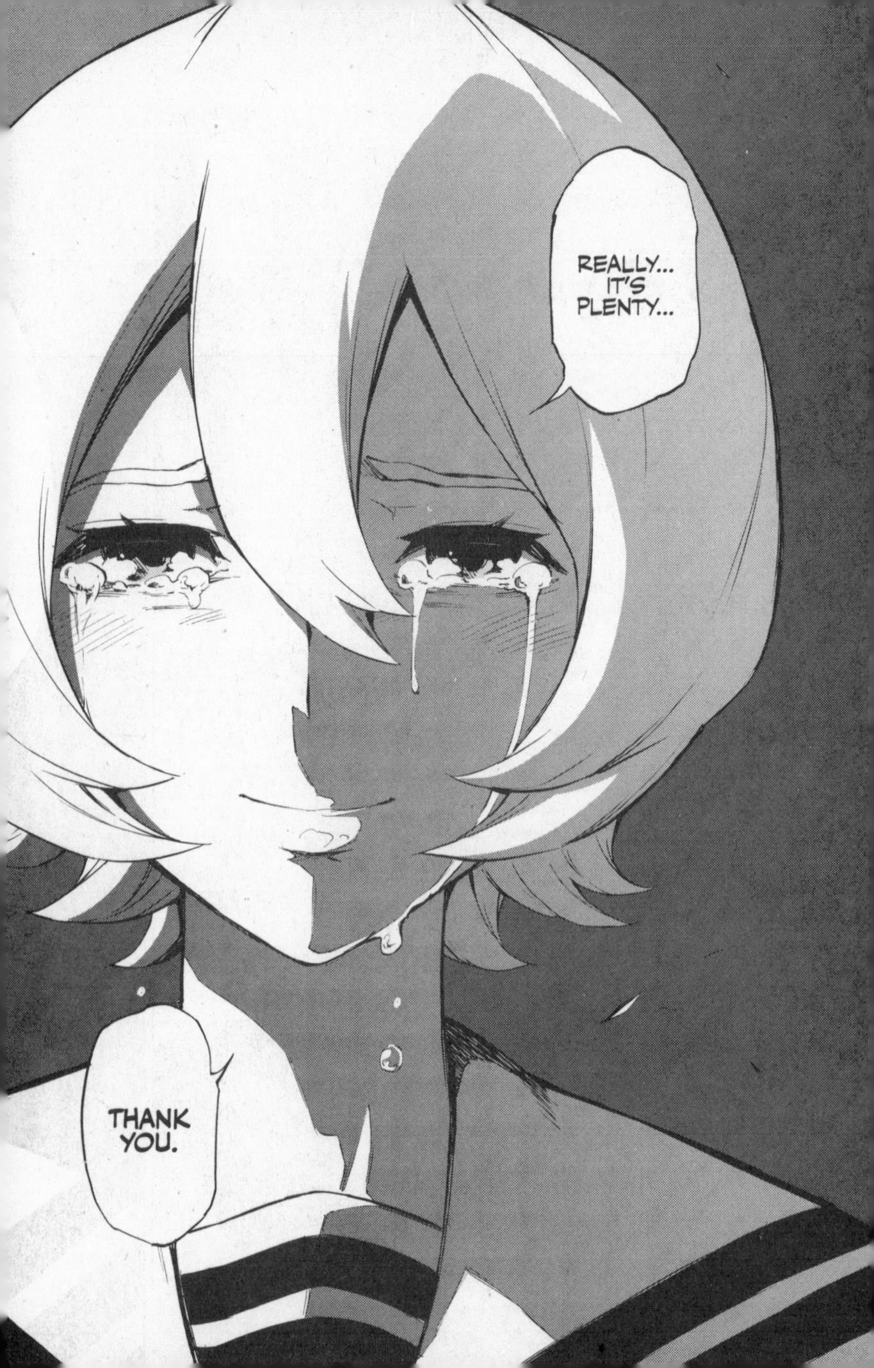
REALLY... IT'S PLENTY...
THANK YOU.

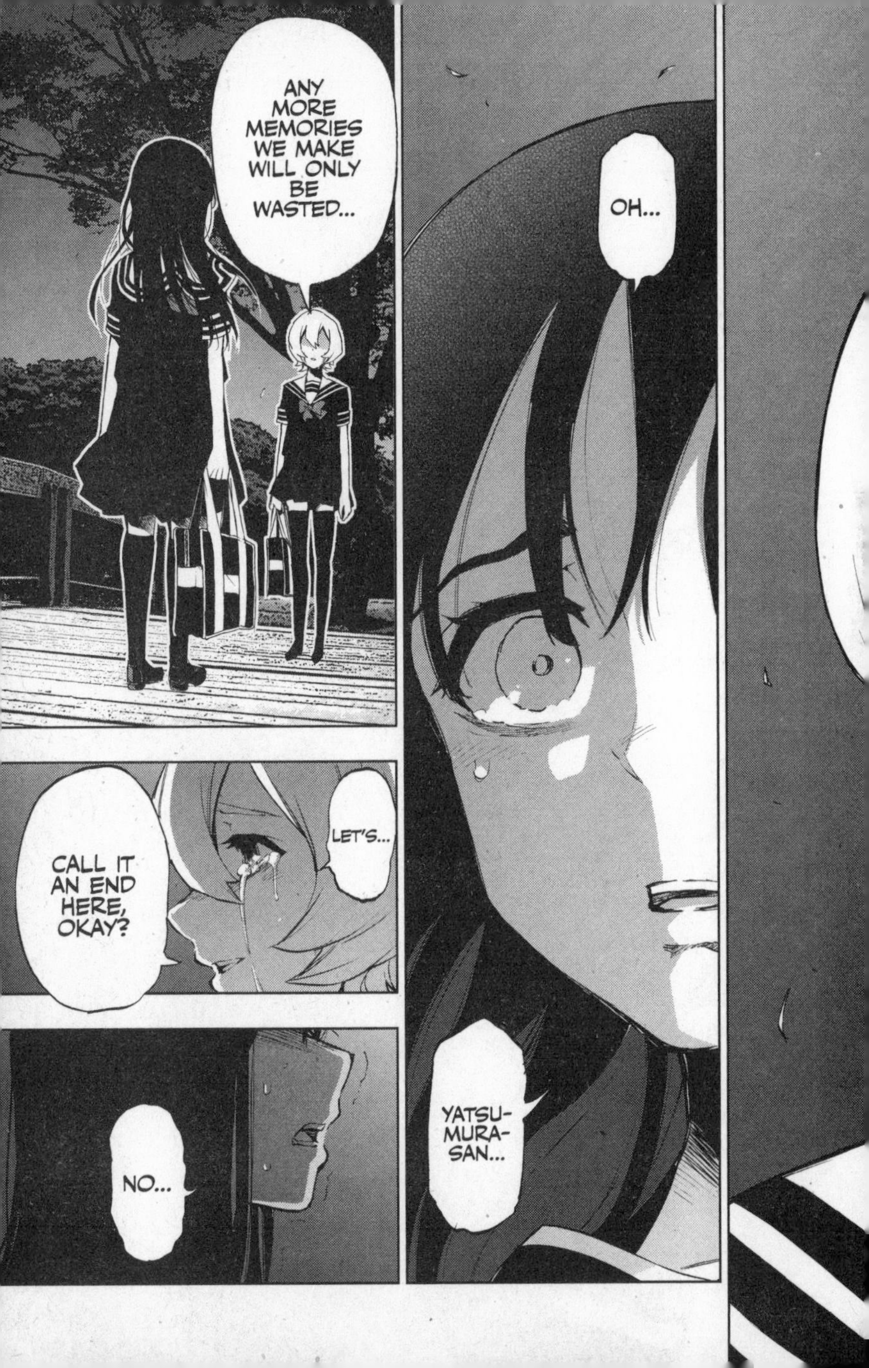
OH...
YATSU-MURA-SAN...
ANY MORE MEMORIES WE MAKE WILL ONLY BE WASTED...
LET'S...
CALL IT AN END HERE, OKAY?
NO...

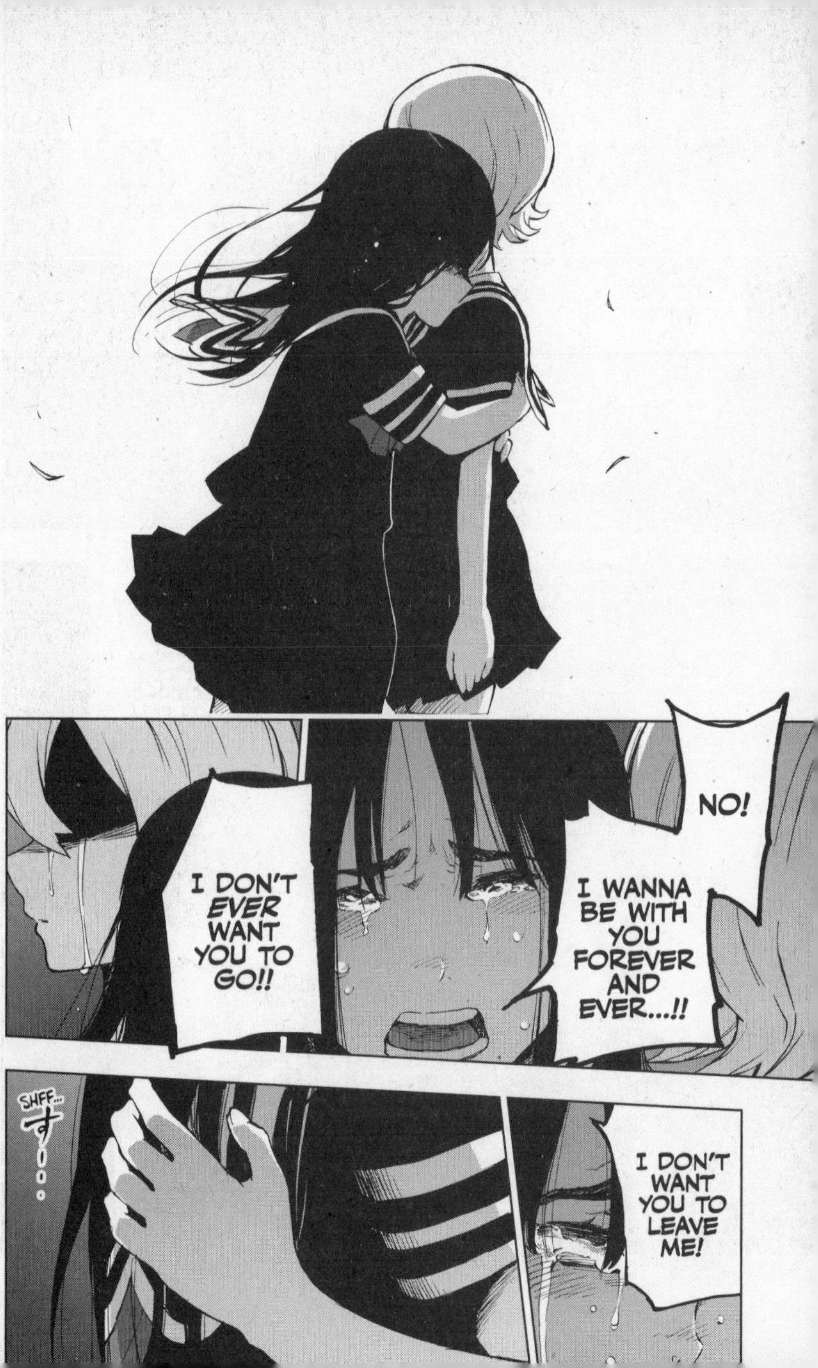
NO!
I WANNA BE WITH YOU FOREVER AND EVER...!!
I DON'T *EVER* WANT YOU TO GO!!
I DON'T WANT YOU TO LEAVE ME!
SHFF...
す

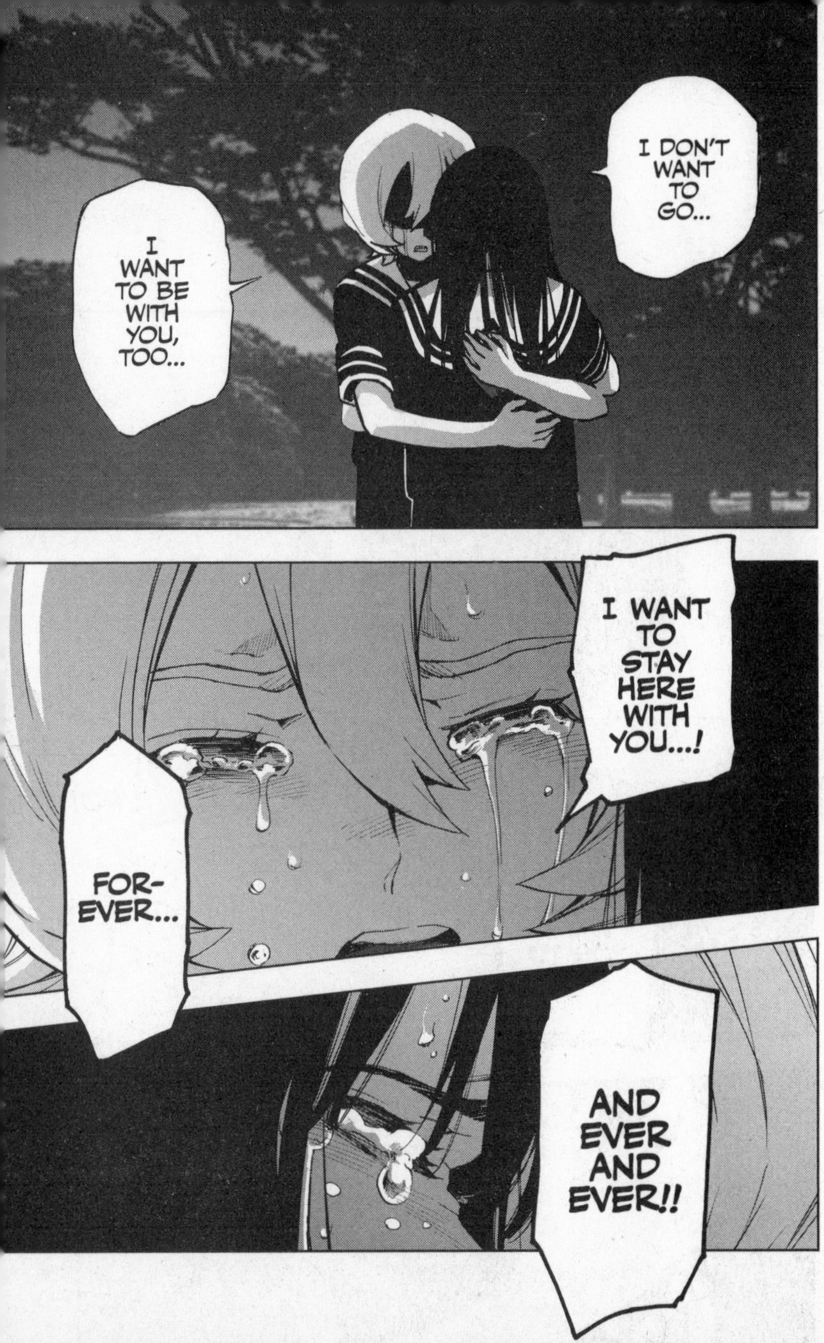
I DON'T WANT TO GO...
I WANT TO BE WITH YOU, TOO...
I WANT TO STAY HERE WITH YOU...!
FOR-EVER...
AND EVER AND EVER!!

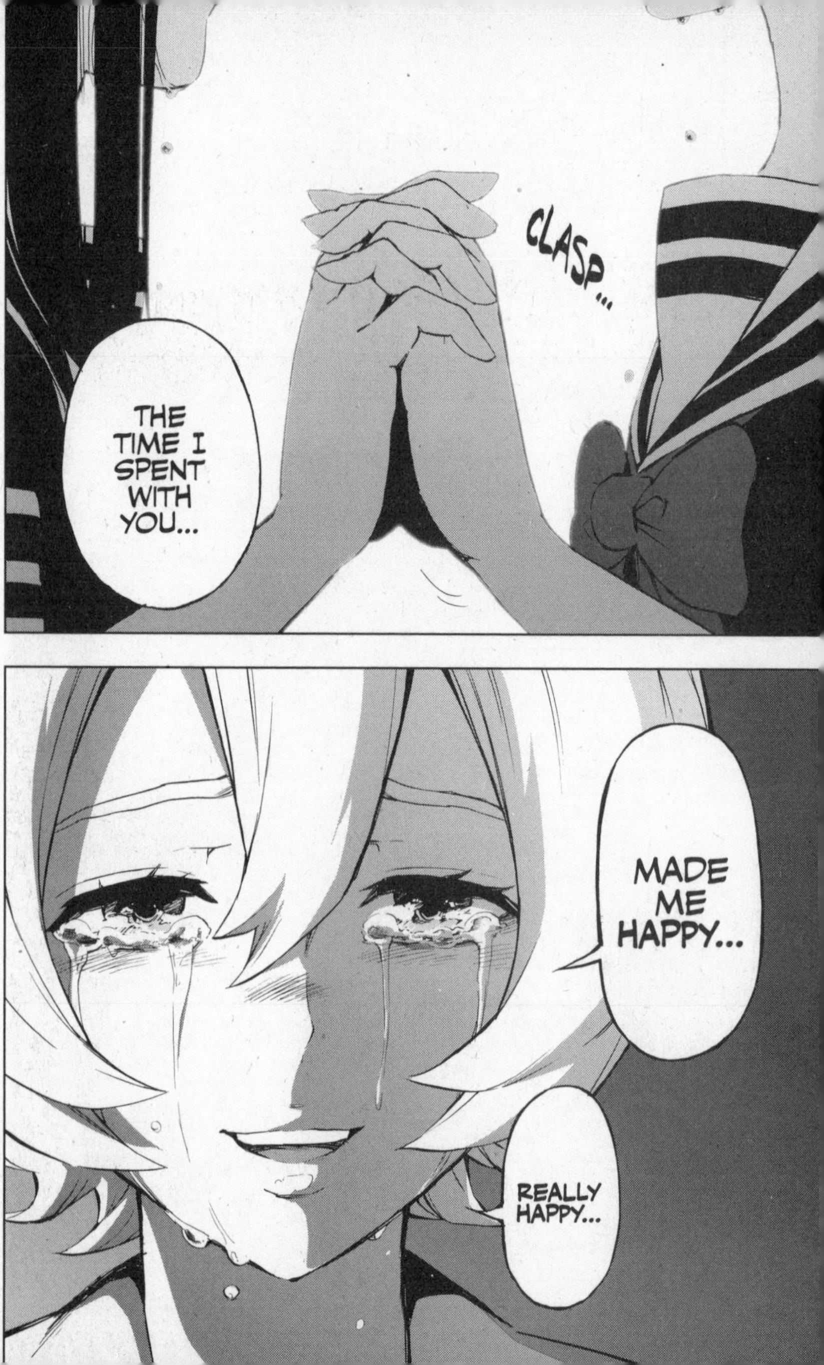
CLASP...
THE TIME I SPENT WITH YOU...
MADE ME HAPPY...
REALLY HAPPY...

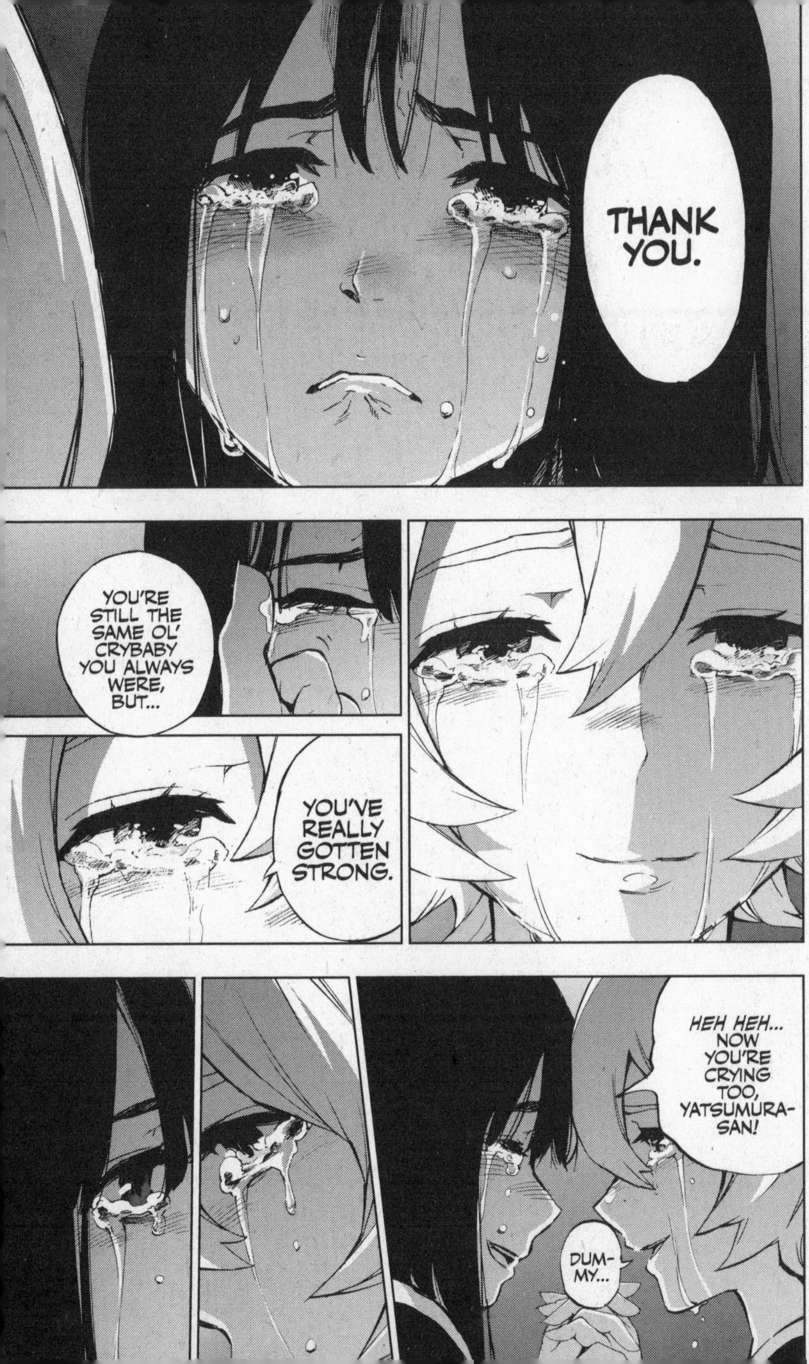
THANK YOU.
YOU'RE STILL THE SAME OL' CRYBABY YOU ALWAYS WERE, BUT...
YOU'VE REALLY GOTTEN STRONG.
HEH HEH... NOW YOU'RE CRYING TOO, YATSUMURA-SAN!
DUM-MY...

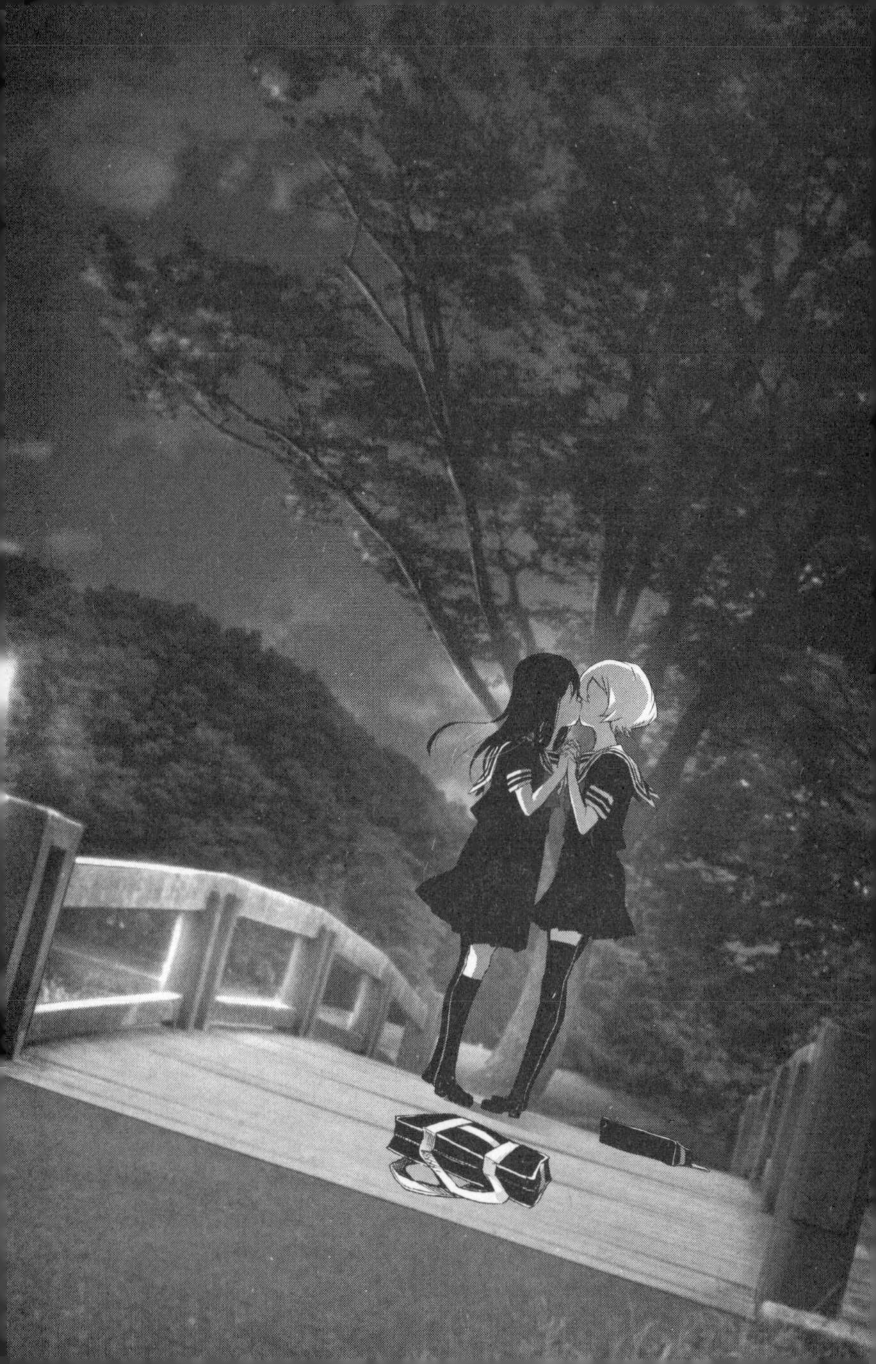

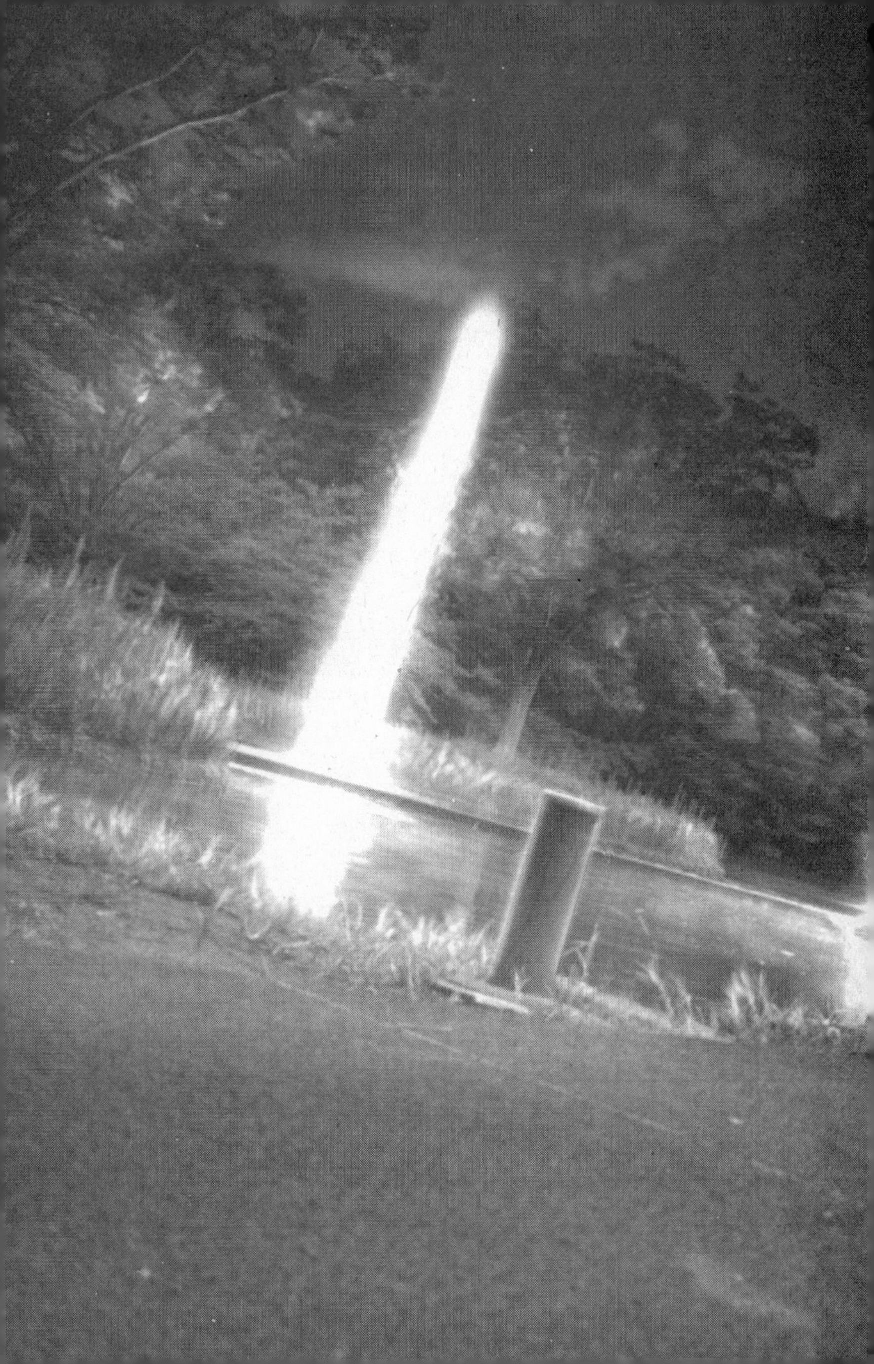

MAGICAL
GIRL SITE

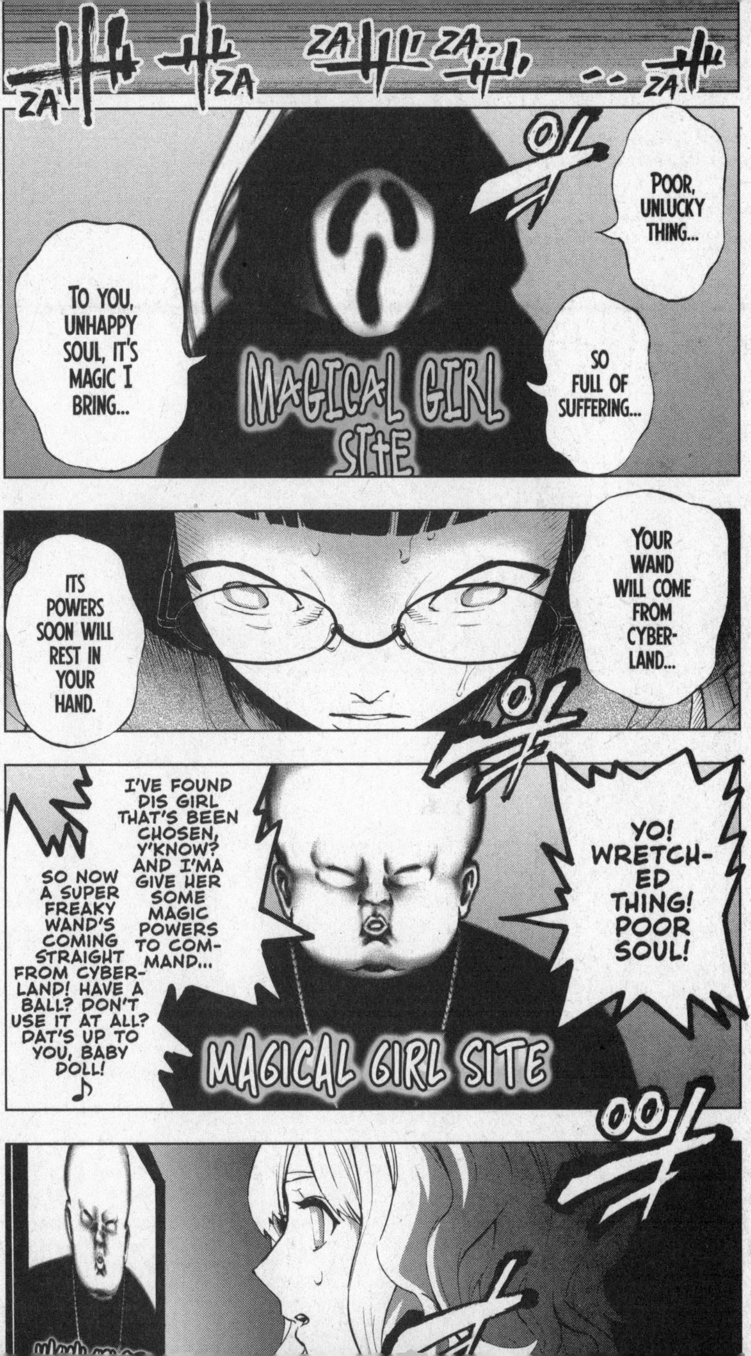
ZA
ZA..
ZA
ZA
ZA
POOR, UNLUCKY THING...
SO FULL OF SUFFERING...
TO YOU, UNHAPPY SOUL, IT'S MAGIC I BRING...
MAGICAL GIRL SITE
YOUR WAND WILL COME FROM CYBER-LAND...
ITS POWERS SOON WILL REST IN YOUR HAND.
YO! WRETCH-ED THING! POOR SOUL!
I'VE FOUND DIS GIRL THAT'S BEEN CHOSEN, Y'KNOW? AND I'MA GIVE HER SOME MAGIC POWERS TO COM-MAND...
SO NOW A SUPER FREAKY WAND'S COMING STRAIGHT FROM CYBER-LAND! HAVE A BALL? DON'T USE IT AT ALL? DAT'S UP TO YOU, BABY DOLL! ♪
MAGICAL GIRL SITE

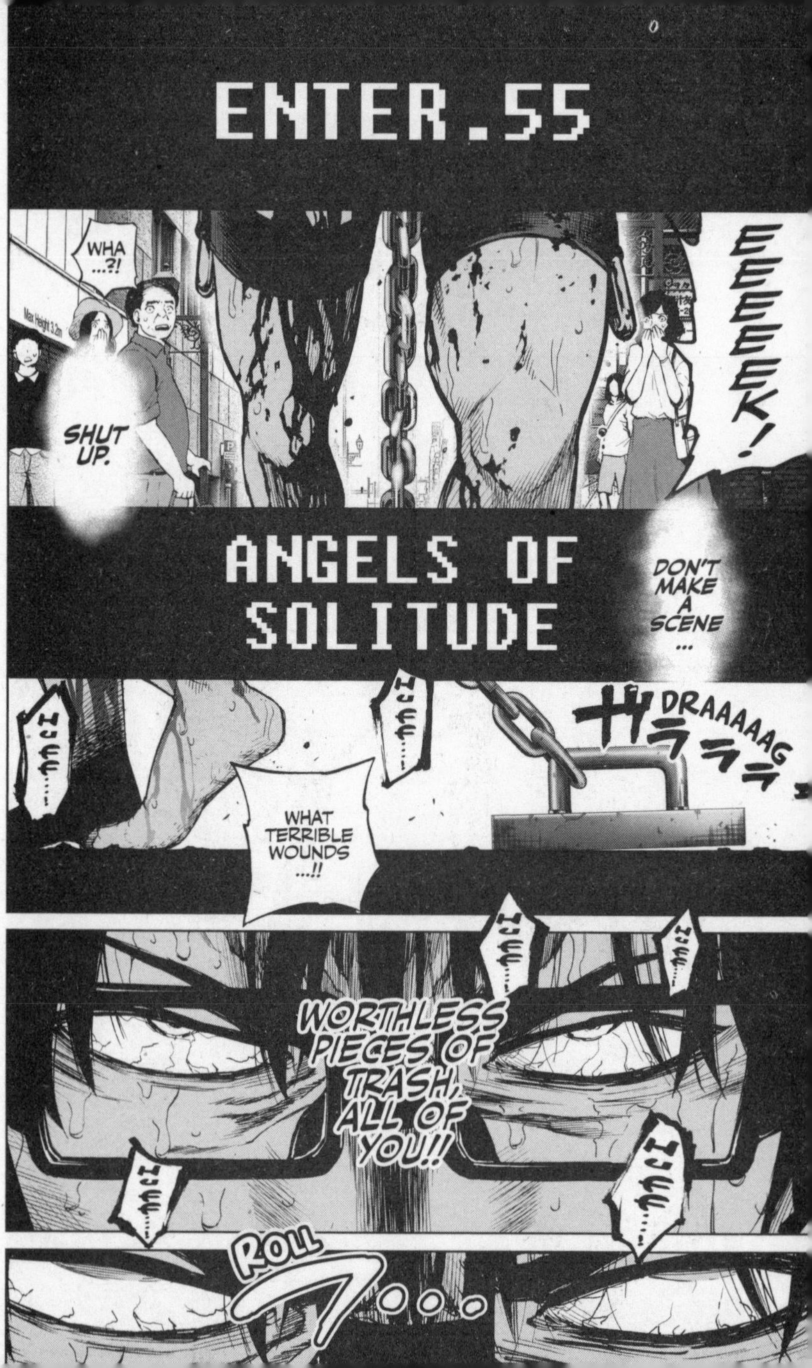
ENTER.55
EEEEEK!
WHA ...?!
Max Height 3.2m
SHUT UP.
ANGELS OF SOLITUDE
DON'T MAKE A SCENE ...
ザラララ
DRAAAAAG
HUFF...
WHAT TERRIBLE WOUNDS ...!!
HUFF...
HUFF...
HUFF...
WORTHLESS PIECES OF TRASH, ALL OF YOU!!
HUFF...!
HUFF...
ROLL

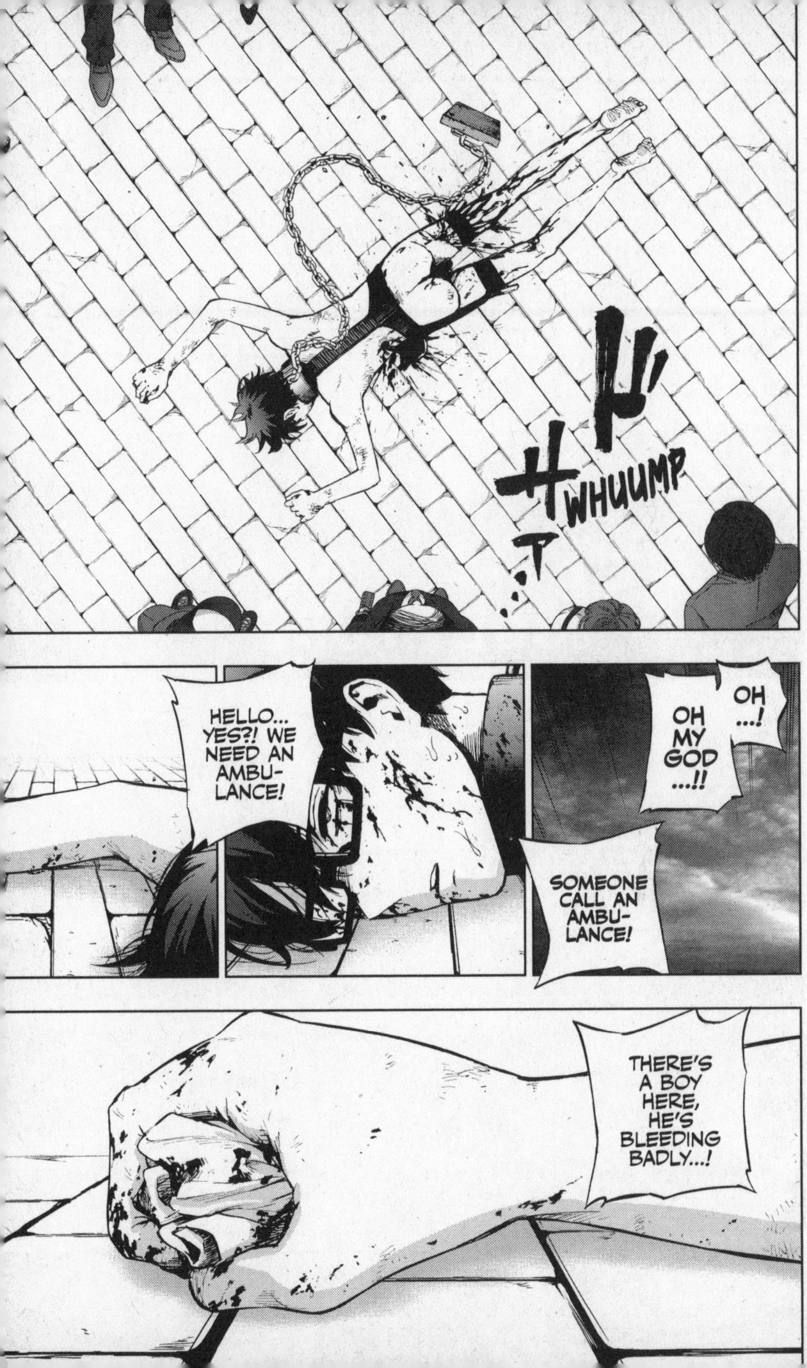
WHUUMP
OH ...!
OH MY GOD ...!!
SOMEONE CALL AN AMBULANCE!
HELLO... YES?! WE NEED AN AMBULANCE!
THERE'S A BOY HERE, HE'S BLEEDING BADLY...!

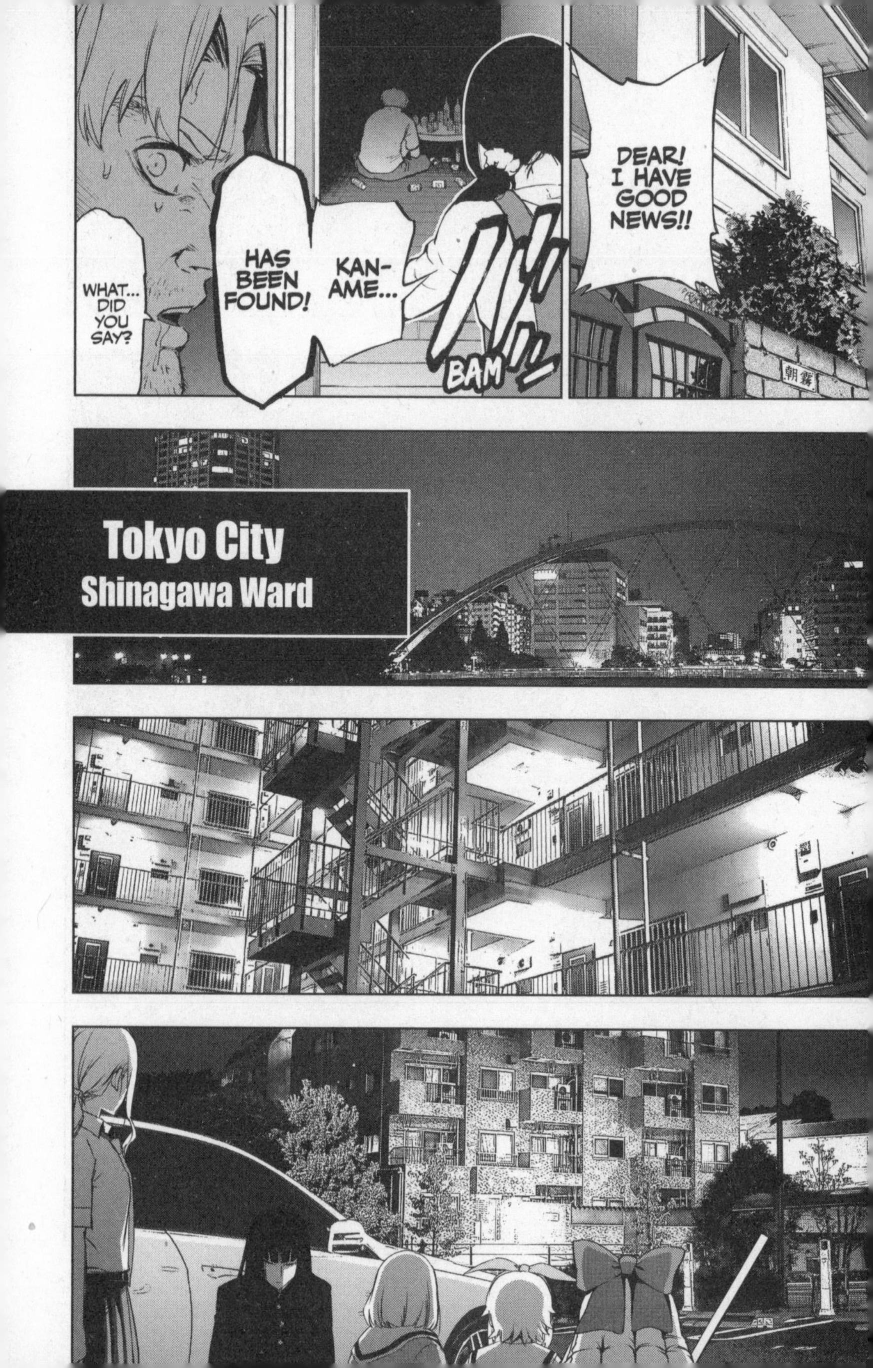
DEAR! I HAVE GOOD NEWS!!
朝霧
BAM
KAN-AME...
HAS BEEN FOUND!
WHAT... DID YOU SAY?
Tokyo City
Shinagawa Ward

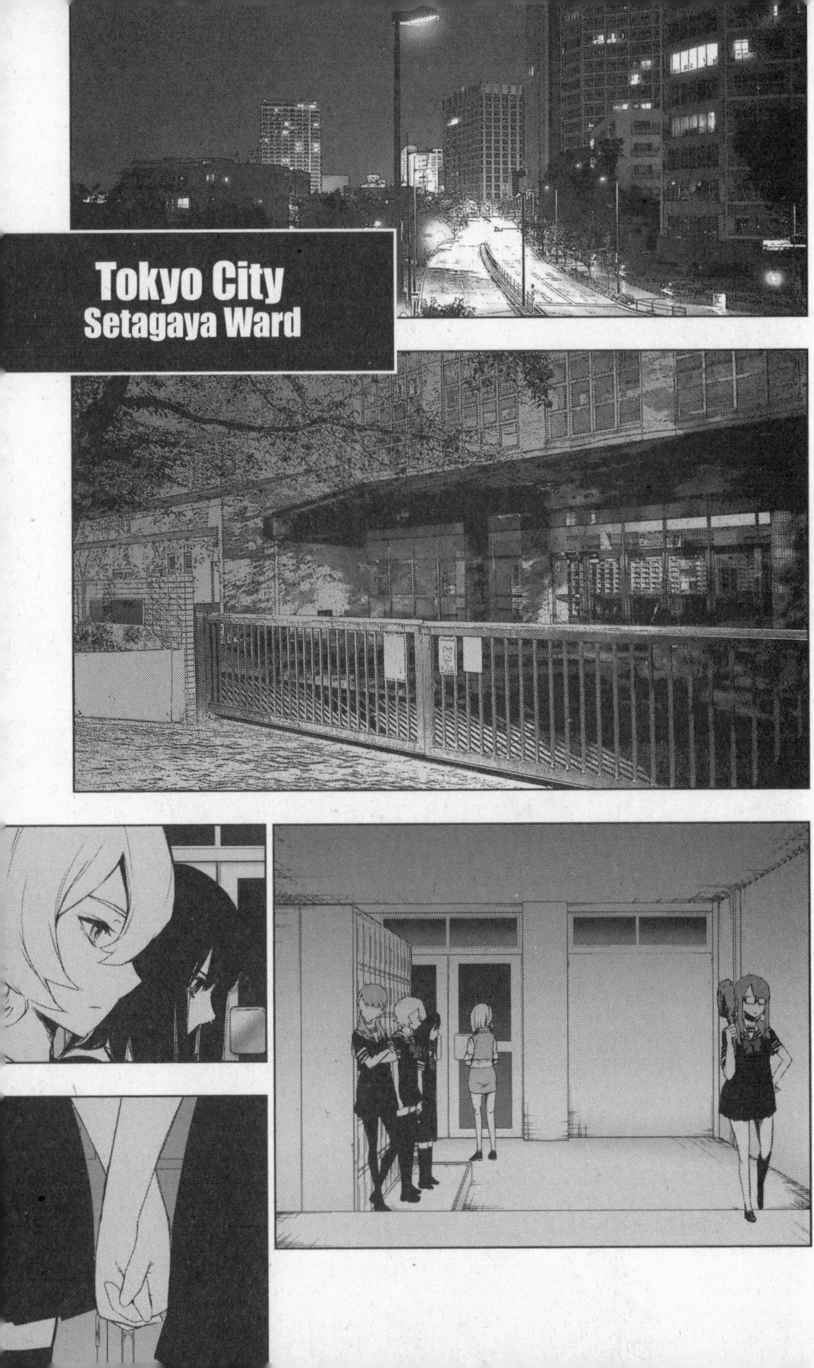
Tokyo City
Setagaya Ward

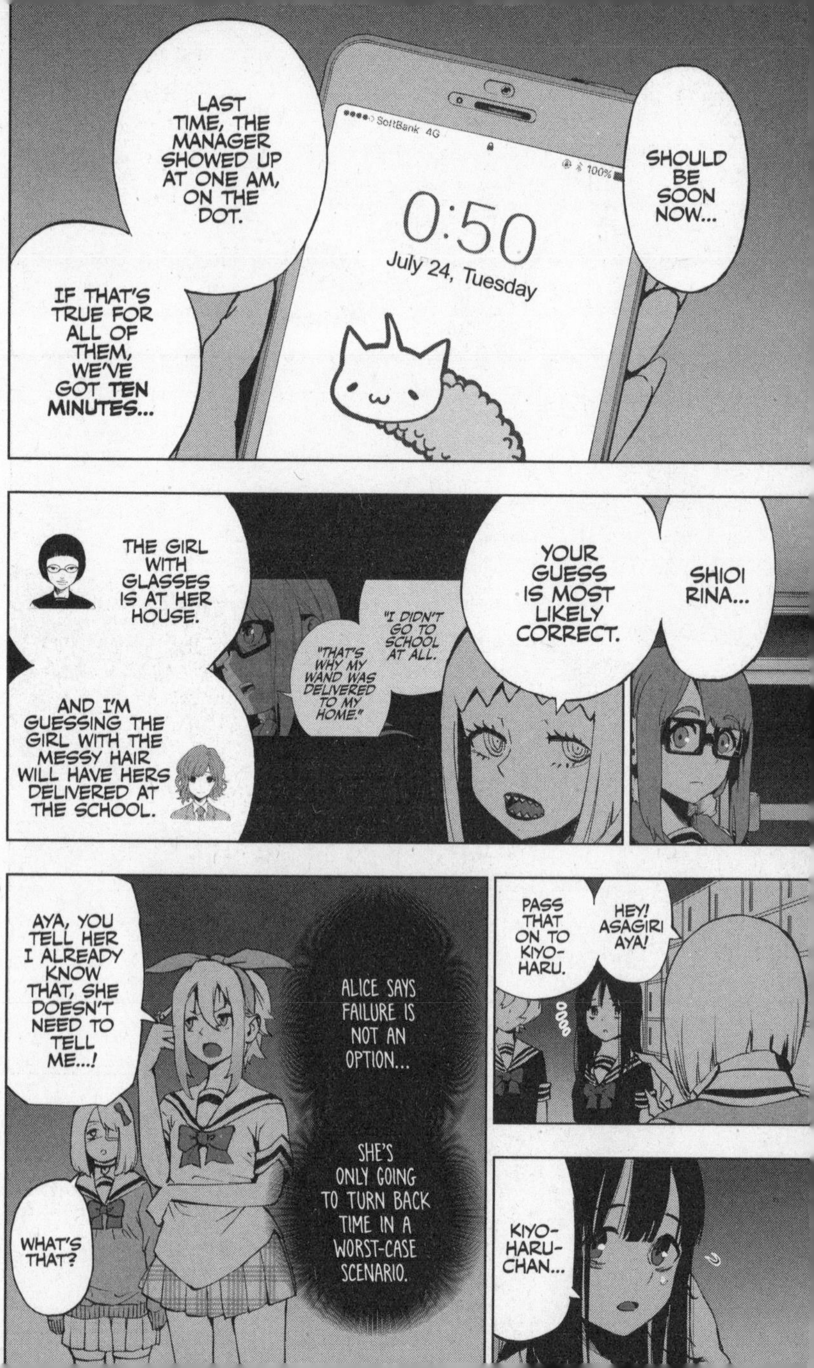
SHOULD BE SOON NOW...
SoftBank 4G
100%
0:50
July 24, Tuesday
LAST TIME, THE MANAGER SHOWED UP AT ONE AM, ON THE DOT.
IF THAT'S TRUE FOR ALL OF THEM, WE'VE GOT TEN MINUTES...
SHIOI RINA...
YOUR GUESS IS MOST LIKELY CORRECT.
"I DIDN'T GO TO SCHOOL AT ALL.
"THAT'S WHY MY WAND WAS DELIVERED TO MY HOME."
THE GIRL WITH GLASSES IS AT HER HOUSE.
AND I'M GUESSING THE GIRL WITH THE MESSY HAIR WILL HAVE HERS DELIVERED AT THE SCHOOL.
HEY! ASAGIRI AYA!
PASS THAT ON TO KIYO-HARU.
KIYO-HARU-CHAN...
ALICE SAYS FAILURE IS NOT AN OPTION...
SHE'S ONLY GOING TO TURN BACK TIME IN A WORST-CASE SCENARIO.
AYA, YOU TELL HER I ALREADY KNOW THAT, SHE DOESN'T NEED TO TELL ME...!
WHAT'S THAT?

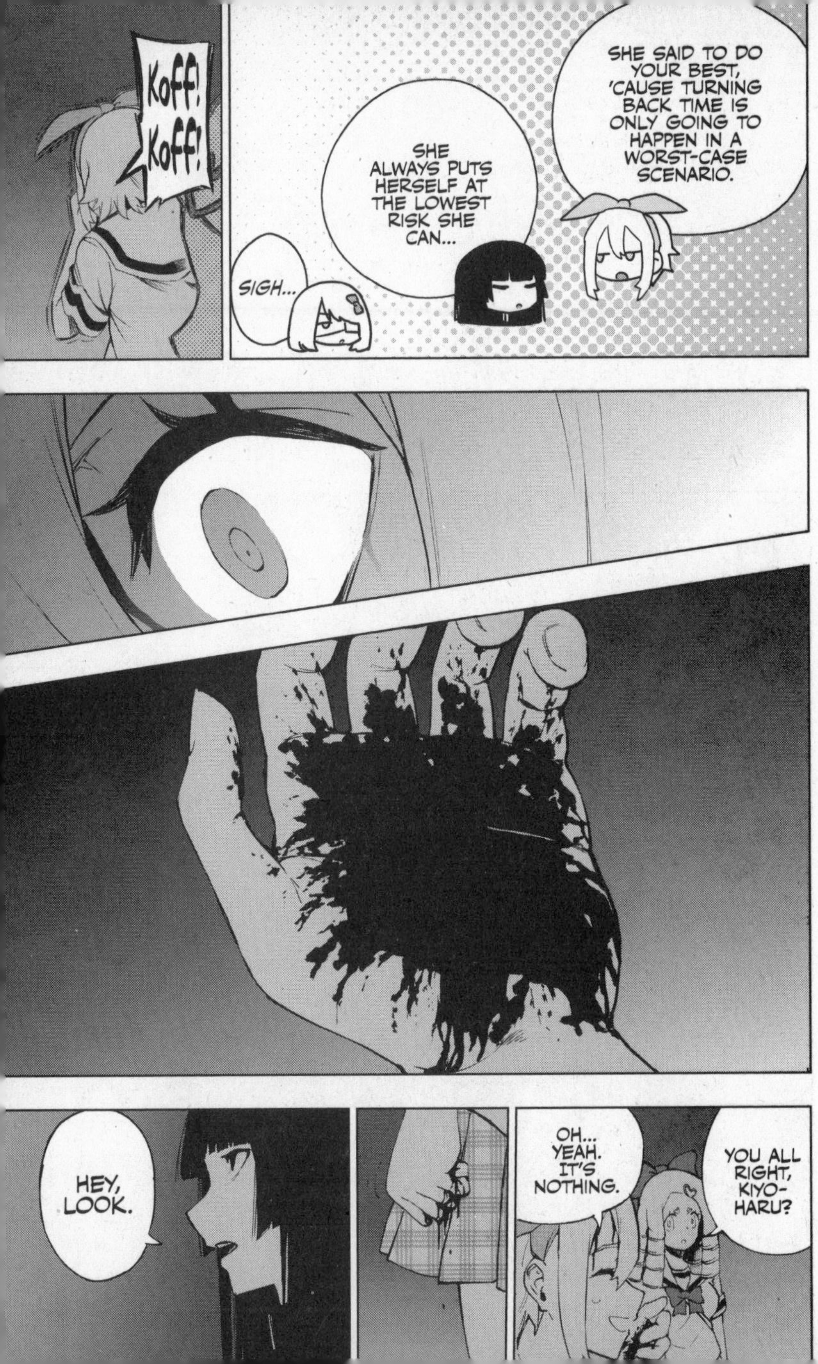
SHE SAID TO DO YOUR BEST, 'CAUSE TURNING BACK TIME IS ONLY GOING TO HAPPEN IN A WORST-CASE SCENARIO.
SHE ALWAYS PUTS HERSELF AT THE LOWEST RISK SHE CAN...
SIGH...
KOFF! KOFF!
YOU ALL RIGHT, KIYO-HARU?
OH... YEAH. IT'S NOTHING.
HEY, LOOK.

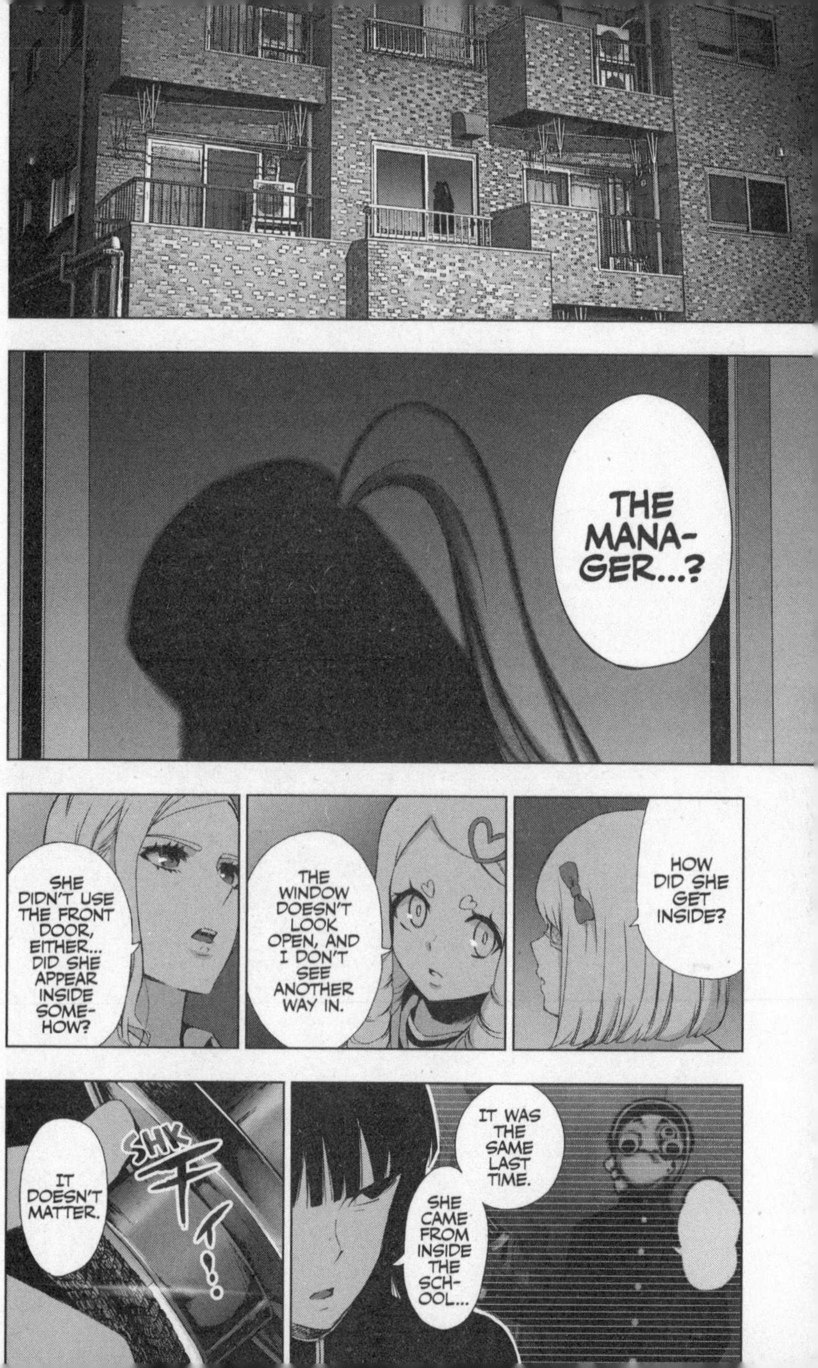
THE MANA-GER...?
HOW DID SHE GET INSIDE?
THE WINDOW DOESN'T LOOK OPEN, AND I DON'T SEE ANOTHER WAY IN.
SHE DIDN'T USE THE FRONT DOOR, EITHER... DID SHE APPEAR INSIDE SOME-HOW?
IT WAS THE SAME LAST TIME.
SHE CAME FROM INSIDE THE SCH-OOL...
SHK
IT DOESN'T MATTER.

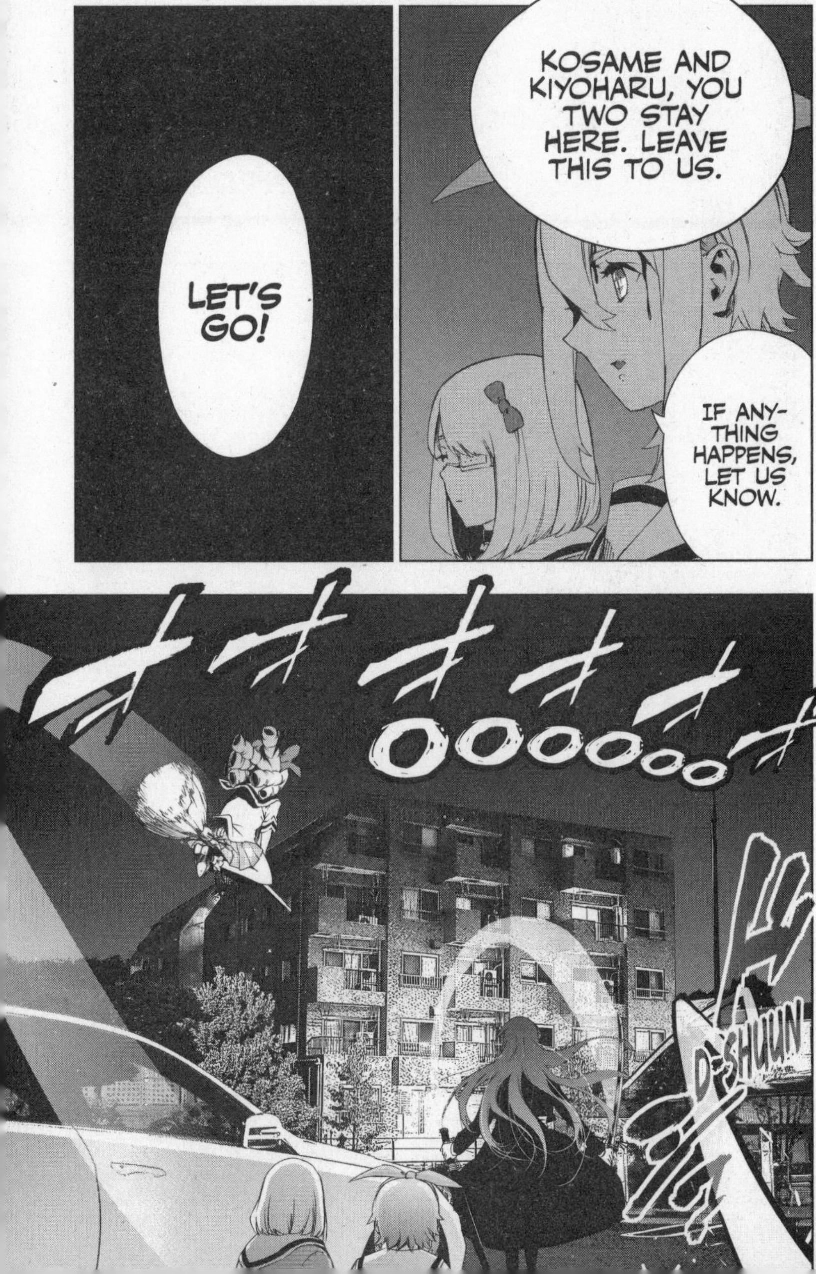
KOSAME AND KIYOHARU, YOU TWO STAY HERE. LEAVE THIS TO US.
IF ANYTHING HAPPENS, LET US KNOW.
LET'S GO!
OOOOOoo
D-SHUUN

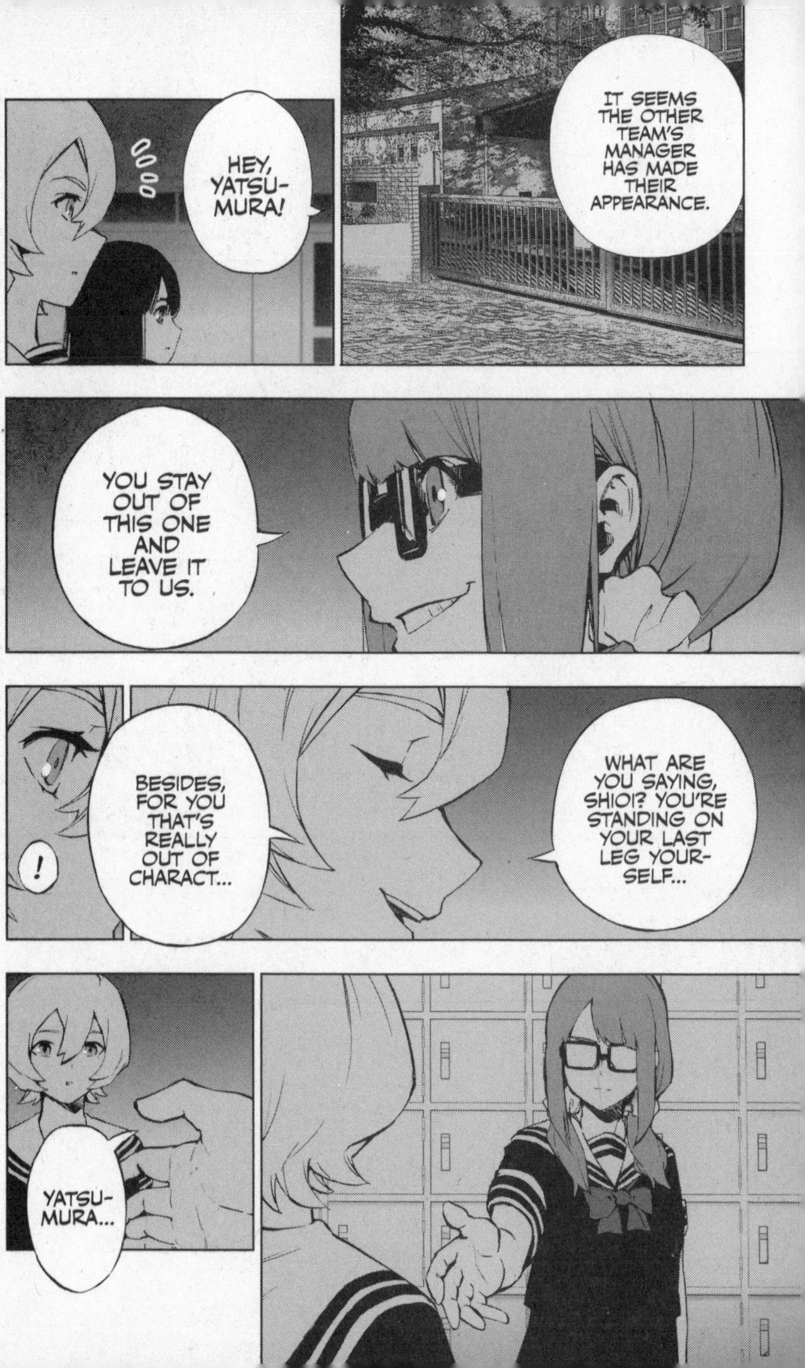
IT SEEMS THE OTHER TEAM'S MANAGER HAS MADE THEIR APPEARANCE.
HEY, YATSU-MURA!
YOU STAY OUT OF THIS ONE AND LEAVE IT TO US.
WHAT ARE YOU SAYING, SHIOI? YOU'RE STANDING ON YOUR LAST LEG YOUR-SELF...
BESIDES, FOR YOU THAT'S REALLY OUT OF CHARACT...
!
YATSU-MURA...

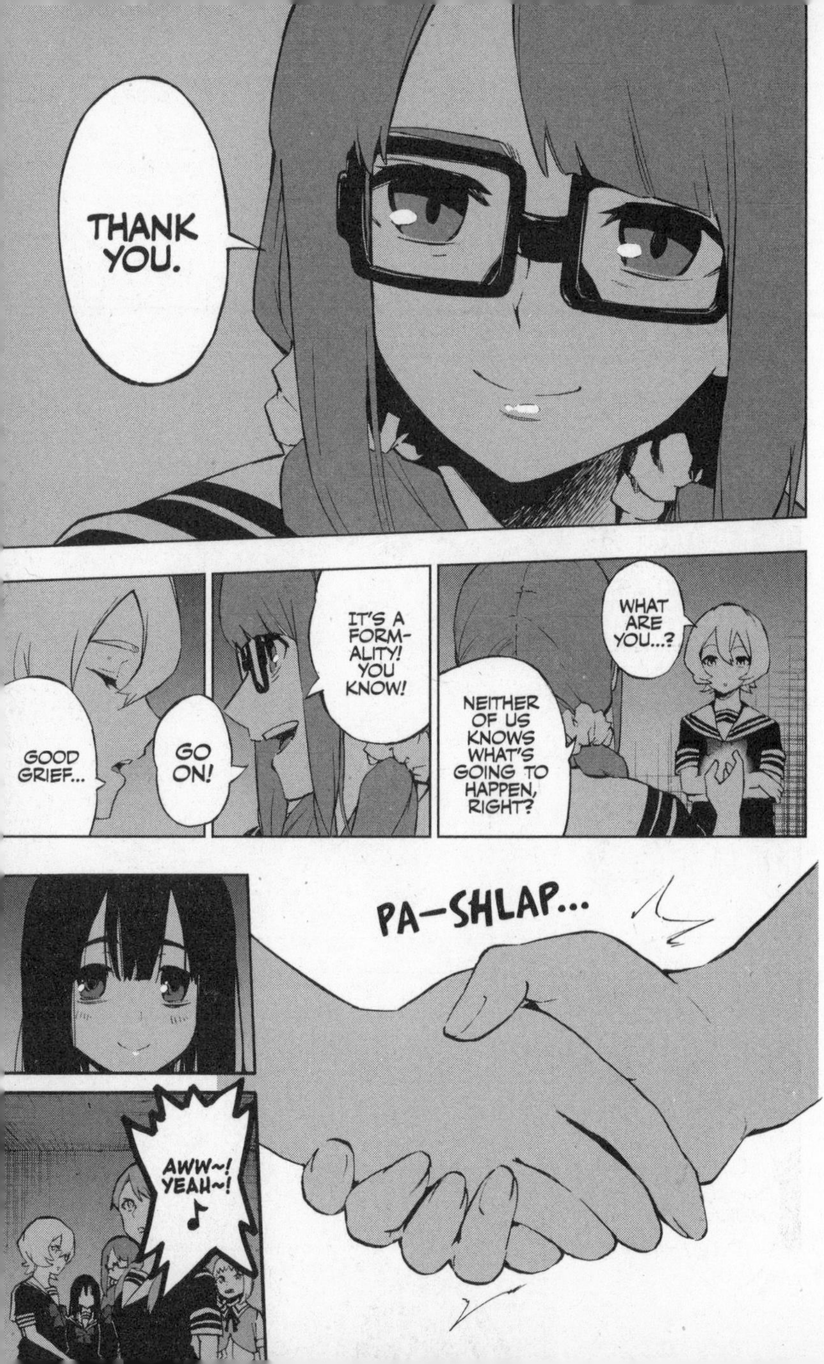
THANK YOU.
WHAT ARE YOU...?
NEITHER OF US KNOWS WHAT'S GOING TO HAPPEN, RIGHT?
IT'S A FORMALITY! YOU KNOW!
GO ON!
GOOD GRIEF...
PA-SHLAP...
AWW~! YEAH~! ♪

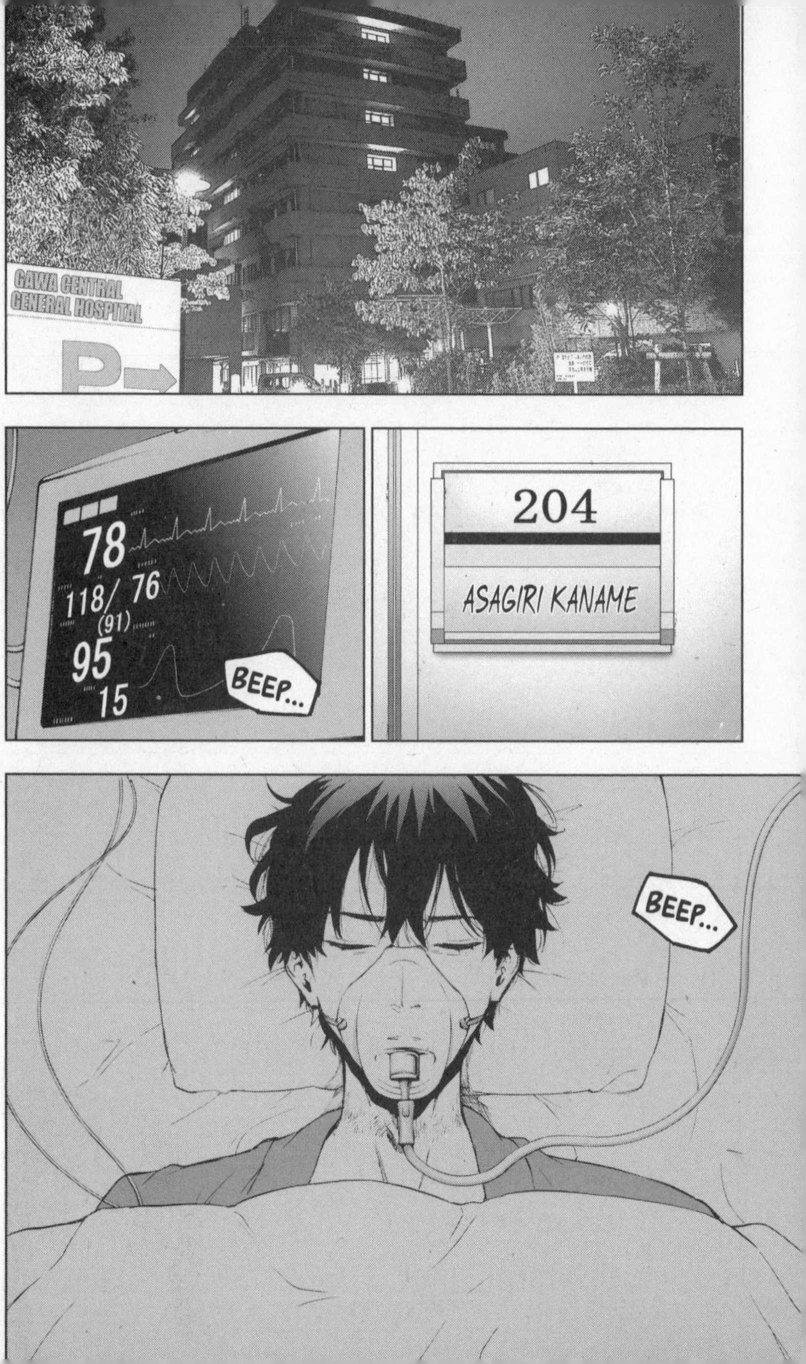
GAWA CENTRAL
GENERAL HOSPITAL
P
204
ASAGIRI KANAME
78
118/ 76
(91)
95
15
BEEP...
BEEP...

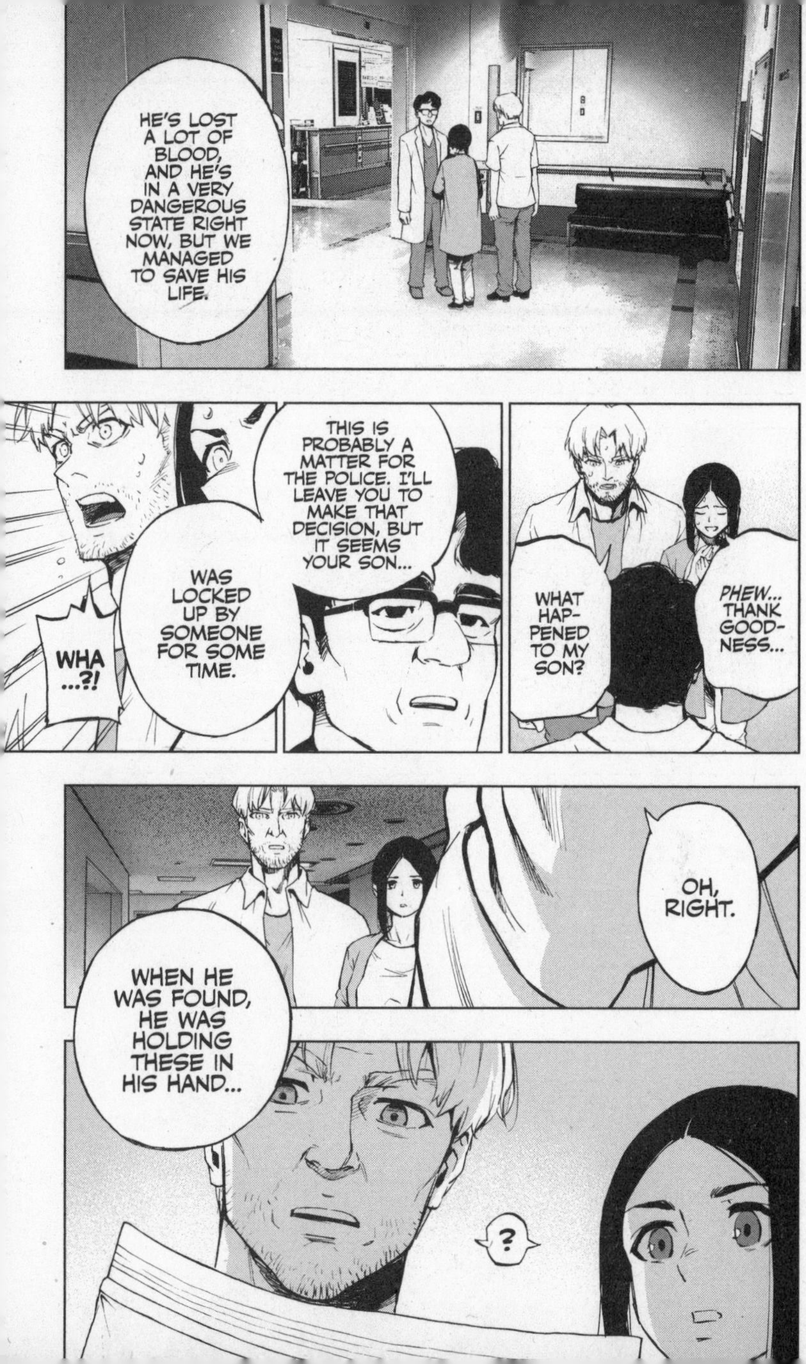
HE'S LOST A LOT OF BLOOD, AND HE'S IN A VERY DANGEROUS STATE RIGHT NOW, BUT WE MANAGED TO SAVE HIS LIFE.
PHEW... THANK GOODNESS...
WHAT HAPPENED TO MY SON?
THIS IS PROBABLY A MATTER FOR THE POLICE. I'LL LEAVE YOU TO MAKE THAT DECISION, BUT IT SEEMS YOUR SON...
WAS LOCKED UP BY SOMEONE FOR SOME TIME.
WHA...?!
OH, RIGHT.
WHEN HE WAS FOUND, HE WAS HOLDING THESE IN HIS HAND...
?

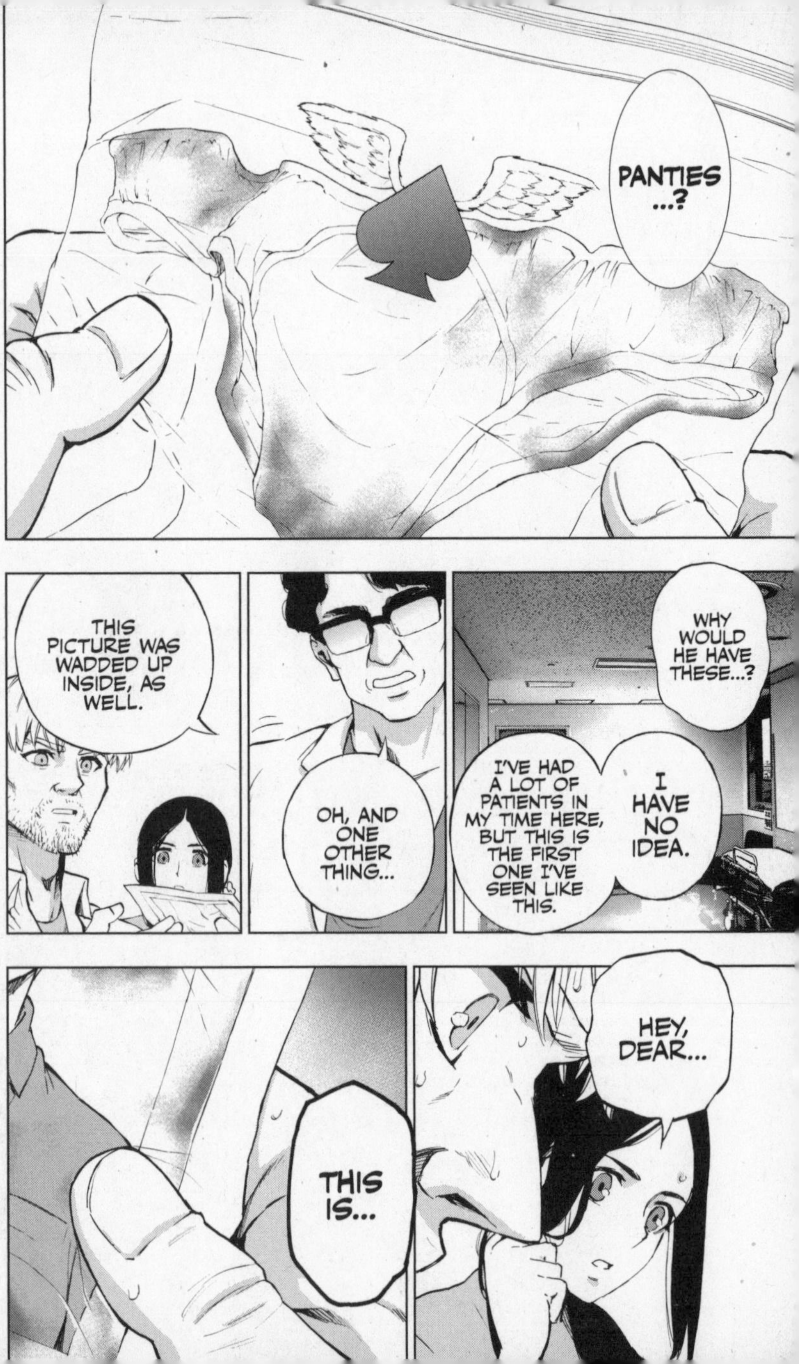
PANTIES ...?
WHY WOULD HE HAVE THESE...?
I HAVE NO IDEA.
I'VE HAD A LOT OF PATIENTS IN MY TIME HERE, BUT THIS IS THE FIRST ONE I'VE SEEN LIKE THIS.
OH, AND ONE OTHER THING...
THIS PICTURE WAS WADDED UP INSIDE, AS WELL.
HEY, DEAR...
THIS IS...

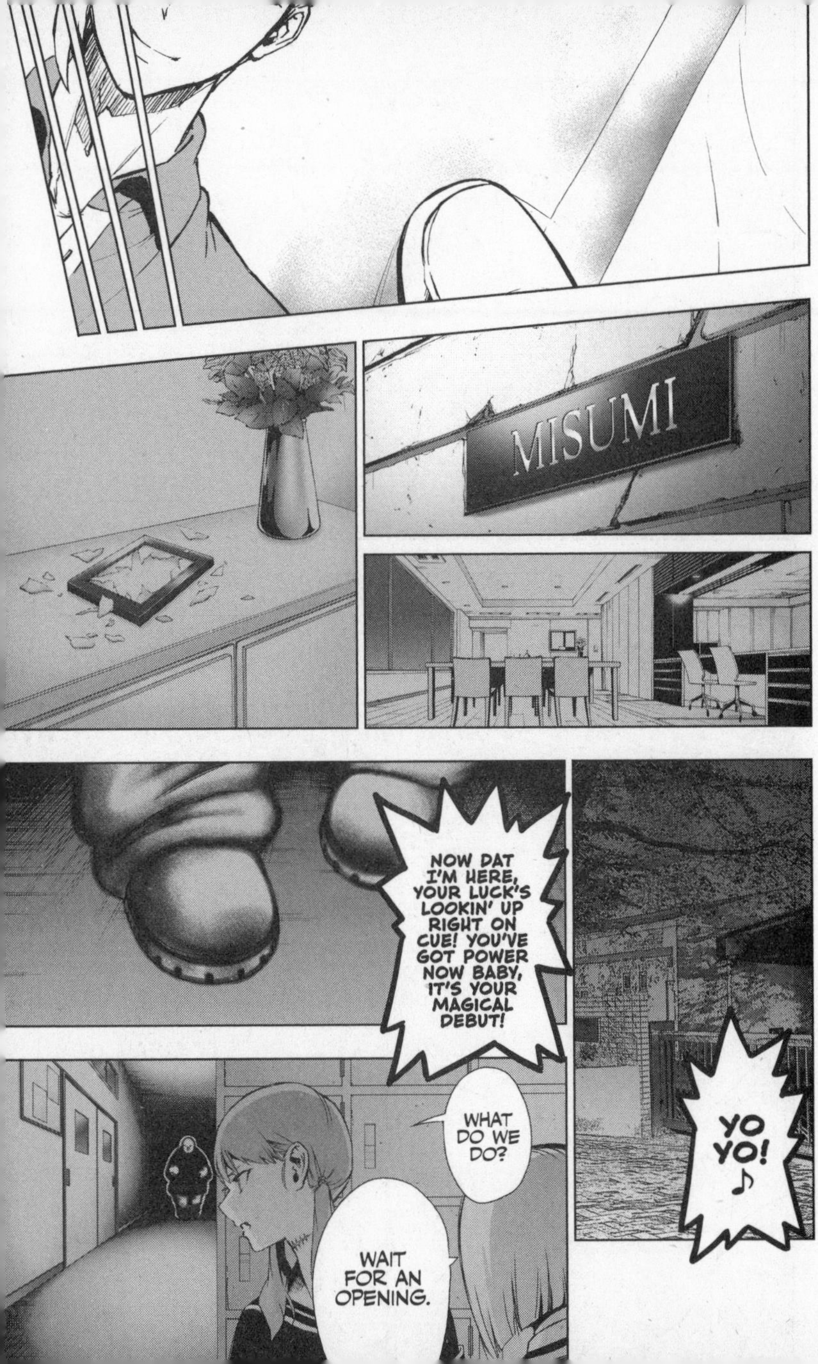
MISUMI
YO YO! ♪
NOW DAT I'M HERE, YOUR LUCK'S LOOKIN' UP RIGHT ON CUE! YOU'VE GOT POWER NOW BABY, IT'S YOUR MAGICAL DEBUT!
WHAT DO WE DO?
WAIT FOR AN OPENING.

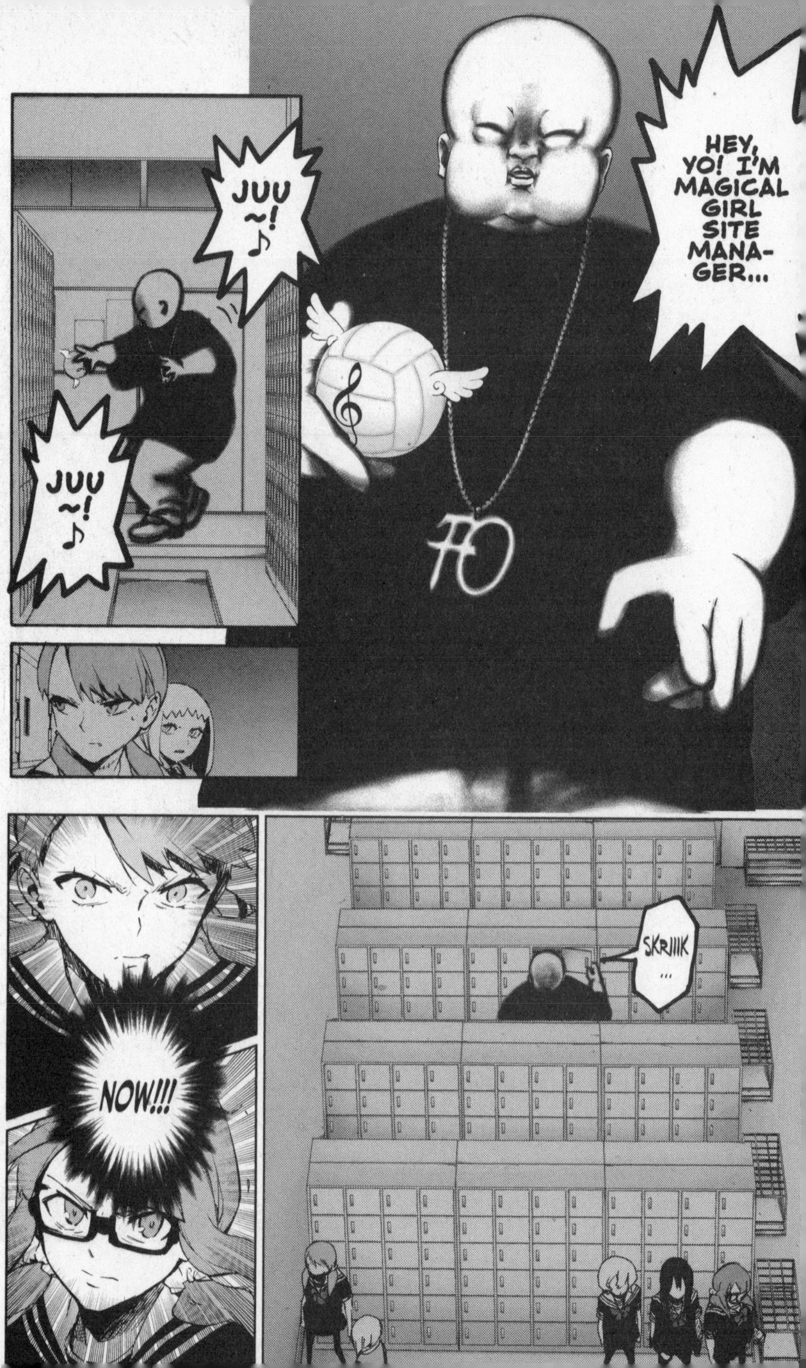
HEY, YO! I'M MAGICAL GIRL SITE MANA-GER...
JUU ~! ♪
JUU ~! ♪
SKRIIK ...
NOW!!!

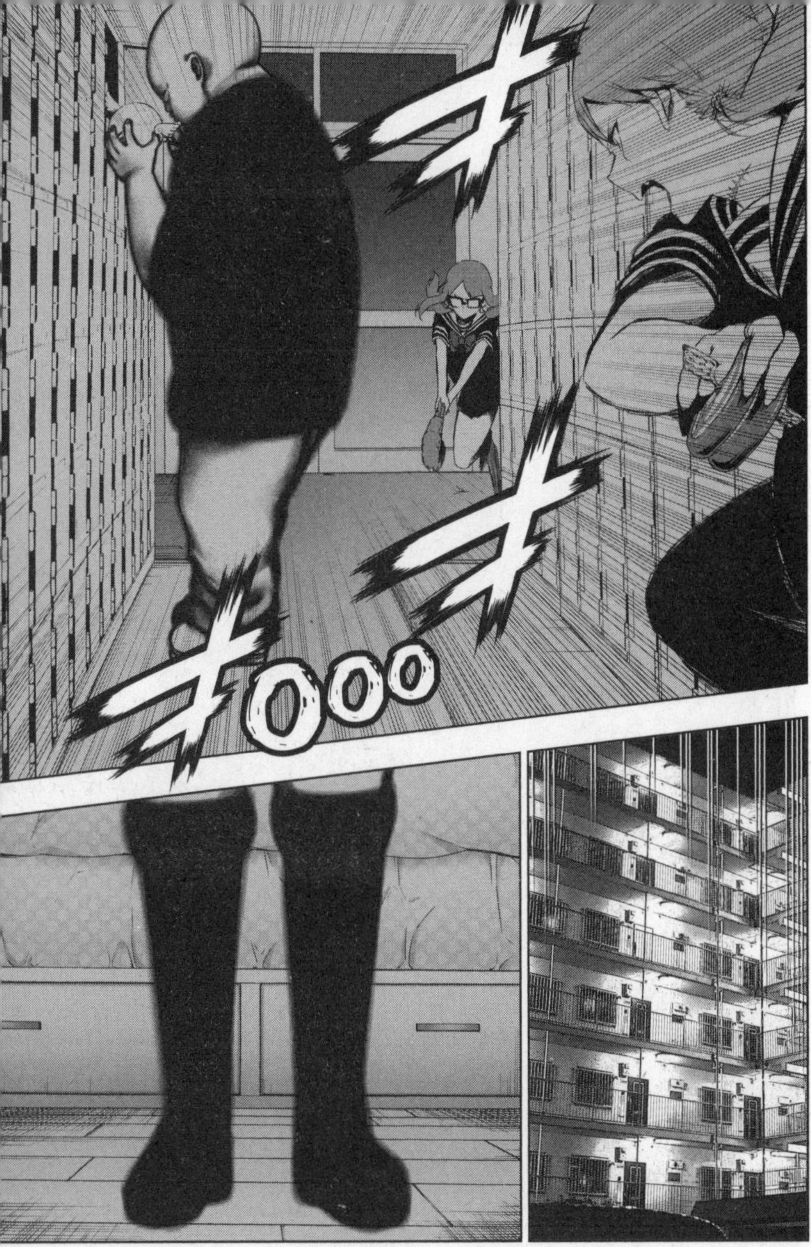

SHUFFLE
POU...

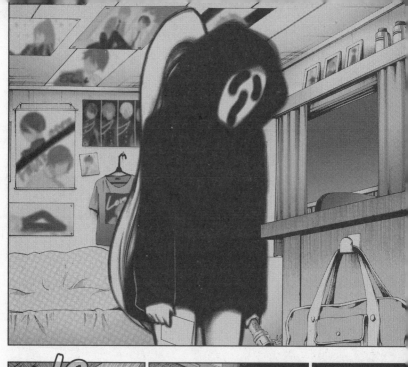

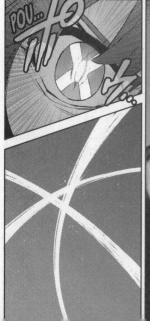

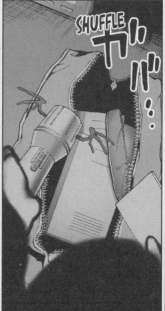

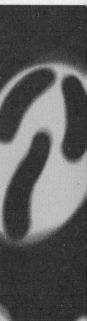

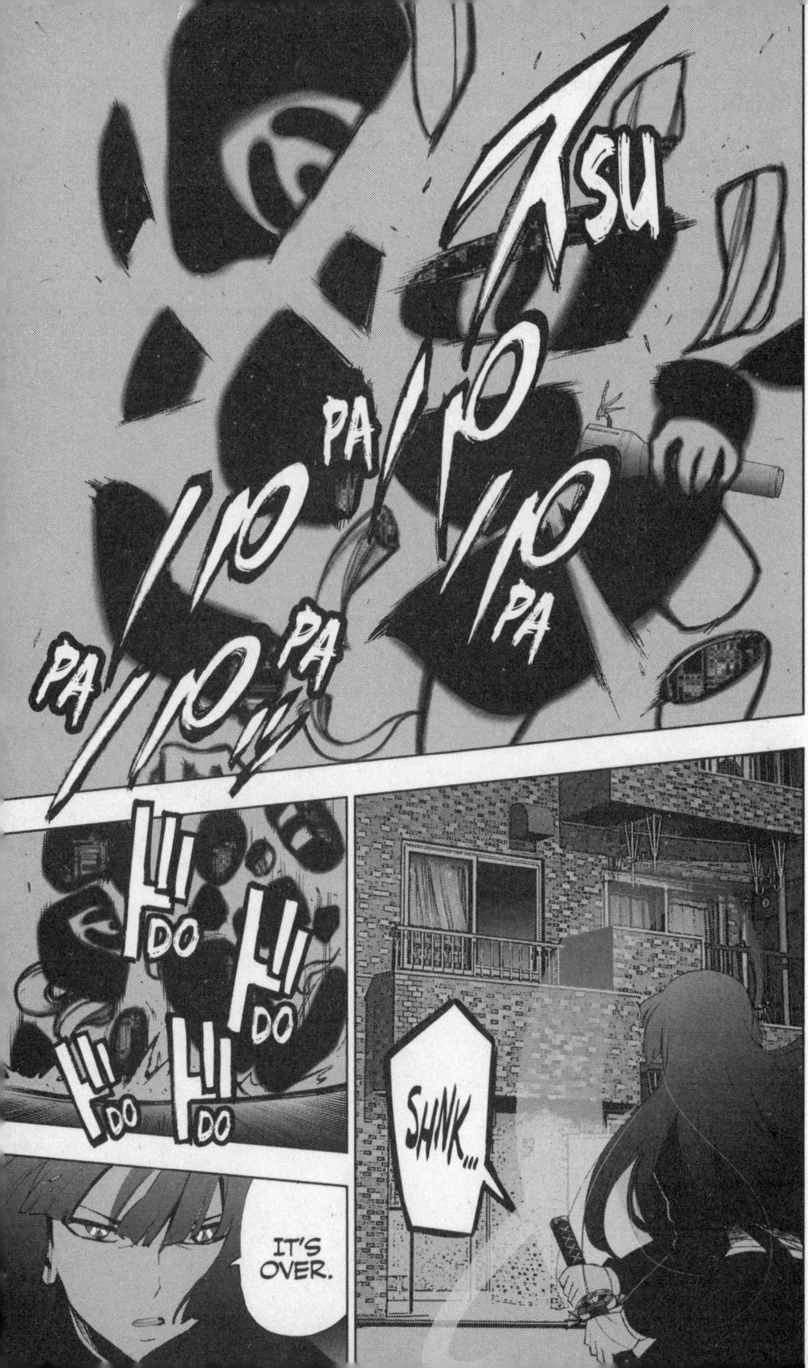
SU
PA
PA
PA
PA
SHINK...
DO
DO
DO
DO
IT'S OVER.

LET'S GRAB THE WAND BEFORE SHE NOTICES.

OKAY.

HYUUUUUUN

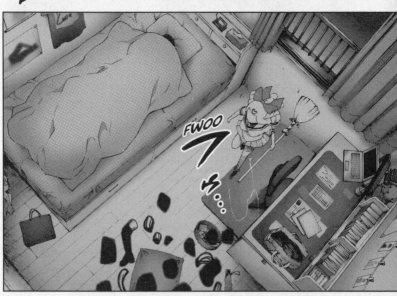

FWOO

HA! I KNEW IT...

SHWUP

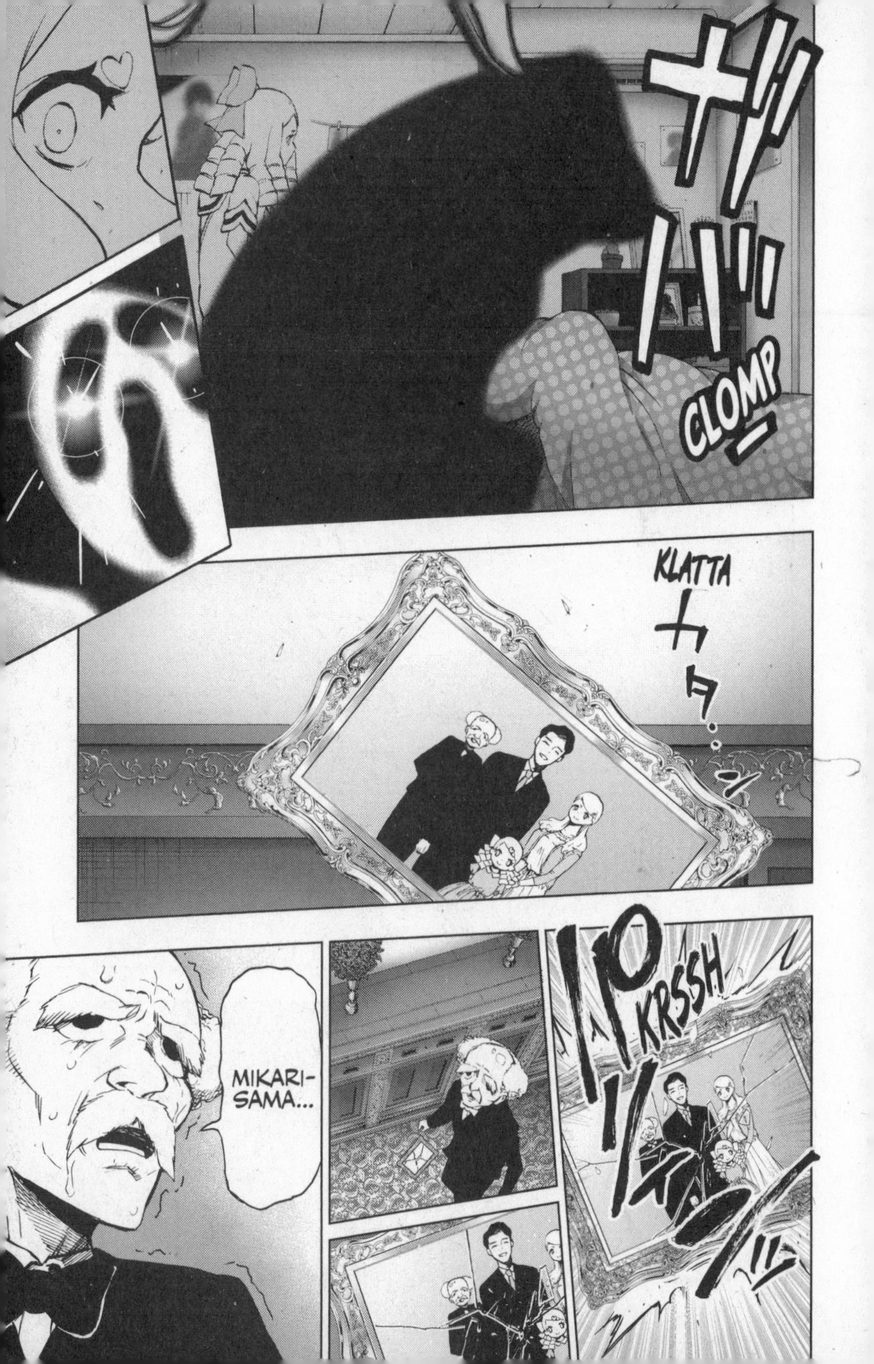
CLOMP
KLATTA
KRSSH
MIKARI-SAMA...

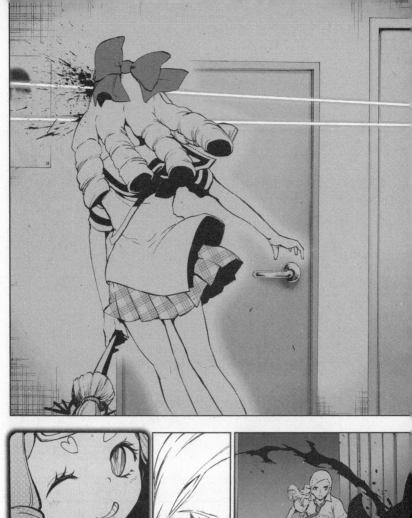

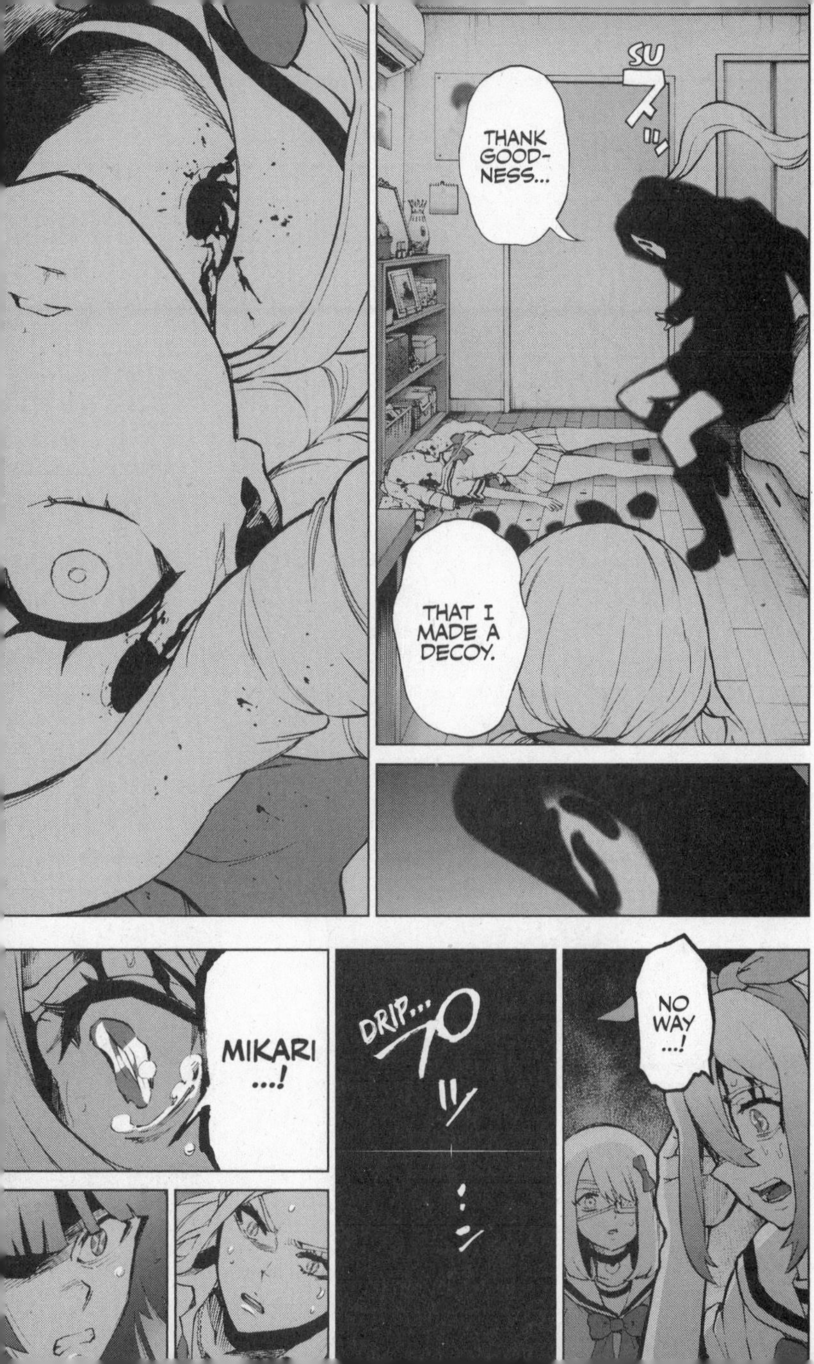
SU
THANK GOODNESS...
THAT I MADE A DECOY.
NO WAY ...!
DRIP...
MIKARI ...!

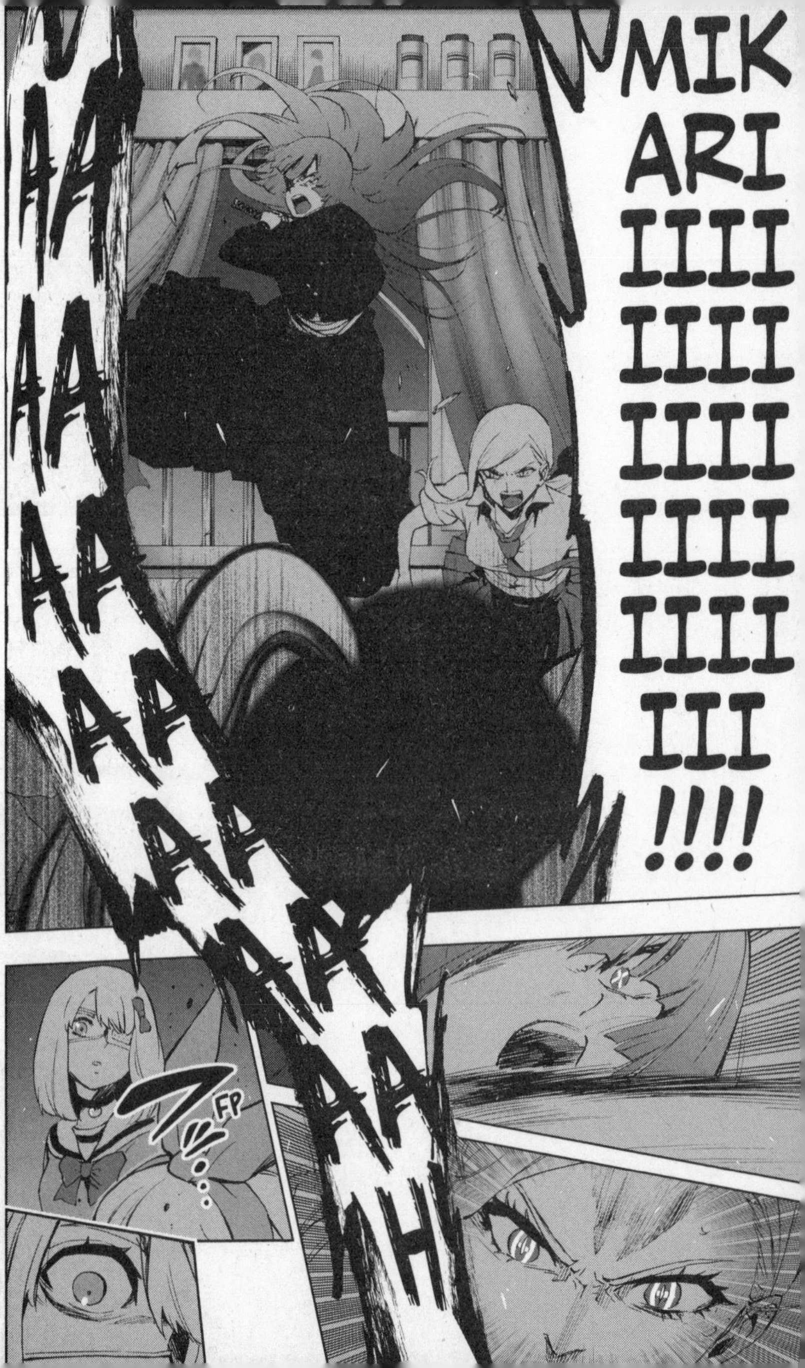
MIKARIIIIIIIIIIIIIIIIIIIII!!!!
AAAAAAAAAAAAAAAAAAAAH!
FP

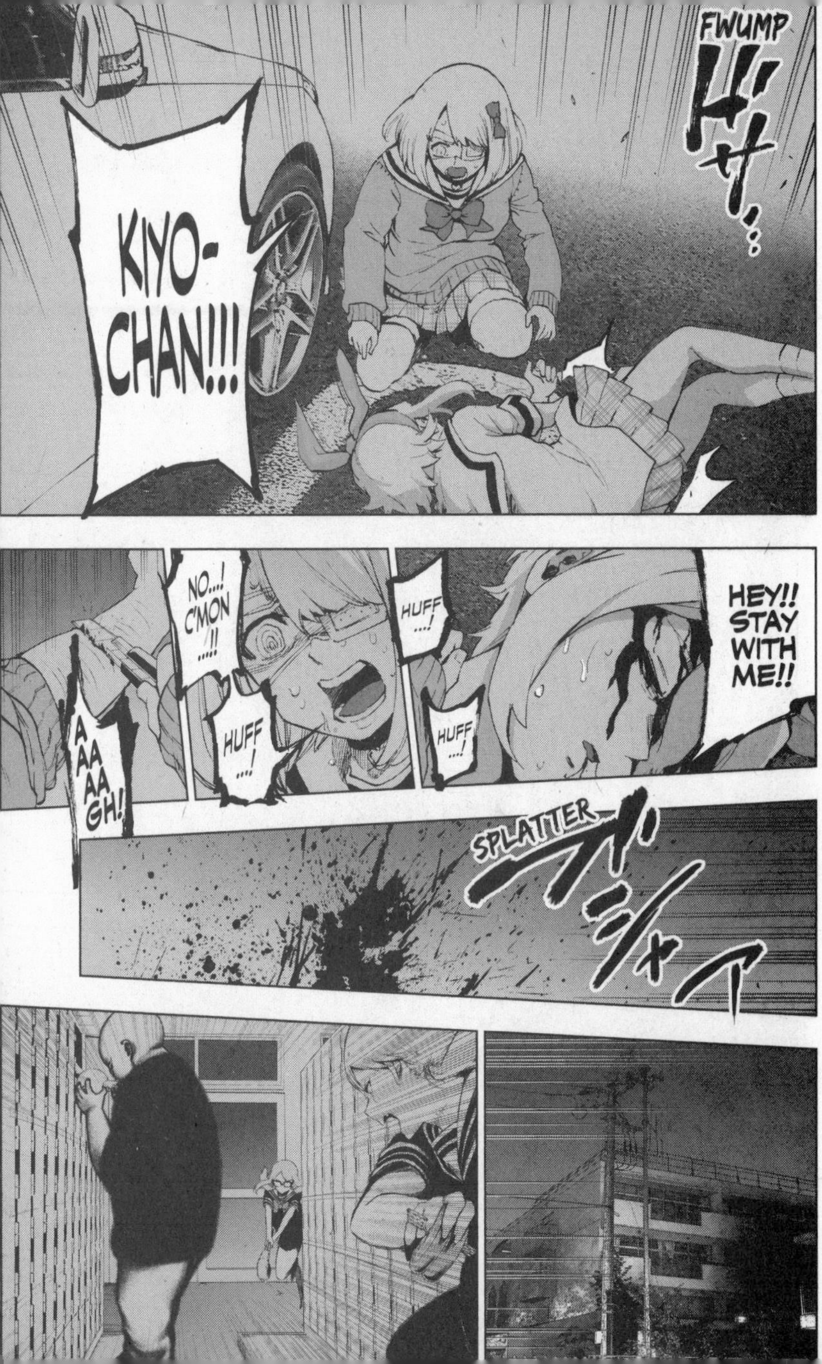
FWUMP
KIYO-CHAN!!!
HEY!! STAY WITH ME!!
HUFF...!
HUFF...!
NO...! C'MON...!!
HUFF...!
AAAAAGH!
SPLATTER

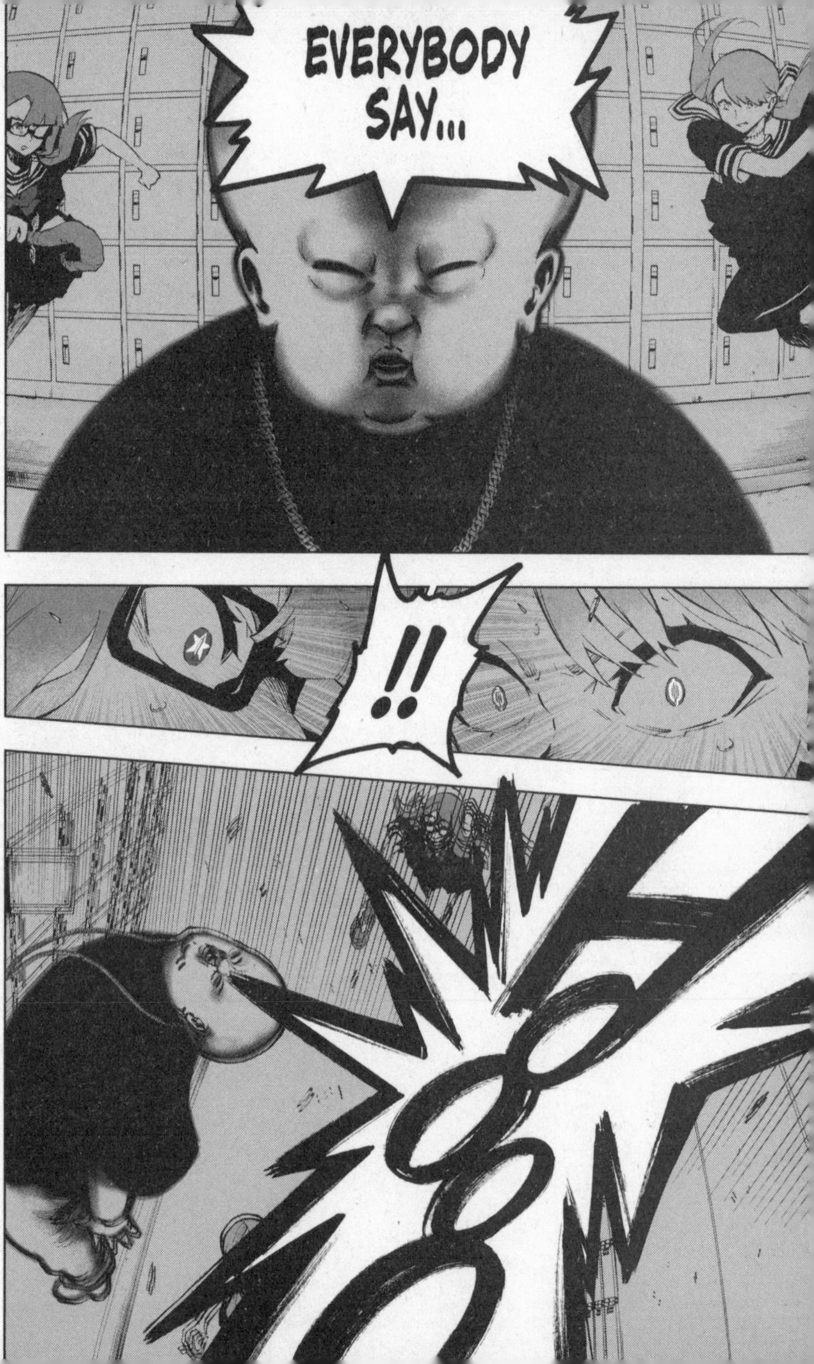
EVERYBODY SAY...
!!

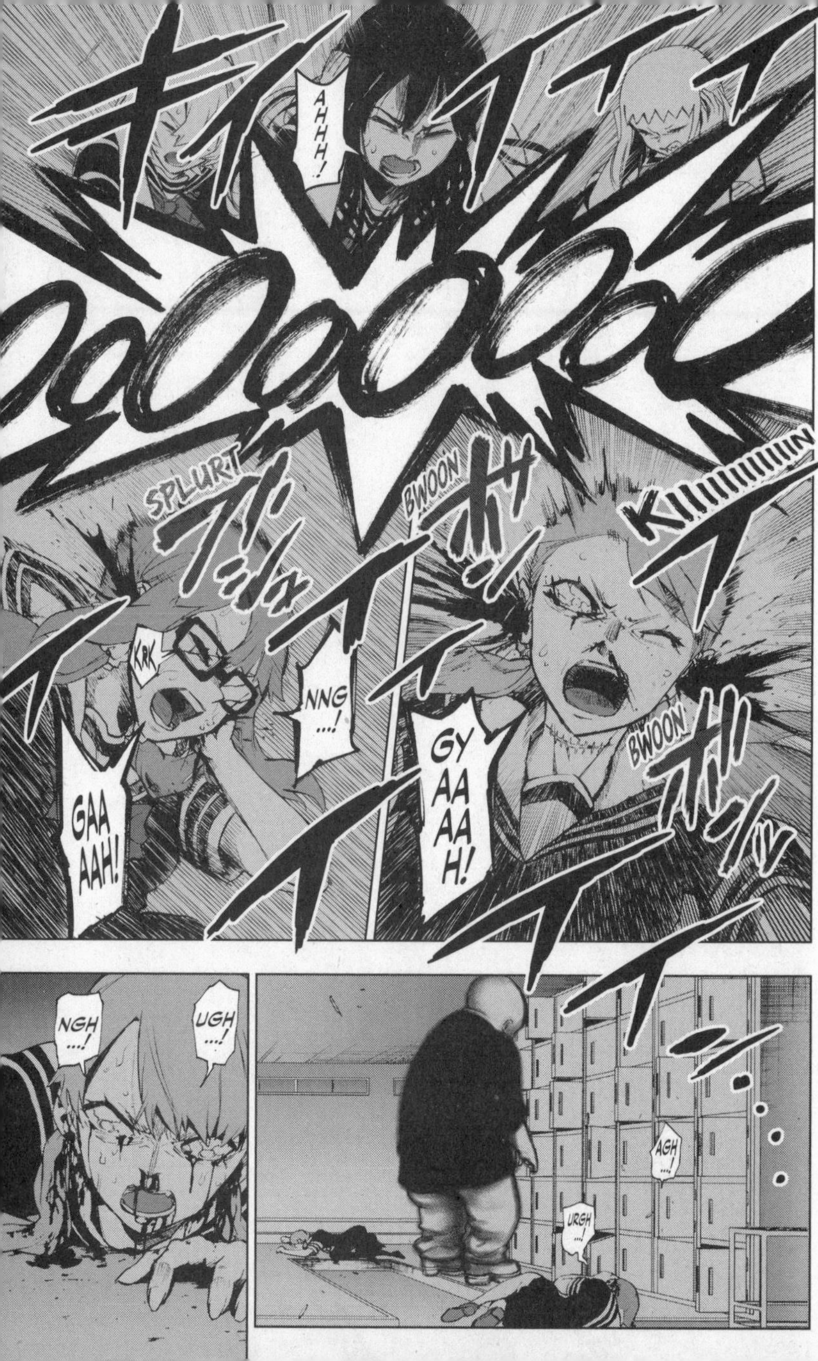
AHHH!
KIIIIIIIIIIN
BWOON
GY AA AA AA H!
BWOON
SPLURT
KRK
NNG ...!
GAA AAH!
AGH ...!
URGH ...!
UGH ...!
NGH ...!

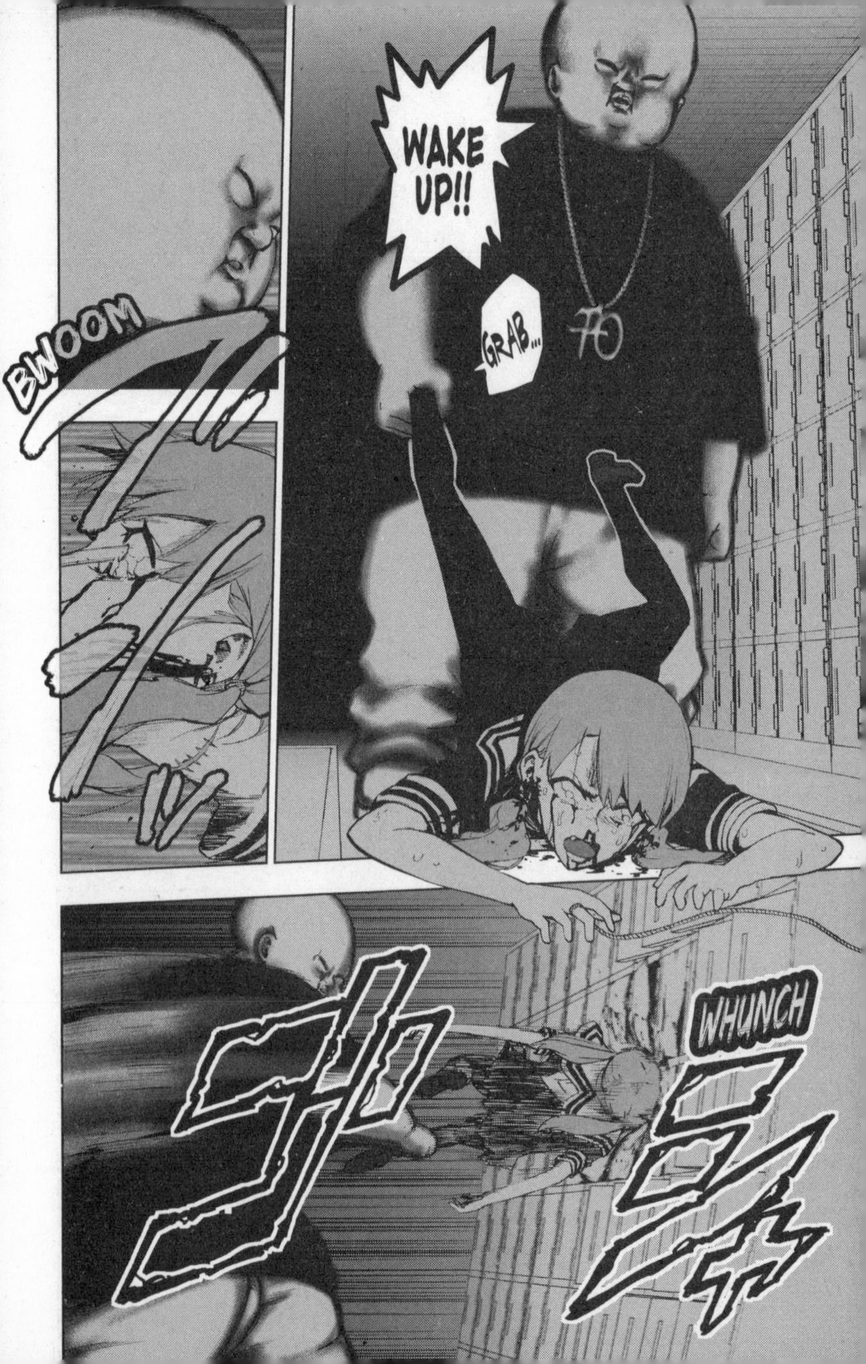
WAKE UP!!
GRAB...
BWOOM
WHUNCH

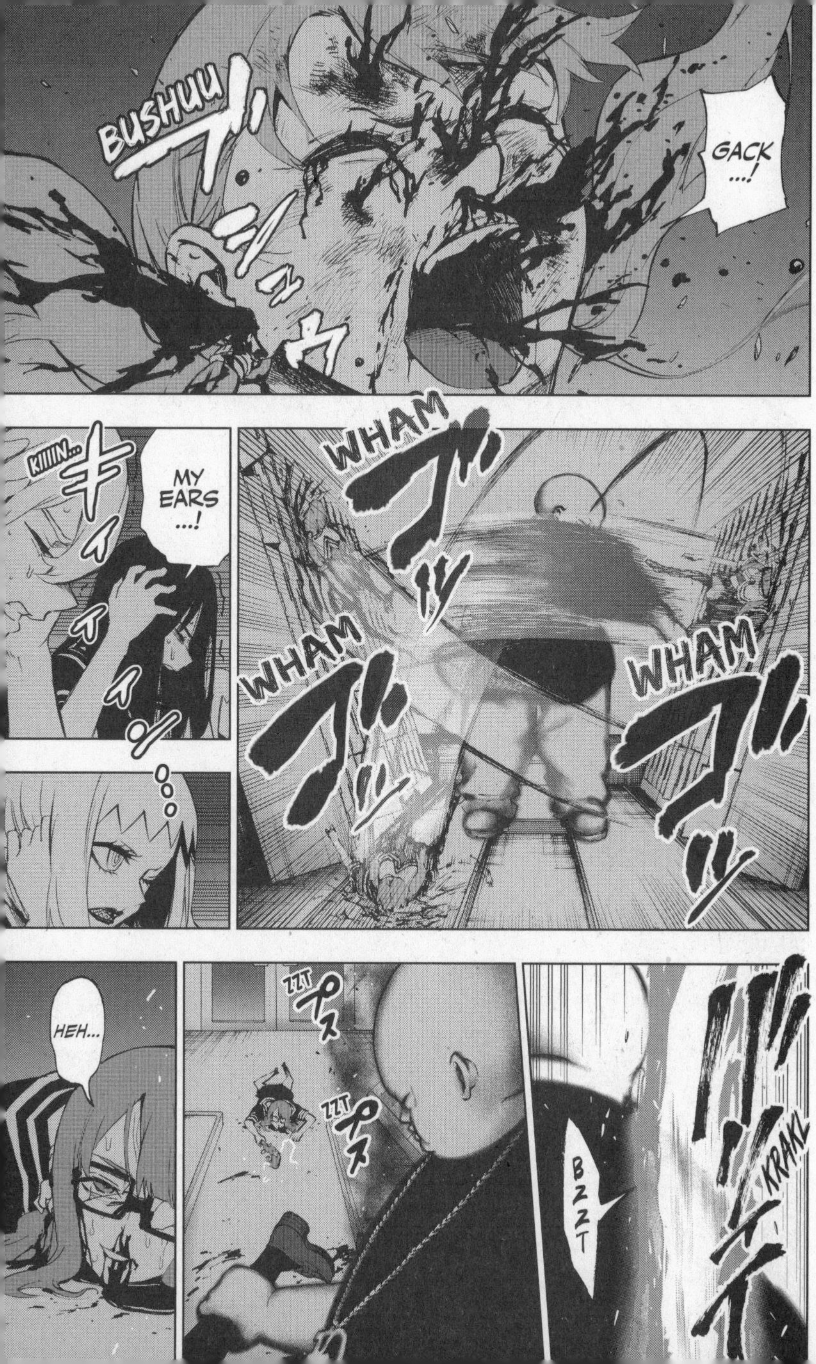
GACK ...!
BUSHUU
WHAM
WHAM
WHAM
MY EARS ...!
KIIIIN...
...
KRAKL
BZZT
ZZT
ZZT
HEH...

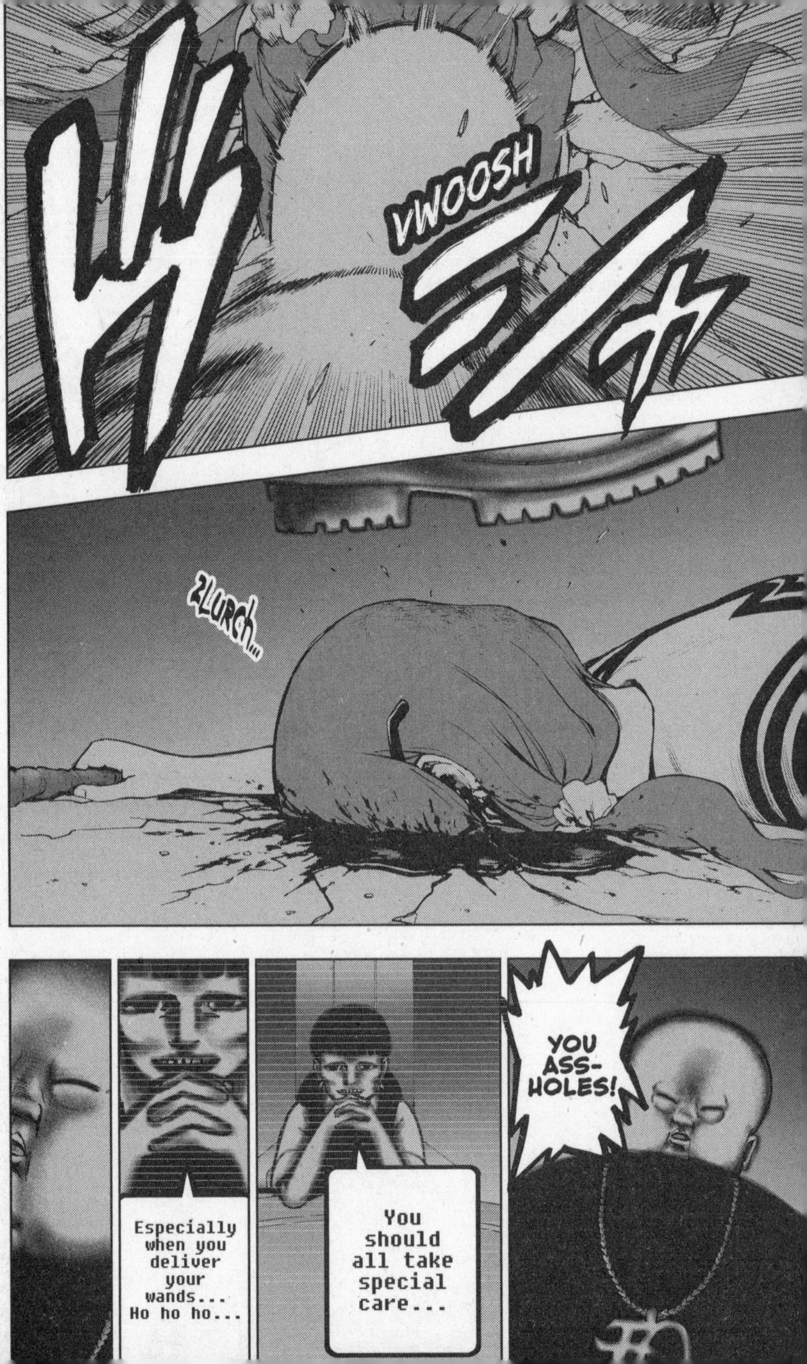
VWOOSH
ZLURCH...
YOU ASS-HOLES!
You should all take special care...
Especially when you deliver your wands... Ho ho ho...

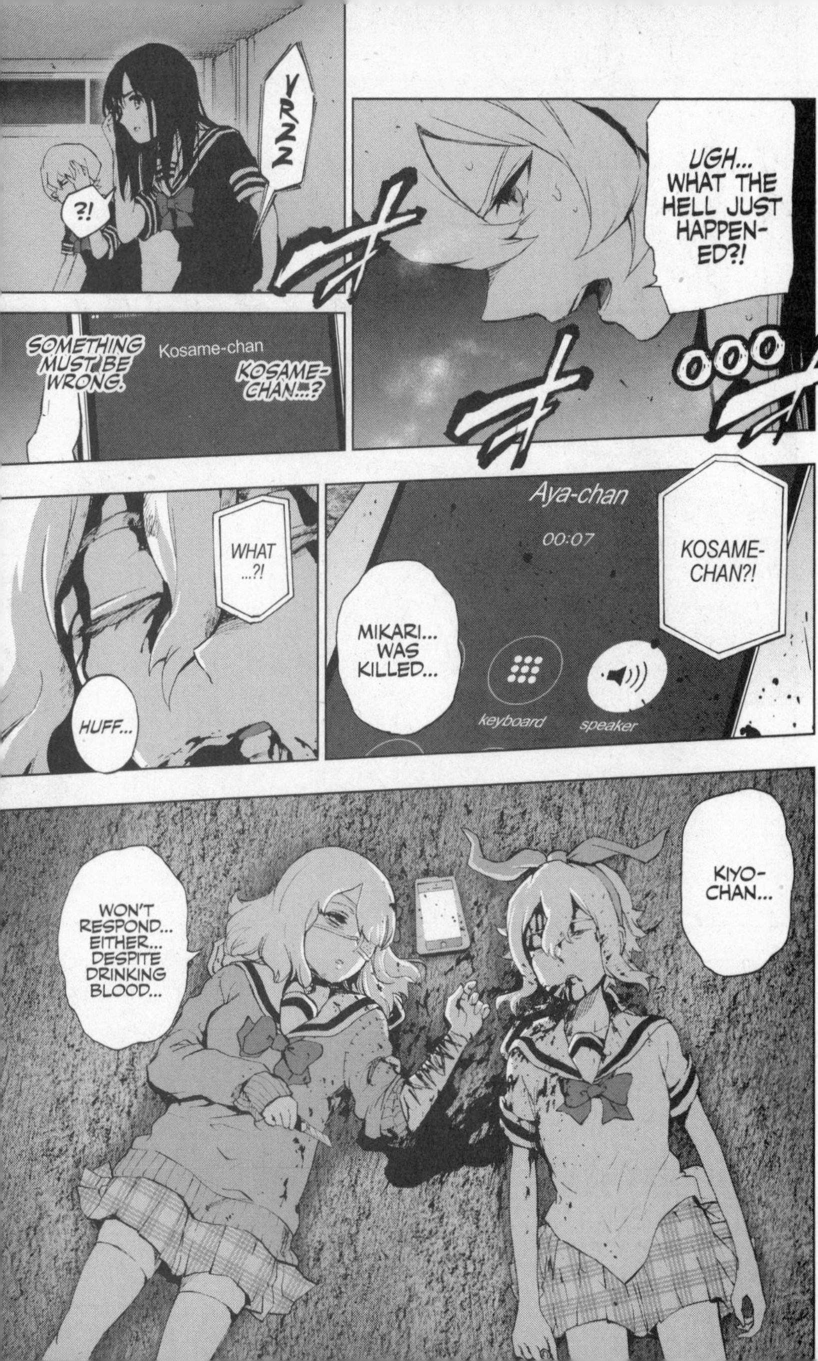
UGH... WHAT THE HELL JUST HAPPENED?!
OOO
VRZZ
?!
KOSAME-CHAN...?
Kosame-chan
SOMETHING MUST BE WRONG.
Aya-chan
00:07
KOSAME-CHAN?!
MIKARI... WAS KILLED...
keyboard
speaker
WHAT ...?!
HUFF...
KIYO-CHAN...
WON'T RESPOND... EITHER... DESPITE DRINKING BLOOD...

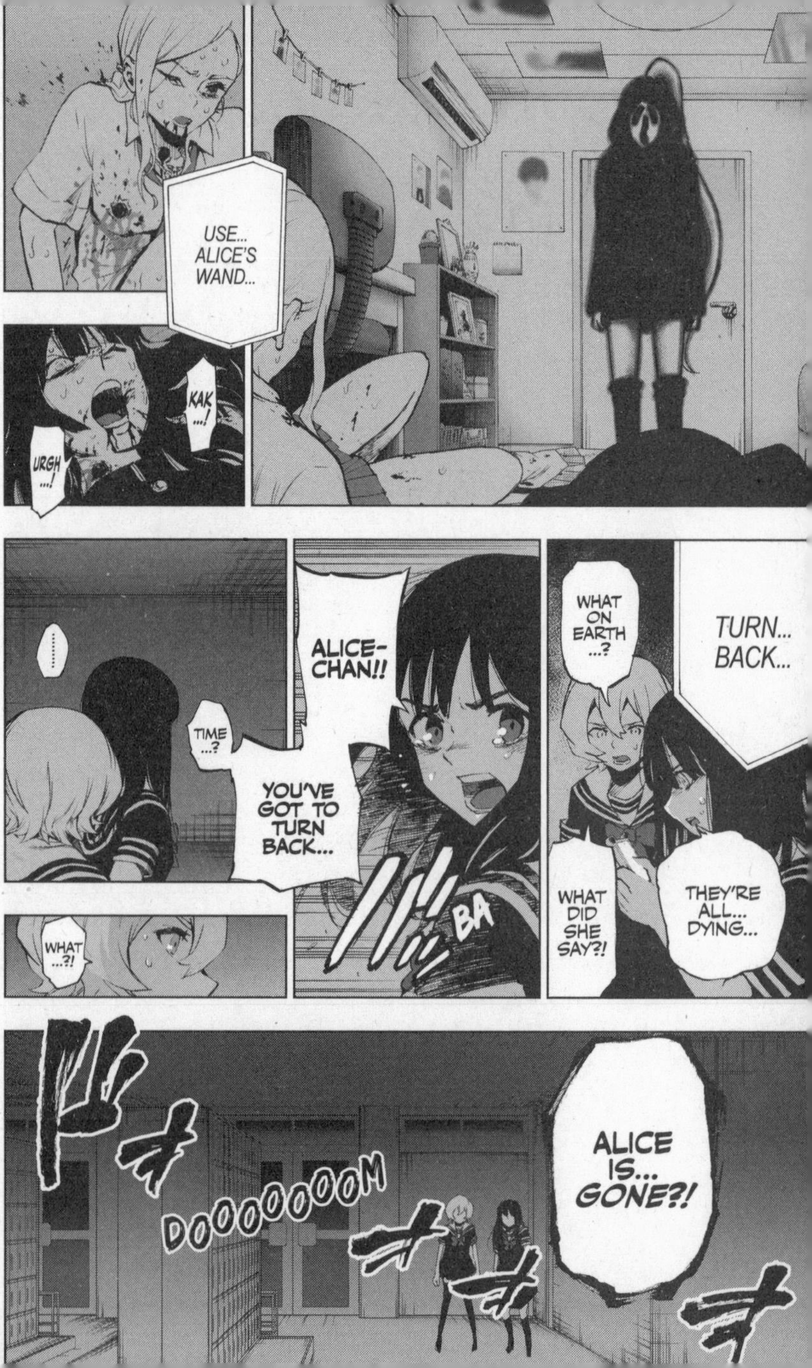
USE... ALICE'S WAND...
KAK ...!
URGH ...!
TURN... BACK...
WHAT ON EARTH ...?
THEY'RE ALL... DYING...
WHAT DID SHE SAY?!
ALICE-CHAN!!
YOU'VE GOT TO TURN BACK...
BA
......
TIME ...?
WHAT ...?!
ALICE IS... GONE?!
DOOOOOOOOM

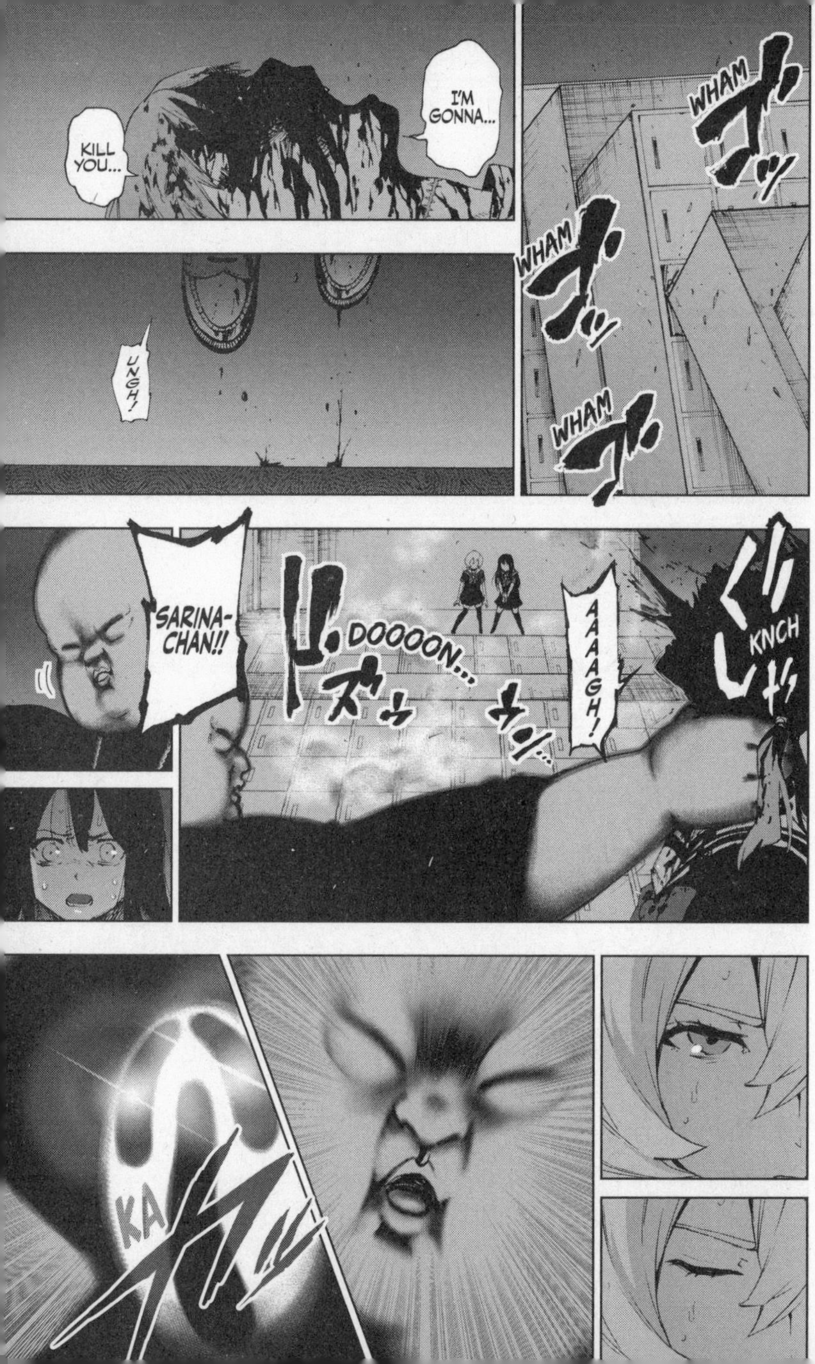
WHAM
WHAM
WHAM
I'M GONNA...
KILL YOU...
UNGH!
KNCH
AAAAGH!
DOOOOON...
SARINA-CHAN!!
KA

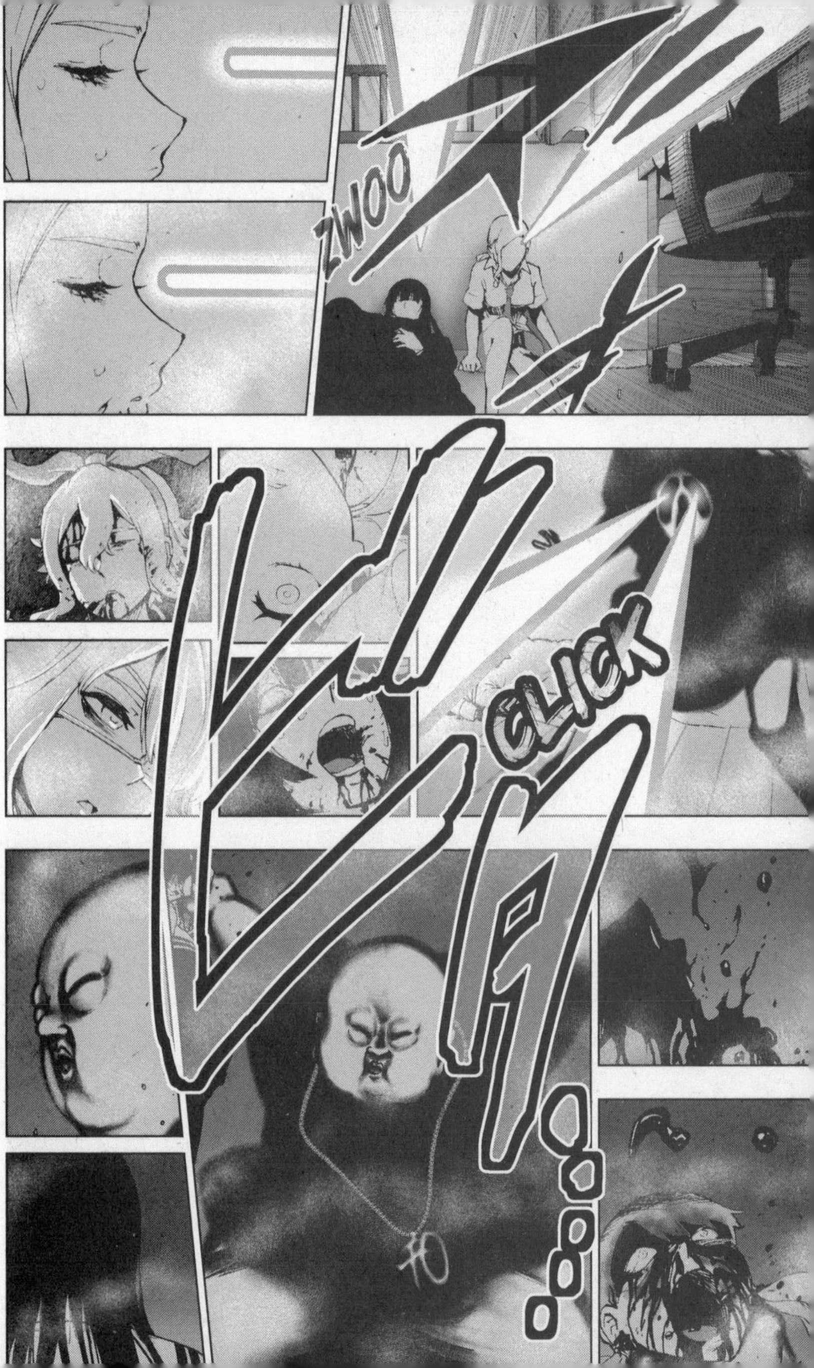
ZWOO
CLICK

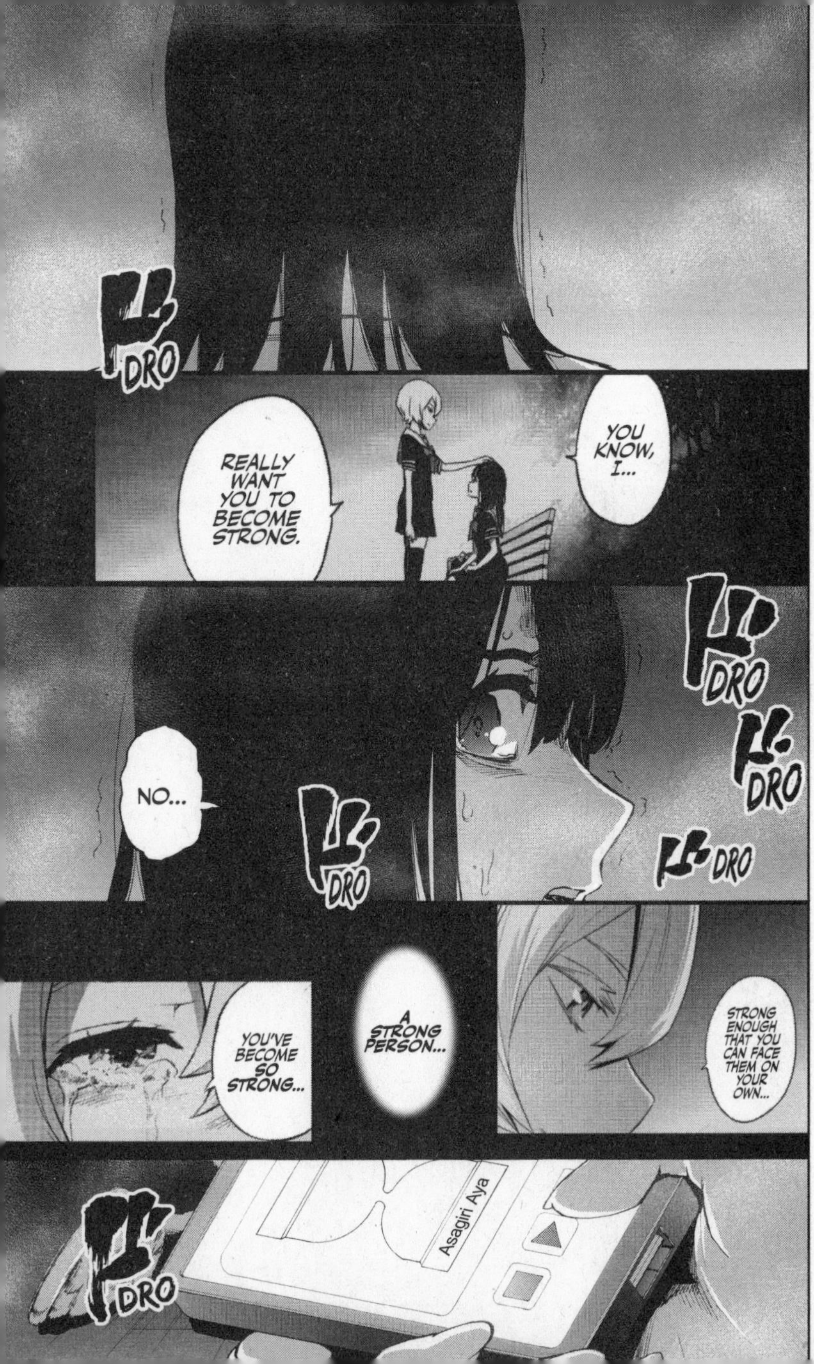
DRO
YOU KNOW, I...
REALLY WANT YOU TO BECOME STRONG.
DRO
DRO
DRO
DRO
NO...
STRONG ENOUGH THAT YOU CAN FACE THEM ON YOUR OWN...
A STRONG PERSON...
YOU'VE BECOME SO STRONG...
Asagiri Aya
DRO

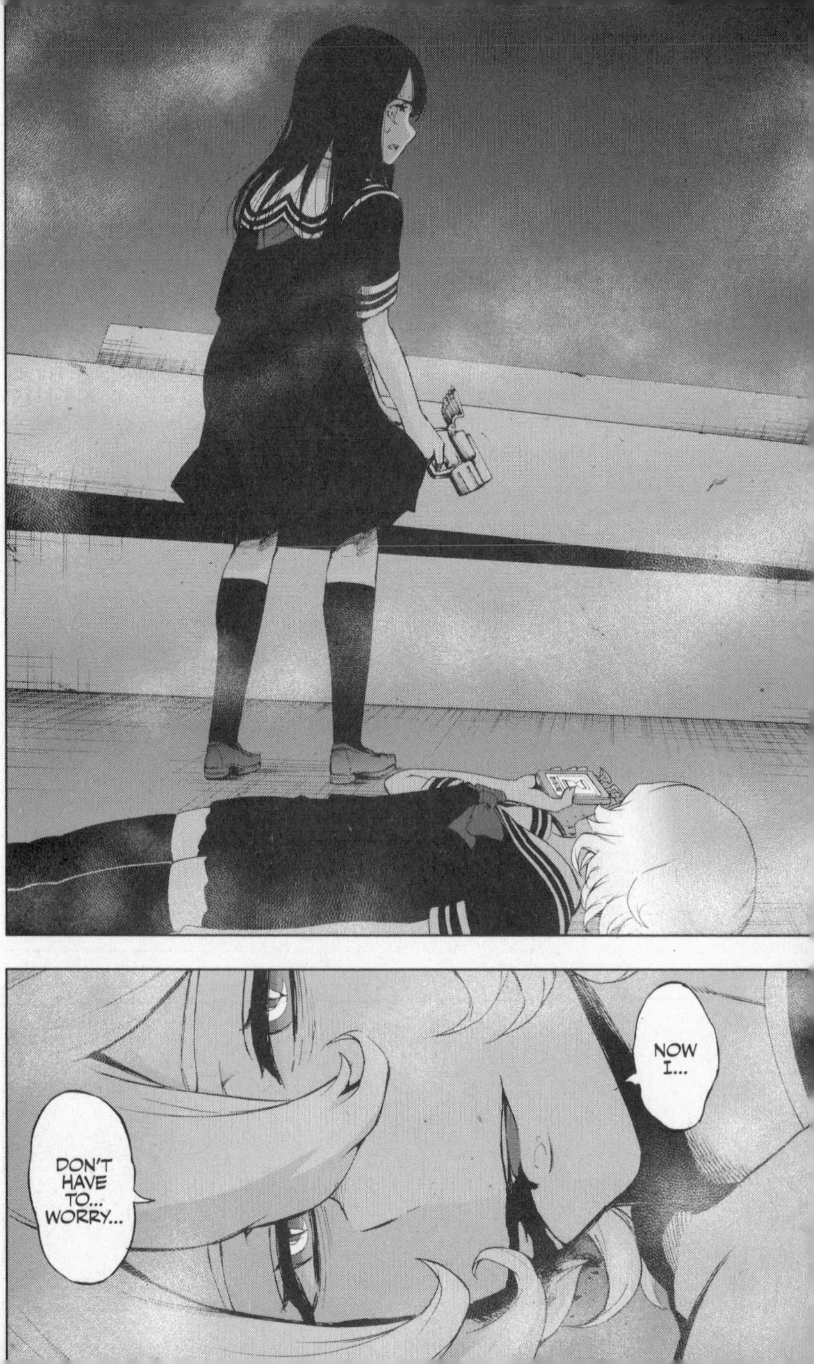
NOW I...
DON'T HAVE TO... WORRY...

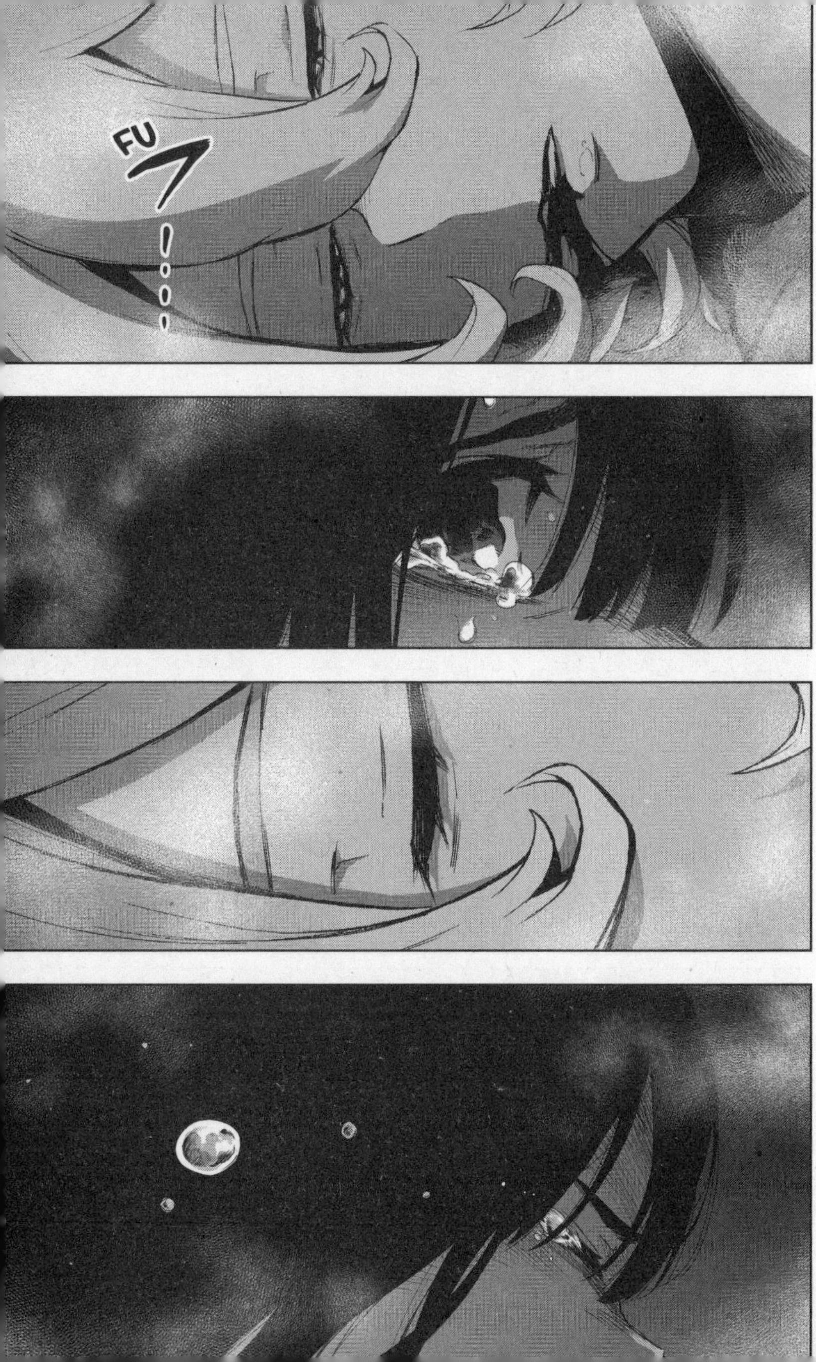
FU ヘ !...

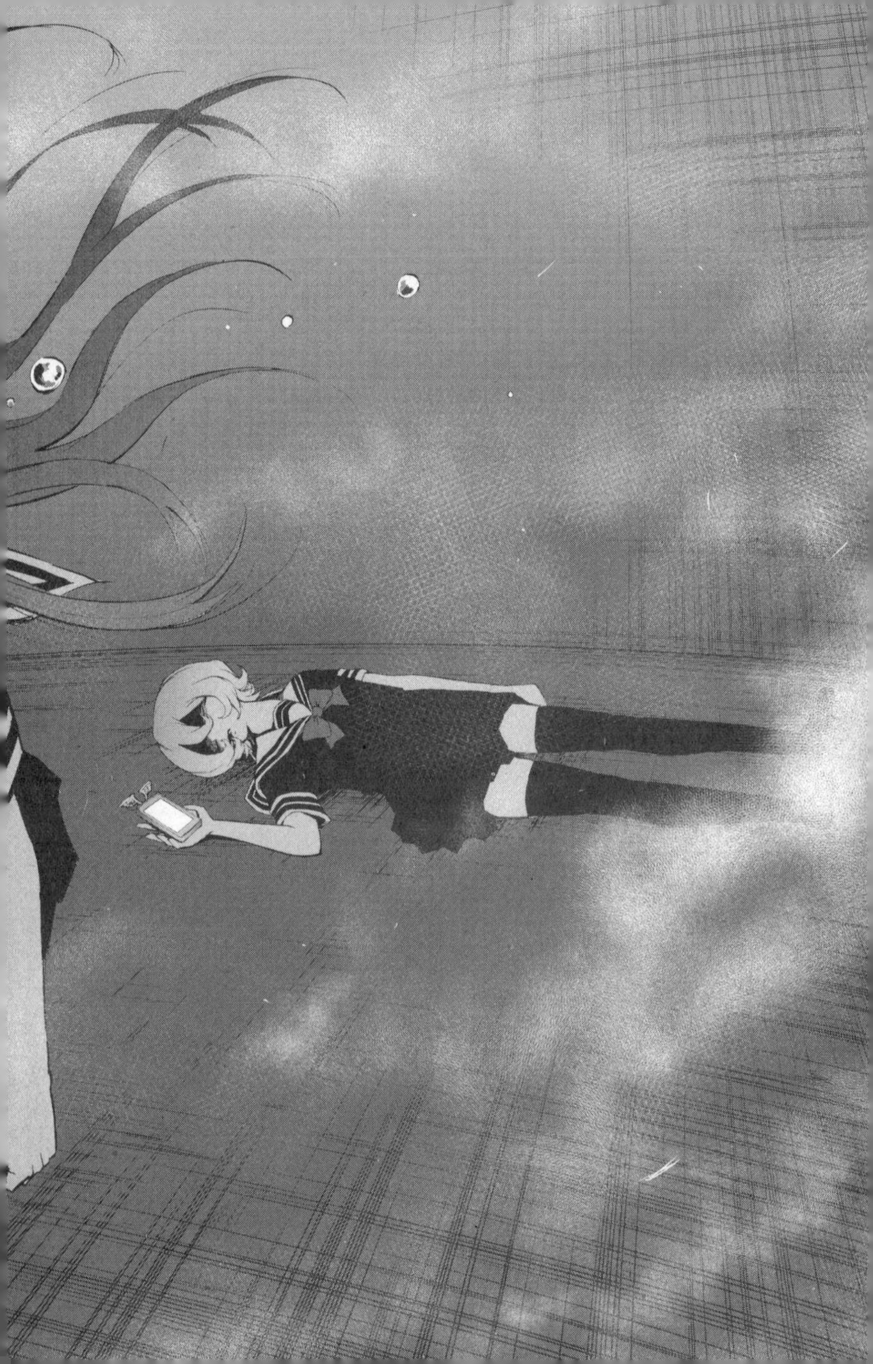

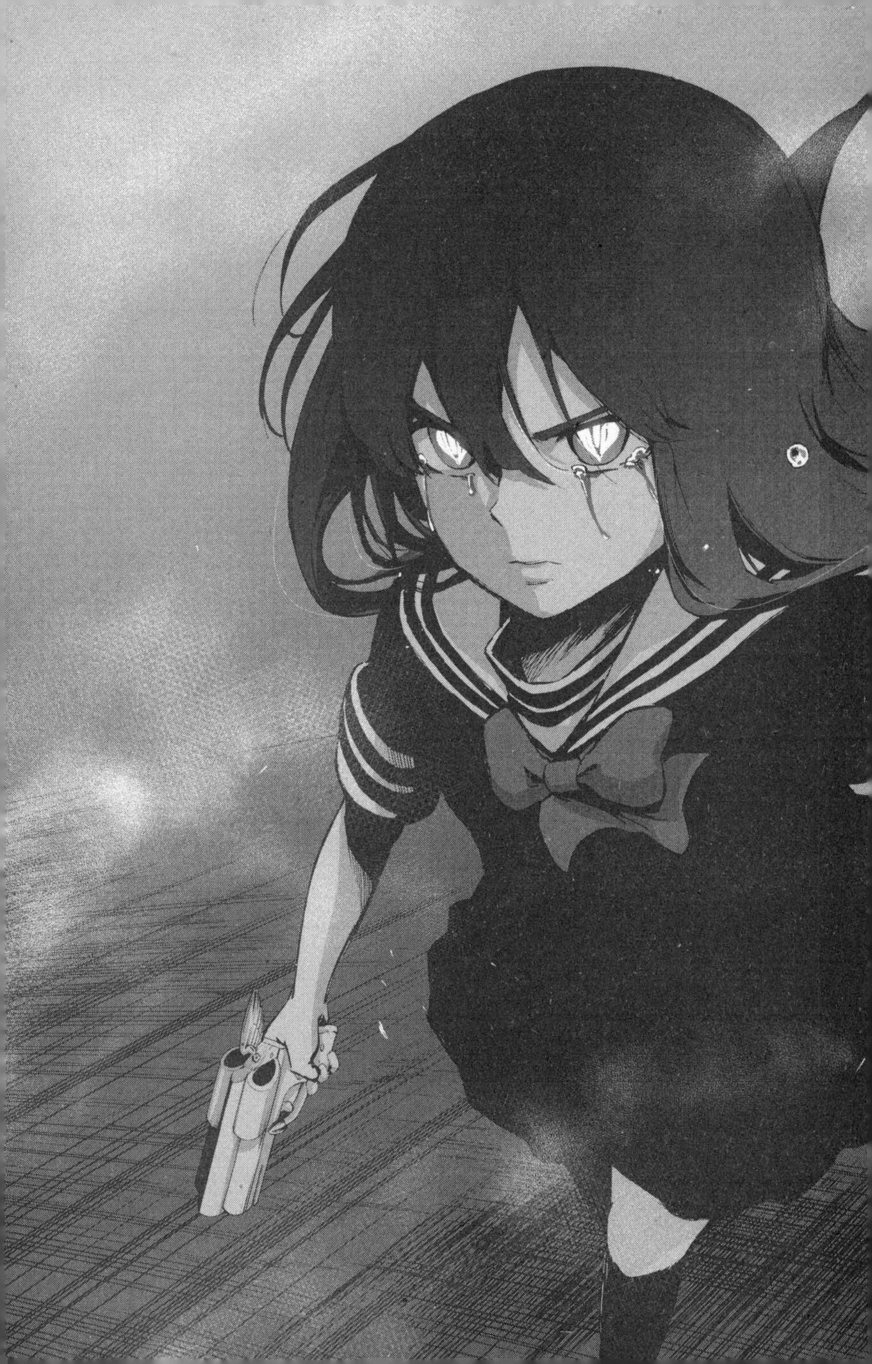

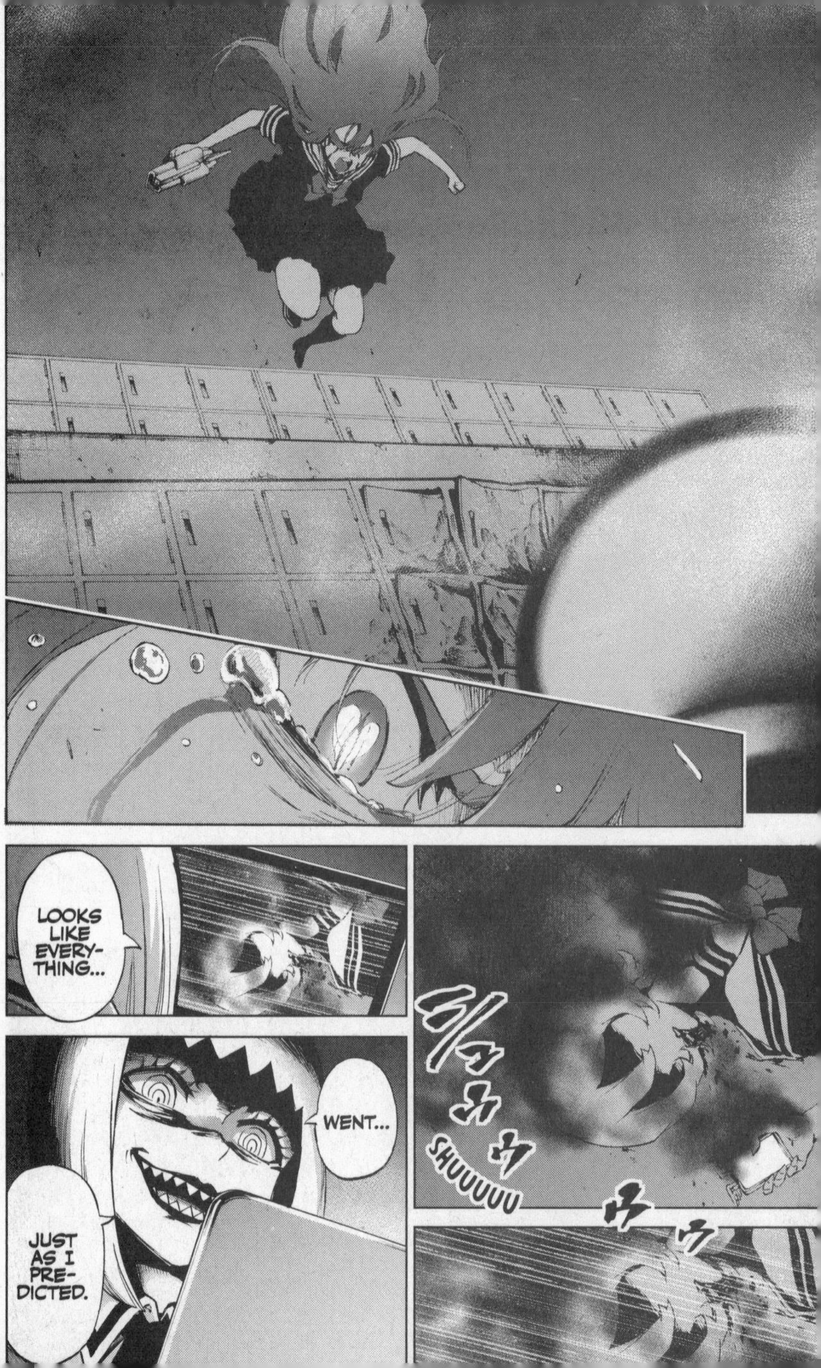
SHUUUUU
LOOKS LIKE EVERY-THING...
WENT...
JUST AS I PRE-DICTED.

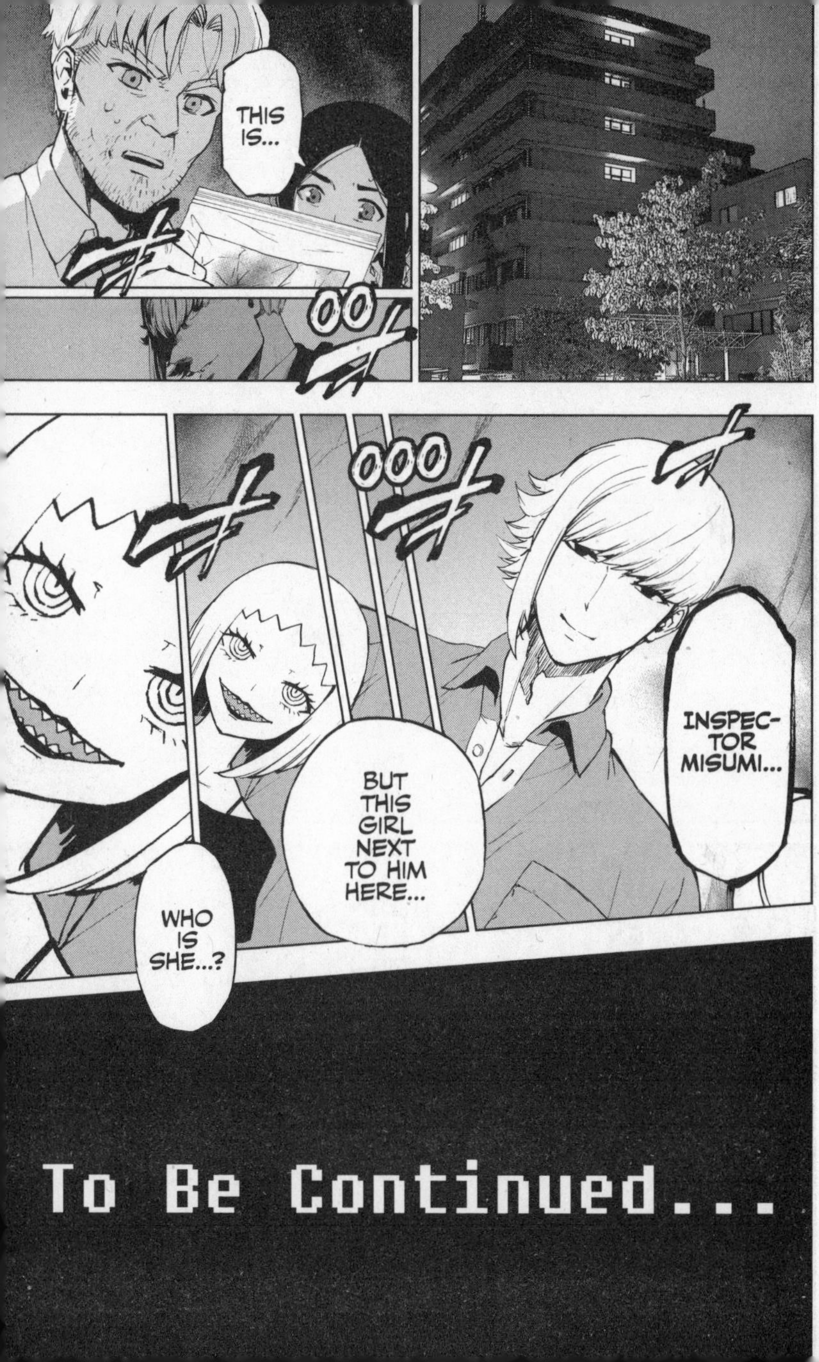
THIS IS...
INSPECTOR MISUMI...
BUT THIS GIRL NEXT TO HIM HERE...
WHO IS SHE...?
To Be Continued...

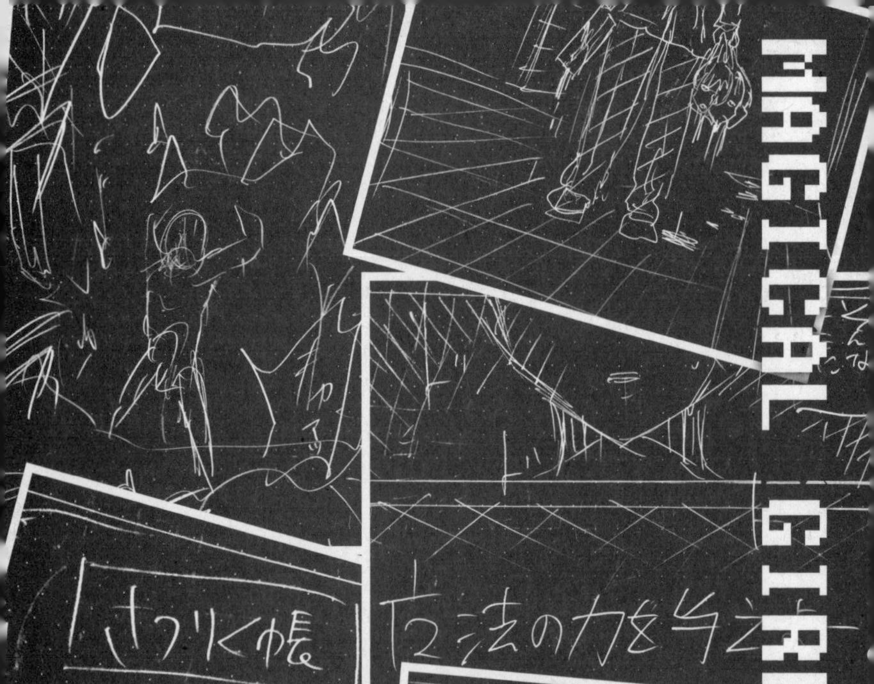
MAGICAL GIRL SITE
Volume 9
COMING SOON!

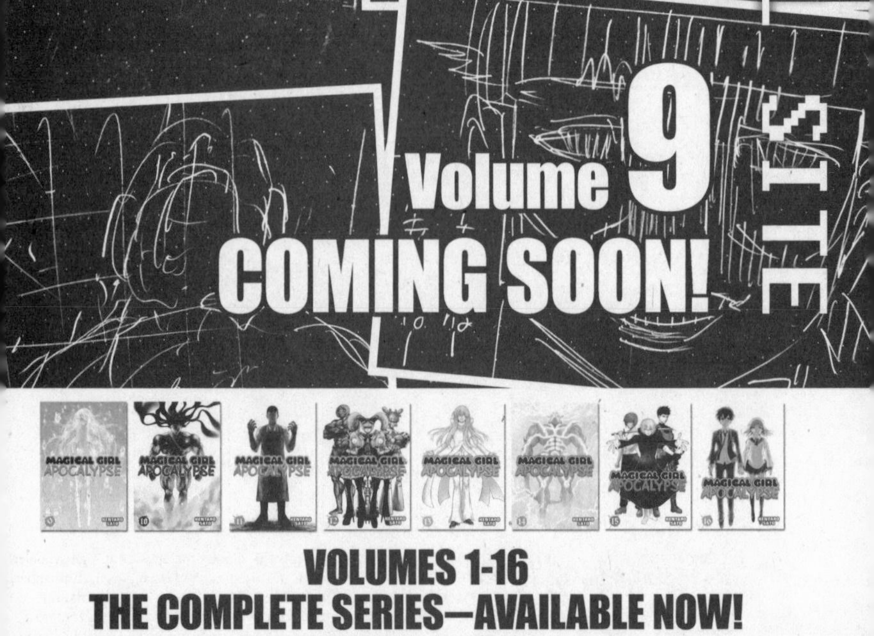
MAGICAL GIRL APOCALYPSE
KENTARO SATO